# REWOLUCJA

ALSO BY ROBERT E. BLOBAUM

*Feliks Dzierżyński and the SDKPiL:*
*A Study of the Origins of Polish Communism*

# REWOLUCJA

## Russian Poland, 1904–1907

### Robert E. Blobaum

CORNELL UNIVERSITY PRESS

ITHACA AND LONDON

Cornell University Press gratefully acknowledges a subvention
from the Eberly College of Arts and Sciences of West Virginia
University, which aided in bringing this book to publication.

First published 1995 by Cornell University Press.


Printed in the United States of America

♾ The paper in this book meets the minimum requirements of the
American National Standard for Information Sciences—Permanence
of Paper for Printed Library Materials, ANSI Z39.48-1984.


Library of Congress Cataloging-in-Publication Data

Blobaum, Robert.
  Rewolucja : Russian Poland, 1904–1907 / Robert E. Blobaum.
    p.  cm.
  Includes bibliographical references and index.
  ISBN 978-1-5017-0713-1
  1. Poland—History—Revolution, 1904–1907.  I. Title.
DK4385.B57  1995
943.8'033—dc20

94-33165

# CONTENTS

# Illustrations

# PREFACE

This book, which is about dramatic change and transformation in a turbulent era of Polish history, was researched and written against the backdrop of an equally profound and revolutionary turn of events in contemporary Poland. Although the first conceptual seeds were planted in 1980 during work on an earlier book, I could not begin the present undertaking until that project's completion in 1984. In Poland, the first "self-limiting" revolution of Solidarity had come and gone, while many of the repressive features of martial law, imposed by General Wojciech Jaruzelski at the end of 1981, remained in place. Three periods of research in Poland followed: in 1985–1986, at the height of the so-called normalization; in 1988, on the eve of the Polish "Round Table" negotiations; and in 1991, during the Republic of Poland's first truly free parliamentary elections since the interwar era. The crisis and then collapse of communism in Poland influenced, at the very least, the circumstances of my research, if not my thinking about it. While I have tried to remain cognizant of the dangers "presentism" poses to historical analyses, I have found the social science methodologies that have informed the best scholarship of more recent events, as well as contemporary debates about such critical issues as the meaning and nature of "civil society," not without value in pondering the causes and significance of an earlier, and admittedly different, revolution.

The revolutionary upheavals of the early twentieth century in Russian Poland—or, more accurately, in the Kingdom of Poland that the Congress of Vienna had created in 1815—have not been well illuminated by historians. The Polish upheavals of 1904 to 1907, although characterized by an undeniable specificity, have been eclipsed by their concurrence with revolution throughout the vast Russian Empire. Until recently, Western students of late imperial Russian history, when dealing with the Revolution of 1905, have focused almost exclusively on the central Russian provinces, and more particularly on Moscow and St. Petersburg. If the peripheral "borderlands," including Russia's Polish provinces, were discussed at all, it was usually in reference to developments at the center. This is not to say that such crucial events as "Bloody Sunday" and the proclamation of the October Manifesto were without influence in Russian Poland, only that these events occurred within an economic, social, cultural, and political context that in many ways was vastly different from what prevailed in the empire's Russian heartland. Hence, the revolution in the Kingdom of Poland, more often than not, took its own route, with a point of departure in the final months of 1904, several weeks before Bloody Sunday. By certain criteria often applied to the study of revolutions—for example, social mobilization and organization, the incidence of political terror and counterterror, and the formation of alternative governing structures—developments in the "peripheral," Polish provinces were, if anything, more "revolutionary" than elsewhere in the empire, including the two Russian capitals. The paucity of Western-language literature on the Revolution of 1905 in Poland thus provided one important justification for my work.

At the same time, Polish historiography, in its nationalist, romantic, and Marxist variants, at home or in emigration, had excessively politicized this initial chapter of twentieth-century Polish history. Consequently, the upheavals of 1904 to 1907 were conventionally rendered as struggles between and among political personalities, ideologies, tactics, and parties. Such partisan historical writing, which reached its apogee in the Polish People's Republic, culminated in the "definitive" second edition of Stanisław Kalabiński and Feliks Tych's *Czwarte powstanie czy pierwsza rewolucja: Lata 1905–1907 na ziemiach polskich* (Fourth uprising or first revolution: The years 1905–1907 on Polish lands), published in 1976. Despite the promise implied in Kalabiński and Tych's title that their study would address the transitional social and political significance of the revolution, *Czwarte powstanie* remained preoccupied with issues of political "treachery" and ideological (i.e., Marxist-Leninist) "correctness." Aside from the occasional inclusion of a statistical table, the social history of the revolution in Russian Poland remained in relative obscurity. Movements among urban workers, middle school and university students, agrarian laborers and small peasant proprietors, Catholic clergy and religious communities, and professional groups, as before, were readily assigned to the influence of one or more of the competing political agents and thus denied any tangible significance in their own right. The same tendentiousness also applied to the numerous "local histories" of the revolution written in the 1960s and

1970s, although in hindsight the best works in this genre, by Halina Kie-purska (on Warsaw) and Władysław Lech Karwacki (on Łódź), were be-ginning to break away from the traditional mode.

My purpose became twofold as work proceeded: to examine the revo-lutionary upheavals in the Kingdom of Poland in their own light, "eman-cipated" as it were from dubious Russian revolutionary "parentage," and to study far more carefully the Polish revolution's social actors, much neglected in the political preoccupations of Polish historians. By the time I embarked on the lengthy journey that, I hoped, would lead me to an ideal intersection of social and political history, a new generation of Polish historical writing relieved me of the overly ambitious task of rewriting the entire history of the revolution from the bottom up. In the late 1970s and especially in the 1980s, important studies, informed by the methodologies of modern social historical research well established in the West, began to appear in Poland; and if they did not focus on the revolution per se, they nevertheless helped define many of its principal issues within a larger social historical context. These works, by Anna Żarnowska and Władysław Lech Karwacki on labor history and workers' culture, Elżbieta Kaczyńska and Jan Molenda on urban and rural crowd behavior, Maria Nietyksza on urban demography, Krzysztof Groniowski on agrarian labor, Andrzej Chwalba, Maria Kowalska, and Tadeusz Krawczak on popular religious conscious-ness, Józef Ryszard Szaflik and Jolanta Niklewska on volunteer firemen and private middle schools, and Jerzy Jedlicki on the origins of modern Polish political culture, marked a radical historiographic breakthrough. Even the era's political parties were subjected to new and objective social analysis, especially in the work of Paweł Samuś on socialist party organiza-tion in Łódź and that of Tadeusz Wolsza on the nationalist movement in the countryside. Meanwhile, historians working on similar and related topics in Western languages lagged far behind the Polish historians until after 1980 and the publication of studies by Richard Lewis on agrarian revolutionary movements and Stephen Corrsin on turn-of-the-century Warsaw.

Significant gaps in the literature remained, however, and a good deal of original research was still necessary to fill them. As a glance at the notes will attest, this book does not lack for primary archival materials retrieved from central, provincial, local, and diocesan repositories. A legitimate ques-tion may be raised about the dependability of these materials, especially those of an administrative, police, military, and judicial nature. I hope I have been able both to distance myself from the attitudes and biases of those who composed and left written comments on these documents and, even better, to submit those attitudes to critical examination where appro-priate.

Perhaps of greater significance are my points of emphasis in this study, as indicated in the chapter titles. My decision to devote three lengthy chapters to largely Polish popular movements—among urban and industrial workers, the postemancipation peasantry, and students in higher and secondary educational institutions, respectively—is easily justifiable. These movements "made" the revolution in Russian Poland and, to a certain extent, helped to "unmake" it as well. The apparatus of imperial Russian state authority, although hardly the monolithic and monstrous Leviathan of contemporary and later caricature, was another obvious and principal actor in the revolutionary drama which required my considerable attention. The role of the Roman Catholic Church in Russian Poland, as the most important social and political actor among the Polish elite, demanded close analysis. So, too, did the main political parties of the era, although in this context I consider their importance less in terms of traditional political history and more for their role as vehicles in creating a modern political culture.

This is not to deny the significance of other "supporting" social and political actors who remained far from passive during these fateful years. Among the elite, this would include the landowning nobility and the entrepreneurial bourgeoisie and, among the popular classes, the small masters and journeymen in the artisanal trades. An even stronger case may be made for including separate chapters on the intelligentsia, which in Poland as elsewhere in central and eastern Europe acted as something of a social substitute for a Western-style middle class, and on the Kingdom's non-Polish minorities, which together constituted over one-quarter of the population. Given the constraints of a single volume, however, I found myself compelled to limit my discussion of these groups and incorporate my analysis of their roles into relevant parts of the text, while conceding that they deserve more detailed treatment than I have been able to afford them.

Finally, in striving for a comprehensive and integrated account of Poland's revolutionary upheavals of the early twentieth century, my greatest hope is that this work will expand the horizons of a discussion hitherto confined by constraints of language, geography, and politics. For this very reason, I have adopted a straightforward narrative style to present my research, one that sacrifices theoretical abstraction and mounds of statistical data for readability. This work quite easily could have taken on a quantitative bent (especially in the chapters on workers and peasants) that might have served the needs of a narrow and specialized audience but would have interfered with a clear articulation of the fundamental social and political issues of the revolution in Russian Poland. I have thus confined my quantifications to the outer parameters of the subject matter at hand, while referring the reader to the relevant specialized literature wherever possible. In other words, this contemporary historian, though ever mindful of the influence of modern social science on reconstructions of the past, nevertheless freely admits a first loyalty to a tradition of historical writing more appropriately associated with the humanities.

Acknowledgment sections usually end with expressions of gratitude to the members of one's family for their indulgence and support. I owe my family more than that. The strains of travel, physical separation, and the sheer absorption of time that a project of this nature demands are not easily borne and often take a greater toll on those closest to an author than on the author himself. I have burdened my wife, Vicki, with untimely departures, all of my chapter drafts, and too much of the responsibility for child care. Before departing on my first research trip to Poland for this project, I escorted my daughter Anna to her third-grade class. Soon, too soon, I will be seeing her off to college. Her brother Charles, ten months old when this project began, has experienced too many of the adventures of Little League baseball, and much else as well, in the absence of his father. Lindsay, who came into my life midway through this project, has joined her siblings in learning that the true meaning of "research" is departure. I have not spared Katherine, my youngest, either, whether in the months before her birth or in the two years since. Still, despite all the birthdays, band concerts, school plays, and other events that have gone on without me, there has been no grumbling, even now as we begin to discuss plans for the "next project." The only way I can begin to acknowledge such support is to dedicate this book to my family.

West Virginia University has also provided ongoing support to this project, but of a quite different nature. In fact, were it not for a generous subvention from the Eberly College of Arts and Sciences, this book might have been partitioned into so many articles. I have Dean Gerald E. Lang to thank for the subvention, as well as for his readiness to agree to lengthy leaves to research and write this book. The West Virginia Faculty Senate provided two summer research grants, and the Office of International Programs a third. The latter unit helped fund the reproduction of photographs and illustrations housed in the Muzeum Niepodległości (Museum of Independence) in Warsaw, which were selected for this book with the help and permission of its director, Dr. Andrzej Stawarz. Two chairs in the Department of History, Robert Maxon and Ronald Lewis, had sufficient faith in my research to add their support to my many supplications within and without and have allowed me to pursue my agenda by limiting the duties and obligations that can easily overwhelm a faculty member. Finally,

Allison Hanham and her skillful manipulation of a computer technology that I cannot begin to comprehend, assisted me in drafting an intelligible map to familiarize the nonspecialist with an unfamiliar place.

A good deal of the major funding for this project, especially for the extended stays in Poland, has come from the International Research and Exchanges Board, with funds provided by the Andrew W. Mellon Foundation, the National Endowment for the Humanities, and the U.S. Department of State. The Joint Committee on Eastern Europe of the American Council of Learned Societies and the Social Science Research Council also provided generous support in the form of a postdoctoral research grant, as did the National Endowment for the Humanities in funding my participation in a summer seminar at Brandeis University on religion in imperial Russia. An earlier version of Chapter 7, which was published as "The Revolution of 1905–1907 and the Crisis of Polish Catholicism" (*Slavic Review* 47, no. 4 [1988]), is reprinted here, with modifications, by permission of the American Association for the Advancement of Slavic Studies. While none of these organizations is responsible for the views expressed in this book, all have certainly helped provide an opportunity for such expression, for which I am most grateful.

Before this book made its way to the anonymous readers for Cornell University Press, whose advice helped shape the final version, various parts of the manuscript benefited from the reading and comment of friends, students, and colleagues. Rosemarie Zagarri, Ron Lewis, Greg Monahan, and George L. Simpson assisted me in keeping this study within frames of reference accessible to interested nonspecialists. Graduate students at West Virginia University, especially Charles Steele, Wolf Heidenmann, and Jean M. Crumrine, when asked to critique the manuscript, were boldly unsparing in pointing out its faults to their professor. The most valuable assistance came from my colleagues in the field, however, some at my direct request, some as coparticipants or commentators on professional panels that served as forums to float more than one trial balloon. Walter Pintner, Norman Naimark, Anna Cienciala, John J. Kulczycki, Neal Pease, Gregory Freeze, Richard Lewis, E. Anthony Swift, Padraic Kenney, Stephen Corrsin, Michael Jakobson, and William Chase have all had a hand in this, whether they realize it or not, and I thank them for their help.

I owe a special debt of gratitude to my colleagues in Poland, beginning with Janusz Żarnowski, who invited me into both his home and his seminar in modern Polish social history at the Institute of History at the Polish Academy of Sciences. At the latter, I had an opportunity to discuss a multitude of issues with Władysław Lech Karwacki, Jan Molenda, Elżbieta Kaczyńska, Walentyna Najdus, and Ludwik Hass, not to mention invited guests such as Jerzy Jedlicki and Daniel Olszewski. Two students in that seminar, Tadeusz Wolsza and Włodzimierz Mędrzecki, have since earned their doctorates and are leaving their own mark on the field, in many ways surpassing their older colleagues and former mentors (I include myself in that category). It was through Professor Żarnowski that I became involved in another seminar at Warsaw University, directed by his wife, Anna Żarnowska, which also included labor historians Andrzej Szwarc and Jarosław Paskudski. Working in the company of these people can only be described as exhilarating, and the hospitality shown me during each research visit went beyond the norms of mere collegiality. I am grateful for their intellectual stimulation and, even more so, for their warmth and acts of kindness, which helped get me through more than one long and lonely Warsaw winter night.

ROBERT E. BLOBAUM

*Morgantown, West Virginia*

# A Note on Dates, Names, and Sources

Historians of imperial Russia are well acquainted with the problems of dating before the Soviet regime's adoption of the Gregorian, or New Style, calendar, but in the case of the Kingdom of Poland, the matter is even more complex. Exclusive use of the Julian, or Old Style, calendar in Poland was confined mainly to internal correspondence and documents among state agencies. Proclamations to the population and other public documents usually were dated according to both calendars, although on occasion only the New Style date, thirteen days past the Old Style date, appeared. As for the population at large, with its historic ties to the Latin culture of the West, its reliance on the New Style calendar was practically uniform. I have therefore followed social rather than administrative usages, and all dates are rendered in the New Style throughout the narrative. In source citations, however, particularly where an official document was dated according to the Old Style, I maintain the original while providing the New Style version in parentheses.

These same official documents, composed in the Russian language, also posed a dilemma in deciphering Polish surnames and place names. I spent many hours attempting to locate on past and present maps the exact spelling of the Polish name of this or that small village, whose only rendition in the sources was in Russian. Because time and historical atlases are frequently unkind to smaller communities, I was not always successful: I was forced into more than one educated guess. A similar problem cropped up when the only reference to a particular individual—for example, in a police protocol—was in Russian. For the most part, the names were easily rendered back into Polish and the Latin alphabet, thanks to common Slavic consonant clusters, but undoubtedly my retransliterations are not error-free.

Jewish names, often poorly transliterated by the Russian authorities, posed an especially difficult chore in this regard, for which I beg the reader's indulgence.

Finally, the archival collections cited in this book have changed over time, usually though the accretion of new documents. Entire *sygnatury* (portfolios of documents known to my colleagues in Russian history as "fonds") have been recataloged and renumbered, sometimes more than once, as have the individual documents contained therein. Consequently, most source citations made by researchers in the late 1960s are no longer valid today; and with another archival reorganization currently in progress as entire collections are being relocated, those made today may not be valid tomorrow. Therefore, I have identified the vast majority of these documents more completely than would usually be the case, both as a hedge against further change and as a more precise aid to future research.

# ABBREVIATIONS AND ACRONYMS

## Archives and Collections

| | |
|---|---|
| ADK | Archiwum Diecezjalne w Kielcach (Diocesan Archive in Kielce) |
| | AK: Akta Konsistorskie (Documents of the Consistory) |
| | KD: Konferencje Dekanalne (Conferences of the Deaconate) |
| ADP | Archiwum Diecezjalne w Płocku (Diocesan Archive in Płock) |
| | PWD: Papiery Władzy Duchownej (Papers of the Bishop) |
| AGAD | Archiwum Główne Akt Dawnych (Main Archive of Old Documents) |
| | AB: Zbiór Anny Branickiej (Anna Branicka Collection) |
| | KGGW: Kancelaria Gubernator Generała Warszawskiego (Chancellory of the Warsaw Governor-General) |
| APK | Archiwum Państwowe w Kielcach (State Archive in Kielce) |
| | TGGK: Tymczasowy Generał Gubernator Kielecki (Provisional Governor-General of Kielce Province) |
| APL | Archiwum Państwowe w Lublinie (State Archive in Lublin) |
| | KGL: Kancelaria Gubernatora Lubelskiego (Chancellory of the Lublin Governor) |
| APŁ | Archiwum Państowe w Łodzi (State Archive in Łódź) |
| | KGP: Kancelaria Gubernatora Piotrkowskiego (Chancellory of the Piotrków Governor) |
| | TGGP: Tymczasowy Generał Gubernator Piotrkowski (Provisional Governor-General of Piotrków Province) |
| APW | Archiwum Państwowe m. st. Warszawy (State Archive in Warsaw) |
| | WGZZ: Warszawski Gubernialny Zarząd Żandarmerii (Office of the Warsaw Provincial Gendarmes) |
| | WWO: Warszawski Wydział Ochrony Porządku i Bezpieczeństwa Publicznego (Warsaw Office of the Okhrana) |

ZOW: Zarząd Oberpolicmajstra Warszawskiego (Office of the Warsaw Superintendent of Police)

CA PZPR  Centralne Archiwum Polskiej Zjednoczonej Partii Robotniczej (Central Archive of the United Polish Workers Party)

### Abbreviations and Polish Acronyms Employed in the Text and Notes

CKR  Centralny Komitet Robotniczy (Central Workers Committee of the Polish Socialist Party)

Endecja  Acronym for the Stronnictwo Demokratyczno-Narodowe (National Democratic Party)

LSDP  Lithuanian Social Democratic Party

NKK  Narodowe Koło Kolejarzy (National Circle of Railroad Employees)

Pedecja  Acronym for the Związek Postępowo-Demokratyczny (Progressive Democratic Union)

PPS  Polska Partia Socjalistyczna (Polish Socialist Party)

PZL  Polski Związek Ludowy (Polish People's Union)

SDKPiL  Socjaldemokracja Królestwa Polskiego i Litwy (Social Democratic Party of the Kingdom of Poland and Lithuania)

SDPA  Special Deputy to the Warsaw Governor-General for Police Affairs

SRCh  Stowarzyszenie Robotników Chrześcijańskich (Association of Christian Workers)

TON  Towarzystwo Oświaty Narodowej (Society for National Education)

WGG  Warsaw Governor-General

Zet  Acronym for the Związek Młodzieży Polskiej (Union of Polish Youth)

# CHAPTER ONE

# RUSSIAN STATE, POLISH SOCIETY

The origins of the Revolution of 1905 in Russian Poland can be traced back to developments in the final phase of an earlier but far different upheaval, the January Insurrection of 1863–1864. As tsarist Russia suppressed this last of a series of challenges by the Polish nobility, or *szlachta,* to its hegemony in central Poland, it set in motion forces that were to reshape Polish society and redefine Polish politics for decades to come. The January Insurrection was therefore an authentic historical watershed, the culminating point of the turbulent romantic era of Polish history and the point of departure for a new period, the contours of which would not be clearly visible until some forty years later.

The insurrection that erupted in January 1863 resulted from frustration and disappointment with the limited concessions offered the Kingdom of Poland by Alexander II shortly after he succeeded to the Russian and Polish thrones in 1855. Since the suppression of the November Insurrection of 1830–1831, the Kingdom had suffered the "iron rule" of Nicholas I and his viceroy in Warsaw, Gen. Ivan F. Paskevich. The Kingdom's autonomous status within the Russian Empire, supposedly guaranteed by agreements reached at the Congress of Vienna in 1815, had been reduced to a legal fiction. In effect, the country was ruled by military decree for almost a quarter of a century. Then came the disastrous defeats of the Crimean War, also inherited by Alexander from his father, which convinced the new tsar that limited reforms were necessary in Poland to avoid a prospective uprising. Consequently, Alexander issued an amnesty for Poles exiled to Siberia in 1831, reopened institutions of higher learning, and restored the right of assembly to permit participation of the Polish elite in the statewide debate on planned reforms, especially peasant emancipation.

Unfortunately, Alexander's relaxations, designed to secure greater stability and loyalty to the throne in the Kingdom, had the opposite effect. Legally recognized organizations with moderate yet undisguisedly political aims, such as the Agricultural Society and the Warsaw City Delegation, emerged, emboldening radicals to form conspiratorial circles and organize patriotic street demonstrations. To contain the growing political unrest and restore discipline, the tsar in 1861 turned to the aristocrat Aleksander Wielopolski, an arrogant and determined "realist" who believed he could manage the crisis by continuing to hold out the carrot of reform while selectively applying the stick of repression. As head of the country's civil administration, Wielopolski imposed martial law, forced the disbanding of the Agricultural Society and the City Delegation, and undertook a series of preventive arrests. Finally, on January 14, 1863, Wielopolski announced the draft of thirty thousand young men into the military service in an effort to force the opposition out into the open.

Instead, that opposition retreated to the underground, where it formed an insurrectionary government and launched a guerrilla war that harassed the Russian army for sixteen months. As the insurrection quickly spilled over to Lithuania and Byelorussia, the eastern borderlands of the prepartition Polish Commonwealth, both sides sought to win the support of the peasantry by offering more favorable terms of emancipation. In this single most important social issue of the insurrection, the tsar had the last word. Aided by a massive bureaucracy that could implement his escalating promises to the peasants, Alexander outbid an insurrectionary government forced to operate in the shadows and whose authority was limited to territory that it never held for more than a few days at a time. With the emancipation decrees of March 2, 1864, the autocracy effectively took the wind out of the sails of the insurrection and left it without a popular base of support. The denouement came five weeks later, with the capture of Romuald Traugutt, the last "dictator" of the insurrectionary government. Organized Polish resistance came to an end.[1]

## Russian Reaction to the January Insurrection

Abrupt changes in Russian policy toward the Kingdom followed the suppression of the insurrection. The modest relaxations and limited reforms

1. From the vast literature on the January Insurrection, see R. F. Leslie, *Reform and Insurrection in Russian Poland* (London, 1963); Stefan Kieniewicz, *Powstanie styczniowe* (Warsaw, 1972); and Franciszka Romotowska, *Rząd narodowy Polski w latach 1863–1864* (Warsaw, 1978).

of the pre-January period now gave way to harsh retaliation for Polish "ingratitude." Especially targeted for retribution were the gentry and the Catholic clergy, perceived by the Russian authorities as the leading social forces behind the rebellion. More than six hundred persons of predominantly gentry origin were sent to the gallows. Tens of thousands were exiled to Siberia, where a significant proportion served out hard-labor terms. Some ten thousand others escaped similar punishment by fleeing the country.[2] Economic deprivation went hand in hand with political revenge. The government confiscated 1,660 estates in the Kingdom and 1,794 estates in Lithuania from the Polish gentry. Another eight hundred estates, belonging to property owners considered politically unreliable, were forcibly sold at auction. Moreover, to maintain post-insurrectionary Russian armies of occupation, contributions totaling thirty-four million rubles were levied on those gentry who remained on the land. One historian estimates that 250,000 lives were affected by the various measures of repression.[3] Together they dealt a devastating blow to the traditional Polish elite.

The Roman Catholic Church was simply terrorized into submission. Some members of the hierarchy were kidnapped and held hostage in the depths of Russia; others were forcibly removed from their ecclesiastical offices. By 1870, not one Polish bishop in the entire Kingdom remained in his diocese, and, for several years thereafter, the episcopate ceased to function. In the meantime, hundreds of lower clergy joined their gentry countrymen in tsarist prisons, Siberian exile, and forced emigration. The autocracy also found a pretext to end its limited toleration of the Uniate (or Greek Catholic) Church in the Kingdom's eastern provinces. For centuries, the Uniate faithful had been considered by the autocracy as religious renegades from the officially recognized Orthodox Church and were largely persecuted out of existence in the Ukraine and Byelorussia. In 1839, Nicholas I severed all contact between the Uniate Church and the Vatican as a first step toward introducing that persecution into the "autonomous" Kingdom. Now, in 1875, the Uniates who remained in the Chełm and Podlasie regions of the Kingdom were disenfranchised, and hundreds of thousands were "reconverted" to Orthodoxy by coercive means. Any hopes for political or moral assistance from Rome were dashed in 1882 when a modus vivendi was reached between the Russian government and the Vatican. Abandoned by Leo XIII to the mercies of the Russian caesar and fearing

---

2. Jerzy Borejsza, "Rewolucjonista polski: Szkic do portretu," in *Polska XIX wieku: Państwo-społeczeństwo-kultura*, ed. Stefan Kieniewicz (Warsaw, 1982), p. 298.
3. Władysław Pobóg-Malinowski, *Najnowsza historia polityczna Polski*, vol. 1 (1864–1914), 2d ed. (London, 1963), pp. 16–17.

further deprivations, the Polish church went into a decades-long hibernation.[4]

Meanwhile, the legal fiction of the Kingdom's autonomous status was dropped. As an immediate consequence of the failed insurrection, thousands of Poles were purged from the civil administration and replaced by Russians. All separate administrative institutions that had survived the reign of Nicholas I were then quickly eliminated. With the death of Count Berg in 1874, the office of viceroy was discontinued and replaced with that of the Warsaw governor-general, which was invested with broad civil and military authority over the administration of the Kingdom's ten *gubernii*, or provinces.[5] Shortly thereafter, "Vistulaland" supplanted the "Kingdom of Poland" in Russian bureaucratic parlance as the country's official designation.

Until 1914, Russian Poland was ruled under a system of exceptional, emergency legislation, beginning with the declaration of martial law by Wielopolski in 1861. Emergency rule allowed the autocracy to deny the Kingdom the advantages of recent Russian legal reforms, such as elected justices of the peace and trial by jury for criminal cases, as well as such reforms of local government as the establishment of elected city councils and *zemstvo* assemblies in the countryside. At the same time, the Warsaw governor-general was empowered to issue binding decrees affecting state security and to levy a variety of administrative penalties if those decrees were violated. The Warsaw governor-general could also arbitrarily transfer the trial of civilians to military courts and order deportations to Siberia without the verdict of any court. Separate Polish scientific, cultural, economic, and philanthropic organizations could not be formed without his express permission, which in turn had to be confirmed by St. Petersburg. Moreover, the political press was absolutely prohibited (with the exception of government-sponsored newspapers), and nonpolitical publications were forced to submit to strict preventive censorship.[6]

In the gubernii, governors served as the highest administrative authority

4. For more on the post-January repressions as they affected the Roman Catholic Church, see Ryszard Bender, *Społeczne inicjatywy chrześcijańskie w Królestwie Polskim, 1905–1918* (Lublin, 1978), pp. 29–41.

5. Russian-style gubernii had already been introduced into the Kingdom under Nicholas I and were named after provincial administrative centers, in this case, Kalisz, Piotrków, Warsaw, Łomża, Płock, Radom, Kielce, Siedlce, Lublin, and Suwałki.

6. For a general discussion of Russian repressive measures after the January Insurrection, see Piotr Wandycz, *The Lands of Partitioned Poland, 1795–1918* (Seattle, 1974), pp. 193–196; Marian Kukiel, *Dzieje Polski porozbiorowej, 1795–1921*, 3d ed. (Paris, 1983), pp. 424–427, 450–452; and Henryk Wereszycki, *Historia polityczna Polski, 1864–1918*, 2d ed. (Paris, 1979), pp. 57–70.

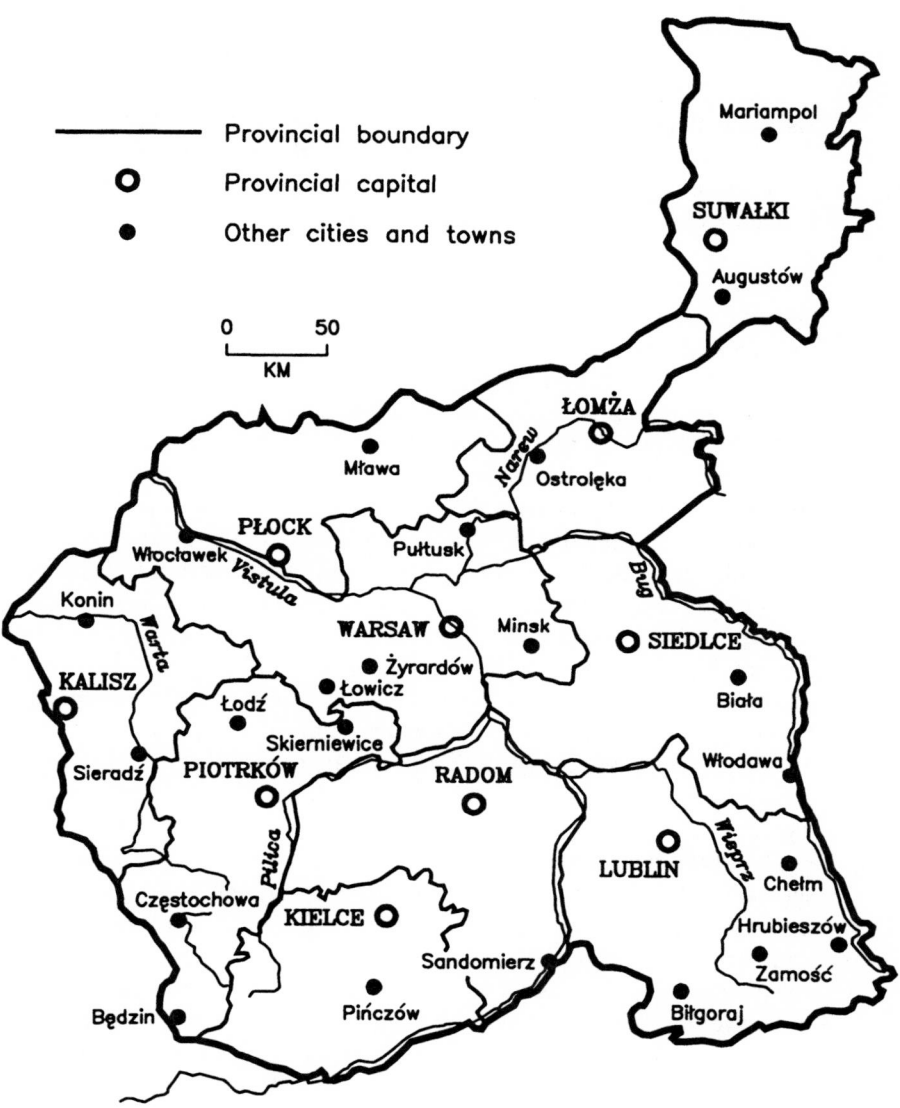

Map of the Kingdom of Poland in 1897

and together with their executive organs supervised the work of provincial-level departments. The provinces, in turn, were divided into Russian-style *uezdy*, or counties, headed by *nachal'niki* (chiefs) appointed by the Ministry of Internal Affairs, but subordinate to the governors. Despite provisions in the emancipation decrees for self-governing institutions in Polish villages and communes, the county nachal'niki regularly intervened and exercised a decisive influence in their affairs. Magistrates, headed by appointed mayors, governed the cities under the supervision of the provincial governors.

A massive and overlapping police bureaucracy ran parallel with the civil-military apparatus. Beginning in 1866, offices of the gendarmes were organized at the provincial and county levels, subordinate to the central office of the Warsaw Regional Gendarmes, which, in turn, was headed by the special deputy to the Warsaw governor-general for police affairs. The unique institution of the Land Guard was also introduced into the Kingdom at this time, charged primarily with preserving law and order in the Polish countryside. The Land Guards were headed by captains who, from their headquarters in the county seats, supervised units in various precincts. In provincial capitals, the chief of police also doubled as head of the county Land Guard. Police forces in major urban areas such as Warsaw and Łódź were entrusted to superintendents of police, whose powers rivaled those of the provincial governors. Beyond the regular police, some two hundred agents of the reorganized secret police, the notorious Okhrana, functioned as the "eyes and ears" of the autocracy in the Kingdom, alert to any sign of independent activity, whether political or nonpolitical.[7] If this were not enough to keep the Kingdom subdued, 240,000 soldiers occupied the country.

The retributive measures of Alexander II's reign, though they eliminated separate Polish institutions and completely incorporated the Kingdom into the empire, did not yet imply the systematic russification of the population. That became official state policy only during the reign of his successor, Alexander III (1881–1894). With the appointment of Iosif Gurko as Warsaw governor-general in 1883, the Kingdom was subjected to a dozen years of intense "denationalization" by which the Russian bureaucracy strove to divest the Poles of their national character. Through a series of arbitrary decrees, the Polish language was eliminated from all levels of administration and the courts; even the "self-governing" institutions in the villages

7. On the establishment of the Okhrana after the assassination of Alexander II in 1881 and its activities in Russian Poland, see Elżbieta Kaczyńska and Dariusz Drewniak, *Ochrana: Carska policja polityczna* (Warsaw, 1993).

and communes were not spared. At the same time, Poles were completely purged from the upper and middle administrative ranks. Henceforth, they would be permitted to serve only in the lower levels of the postal and railroad bureaucracies. Moreover, all legally registered associations, including the Roman Catholic Church, were now required to conduct internal correspondence in the Russian language, making it easier for the police to keep tabs on them. Of course, all business with the state authorities had to be transacted in Russian. Polish street and building signs came down and were replaced by Russian-language equivalents. The names of towns were also changed; for example, Puławy in Lublin Province became Novo-Aleksandria. In short, when the nightmare of Gurko's tenure as Warsaw governor-general came to an end in 1894, the only places where Polish remained a public language were a few state-owned theaters in Warsaw.[8]

The russifiers took principal aim, however, at the Kingdom's separate educational institutions. Already in 1867 a tsarist edict liquidated all traces of autonomy in the educational system as Russians took over the administration of the schools. Two years later, the Warsaw Main School, a Polish institution of higher learning earlier conceded by Alexander II, was transformed into an imperial Russian university and its faculty purged. Fluency in Russian became necessary for admission, a criterion that openly discriminated against Polish applicants. Also beginning in 1869, public secondary schools were required to use Russian as the language of instruction for all subjects with the exception of religion. Polish could be studied as an elective "foreign language" in gymnasia that had received permission from the Ministry of Internal Affairs, but only up to the sixth form. Even then, Russian was employed as the language of instruction. To implement these policies, teachers were recruited from Russia with the aid of substantial bonuses and other incentives. According to official expectations, once a sufficient number of Russians were hired, the employment of Polish teachers in the state-run secondary schools would be terminated.[9]

The task of consolidating and extending the russified school system fell to Aleksandr Apukhtin, curator of the Warsaw School District during the Gurko era. Before Apukhtin's appointment, public elementary schools were considerably less affected by the "denationalization" measures. Compulsory study of Russian had been introduced, as had textbooks that eliminated references to "Poland." Otherwise, the authorities concentrated on the teachers seminaries where Russian replaced Polish as the language of in-

---

8. Wandycz, *Lands of Partitioned Poland,* p. 267.
9. Edmund Staszyński, *Polityka oświatowa caratu w Królestwie Polskim od powstania styczniowego do I wojny światowej* (Warsaw, 1968), pp. 3–19.

struction. Under Apukhtin, however, Russian became the instructional language for all subjects in the elementary schools with the exception of Polish grammar and religious studies. New teachers were hired, moreover, according to political rather than pedagogic criteria. The same criteria determined advancement and bonuses. Heads of provincial and city school directorates, for example, had at their disposal discretionary funds that they used to reward the most loyal agents of russification.[10]

Apukhtin also sought to fill in the few cracks of Polishness that remained in the system of public secondary education. He began his tenure with another purge, this time of Russian teachers suspected of harboring sympathies for the Poles. And though he was unable to root out Polish language and religious studies from the gymnasia, he did succeed in organizing Orthodox chapels and choirs in the secondary schools. Apukhtin also planted political informers in the schools to "maintain student discipline." To increase police supervision of the students' extracurricular activities, he introduced both mandatory uniforms and on-campus residency requirements.

Apukhtin's final "achievement" was to bring the education of Catholic clergy into the orbit of the russified state system. By the 1880s the training of clergy in the seminaries came to include compulsory study of Russian and the use of Russian for the instruction of history.[11] In the private schools (largely confined to the secondary level), russification never advanced as far as in the state schools. Nevertheless, their curricula were made subject to the approval of the state authorities. In addition, access to Russian institutions of higher learning for graduates of private secondary schools required passing examinations identical to those necessary for matriculation at the state-run boys' gymnasia. A similar curriculum was therefore adopted in the private schools, with Russian as the primary language of instruction. Private secondary schools for girls possessed more latitude to use the native language, but only because their graduates—like their counterparts in the state-run girls' gymnasia—were denied access to higher education.[12]

The Gurko-Apukhtin era in the Kingdom, especially when coupled with simultaneous efforts at germanization in Prussian Poland, constitutes one

10. Eugenia Podgórska, *Szkolnictwo elementarne w Łodzi w latach 1808–1914* (Łódź, 1966), pp. 67–91.

11. Bender, *Społeczne inicjatywy*, pp. 38–40.

12. Staszyński, *Polityka oświatowa*, pp. 187–193. For more on women's educational opportunities in Russian Poland before 1905, see Adam Winiarz, "Kształcenie i wychowanie dziewcząt w Księstwie Warszawskim i Królestwie Polskim, 1807–1905," in *Kobieta i edukacja*, ed. Anna Żarnowska and Andrzej Szwarc, vol. 2, pt. 2 (Warsaw, 1992), pp. 17–22.

of the bleaker periods of Polish history. To a much greater extent than its German counterpart, however, the ubiquitous machinery of Russian government in the Kingdom possessed significant defects that, although they did not make life any more tolerable, did permit the Poles considerable room to maneuver. Particularly at the lower levels of the Russian bureaucracy, corruption was rife and officials could easily be bribed to bend the rules. This was particularly the case among the poorly paid and understaffed police forces in both urban and rural areas. The Russian authorities were also notoriously capricious. Although their permission was required for almost everything, frequently the decision of one official could be ignored by turning with the same request to another of the same rank. Higher-ranking bureaucrats commonly overturned decisions of subordinates, a practice that encouraged appeals. Finally, with the passing of Gurko and Apukhtin from the scene in the mid-1890s, the perspectives of the central government in St. Petersburg and those of the provincial government in the Kingdom began to diverge significantly. In other words, Russian government in the Kingdom was hardly monolithic.

The Russian bureaucracy was also insufficiently financed to fulfill the tasks imposed on it. Despite the russification of the country's educational system, for example, there were too few schools and pedagogic personnel at all levels to carry out the official policy of mass "denationalization." The autocracy simply lacked the resources to achieve such an end. The public elementary school system was woefully underfunded and failed to keep pace with population growth. By the turn of the century, only 18 percent of the Kingdom's school-aged children received primary education. The state-run secondary schools were better funded, but their small number (fifty-four in the entire Kingdom in 1904), high tuition, and difficult entrance examinations effectively confined enrollment to the children of a narrow elite. In 1900, only a fraction of a percent of the total population had attended a state secondary school.[13] Neither the few legally registered private schools nor an underground network of "secret schools" could hope to fill such a huge gap left by the state. Hence, the end result of Russian educational policies was not increased literacy in Russian among the general population but high rates of general illiteracy (69.5 percent of the total population, according to the census of 1897).[14]

---

13. Staszyński, *Polityka oświatowa*, pp. 88, 95–96.

14. Estimation of literacy in Russian Poland, however, is extremely problematic. The literacy rates based on the 1897 census, and repeated in much of the literature, should be revised upward, in that they include children under the age of ten, a significant cohort of the population. The census also discounted literacy in Yiddish and Hebrew, which disqualified a significant proportion of Jews. Finally, admitting literacy in Polish may have been considered

In short, when the Gurko-Apukhtin era came to a close, the Russian bureaucracy had failed to transform the population of the Kingdom into docile, loyal subjects of the tsar. Rather, the Kingdom was undergoverned, especially at the local level, where state authority came into direct contact with society. This undergovernance hindered the effective implementation of policy and promoted among the general population an impression of contradiction and ineptitude. At the same time, the very pretensions of tsarist government in the Kingdom, too underfinanced and inadequately staffed to inspire fear and respect, nevertheless managed to create a sizable gulf between the Russian governing class and the society over which it ruled, a gulf that could not be bridged by the minor relaxations and tiny concessions offered in subsequent years. How large that gulf actually was, however, became apparent a decade later, during the Revolution of 1905.

### The Impact of Agrarian Reform

The emancipation of the peasantry in Russian Poland, although in its final version at significant variance with the autocracy's original intentions, was the single most important reform carried out by the imperial bureaucracy in the post-January period. Forced by the insurrection into a bidding war for peasant support—not only in the Kingdom but also in adjacent Lithuanian, Byelorussian, and Ukrainian provinces—the autocracy began making good on its promises even before the insurgents had been completely suppressed. The tsar and his advisers believed that quick implementation of the favorable terms offered the peasants would win them over permanently to their Russian benefactors. At the same time, the Russian authorities were determined to punish the Polish gentry for its leading role in the revolt, and a generous emancipation settlement would seriously undermine the economic base of the country's traditional elite. Motivated by immediate political calculations and a general desire for revenge, the emancipation nevertheless had unforeseen social, economic, and political consequences that created a quite different set of problems for Russian rule in the Kingdom.

The decrees of March 2, 1864, immediately liquidated all peasant obli-

---

by many respondents to be synonymous with admitting involvement in an illegal activity. For a discussion of literacy in Russian Poland, see Egon Vielrose, "Szacunek analfabetyzmu w zaborze rosyjskim," *Przeszłość Demograficzna Polski* 9 (1976): 3–16. I also thank Stephen D. Corrsin for sharing with me his unpublished manuscript "Levels of Literacy among Poles and Jews in Late Nineteenth-Century Warsaw."

gations to the manor. In contrast to the rest of the Russian Empire, there was no transitional phase of "temporary obligation." Further, the peasants in the "western provinces" and the "Vistulaland" received as freeholds the lands they used, together with holdings "illegally" enclosed by the nobility since 1846. As fully recognized landowners, they were also granted individual titles to their property free of charge as a gift of the tsar. The Russian muzhik, again by contrast, made redemption payments stretched out over forty-nine years while being denied individual property rights. Instead, title to "peasant land" in Russia after the emancipation was held collectively by peasant communes. Polish peasant proprietors paid a hefty land tax, double that prevailing for Russian peasants, but not exceeding two-thirds of the former rent or ransom. Financially, too, they came out ahead of their Russian counterparts.

The landless peasantry in the Kingdom, on the other hand, derived little benefit from the emancipation other than their immediate personal freedom. The majority remained without land while a minority, not exceeding 140,000 peasants, were granted small plots averaging about three *morgs* (four acres), too little to sustain their new proprietors over the long term.[15] The expectation that the national domains would be divided among the landless went largely unrealized. Only 27 percent of the crown lands, for example, passed into peasant hands, while 60 percent was granted in entail to Russian dignitaries.[16] The great latifundia of the titled aristocracy, the most logical source of land for the landless, were left relatively untouched as a reward for that group's continued loyalty to the tsar during the insurrection. Actual peasant landholding therefore increased only marginally (between 5 and 8 percent) after the emancipation, and at least 220,000 peasants remained propertyless.[17]

In the end, the emancipation left 56.5 percent of the Kingdom's arable land in the hands of the Polish nobility, even after the confiscation of considerable gentry property.[18] The great latifundia, as already mentioned, were little affected. The Russian officials who staffed the local liquidation committees and carried out the reform rewarded the political loyalty of the owners of large estates by making favorable determinations concerning the value of lost labor and rents for the purpose of subsequent compensation. The great landowners, moreover, possessed the necessary capital to adjust

15. Stefan Kieniewicz, *The Emancipation of the Polish Peasantry* (Chicago, 1969), p. 177.
16. Wandycz, *Lands of Partitioned Poland*, pp. 197–198.
17. Kieniewicz, *Emancipation of the Polish Peasantry*, p. 177; see also Krzysztof Groniowski, *Kwestia agrarna w Królestwie Polskim, 1871–1914* (Warsaw, 1966), pp. 106–107.
18. Józef Buszko, *Historia Polski, 1864–1918* (Warsaw, 1979), p. 14.

to the new postemancipation conditions. Not only could they afford to bribe corrupt officials and defend themselves against peasant claims in lengthy court litigation, but they could also switch more easily from compulsory to hired labor and were able to invest in mechanical sowers, reapers, and threshers as those became available. The subsequent increase in productivity on the latifundia more than offset the impact of higher land taxes. Not surprisingly, the latifundia owners continued to stand in the forefront of economic life in the Polish countryside.

The smaller gentry estates, however, particularly those that had relied on serf labor, were devastated by the emancipation settlement. The same Russian bureaucrats who rewarded latifundia owners for their political loyalty during the insurrection punished rank-and-file gentry for their collective "treason" by making arbitrary undervaluations of gentry losses in labor and rents. Subsequent indemnification arrangements therefore left most of the gentry in a worse financial situation than before the agrarian reforms. In addition, the method of indemnification was carefully calculated to bring profit to the Russian regime. Compensation took the form of negotiable bonds carrying a 4 percent rate of interest and an amortization period of forty-two years. The bonds, the value of which quickly depreciated, were financed by the new and relatively high land taxes imposed primarily on peasant proprietors. In the end, the authorities would collect 110 million rubles through land taxes while paying only 64 million rubles in compensation to noble landlords.[19]

As a whole, the gentry lacked sufficient capital to absorb the losses incurred, let alone to adapt to new conditions. Many had to accede to peasant claims on disputed land or went bankrupt fighting such claims in court. Escalating demands by Russian bureaucrats for bribes also took their toll. The imposition of high land taxes, the new cost of hiring farm laborers, and the inability to compete with the large estates all eventually led to the outright sale and parceling of gentry property.

The resulting exodus of the gentry from the land was a slow, gradual process in the first two postemancipation decades. Then, with the collapse of local grain prices by 50 to 60 percent in the 1880s, as cheap American and Russian grain became available to European markets, gentry departures became a mass phenomenon. By 1890, noble landholding had declined to 47 percent of the total tilled area, representing a loss of nearly two million acres since the emancipation. During the same period, total peasant landowning rose by 8.1 percent, although the sale and parceling of gentry land

19. Wandycz, *Lands of Partitioned Poland*, pp. 197–198.

accounted for only a small part of the increase.[20] Lacking access to state credit institutions until the 1890s, the peasantry gained little immediate advantage from the gentry's economic plight. Instead, urban merchants and industrialists proved the main purchasers of gentry property.

A more important source for the increase of peasant landownings in the first twenty-five years after the emancipation was the liquidation of traditional easement rights, or "servitudes," for which the peasantry received compensation in land. The emancipation decrees of 1864 specified that servitudes would remain in force only temporarily, that is, until the government assessed their value and adopted regulations to fix the means of their conversion. This provisional arrangement, affecting private estates only, left 65 percent of the peasants with grazing rights, 55 percent with fuel rights, 39 percent with timber rights, and 21.5 percent with gathering rights.[21] In state forests and crown lands, by contrast, the servitudes were entirely and immediately abolished, but only a small percentage of peasants were compensated in the form of land transfers.

Although the 1864 decrees anticipated the conversion of all easement rights on private estates, the authorities soon recognized that the servitudes issue, already a source of contention between village and manor, served Russian interests by maintaining a state of friction in the Polish countryside. Consequently, the authorities did nothing to accelerate a final solution to the problem. In 1872 the government decided that the conversion of easement rights would best be left to agreements privately negotiated between the former lords and the villages and subsequently ratified by the appropriate state authorities. This solution allowed Russian officials to act ostensibly as mediators, although in reality they frequently considered opposing claims in accordance with the respective bribes or delayed cases that held the potential for substantial personal profit. The process of conversion was therefore excruciatingly slow, and it exacerbated existing conflicts. Between 1864 and 1912, approximately two-thirds of all peasant farms underwent some changes in servitudes, for which they were compensated with land in varying amounts.[22] Despite such partial liquidation of servitudes, a similar percentage of peasant farms continued to retain some form of easement rights up to World War I.[23] Even where conversion had occurred, the peasants were frequently dissatisfied and ignored the

20. Groniowski, *Kwestia agrarna w Królestwie Polskim*, pp. 76–77; Kieniewicz, *Emancipation of the Polish Peasantry*, pp. 221–222.
21. Kieniewicz, *Emancipation of the Polish Peasantry*, pp. 178–179.
22. Groniowski, *Kwestia agrarna w Królestwie Polskim*, p. 142.
23. Jan Molenda, "Carat i klasy posiadające w walce z rewolucją 1905–1907 r. na wsi polskiej," *Przegląd Historyczny* 46, 1–2 (1955): 138.

results, prompting widespread "illegal" trespassing and sporadic outbursts of resistance to state intervention.[24] Hence, the conflict over servitudes, while mobilizing the peasants against the manor, could and did rebound against the authorities as well.

Another part of the agrarian reform which departed even more significantly from original intentions related to local government. Before the January Insurrection, administration on the communal level had been entrusted to a *wójt* (mayor) who served simultaneously as a paid agent of the local landlord. With the emancipation decrees, this system was abolished and replaced by a two-tiered administration designed to end the nobility's domination of local affairs. At the lower level of the *gromada* (community or "small commune"), an assembly composed exclusively of peasants elected a *sołtys* (elder) who carried out those resolutions of the assembly confirmed by the authorities. At the higher level, several gromady constituted a *gmina* ("large commune"). In addition to the peasants, the gmina assembly included owners of adjoining estates and other nonpeasant settlements. The gmina assembly, in turn, elected the wójt, the *pisarz* (a clerk who saw to the day-to-day administration of communal affairs), and two plenipotentiaries. At both the gromada and gmina levels, landless peasants and smallholders possessing less than 1.5 and 3 morgs respectively were excluded from participation in the assemblies.

These institutions of self-government in the Polish countryside, initially designed to empower the peasantry at the expense of the manors, were gradually transformed into instruments of the ruling bureaucracy. Centralization and merger of gminy provided one means to this end. Of the 3,083 gminy in existence in 1864, only 1,287 remained forty years later.[25] The contraction of gminy made it easier for centrally appointed county officials to interfere in local affairs. By the 1880s the nachal'niki were regularly rejecting the results of local elections, suspending elected officials from their duties, declaring assembly resolutions invalid, and through the timely presence of the county Land Guard at assembly meetings, applying pressure on the peasants to act in a way prescribed by the Russian bureaucracy, especially in matters of taxation.[26] During the Gurko-Apukhtin era, county chiefs also acquired the power to appoint the communal pisarz, turning a previously elected official into yet another agent of the bureaucracy in the

24. On the conflict over servitudes in the late nineteenth century, see Helena Brodowska, *Ruch chłopski po uwłaszczeniu w Królestwie Polskim, 1864–1904* (Warsaw, 1967), pp. 65–109.

25. Jan Borkowski, *Chłopi polscy w dobie kapitalizmu* (Warsaw, 1981), p. 23.

26. Richard D. Lewis, "Revolution in the Countryside: Russian Poland, 1905–1906," *Carl Beck Papers in Russian and East European Studies* 506 (1986): 3.

"A Peasant before a State Official." Contemporary drawing by Jan Olszewski.
(Muzeum Niepodległości 35864)

Polish countryside. Most debilitating, however, was the introduction of Russian as the official language of local "self-government" as well as the language of instruction at village schools funded by the gminy. By the 1890s, self-government had come to mean the rural community's rubber-stamping of resolutions drawn up by an alien bureaucracy in a language incomprehensible to the villagers. Not surprisingly, peasant participation in meetings of communal assemblies declined precipitously, especially among members of the postemancipation generation.[27]

Despite the shortcomings of the agrarian reforms, most Polish peasants experienced an immediate improvement in their standard of living in the first decade after the emancipation. A continuing rise in grain prices throughout the 1870s contributed to their relative prosperity, while better nutrition through increased consumption lowered mortality rates.[28] Peasant

27. Brodowska, *Ruch chłopski,* pp. 136–140.
28. Tadeusz Sobczak, *Przełom w konsumpcji spożywczej w Królestwie Polskim w XIX wieku* (Wrocław, 1986), p. 254.

farmers were not induced by the favorable conditions, however, to introduce more intensive methods of land cultivation. In 1877, peasant farms of less than twenty hectares (approximately fifty acres) accounted for 80 percent of all peasant property holdings.[29] Such small plots discouraged the use of mechanical threshers, seeders, and reapers. Moreover, only a fraction of the peasant farms used iron ploughs, and iron harrows remained practically unknown up to World War I. As a result, total grain production and average yields increased only marginally. In this regard, the Kingdom even lagged behind neighboring Galicja under Austrian rule, considered by many to be the most poverty-stricken, "backward" corner of Europe.

Grain production also failed to keep pace with rapid population growth, a process that had begun in the 1870s. In 1860, the Kingdom of Poland had an estimated 4.8 million inhabitants. According to official censuses taken in 1897 and 1907, the population increased to 9.2 and 11.5 million inhabitants respectively.[30] As a result, the output of grain per inhabitant actually declined so that by the beginning of the twentieth century the Kingdom had become a net importer of grain for the first time in its history.[31]

The demographic explosion, in turn, placed enormous pressures on the land. Principally through subdivision, the number of peasant holdings increased from 593,000 in 1870 to 717,000 in 1899, and the average size of peasant holdings declined.[32] By 1907, almost 90 percent of all peasant landowners possessed farms of five hectares (12.4 acres) or less. At the same time, the landless population doubled. In 1891 the Warsaw Statistical Committee estimated that there were 827,000 landless peasants (together with families), or 13.2 percent of the rural population, compared with 590,000 in 1864. By 1901, that number had grown to 1,220,333, or 18.1 percent of all rural inhabitants.[33]

The great estates and, to a considerably lesser extent, the larger peasant farms could provide employment for only part of the rapidly expanding rural proletariat and semiproletariat. Moreover, as a readily available source of cheap labor, farm workers received abysmally low wages, which were

29. Juliusz Łukasiewicz, "Drogi rozwoju rolnictwa na ziemiach polskich," in *Polska XIX wieku*, ed. Kieniewicz, p. 22.
30. Włodzimierz Wakar, *Rozwój terytoryalny narodowości polskiej*, vol. 2 (Kielce, 1918), p. 11.
31. Łukasiewicz, "Drogi," p. 44.
32. Kieniewicz, *Emancipation of the Polish Peasantry*, p. 189.
33. Krzysztof Groniowski, *Robotnicy rolni w Królestwie Polskim, 1871–1914* (Warsaw, 1977), pp. 29, 48.

paid both in money and in kind. At the beginning of the twentieth century, the average annual monetary wage of an *ordynariusz* (a full-time farm worker) was twenty-two rubles, supplemented by 10.8 bushels of grain. Full-time farm workers were also granted a small amount of land (averaging one-third of an acre) in order to grow potatoes, the principal staple in their diet, and usually the right to raise a cow, a hog, a few goats, and chickens at their employer's expense. Occasionally, a farm worker also received specified amounts of wood and salt as part of his wage. The total value of the average annual earnings of a farm worker in money and kind has been estimated at 157 rubles, which fell well below the average annual wage of 240 rubles paid in industry.[34] Of course not all landless peasants could find full-time employment in the countryside, especially when faced with the competition of peasant smallholders seeking seasonal, part-time employment.

The already-mentioned collapse of local grain prices in the 1880s, which drove many gentry proprietors from the land, had a less dramatic but still significant impact on the peasantry and contributed to the general impoverishment of the Polish countryside. Peasant farm income declined, and the previously impressive growth of peasant consumption slowed considerably. Fortunately, the agricultural depression produced no famines, but market conditions discouraged peasant farmers from expanding grain production even through traditional, extensive methods. Moreover, the growth of the hog population stagnated, and the cattle population actually declined.[35] After 1896, grain prices stabilized and then began to rise, but it would take years for peasant agriculture to recover from the crisis.

In the meantime, hundreds of thousands had already left the land. Some went to Prussia's Polish provinces in search of employment, only to be expelled by Bismarck in 1885. They returned with the relaxation of immigration policies after 1890, so that by 1914, some 400,000 "seasonal" farmhands from the Kingdom were employed by German agriculture.[36] Between 1890 and 1904, another 127,000 emigrated permanently from the Kingdom to new homes in the Ruhr industrial region of Germany, Canada, Brazil, and above all, the United States.[37] Most important, however, they were lured by the expectation of higher wages and social mobility to the

---

34. Ibid., pp. 69–75.
35. On the crisis afflicting Polish agriculture in the 1880s and 1890s, see Juliusz Łukasiewicz, *Kryzys agrarny na ziemiach polskich w końcu XIX wieku* (Warsaw, 1968).
36. Kieniewicz, *Emancipation of the Polish Peasantry*, p. 193. According to Kieniewicz, these "seasonal" farmhands worked ten to eleven months a year.
37. Borkowski, *Chłopi polscy w dobie kapitalizmu*, p. 44.

dynamically expanding industrial centers of the Kingdom itself, sparking an internal migration of unprecedented proportions which was to change the social, economic, cultural, and political complexion of the country.

## Industrialization and Urbanization

The industrial revolution, as it spread eastward, came to the Kingdom of Poland in the second half of the nineteenth century, transforming the country—at least temporarily—into the most economically advanced region of the Russian state. Until the late 1890s, the total value of industrial production in the Kingdom actually exceeded that of the rest of the Russian Empire.[38] Stimulated initially by railroad construction and the expansion of the domestic market, and subsequently by sales in a much larger Russian market, industrialization of the Kingdom progressed through two distinct stages in the relatively short period of fifty years. In many ways, the Kingdom's industrial revolution with its accompanying social and demographic transformations followed the classic English model; in others, local conditions and geographic factors imbued these processes with peculiarly Polish characteristics.

The starting point of the Kingdom's industrial revolution is subject to debate. The most recent consensus focuses on the year 1850, when the lifting of tariff barriers between the Kingdom and the empire eased the access of Polish industry to potentially lucrative Russian markets. Of course, industrial enterprises existed in the Kingdom already in the first half of the nineteenth century, and in mining and metallurgy many were owned and operated by the state. In the absence of cheap transportation and sufficient local demand, however, a considerable number of these undertakings—and particularly those under state management—proved unprofitable and were abandoned or allowed to stagnate. Railroad construction, which began in the 1850s, soon facilitated the movement of raw materials and finished goods, while the favorable economic conditions in agriculture and the demographic increase after the emancipation of the peasantry led to a dramatic expansion of the domestic market. The first industries to tap that market, food processing and textiles, were also the first to be transformed through mechanization and the adoption of the factory system of industrial organization. By 1864 almost all the country's sugar refineries had converted from wind and water power to steam, and,

38. Ireneusz Ihnatowicz, "Przemysł, Handel, Finanse," in *Polska XIX wieku,* ed. Kieniewicz, p. 82.

by 1875, the cotton-spinning industry was completely mechanized. Owing to state neglect and inadequate investment, mining and metallurgy were the last industries to experience technological modernization. The sale of concessions in the form of long-term leases to foreign investors, coupled with the imposition of protective tariffs on imported coal and pig iron in the 1870s, led to the emergence of a modern heavy-industrial base in the Kingdom by 1890.[39]

In the first phase of the Kingdom's industrial revolution, up to around 1880, the main catalysts of economic change were the development and expansion of local markets, the growth of per capita domestic consumption, and native capital accumulation and investment. The Kingdom's incorporation into the Russian customs system became significant only later; until 1880, the country's trade with western Europe remained more important than its trade with the Russian Empire.[40] At that point, the eastward movement of Polish industrial goods began, led by textiles. This reorientation of Polish industry from production for domestic consumption to production for "export" was spurred by the seemingly limitless possibilities for profits in the huge Russian market. Once that market emerged and began to expand, Polish industry, at least initially, faced little competition in its efforts to capture it. Until the 1890s, Russia's semiprotectionist trade policies favored the more advanced Polish industries as well as infant Russian industries not yet able to satisfy consumer demand. Simultaneously, the agrarian crisis of the 1880s and 1890s dramatically slowed the growth of domestic consumption in the Kingdom and prompted a search for new sales markets. As a result, the Kingdom's trade with Russia increased elevenfold in the period 1880–1910.[41] Driven primarily by "exports" until the late 1890s, this trade led to a lasting dependence of certain industries on Russian sales. By 1900, 75 percent of the production of the Kingdom's textile industry was sold on "eastern" markets.[42] In addition, the Kingdom exported large quantities of pig iron, steel, sugar, paper, and agricultural machines to Russia in the last two decades of the nineteenth century.

Stimulated primarily by sales on Russian markets in the period 1880–1900, Polish industry experienced a second phase of modernization and expansion. Steam turbines, then electric generators continued to transform

39. Irena Pietrzak-Pawłowska, "Przewrót przemysłowy w warunkach kapitalistycznej industrializacji na ziemiach polskich do 1918 r.," in *Uprzemysłowienie ziem polskich w XIX i XX wieku: Studia i materiały*, ed. Irena Pietrzak-Pawłowska (Wrocław, 1970), pp. 57–103.
40. Andrzej Jezierski, *Handel zagraniczny Królestwa Polskiego, 1815–1914* (Warsaw, 1967), p. 121.
41. Ibid., p. 151.
42. Ireneusz Ihnatowicz, *Przemysł łódzki w latach 1860–1900* (Wrocław, 1965), p. 124.

the energy base. Joint-stock companies dominated by foreign capital gradually replaced individual native ownership of the larger enterprises, and
this conversion was accompanied by the creation of informal cartels, particularly in the mining and textile industries. Production became more concentrated, although not on the scale that subsequently prevailed in Russia.
Nevertheless, in the Kingdom's metallurgical industry, the three largest
firms employed 63 percent of the labor force and produced 64 percent of
the country's pig iron and 68 percent of the country's steel.[43] In the textile
industry, great firms employing over a thousand workers accounted for
over half of the total value of production and an equal percentage of the
labor force.[44] At the same time, production processes became more concentrated in individual factories, reducing the reliance of the textile industry, for instance, on cottage labor at certain stages in the production cycle.

Following the classic British model, the textile industry played a dominant role in the Kingdom's industrial revolution. Concentrated in the Łódź
region of Piotrków Province, with important subcenters in the Warsaw-
Żyrardów and Częstochowa-Sosnowiec regions, the textile industry at the
turn of the century employed over half (121, 481 workers) of the entire
factory labor force and accounted for 44 percent of the total value of
industrial production.[45] Textiles also led Polish industry's offensive on Russian markets and absorbed the largest share of capital investment. The
prosperity of the textile industry was therefore of crucial importance to the
country's economic health, and in Łódź and other parts of Piotrków Province, it affected almost every inhabitant. Extremely vulnerable to changing
market conditions, the Kingdom's textile industry experienced periodic crises that led to sharp declines in sales, factory closings, and high rates of
unemployment. Although the general trend was one of dramatic expansion
(between 1879 and 1913, the value of textile production increased fivefold,
and employment fourfold), the first years of the twentieth century were
characterized by depression and contraction.[46]

"Heavy industry," a term that embraces the mining, mineral, metal, and
metallurgical industries, comprised the second-most-important sector in the
Kingdom's industrial economy at the turn of the century. It was also the
most rapidly expanding one. Of only minimal significance in 1880, heavy

43. Wacław Długoborski, "Górnictwo i hutnictwo do 1918 r.," in *Uprzemysłowienie*, ed.
Pietrzak-Pawłowska, pp. 150–151.
44. Gryzelda Missalowa et al., "Przemysł włókienniczy," in *Uprzemysłowienie*, ed. Pietrzak-Pawłowska, p. 230.
45. Paweł Korzec, *Walki rewolucyjne w Łodzi i okręgu łódzkim w latach 1905–1907* (Warsaw, 1956), pp. 11–12.
46. Missalowa et al., "Przemysł włókienniczy," pp. 226–227.

industry accounted for 27.9 percent of all industrial enterprises and employed 32.8 percent of the industrial labor force by 1911.[47] The Dąbrowa Basin, a geophysical extension of [Prussian] Upper Silesia into the Będzin region of southern Piotrków Province, became the principal center of the mining and metallurgical industries, beginning with the purchase by French capital of four coal mines and the Huta Bankowa steel mill from the Russian state in the late 1870s. Aided by the further influx of foreign, mainly German, capital as well as by Russian protective tariffs, the Dąbrowa Basin by 1890 produced over half the country's pig iron and steel and almost all its coal and zinc.[48] At the same time, Warsaw became a major center of the Kingdom's metal industry, employing 18,000 workers (or 43 percent of the city's industrial labor force) in the first years of the twentieth century.[49] Compared to textiles, heavy industry was considerably less vulnerable to general economic crises, which tended to slow rather than halt its further expansion. For most of the period under consideration, the rapid growth of heavy industry outstripped the influx of new workers. The coal industry, for instance, suffered a perpetual labor shortage.[50]

Food processing, mainly distilling, brewing, milling, and especially, sugar beet–refining, was the Kingdom's third-most-important industrial sector. The oldest and most traditional of the country's industries, food processing was closely tied to the agrarian economy and dominated by small factories on manorial estates up to approximately 1870. Many of these plants collapsed after the emancipation of the peasantry and the loss of servile labor; between 1855 and 1897, the number of distilleries and breweries was cut in half, the number of sugar refineries by 20 percent.[51] As the significance of landed capital in the food industry lessened, merchant and bank capital grew in importance, primarily through the formation of joint-stock companies. Expansion of the industry occurred largely as a result of investments in new technologies and substantial growth in labor productivity. Between 1870 and 1914, sugar and beer production increased eightfold, and alcohol production grew fourfold. Over the same period, however, employment increased by only 40 percent, from 19.3 to 26.6 thousand workers.[52] Unlike textiles and heavy industry, the food processing

47. Pietrzak-Pawłowska, "Przewrót," pp. 81–82.
48. Jan Ziemba, Kształtowanie się proletariatu Zagłębia Dąbrowskiego, 1865–1914 (Warsaw, 1980), pp. 20–25.
49. Anna Żarnowska, Robotnicy Warszawy na przełomie XIX i XX wieku (Warsaw, 1985), p. 18.
50. Ziemba, Kształtowanie się proletariatu Dąbrowskiego, pp. 39–41.
51. Stanisław Wykrętowicz, "Przemysł spożywczy," in Uprzemysłowienie, ed. Pietrzak-Pawłowska, pp. 285–286.
52. Ibid., pp. 288–290.

industry was not geographically concentrated. Distilleries, for example, were scattered throughout the Polish countryside, whereas breweries tended to be located in urban areas. The food processing industry could therefore be as important to the economy of Warsaw, where it was the third-most-important source of industrial employment, as it was to rural Siedlce Province, where the Elżbietów sugar beet manufacturing plant was the largest industrial enterprise, employing 367 workers in 1904.[53]

In line with patterns elsewhere in Europe, industrialization in the Kingdom was accompanied by urbanization. Between 1865 and 1897, the urban population increased by 131.3 percent compared with a 77.2 percent demographic increase for the country as a whole. In 1865, one out of every five inhabitants of the Kingdom lived in a city or larger town; in 1897, one out of every four; in 1913, one out of every three. Urbanization was particularly pronounced on the west bank of the Vistula River, where 80 percent of the urban population resided. Piotrków Province, for example, experienced a 376 percent increase in urban population between 1865 and 1897. By contrast, the proportion of urban inhabitants to total population actually declined in Siedlce Province on the Vistula's east bank. Nevertheless, by 1897, thirty-two cities in the Kingdom had more than ten thousand inhabitants, with Warsaw and Łódź accounting for half of the country's total urban population.

The cities and towns were also primarily responsible for the multinational character of Russian Poland. Although the Polish element dominated the countryside and constituted almost three-quarters of the total population, only 48.2 percent of the urban population was Polish in 1897. Nevertheless, as a result of wage migration from the villages, the Polish element was primarily responsible for the demographic increase in urban areas. This growth occurred primarily at the expense of the Jews, who in 1865 accounted for 47.1 percent of the urban population. Although steadily declining as a percentage of total urban population, Jews still were 38.6 percent of all urban dwellers in 1897 (compared with a 13.7 percent share of the Kingdom's total population). Like the Jews, the German and Russian elements of the population were primarily urban ones, accounting for 6 and 4 percent of the urban population, respectively. The former provided a significant proportion of the capital and skilled labor required by industrialization, especially in the textile industry, while the latter group was made up largely of state officials and their families. The census category of "others" in the urban population would have included French, Czechs,

---

53. Żarnowska, *Robotnicy Warszawy*, p. 20; Urszula Głowacka-Maksymiuk, *Gubernia siedlecka w latach rewolucji, 1905–1907* (Warsaw, 1985), p. 37.

English, Estonians, Ukrainians, and Lithuanians, although the latter two groups were predominantly rural in character, concentrated in the eastern-most counties of the Kingdom.[54]

In 1904 the population of Warsaw, the Kingdom's largest city, stood at more than three-quarters of a million inhabitants, having increased more than three times in less than forty years. The most dynamic growth rates were recorded in the period 1895–1900, when the city's population increased by over 150,000. Natural increase and migration shared equally in stimulating the city's demographic growth, although in the most dynamic years before the turn of century, the latter accounted for 65.3 percent of the increase in population. According to the census of 1897, 47.7 percent of the city's inhabitants were born outside of Warsaw. In the suburbs, where most of the city's larger industrial plants and a sizable proportion of the working-class population were located, that figure stood at 56.1 percent. In comparison with Łódź or the industrial settlements of the Będzin region in the Dąbrowa Basin, migrants to Warsaw came from farther afield; nevertheless, the surrounding Warsaw Province provided the main source, followed by the adjacent counties of Płock and Siedlce provinces. According to official statistics, 44.4 percent of Warsaw's population was "professionally active" (a term that does not embrace family members helping in small artisanal shops, a practice quite common among Warsaw's Jews, who were one-third of the population). Of the city's "professionally active" inhabitants, 36 percent relied on industry and artisanal trades as the main source of income, 19.3 percent on commerce, 12.8 percent on domestic and personal services, 9.9 percent on administration and the free professions, 6.6 percent on day labor, 6.5 percent on transportation and communications, and 4.7 percent on "unearned income."[55]

The growth of Łódź, the Kingdom's second-largest city and center of its textile industry, was even more phenomenal. Little more than a sleepy hamlet at the beginning of the nineteenth century, Łódź counted 33,000 inhabitants by 1865 and 314,000 by 1897. In contrast to Warsaw, Łódź had a large German minority (18 percent of the population in 1897), which played a crucial role in transforming the city into the country's most im-

---

54. For the best overall treatment of the Kingdom's urbanization, see Maria Nietyksza, *Rozwój miast i aglomeracji miejsko-przemysłowych w Królestwie Polskim, 1865–1914* (Warsaw, 1986); see also Ryszard Kołodziejczyk, *Miasta, mieszczaństwo, burżuazja w Polsce w XIX wieku* (Warsaw, 1979).

55. Maria Nietyksza, *Ludność Warszawy na przełomie XIX i XX wieku* (Warsaw, 1971), pp. 26–29, 30–34, 41–43, 138, 149, 155; see also Stephen D. Corrsin, *Warsaw before the First World War: Poles and Jews in the Third City of the Russian Empire, 1880–1914* (Boulder, 1989), for a discussion of the city's ethnically mixed character.

portant industrial center. The city's great textile barons were predominantly of German origin, and Germans were strongly represented among factory technicians and foremen. Nevertheless, that minority was rapidly losing ground to Poles (48.3 percent), many of whom had recently arrived from the countryside, as well as to Jews (31.4 percent), whose numbers had increased both naturally and as a result of migration from the empire's western provinces.[56]

Łódź was a classically proletarian city; in numbers of industrial workers it was third in the Russian Empire, behind Moscow and St. Petersburg, on the eve of the 1905 revolution. According to data compiled by the Factory Inspectorate, 76,500 workers were employed by 547 factories, the vast majority in the textile industry. Another 6,000 cottage workers, classified among 23,000 independent artisans in official statistics, also derived their income from the textile industry. Among the city's textile workers, women formed nearly half the labor force, and the employment of minor children was commonplace until the late 1880s. The city was continually overwhelmed by the onslaught of new migrants from the countryside; well over half of the city's inhabitants in the 1890s were first-generation residents, and the proportion was considerably higher in the unincorporated industrial suburbs of Widzew and Bałuty.[57] Not surprisingly, the growth of institutions such as schools, hospitals, and libraries did not keep pace with population growth, prompting one scholar to refer to Łódź as "the most [culturally] backward city in the Russian state."[58]

Urbanization in the Będzin area of the Dąbrowa Basin, the Kingdom's third major industrial region, was peculiar in that there were no major concentrations of population similar to Warsaw or Łódź. Nevertheless, the population of Sosnowiec, the largest city in the region, increased from nine thousand in 1886 to fifty-seven thousand in 1904.[59] Other centers of urban population, although still treated as rural communes in official statistics, included Dąbrowa, Czeladź, and Zawiercie, not to mention the county seat of Będzin. The region as a whole experienced a fivefold increase in population between 1867 and 1912, with the peak period falling in the last five years of the nineteenth century. In comparison with Warsaw and Łódź, the Polish element was far more dominant in the Dąbrowa Basin, constituting over 86.5 percent of the total population.[60] Like Łódź, the Dąbrowa

---

56. Kołodziejczyk, *Miasta*, p. 79; Korzec, *Walki rewolucyjne*, p. 31.
57. Władysław Lech Karwacki, *Związki zawodowe i stowarzyszenia pracodawców w Łodzi* (Łódź, 1972), pp. 1–19; Ihnatowicz, *Przemysł łódzki*, pp. 89–94.
58. Władysław Lech Karwacki, *Łódź w latach rewolucji, 1905–1907* (Łódź, 1975), p. 9.
59. Kołodziejczyk, *Miasta*, p. 70.
60. Nietykksza, *Rozwój miast*, p. 304.

Łódź as viewed from the south. (Muzeum Niepodległości 39028)

Basin was characterized by the numerical dominance of its working-class population (56.8 percent of total inhabitants in 1897). Yet there was much greater occupational diversity among that population; 27.3 percent of the regional labor force was employed by the mining industry, 17.9 percent by the metal and metallurgical industries, 10.4 percent by the textile industry. Although the organization of educational, cultural, and health-care institutions in the Dąbrowa Basin left much to be desired, the situation was much better than in Łódź. In 1897, 48 percent of the adult population of the Dąbrowa Basin could read and write compared with a less than 40 percent literacy rate in Łódź.[61]

As impressive as the Kingdom's industrialization and urbanization were statistically, they must be viewed in their proper context. To be sure, the total value of industrial production exceeded that of agriculture by the turn of the century. Two-thirds of the population nevertheless continued to live in the countryside, and agriculture remained the major source of income for a majority of the Kingdom's inhabitants. Within industry itself, modern

61. Ziemba, *Kształtowanie się proletariatu Dąbrowskiego*, pp. 34–36, 47–51, 171–172, 188–193; Karwacki, *Związki zawodowe*, pp. 17–18.

Textile workers from Hielle and Dietrich in Żyrardów. (Muzeum Niepodległości 36365)

methods and machines existed side by side with antiquated equipment and more traditional production processes. The transportation of coal directly from the mines, for instance, was based exclusively on human labor and draft animals until World War I. In the textile industry, the abundance of cheap labor and the persistence of the cottage system hindered the introduction of technological innovations, which in turn contributed to a period of stagnation in the first years of the twentieth century.

Similarly, urbanization, which proceeded quite dramatically in the country's western provinces, had only a minimal impact east of the Vistula. Moreover, a substantial portion of the urban population retained social and economic ties to the countryside. In cities like Łódź, adaptation to changing conditions was perhaps more difficult for native urban dwellers continually overwhelmed by peasant migrants than it was for the migrants themselves.

In reality, the Kingdom could be considered "advanced" only in the context of the tremendous backwardness of the entire Russian Empire; compared with western Europe, the Kingdom continued to lag far behind. What is more, by the beginning of the twentieth century, the Kingdom's industry was losing the privileged place in the very Russian sales markets that had stimulated its expansion the previous twenty years. Already in the

Working-class dwellings on the outskirts of Warsaw. (Muzeum Niepodległości 38008)

1890s, during Sergei Witte's tenure as minister of finance, the Kingdom was subjected to discriminatory policies in taxation, state investment, and rail freight rates in order to protect Russian industries from Polish competition. At the same time, the technological gap between Polish and Russian industry began to close, depriving the former of its competitive edge in the eastern markets. Consequently, exports to Russia of Polish manufactured goods, particularly of the textile and metallurgical industries, declined appreciably in the first years of the twentieth century, while imports of Russian industrial products increased. By 1910, for example, pig iron from the Donets Basin had captured 42.8 percent of the Kingdom's market, symbolizing a dramatic shift in the terms of trade.[62]

Partial modernization, uneven development, and overreliance on Russian markets thus characterized the Kingdom's industrial economy just before the 1905 revolution. Not surprisingly, that economy had just entered a state of crisis and adjustment to new market conditions created by Russian industrialization. Economic stagnation rather than expansion was the rule in the first decade of the twentieth century. Nevertheless, the transformational processes of the previous fifty years had already made deep imprints on Polish society, and the long-term trends were irreversible. For better or worse, the Kingdom of Poland had entered the modern industrial age. A

62. Długoborski, "Górnictwo," p. 169.

large but not entirely stabilized class of industrial workers had emerged, constituting about 10 percent of the country's population. Even more than the emancipated peasantry, the factory proletariat was destined to become the new focal point of Polish political strategies.

## The Changing Nature of Polish Politics

In the forty years between the collapse of the January Insurrection and the first rumblings of the 1905 revolution, Polish political thought retained many of the divisions and much of the diversity that had characterized it since the partitions of the eighteenth century. Although some scholars prefer to reduce that diversity to a few easily manageable categories for didactic purposes, actual historical experience reveals many conflicting and converging political tendencies.[63] More important than categories and labels, however, is the social and economic setting in which political thought is formulated. In the Kingdom of Poland at the end of the nineteenth century, peasant emancipation and industrialization revolutionized the context of Polish politics and created conditions favorable to the formulation and adoption of ideologies that anticipated the rise of modern mass movements.

The collapse of the January Insurrection, followed by the dramatic shift in the European balance of power in the wake of the Franco-Prussian War and German unification, brought a definite end to the romantic era of Polish history. Russian retribution removed the szlachta as the dominant force in Polish politics, thereby eliminating the principal social base of the insurrectionary tradition. Shortly thereafter, Prussia's victory over France dashed any lingering hope for assistance from the West. The "Polish question," once at the center of European diplomacy, now disappeared into oblivion. Not surprisingly, demoralization and resignation spread among the politically conscious and active strata of Polish society. At home, conspiracies were denounced as suicidal, the insurrectionary past condemned. Abroad, Władysław Czartoryski closed the "Polish Embassy" at the Hotel Lambert in Paris, the center of efforts for over thirty years to gain diplomatic support for the cause of Polish independence.

Such a political climate gave rise to the philosophy known as "Triple

---

63. See particularly Adam Bromke, *Poland's Politics: Idealism versus Realism* (Cambridge, Mass., 1967). Jerzy Jedlicki's *Jakiej cywilizacji Polacy potrzebują: Studia z dziejów idei i wyobraźni XIX wieku* (Warsaw, 1988) is the most reliable guide to the complexity and diversity of Polish political thought for the entire period of the partitions. More specific to the period embraced by my book are Wilhelm Feldman, *Dzieje polskiej myśli politycznej, 1864–1914* (Warsaw, 1933), and Wereszycki, *Historia polityczna Polski.*

Loyalism.'' Too frequently, Triple Loyalism has been characterized as an abject political prostration at the feet of the three empires that had partitioned Poland. Actually, it was a rather sophisticated program that considered loyal behavior toward the partitioning governments as the necessary, if evil, condition for the continued cultural existence and material progress of Polish lands. Its practitioners, moreover, were not of one mind. For ultramontane conservative periodicals like the Kraków-based *Czas* (Time) or *Dziennik Poznański* (The Poznań Daily) in Prussian Poland, Triple Loyalism meant not only resignation from the ''hopeless'' cause of Polish independence but also entrusting the preservation of the existing social order to Europe's conservative monarchies. By contrast the young Kraków conservatives who made up the Stańczyk group, though opposed to the spirit of Polish irredentism, were nevertheless considerably more accommodating to social and economic change.[64]

In Russian Poland, right-wing loyalism found a natural representative in the figure of Zygmunt Wielopolski, son of the luckless Aleksander Wielopolski, and, as elsewhere on Polish lands, the aristocracy provided its principal constituency. By appealing to the goodwill of the tsar, by seeking a common ground with Russian conservatives based on Pan-Slavism, and by supporting the Russian government's struggle against the revolutionary movement, Wielopolski hoped to gain equal rights for the tsar's Polish subjects and a more decentralized political structure for the Kingdom. Viewed in the light of the tragic aftermath of the January Insurrection and its effect on the collective instinct for self-preservation, Wielopolski's modest program offered a ''realistic'' alternative to total political apathy and quietism. After Leo XIII's concordat with the Russian government in 1883, Wielopolski's program won the tacit support of the reinstated Polish episcopate and became the basis for an informal clerical-conservative alliance.

*Kraj* (The Country), a social and literary weekly published in St. Petersburg and associated primarily with the figures of Włodzimierz Spasowicz and Erazm Piltz, represented a somewhat more moderate strain of loyalism. Like Wielopolski, *Kraj*'s political program emphasized conciliation with Russia, but more in terms of the Russian intelligentsia than the tsarist government. Indeed *Kraj* openly criticized that government, particularly its policies of russification. *Kraj*, too, was influenced by Pan-Slavic currents and acknowledged the hegemonic role of Russia in the Slavic movement. Yet in contrast to Wielopolski and his adherents, its editors polemicized

---

64. For an interesting discussion of the Stańczyk group of Kraków conservatives, see Marcin Król's introduction to *Stańczycy: Antologia myśli społecznej i politycznej konserwatystów krakowskich* (Warsaw, 1985), pp. 5–37.

with conservative Russian Pan-Slavists who accused the Poles of betraying Slavic interests. Finally, *Kraj* was much more emphatic in its promotion of economic and cultural "organic work" as the principal means of assuring the continued existence of the Polish nation. As censorship was much less severe in St. Petersburg than in Warsaw, *Kraj* was able to attract and publish many of the most important Polish authors of the day, including Henryk Sienkiewicz and Eliza Orzeszkowa, making it for a time the most informative and widely read periodical in Russian Poland.[65]

The problem with loyalism and conciliation in Russian Poland, whether of the clerical-conservative or more progressive variety represented by *Kraj*, was that the concessions and goodwill necessary to their minimal political viability were not forthcoming from the Russian side. The Gurko-Apukhtin era of systematic russification could not but undermine Wielopolski's efforts to legitimate Russian rule in Polish eyes, while the majority of educated Russians remained distrustful of even the most moderately formulated Polish policies, always suspecting them as covers for Polish separatism. Unable to demonstrate any concrete political dividends as a result of their policies, the loyalists and conciliationists in Russian Poland failed to attract more than a narrow upper-class following. As for the rank-and-file nobility, or what was left of it after 1864, this potential constituency of conservative politics found it difficult to find common ground with a Russian government that had long abrogated its traditional rights and privileges and had purposefully reduced its property.

Despite these obstacles, loyalism and conciliation were given one last chance with the death of Alexander III in 1894, his succession by Nicholas II, and the departure of Gurko and Apukhtin from the Kingdom. Nicholas's visit to Warsaw in 1897 and the tsar's permission for the unveiling of a monument dedicated to Adam Mickiewicz, the great bard of Polish romanticism, briefly raised the hopes of Polish conservatism for substantive changes in Russian policy. These hopes were dashed within a year, however, by the disclosure and publication of a secret memorial of the new Warsaw governor-general, Prince Imeretinskii, in which Gurko's "liberal successor" ridiculed the political impotence of the Polish conservatives. More damaging to the loyalist-conciliationist camp was the continuation and, in some cases, extension of the denationalization measures of the preceding era.[66]

The decline and gradual disappearance of the Polish szlachta, the tra-

65. On *Kraj*, see particularly Zenon Kmiecik, *"Kraj" za czasów redaktorstwa Erazma Piltza* (Warsaw, 1969).
66. Wandycz, *Lands of Partitioned Poland*, p. 280. In the first years of the twentieth century, for example, the provincial Russian bureaucracy made an unsuccessful effort to eliminate Polish as a permitted language for the instruction of religion.

Triumphal Gate and street decorations on the occasion of the visit of Tsar Nicholas II to Warsaw, 1897. (Muzeum Niepodległości 22412)

ditional social base for all political activity, whether conservative or revolutionary, made it increasingly unlikely for that group to play an influential, let alone leading, role in any case. Driven from the land by Russian policies and adverse economic conditions, many bankrupt noblemen migrated to the cities in the 1880s. According to the imperial census of 1897, two-thirds of those officially classified as gentry lived in cities, where they made up the majority of recruits for a newly emerging urban intelligentsia.[67] Indeed, this first generation of intelligentsia of noble descent coincided roughly with the first generation of industrial workers of peasant background; both came to the cities in search of work. Some displaced gentry found employment in the lower levels of the state administration, particularly the postal and rail bureaucracies. Others were able to turn to the private sector or to the free professions, and a narrow stratum— the "creative intelligentsia"—earned a living from cultural pursuits or journalism. It was among this intelligentsia, in its first generation careerminded and apolitical, that the liberal philosophy of Warsaw positivism with its emphasis on "organic work" found its principal audience.[68]

67. Janina Żurawicka, *Inteligencja warszawska w końcu XIX wieku* (Warsaw, 1978), p. 54.
68. On Warsaw positivism, see Stanislaus Blejwas, *Realism in Polish Politics: Warsaw Positivism and National Survival in Nineteenth-Century Poland* (New Haven, 1984).

Compared to Triple Loyalism, the positivism of August Comte as it applied to Polish conditions was considerably more forward-looking. Harking back to the traditions of the Polish Enlightenment, Warsaw positivism based itself on a firm belief in reason, science, material progress, and education as keys to the nation's future. Reformist in outlook, but politically passive, Warsaw positivism rejected both political loyalism and insurrectionary irredentism. Instead, positivism called on the "enlightened classes" to participate in "organic work" that aimed at quietly transforming a traditional society into a modern one as the only means of preserving the national existence. Arguing that the only field for Polish "conquests" was in the advance of civilization, Aleksander Świętochowski, Warsaw positivism's leading exponent, wrote, "If a supreme omnipotent force offered us a choice between 500,000 soldiers and the same number of knowledgeable people, we would take the latter."[69]

Superficially apolitical, in practice positivism could not be separated from politics. The positivists' designation of the nascent Polish bourgeoisie as the leading class in the nation's future, as well as their critique of the nobility's role in the nation's past, invited attacks from traditional conservatives. The ultramontane clergy, for its part, accused the positivists of loosening social bonds as a result of their liberal positions on divorce, the emancipation of women, and Jewish assimilation. Positivism's espousal of materialism, modernism, and secular education also brought on a strong clerical reaction.[70]

In time, however, the principal challenge to positivism came from the left of the political spectrum, particularly from the emerging nationalist and socialist movements, which derided Świętochowski and the Warsaw positivists for their apolitical reformism in the face of belligerent russification. Like conservative loyalism, positivism was undermined by the uncompromising nature of Russian policies, which in the latter case rendered meaningful "organic work" next to impossible. The fact that the Kingdom's emerging entrepreneurial bourgeoisie in the last decades of the nineteenth century was largely non-Polish and partially absentee, a varied group more interested in maximizing profits than in playing the philanthropic and cultural role assigned to it by the positivists, further played into the hands of liberalism's leftist opponents. Finally, the coming of age in the late 1880s and early 1890s, of a second, more politically impatient generation

69. Feldman, *Dzieje polskiej myśli politycznej*, p. 153.
70. On the political exchange between the Warsaw positivists and their conservative opponents, see Andrzej Jaszczuk, *Spór pozytywistów z konserwatystami o przyszłość Polski, 1870–1903* (Warsaw, 1986).

of the intelligentsia devoid of personal memories of the tragedy that accompanied the ill-fated January Insurrection, also led to a search for more
activist solutions. Given these circumstances, the intelligentsia in Russian
Poland never did become a real substitute for the native, reforming middle
class of Western tradition, nor would it create a significant political vehicle
of progressive liberalism like the Constitutional Democratic Party in Russia. Nevertheless, both the early nationalists and the socialists owed an
intellectual debt to positivism. The former eventually adopted much of the
positivists' economic and social agenda, and positivism's materialist philosophy and emphasis on scientific method definitely influenced the latter.[71]

The emergence of the modern ideologies of nationalism and socialism
marked a transformation in Polish political thought, if not yet a transformation of Polish political culture. Before the revolutionary period, the nationalist and socialist movements had not attained the status of true mass
movements. Effectively confined to the underground by the Russian
bureaucratic-police system, conspiratorial elites formed primarily from the
intelligentsia dominated both camps in their prerevolutionary phase. As
political ideologies, however, nationalism and socialism already enjoyed
greater popular appeal and a broader social base than either conservative
loyalism or liberal positivism. What set them apart was their call for active
opposition to Russian rule and the existing political status quo at a time
of fluid economic and social change. The ascendancy of nationalism and
socialism also coincided with a general reaction among younger intellectuals to the "realism" of the older generation, symbolized by the neo-
romantic Młoda Polska (Young Poland) movement in literature, theater,
and the arts.

Of the two popular political currents, nationalism proved far more ideologically, and therefore organizationally, cohesive. The birth of the modern
Polish nationalist movement is usually associated with three interrelated
events: the founding of the Warsaw-based populist periodical *Głos* (The
Voice) in 1886, the formation of the Polish League (Liga Polska) by émigré
Polish democrats in 1887, and the creation of a radical student organization
known as "Zet" (a popular acronym for the Union of Polish Youth) in
the same year. The appearance of *Głos,* whose most important contributor
was Jan Ludwik Popławski, signaled the emergence of a new generation
unwilling to accept positivist prescriptions for the nation's survival. Appealing to the radical and democratic aspirations of this generation, *Głos*
called for mass political action as the only effective form of opposition to

71. Blejwas, *Realism in Polish Politics,* pp. 148, 162–163.

russification. Meanwhile, émigré Polish democrats led by Col. Zygmunt Miłkowski (also known by the pseudonym T. T. Jeż) and relatively silent since the collapse of the Paris Commune and many of their revolutionary hopes, seized the organizational initiative. The publication of Miłkowski's brochure "On Active Defense and the National Treasury" was both an antipositivist manifesto and the founding document of the nationalist movement. Shortly thereafter, with funds unexpectedly pouring into Miłkowski's "national treasury," the decision was made to form the Polish League with the aim of coordinating a renewed struggle for Polish independence. Through its energetic emissary and one-time socialist sympathizer Zygmunt Balicki, the Polish League then inspired the organization of Zet, a clandestine organization of Polish students enrolled in universities both at home and abroad. Together with *Głos,* Zet subsequently recognized the leadership of the Polish League in the so-called camp of action.

In its formative stage, Polish nationalism represented a mixture of radical populist, democratic, and socialist elements dedicated to the restoration of a unified Polish state. Both the Polish League and Zet were organized along masonic-like conspiratorial lines that kept the movement lean in terms of active members, if not sympathizers. For example, Zet had only eighty-five members in Russian Poland a year after its creation. Then in 1893, the nationalist movement entered a new phase in its development as a result of an internal coup that wrested leadership from Miłkowski and the émigrés. Engineered by Roman Dmowski, a former Zet activist, with Balicki's cooperation, the coup led to the transformation of the Polish League into the National League (Liga Narodowa), which in turn marked the beginning of far-reaching organizational and ideological changes. Dmowski, whose name became virtually synonymous with Polish nationalism, quickly sought to remove freemasonry's liberal and cosmopolitan traditions from the movement. While recognizing the need for preserving the conspiratorial and elitist nature of the league itself, Dmowski worked to give the rest of the movement a more open character as well as a larger "all-Polish" focus (instead of its previous preoccupation with Russian Poland). This was accomplished through the publication of *Przegląd Wszechpolski* (The All-Polish Review) as the league's leading organ from 1895 to 1905, the formation of the National Democratic Party as the political arm of the movement in 1897, and, under league sponsorship, the creation of satellite organizations such as the Towarzystwo Oświaty Narodowej (TON, Society for National Education).

The ideological changes after Dmowski's coup were even more significant. As seen from successive programmatic documents—Dmowski's *Nasz patriotyzm* (Our patriotism, 1893); the programs of the National

League published in 1897 and 1903 in *Przegląd Wszechpolski*; Balicki's *Egoizm narodowej wobec etyki* (National egoism and ethics, 1902); and Dmowski's *Myśli nowoczesnego Polaka* (Thoughts of a modern Pole, 1903)—the movement abandoned its radical democratic and populist roots for an all-embracing integral nationalism. Gradually, less emphasis was placed on the restoration and reunification of Poland as immediate goals, particularly through an armed insurrection. Instead, more attention was paid to the cultivation of national "instincts" through cultural and educational activities—in other words, through the previously criticized methods of "organic work." The idealistic rhetoric of the not-so-distant past now gave way to calls for realism and "sobriety." Similarly, anticlerical polemics were replaced by efforts to reach a modus vivendi with the Catholic church as a "national institution." The movement also became less tolerant of its political competitors, especially the socialists, as it sought to monopolize expression of the "national interest." At the same time, it became intolerant of other nationalities inhabiting "Polish lands," particularly Jews and Ukrainians. Under Dmowski's leadership, the Polish nationalist movement, popularly known as the "Endecja," evolved into a kind of lower-middle-class populism that characterized other nationalist movements of the period, particularly in central Europe. Yet the Endecja's organizational tentacles reached beyond the lower middle-class into all Polish social groups, making it the most formidable political force in the Kingdom by the time of the revolution.[72]

Polish nationalism's evolution toward a right-wing orientation was occasioned, at least in part, by the rise of an organized socialist movement. Yet from the beginning, Polish socialism was plagued by bitter factionalism resulting from fundamental differences of opinion over two issues: the movement's relationship to the question of an independent Polish state and the efficacy of terror as a form of political struggle. The first issue made its appearance already in 1881 when Bolesław Limanowski broke with the Geneva-based socialist publication *Równość* (Equality), whose internationalist program was inspired by Marxian socialism and the previous shared experiences of many early Polish socialists with Russian populists (*narod-*

---

72. For critical assessments of the Polish nationalist movement, see Władysław Pobóg-Malinowski, *Narodowa Demokracja, 1887–1918: Fakty i dokumenty* (Warsaw, 1933); Jerzy Janusz Terej, *Idee, mity, realia: Szkice do dziejów Narodowej Demokracji* (Warsaw, 1971); and Andrzej Micewski, *Roman Dmowski* (Warsaw, 1971). More partisan to the movement are Stanisław Kozicki, *Historia Ligi Narodowej* (London, 1964), and Tadeusz Bielecki, *W szkole Dmowskiego: Szkice i wspomnienia* (London, 1968). In English, see Alvin Marcus Fountain, *Roman Dmowski: Party, Tactics, Ideology, 1895–1907* (Boulder, 1980), and Adam Bromke, *The Meaning and Uses of Polish History* (Boulder, 1987), pp. 71–88.

*niki*) in the imperial Russian universities. Limanowski, who maintained contacts with Polish democratic circles in emigration and later became a member of the Polish League, argued that the position of *Równość* ignored the national aspirations of the Polish proletariat through its relegation of Polish independence to a mechanical by-product of a distant social revolution. In setting up the rival, but short-lived, Lud Polski (Polish People) organization, Limanowski put the resolution of the Polish question at the top of the "national socialist" agenda.[73]

The internationalist wing of the movement, however, was the first to set up a functioning organization on Polish soil known simply as "Proletariat," later called the "Great Proletariat" to distinguish it from its successors. The organization was led by Ludwik Waryński, whose profound belief in the necessity of common action with Russian revolutionary groups to overthrow the tsarist government led to an alliance with the People's Will, the terrorist offshoot of the narodniki responsible for the assassination of Alexander II in 1881. Cooperation between the two groups ended in mass arrests by the police in 1886 and the collapse of the Great Proletariat after less than five years of existence. In the meantime, however, Waryński and his comrades had managed to spread socialist propaganda and make organizational inroads among the movement's principal designated audience, the industrial workers of Warsaw, Łódź, and Żyrardów. Downplaying, if not completely negating, the Polish question from ideological conviction, the leaders of the Great Proletariat mobilized workers by concentrating on their immediate socioeconomic concerns and the organization of mutual aid in the event of strikes.[74]

After the liquidation of the Great Proletariat, a variety of groups emerged to compete for its legacy. The Second Proletariat, created in 1888, departed from the traditions of its namesake in two important respects. Its leadership in the Kingdom, headed by Ludwik Kulczycki, relied on terrorist tactics as the primary means of political struggle against the Russian autocracy, whereas Waryński and his collaborators had viewed terror only as an an-

73. On Limanowski's long career, see K. J. Cottam, *Bolesław Limanowski, 1835–1935: A Study in Socialism and Nationalism* (Boulder, 1978). For a more general discussion of the early Polish socialist movement's collisions and compromises with nationalism, see Ulrich Haustein, *Sozialismus und die nationale Frage in Polen* (Cologne, 1969), and the still-valuable account of Feliks Perl, *Dzieje ruchu socjalistycznego w zaborze rosyjskim do powstania PPS* (1910; reprint, Warsaw, 1958).

74. On the Great Proletariat, Norman Naimark, *The History of the "Proletariat": The Emergence of Marxism in the Kingdom of Poland* (Boulder, 1979), views Waryński's party in a much broader perspective than either Lucjan Blit, *The Origins of Polish Socialism: The History of the First Polish Socialist Party, 1878–1886* (London, 1971), or Leon Baumgarten, *Dzieje Wielkiego Proletariatu* (Warsaw, 1965).

cillary weapon for use against traitors and spies. In addition, the Second Proletariat, especially through its Geneva-based theoretical publication *Przedświt* (Pre-Dawn), rejected Waryński's emphasis on the necessity of cooperation with the Russian revolutionary movement. It believed that the Kingdom was far riper for revolution than Russia, given its more advanced industrialization, its more settled urban proletariat, and its long-standing tradition of rebellion against tsarist rule. Indeed, *Przedświt* discounted any revolutionary possibilities in Russia whatsoever after the final collapse of the remnants of the People's Will organization. The Union of Polish Workers, also organized in 1888, was somewhat closer in spirit to the Great Proletariat. Rejecting the terrorist tactics of Kulczycki and the "national socialism" of *Przedświt*, the Union of Polish Workers concentrated on economic agitation and illegal trade union activity. Its avoidance of political forms of struggle, however, marked an equally significant departure from the traditions of Waryński's party.[75]

The largely unplanned outbreak of a general strike in the Łódź textile industry in 1892, accompanied by street rioting and a brief but bloody struggle from makeshift barricades with Russian troops, caught the various Polish socialist groups by surprise. The suppression of the Łódź riots and mass arrests of socialist activists served as an immediate spur for the liquidation of factions and for the temporary unification of the movement. In emigration, Limanowski and the editorial board of *Przedświt* seized the initiative in November to create the Union of Polish Socialists Abroad, which was then entrusted with the task of drawing up a program for a united organization. A few months later, representatives of the Union of Polish Workers and the Second Proletariat, preferring that unification take place in the Kingdom, held a conference in Warsaw that called into existence the Polish Socialist Party (Polska Partia Socjalistyczna—PPS). The new party, however, was soon decimated by arrests, leaving the formulation of programmatic principles completely in the hands of the émigrés.

The semblance of socialist unity proved short-lived. The publication of a party program in *Przedświt* in July 1893, largely the work of Stanisław Mendelson, the organ's chief editor, reflected the views of the émigrés. By assigning priority to the creation of an independent Polish democratic republic, *Przedświt* and the Union of Polish Socialists Abroad reopened old

---

75. On the Second Proletariat, see Jerzy Borejsza, "Powstanie II Proletariatu i początki jego działalności," *Z Pola Walki*, 2 (1958): 21–56, and L. J. Wołkiewicz, "Z dziejów II Proletariatu, 1889–1890," *Z Pola Walki*, 4 (1975): 89–116. On the Union of Polish Workers, see Feliks Tych, *Związek Robotników Polskich, 1889–1892: Anatomia wczesnej organizacji robotniczej* (Warsaw, 1974).

wounds. Shortly thereafter, a rival "Zurich group" led by Rosa Luxemburg and Leon Jogiches began publishing *Sprawa Robotnicza* (The Workers' Cause), which condemned the "nationalism" of *Przedświt*. At home, dissident elements allied with *Sprawa Robotnicza*, consisting mainly of former members of the Union of Polish Workers, quit the PPS in 1894 to form the Social Democracy of the Kingdom of Poland (SDKP, after 1900 called the SDKPiL as a result of a merger with a small socialist group from Lithuania led by Feliks Dzierżyński). The lines quickly hardened as a result of bitter polemical exchanges between Social Democrats and "social patriots," leaving the long-desired unity of Polish socialism a shambles. To complicate matters even further, Ludwik Kulczycki and his adherents withdrew from the PPS in 1900 in protest of the party's theoretical rejection of terrorism as well as its neglect of social issues. Yet another organization was created, the PPS-Proletariat (sometimes called the Third Proletariat), which vied with both the PPS and the SDKPiL. When one includes the General Jewish Workers Union, popularly known as the Bund, a Marxist organization active among the Jewish urban poor in Russia's western provinces and itself soon to be challenged by a Zionist-socialist movement, at least four socialist organizations competed for influence in Russian Poland at the turn of the century.[76]

If the socialists in the Kingdom of Poland were divided, at least they were active. This was particularly true of the Bund and the PPS. Already by 1892, Jewish socialists had established an efficient organization centered in Vilna, and its theoretical refinement of and experience with "agitation" among Jewish workers influenced both Russian and Polish socialist organizations as they emerged. Although the Bund's activity in the Kingdom of Poland was somewhat peripheral to its main arena in the empire's western borderlands, its organizations in Warsaw and Łódź were the equal of those of any Polish socialist party on the eve of the 1905 revolution.[77] For its part, the PPS developed a stable organization and an efficient smuggling operation between 1894 and 1900, owing in part to the efforts of Józef Piłsudski, a native of Lithuania and editor of the clandestine *Robotnik* (The Worker). By the end of 1903, the PPS could boast of organized activity in Warsaw, Łódź, the Dąbrowa Basin, Radom, Lublin, and Kalisz; the circulation of party appeals in up to twenty thousand copies; and an annual

---

76. For a factually accurate but ideologically biased account of the PPS-SDKPiL split, see Jan Kancewicz, *Rozłam w polskim ruchu robotniczym na początku lat dziewięćdziesiątych XIX wieku* (Warsaw, 1961).

77. On the activities and evolution of the early Bund, see Henry J. Tobias, *The Jewish Bund in Russia: From Its Origins to 1905* (Stanford, 1972).

budget of eighteen thousand rubles.[78] By contrast, the SDKPiL remained largely confined to Warsaw and Łódź; its appeals were published in usually fewer than five thousand copies; and its activity was financed by a meager budget of fifteen hundred rubles.[79] The organizational apparatus of the PPS-Proletariat was even weaker than that of the SDKPiL, and it displayed no signs of political existence outside of Warsaw.

Despite disunity within the movement, the socialist parties, considered together, posed more than an irritant to the Russian authorities and represented a serious challenge to the Polish nationalist movement. The former considered the socialists, particularly the PPS with its militant striving for independence, the chief threat to the political order in the Kingdom. The latter, seeing in the socialist movement's slogans of class struggle a negation of its own efforts to achieve social solidarity in pursuit of "national goals," began courting the traditional elite while simultaneously initiating its own organizational activity among Polish workers. Again, the PPS posed the principal danger, in part because of the perceived radicalism of its social program, but also because of its active disputation of the Endecja's self-proclaimed monopoly on patriotism. Dmowski and the Endecja countered by pointing to Jewish involvement in the socialist movement as evidence of its "alien" character. The competition for popular support had definitely been joined between nationalists and socialists on the one hand, and among socialists on the other. In the process, the existence of a repressive, autocratic Russian government was sometimes forgotten, lost amid heaps of polemical invective, a telling sign of political immaturity among an ambitious but divided intelligentsia at the head of the emerging popular movements.

As the twentieth century began, hardly anyone save a handful of radical socialists anticipated revolution in the Kingdom of Poland, let alone in the Russian Empire. On the surface, all was relatively calm. Agriculture was

---

78. On the PPS before the Revolution of 1905, see Jan Kancewicz, *Polska Partia Socjalistyczna w latach 1892–1896* (Warsaw, 1984); the first chapters of Anna Żarnowska, *Geneza rozłamu w Polskiej Partii Socjalistycznej, 1904–1906* (Warsaw, 1965); and the biography of the young Piłsudski by Władysław Pobóg-Malinowski, *Józef Piłsudski, 1867–1914* (London, 1964). The first chapters of Wacław Jędrzejewicz, *Piłsudski: A Life for Poland* (New York, 1982), are based largely on Pobóg-Malinowski's account.

79. The principal works on the evolution of the SDKPiL are Bronisław Radlak, *Socjaldemokracja Królestwa Polskiego i Litwy w latach 1893–1904* (Warsaw, 1979); Georg W. Strobel, *Die Partei Rosa Luxemburgs, Lenin und die SPD: Der polnische "europäische" Internationalismus in der russischen Sozialdemokratie* (Wiesbaden, 1974); and Robert Blobaum, *Feliks Dzierżyński and the SDKPiL: A Study of the Origins of Polish Communism* (Boulder, 1984).

recovering from its prolonged slump, promising the renewed expansion of the domestic market for industrial goods. The grievances of the peasantry, though considerable, did not threaten agrarian revolt. Strikes were occurring with greater frequency in industrial centers, but workers' demands remained confined to immediate economic issues. The old elite seemed content to follow the path of loyalism and conciliation, despite major setbacks, or simply ignored the state altogether and pursued "organic work." The patriotic and insurrectionary methods of the Polish nobility may have been transferred after a generation or two to the urban intelligentsia at the head of illegal political movements, but their "parties" still bore more resemblance to conspiratorial sects than to modern mass organizations. The Russian authorities kept close tabs on the situation in the Kingdom but were not overly concerned.

Yet they should have been. For just below the surface seethed a society that had changed greatly since the January Insurrection. The peasants, once emancipated with land, became less politically pliable. Instead, as independent proprietors, they displayed growing resentment of the Russian bureaucracy's interference in local rural affairs. They were thus partially reconciled to the remnants of the szlachta, whose declining wealth and influence nevertheless served to mitigate ancient class divisions in the countryside. The industrial workers, though chiefly concerned about wages and working conditions, ran up against repressive Russian police measures whenever they tried to improve their lot through the "illegal" means of collective action. Petty discrimination against the Kingdom's industry exacerbated social tensions by increasing unemployment. While the nonnative and absentee captains of Polish industry could only protest such measures to the Russian government (or just as likely, to foreign embassies and consulates), they also led a group of ethnically Polish entrepreneurs to support the national movement with financial contributions, if not direct participation. Finally, the vast majority of Poles may have reconciled themselves to Russian rule, but they could never accept russification and the attempted eradication of their language, religion, history, and culture. Opposition to russification united all groups in society, from conservative clericalists to revolutionary socialists, and led to the creation of informal networks of passive resistance and ultimately, to alienation from the ruling regime. Thus the situation in the Kingdom was far more delicate than the Russian bureaucracy imagined. The Kingdom may not have been pregnant with revolution, but general dissatisfaction had drawn increasing numbers into active opposition to the regime. When that regime belatedly discovered, in the course of 1904, how widespread that opposition actually was, it came as a something of a shock.

# The Making of a Revolution, 1904

On Sunday morning, November 13, 1904, more than a thousand people crowded into the parish church of All Saints on Grzybowski Square in what was then the solidly working-class Zachodna district of Warsaw, a couple of blocks north of aleje Jerozolimskie (Jerusalem Boulevard). Some were there to attend the regularly scheduled Mass, others to participate in a political demonstration organized by the Polish Socialist Party against the Russo-Japanese War and the mobilization of reservists for the Far Eastern front. Days earlier, the Warsaw Workers' Committee of the PPS had issued separate appeals to Polish and Jewish workers as well as to students at Warsaw University and the Warsaw Polytechnical Institute, informing them of the location, time, and avowed purpose of the planned demonstration. The Warsaw protest, the Socialists proclaimed, was to serve as a political example for the rest of the country. The PPS appeals also found their way, as if by design, into the hands of the Russian authorities.[1] On November 12, police raided two meetings of members of the Jewish section of the PPS, arresting twenty who had gathered to discuss preparations for the Grzybowski Square demonstration. On the same day, police and Cossack units were placed on alert and given instructions to disperse the crowd and arrest "the guilty."[2]

Neither the unwitting Catholic parishioners, nor the police, nor indeed the majority of those who turned up for the demonstration were aware of what was in store for them that Sunday. A month earlier, members of the

1. APW WGZŻ 934.
2. AGAD KGGW 2384, Warsaw Superintendent of Police to the WGG, October 27 (November 9) and October 30 (November 12), 1904.

Central Workers Committee of the PPS, then under the leadership of Józef Piłsudski, had conferred in Kraków and resolved to respond to Russian mobilization orders with a "tactic of deeds." For months Piłsudski had sought to create a special paramilitary organization that, he hoped, would provoke a general uprising by carrying out a series of armed actions against Russian state institutions and personnel. Until October, his plans had met with apprehension among his closest collaborators and open opposition within the party's Warsaw organization, although workers' self-defense circles had been formed in April to protect PPS demonstrations against the "brutality" of the authorities. In Kraków, however, the party leadership concluded that the self-defense circles should also engage in limited terrorist-style actions against the most hated representatives of the regime. Although the self-defense circles were still far from the paramilitary units Piłsudski had in mind, he nevertheless assumed responsibility for the smuggling of men, arms, and ammunition into the Kingdom from Kraków, while Józef Kwiatek, a leading member of both the party's Jewish section and the Warsaw Workers Committee, took direct charge of operations in the country.[3]

Before the self-defense circles of "tens" could be properly armed and trained in the tactics of what essentially would become urban guerrilla warfare, a small PPS demonstration on Leszno Street numbering fewer than three hundred participants was dispersed by Cossacks on October 28, leaving some eighty injured. At that point, Kwiatek and the Warsaw leadership decided that the next demonstration, designated for November 13 on Grzybowski Square, would be "armed."[4] Sixty men were assigned the task of "defending" the demonstration in the furious planning that preceded it.

Thus, at half past twelve on that fateful Sunday, before the crowd began to file out of All Saints, a central group of PPS *bojowcy* (fighters) took their places in front of the church and began to intone the revolutionary hymn "Warszawianka" while Stefan Okrzeje, destined to become a martyr to the cause of "armed struggle" against Russian rule, unfurled a small red banner with the slogan "PPS: We don't want to be soldiers of the tsar!"[5] As some seventy to eighty regular police and mounted Cossacks moved to disperse the demonstrators, mainly student sympathizers of the

3. Władysław Pobóg-Malinowski, *Józef Piłsudski, 1867–1914* (London, 1964), pp. 288–290; Jerzy Pająk, *Organizacje bojowe partii politycznych w Królestwie Polskim, 1904–1911* (Warsaw, 1985), pp. 44–55; Henryk Piasecki, *Żydowska organizacja PPS, 1893–1907* (Wrocław, 1978), p. 106.
4. Pobóg-Malinowski, *Józef Piłsudski*, p. 291; Bronisław Żukowski, "Pamiętniki bojowca," *Niepodległość* 1 (October 1929): 120.
5. Halina Kiepurska, *Warszawa w rewolucji 1905–1907* (Warsaw, 1974), p. 60.

PPS, they were met with a volley of bullets from the revolvers and Brownings carried by the sixty bojowcy. The police and Cossacks returned the fire, primarily into the crowd of departing parishioners with whom the demonstrators had merged. In the resulting melee, twenty-seven civilians were wounded and six killed. Only one policeman lost his life in the exchange, although five others suffered injuries. More than six hundred persons were arrested, including more than two hundred trapped inside the church. Fifty were subsequently deported from Warsaw, thirty-two jailed for two to six weeks, and twenty-four imprisoned for more than two years before standing trial. The remainder were released the day after the demonstration, including fifty bojowcy whom police interrogators failed to identify.[6]

Those involved in the planning of the "armed demonstration" on Grzybowski Square believed that the firing of shots would mobilize the population and perhaps even ignite a general revolt. In this they were very much mistaken. Public outrage over the incident was directed as much at the PPS as at the tsarist government. The demonstration was roundly condemned by conservatives led by the archbishop of Warsaw, Wincenty Popiel. The press of the Endecja claimed that the demonstration was inspired by and served foreign interests ("English and perhaps Japanese").[7] The SDKPiL accused its rival of "political adventurism" and of organizing a "street tumult" that had led to the deaths of persons "having nothing in common with the socialist movement."[8]

The incident on Grzybowski Square therefore did not become a Polish version of Bloody Sunday, despite the intentions of its leading organizers. At the same time, however, it did not occur in a vacuum. The Grzybowski Square demonstration was in fact only one of eighty antiwar protests organized in the Kingdom in 1904, eighteen of which occurred in Warsaw.[9] Nor was the movement against the war and mobilization the only expression of discontent with Russian policies in 1904. Disturbances in the schools, mounting labor unrest, "illegal" Polish-language resolutions of rural communal assemblies, and the steady, if not spectacular, growth of opposition parties all bore witness to a growing crisis. The skirmish on Grzybowski Square between police and PPS gunmen may not have launched a revolution, but it certainly dramatized the heightening tensions

---

6. AGAD KGGW 2384, Warsaw Superintendent of Police to the WGG, November 11 (24), 1904; APW WGZŻ 934; Pająk, *Organizacje bojowe*, p. 49.
7. Kiepurska, *Warszawa w rewolucji*, p. 60.
8. AGAD AB, druk 249.
9. Anna Żarnowska, *Robotnicy Warszawy na przełomie XIX i XX wieku* (Warsaw, 1985), p. 245.

between the Russian governing class and the society over which it ruled. Meanwhile, a real explosion, ignited by spontaneous social combustion rather than political calculation, was only two months away.

### Opposition to the Russo-Japanese War and Mobilization

On February 8, 1904, the Japanese surprise attack on the Russian naval base at Port Arthur marked the beginning of a war in the Far East that would last nearly eighteen months. Within two weeks of the outbreak of hostilities, on February 21, a patriotic demonstration orchestrated by the Russian authorities in Warsaw to show support for the war effort was disrupted by club-wielding counterdemonstrators organized by the PPS and the Jewish Bund. Two days earlier, Polish and Jewish students walked out of the Warsaw Polytechnical Institute rather than participate in a pro-government demonstration.[10] In subsequent weeks, three gmina assemblies in Łomża and Warsaw provinces refused to assign 10 percent of community funds to aid the cause of Russian arms in the Far East, despite considerable pressure applied by county chiefs.[11] In Radom on March 11, five Polish "patriots" were jailed for three months each for disrupting a spectacle at the local theater which had been staged to raise contributions for the war.[12]

From the beginning, the attitude of the population in the Kingdom toward the war in the Far East, according to the head of the country's gendarmerie, ranged from "indifferent to hostile."[13] The response of the clandestine Polish parties to the news of the outbreak of the Russo-Japanese War was of course predictable. The SDKPiL, in an appeal of its main directorate, used the occasion to declare war on the tsarist government.[14] The Central Workers Committee of the PPS portrayed the war as one of Japanese defense against Russian imperial aggression and declared that "a Japanese victory is our victory."[15] The central committee of the National League was more subdued. Its appeal argued that although Rus-

10. AGAD KGGW 2308, Warsaw Superintendent of Police to the WGG, February 11 (24), 1904.
11. AGAD KGGW 2307; Herman Rappaport, ed., *Narastanie rewolucji w Królestwie Polskim w latach 1900–1904* (Warsaw, 1960), pp. 499–500.
12. AGAD KGGW 2255, Report of the SDPA to the WGG, February 26 (March 11), 1904.
13. AGAD KGGW 2308, Report of the SDPA to the WGG, March 9 (22), 1904.
14. T. Daniszewski, ed., *SDKPiL w rewolucji 1905 roku: Zbiór publikacji* (Warsaw, 1955), pp. 5–6.
15. Rappaport, *Narastanie rewolucji,* pp. 488–490.

sian losses in the war with Japan were beneficial to Poland, the war in the Far East would not change the map of Europe. Nevertheless, the nationalists believed that the best tactic was to use the war to build up "our own forces" and not to permit the spilling of one drop of Polish blood "for someone else's cause."[16] In the eyes of the authorities, all these groups, together with the Bund, were guilty of conducting a widespread propaganda campaign against the Russian government.

Genuine support for the Russian war effort was confined to a small group of conservative loyalists. Archbishop Popiel, anticipating official gratitude and concessions for the Roman Catholic Church, sponsored the formation of a committee of fourteen prominent clergy and laymen to solicit contributions for sending a "sanitary train" of medical supplies and personnel to the front. Funds came in at a trickle, however, and by mid-April, only seventy thousand rubles had been collected.[17] The lower clergy, for its part, generally refrained from active participation in the hierarchy's fund-raising initiative and maintained a "passive" attitude toward the war. Priests in Siedlce Province, in a rare display of clerical opposition to the authorities, refused to read the government's wartime proclamations until directly forced to do so by the police.[18] In Radom Province, even the Polish upper classes, the traditional bastion of loyalism, failed to respond to the archbishop's appeal.[19] Meanwhile, politically inspired vandals attacked the Warsaw homes of several conservatives authorized by the archbishop to collect contributions for the sanitary train.[20]

To the Russian bureaucracy, the attitudes of the urban lower classes and student population toward the war were not only dismaying but the source of considerable alarm. The governor of industrialized Piotrków Province reported that the sympathies of the workers "are entirely on the side of Japan."[21] In Warsaw, rumors of the fall of Port Arthur published in the legal daily *Kurier Poranny* (Morning Courier) on March 14 were enough to set off a demonstration against the war involving some four hundred workers.[22] Students were even more active in their opposition to Russia's cause in the Far East. The example of the Warsaw Polytechnical Institute in February quickly spread to other institutions of higher and secondary

---

16. Ibid., pp. 490–492.
17. AGAD AB, druk 3.
18. AGAD KGGW 2308, Report of the SDPA to the WGG, March 13 (26), 1904.
19. AGAD KGGW 2308, Radom Governor to the SDPA, February 29 (March 13), 1904.
20. AGAD KGGW 2280, Warsaw Superintendent of Police to the WGG, March 18 (31), 1904.
21. AGAD KGGW 2308, Piotrków Governor to the WGG, February 28 (March 12), 1904.
22. Rappaport, *Narastanie rewolucji*, p. 497.

education in the Kingdom. In at least four provinces, Polish and Jewish students boycotted the "patriotic demonstrations" in support of the Russian war effort organized by the school authorities, despite threats of expulsion. In Warsaw, teachers in some city schools received anonymous letters warning them against participating in pro-Russian activities.[23]

Only the peasantry retained the relative confidence of the authorities in the first months of the war. The most optimistic report came from Piotrków Province, where several community assemblies readily assigned 10 percent of their funds for the government's wartime needs.[24] In Radom Province as well, the peasantry appeared "favorably disposed" to the Russian war effort, although "not to the extent among peasants in the empire."[25] The Warsaw provincial governor noted that where the Catholic clergy supported pro-Russian fund-raising activities, the peasantry tended to follow suit.[26] Elsewhere, however, the local authorities were less sanguine in their assessments. The Łomża governor could not vouch for the "real mood" of the province's overwhelmingly peasant population, especially after two gmina assemblies refused to contribute funds for the Russian cause.[27] The attitude of the peasantry of Suwałki Province was generally described as "unenthusiastic" and, in the northern counties inhabited by Lithuanians, "antipathetic."[28] The most discouraging news came from Siedlce Province, where Polish peasants, following the lead of the Roman Catholic clergy, boycotted all "patriotic" activity. Worse, the dissident Uniate peasantry of the province's eastern counties were reported to "openly sympathize with Japan in the hope that a Russian defeat will give them the possibility of openly practicing Catholicism."[29]

In subsequent months, conscription and the mobilization of reservists strengthened the growing antiwar movement. According to the PPS central organ *Robotnik* (The Worker), conscripts from the Kingdom eventually made up 30 percent of the tsarist army on the Far Eastern front.[30] Although such claims were exaggerated, there can be little doubt that the Kingdom,

---

23. AGAD KGGW 2308, Warsaw Superintendent of Police to the WGG, February 11 (24), 1904.
24. AGAD KGGW 2308, Piotrków Governor to the WGG, February 28 (March 12), 1904.
25. AGAD KGGW 2308, Radom Governor to the SDPA, February 29 (March 13), 1904.
26. AGAD KGGW 2308, Warsaw Governor to the WGG, April 2 (15), 1904.
27. AGAD KGGW 2308, Łomża Governor to the SDPA, March 1 (14), 1904.
28. AGAD KGGW 2308, Suwałki Governor to the SDPA, February 27 (March 11), 1904.
29. AGAD KGGW 2308, Report of the SDPA to the WGG, March 13 (26), 1904; see also Robert Blobaum, "Toleration and Ethno-Religious Strife: The Struggle between Catholics and Orthodox Christians in the Chełm Region of Russian Poland, 1904–1906," *Polish Review* 35, 2 (1990): 117.
30. *Robotnik,* no. 58 (January 20, 1905).

accounting for 10 percent of the total population of the Russian Empire, provided a disproportionate share of recruits for the war. Consequently, in comparison with the rest of the empire, resistance to mobilization was far more pronounced, assuming a mass character by the end of the year.

Evasion of military service was particularly widespread among the Jewish population, whose communities traditionally preferred to pay heavy fines rather than deliver recruits to the Russian army. In Piotrków Province, Jewish draft evasion reached such proportions that local authorities feared it might provoke resentment among Polish recruits and eventually lead to "major disorders."[31] Similar situations existed in Radom, Siedlce, and Kielce provinces, where fighting broke out between local Jews and Polish conscripts reporting for duty. Although Jews were frequently victimized by Christian hostility in such incidents—as in Ostrowiec in Radom Province where more than one hundred Jewish homes were ransacked in a July pogrom[32]—there were also several reported cases of violence perpetrated by large Jewish crowds. In the town of Chmielnik in Kielce Province, for example, three thousand Jews armed with rocks and clubs attacked a military escort taking sixteen reservists into active service.[33]

Draft evasion and resistance to mobilization, moreover, was hardly confined to the Jewish population. By October, information reached the Warsaw governor-general that thousands of young men were fleeing the country to escape military service and the prospect of being sent to the Far East, a situation attributed to "fear of death" as well as to "underground propaganda."[34] Official records also include several reports of resistance among reservists to mobilization at induction points purposefully located outside the major cities. When that resistance was actively supported by the local population, as in the small town of Kutno in late October, violent clashes with Russian police and army units were the usual result.[35] Such incidents, however, were exceptional. As a rule, the forms and methods of popular protest against conscription and mobilization were considerably less dramatic, particularly in rural areas. For instance, the wives of peasant conscripts in the gmina of Skępe in Płock Province, supported by their neighbors, informed the local mayor that they would no longer pay taxes, citing the loss of income resulting from their husbands' departure for the

---

31. AGAD KGGW 2382, Piotrków Governor to the WGG, October 30 (November 12), 1904.
32. AGAD KGGW 2431, Radom Governor to the Minister of Internal Affairs, July 16 (29), 1904.
33. Rappaport, *Narastanie rewolucji*, p. 673.
34. Ibid., p. 637.
35. Ibid., pp. 649–651.

front.[36] The gmina assembly of Długoborz in Łomża Province, by contrast, "illegally" resolved to cease its subscription to all government-sponsored publications and to use the money instead to aid widows of those killed in action in the Far East.[37]

Opposition in urban areas was considerably more active, particularly in Warsaw, which by early summer had become the focal point of the growing discontent against the war and Russian military recruitment. This was due in large part to the activity of the PPS and its ability to transform general sentiment against the war into an organized movement.[38] Of the clandestine parties active in the Kingdom, the PPS most clearly recognized the possibilities the war created for political mobilization. The party leadership may have been divided on the ultimate goal of that mobilization, the Old Guard (Starzy) thinking of preparations for a national armed uprising; the Young (Młodzi), of a socialist revolution. Nevertheless, by placing itself at the head of the antiwar movement, the PPS quickly acquired an "active" image that in a situation of growing crisis was bound to reap political dividends. By the end of 1904, the party had tripled its membership in Warsaw, quadrupled it in Łódź, and developed strong local organizations in Kalisz, Lublin, Radom, and Zagłębie.[39]

The antiwar, antimobilization strategy did not come immediately to the divided PPS leadership. At the outset of the war, the Old Guard, led by Piłsudski, Witold Jodko-Narkiewicz, and B. A. Jędrzejowski, pursued an "alliance" with the Japanese, who were expected to finance and arm Polish legions recruited by the PPS. The Japanese were at least willing to explore the possibilities of a more limited collaboration with the PPS, and thus Jodko was able to hold preliminary discussions with Japanese envoys in Vienna, Paris, and London. An invitation was then issued to Piłsudski to make a visit to Tokyo, where his hosts wished to discuss the PPS's capabilities for gathering intelligence information on the situation in Russia and Siberia. Piłsudski agreed to make the trip, kept secret from party leaders inside the country because of their anticipated opposition, in the hope that in exchange for PPS intelligence activity, the Japanese would supply arms and ammunition for a PPS-led uprising in the Kingdom. He arrived in Tokyo in July but failed to persuade his hosts that the PPS possessed an "armed force" capable of inflicting enough damage in the Russian rear

---

36. AGAD KGGW 2385, Report of the SDPA to the WGG, November 1 (14), 1904.
37. Rappaport, *Narastanie rewolucji*, pp. 709–710.
38. Forty-four demonstrations against the war and mobilization, or more than 50 percent of the total in 1904, can be ascribed directly to PPS activity; see Anna Żarnowska, *Geneza rozłamu w Polskiej Partii Socjalistycznej, 1904–1906* (Warsaw, 1965), pp. 18–19.
39. Ibid., pp. 12–14.

to force a transfer of troops from the Far Eastern front. Japanese reservations were undoubtedly influenced by Roman Dmowski, who to Piłsudski's surprise, made a simultaneous visit to the Japanese capital to dissuade Tokyo from supporting insurrectionary activity in the Kingdom, which according to Dmowski, could only turn into a needless bloodbath. Dmowski's argument that the PPS could count on an organized force of fewer than a hundred men, only some of whom possessed handguns, was compelling enough to deter Japanese support.[40]

Having played the Japanese card without much effect, the PPS Old Guard began to pay more attention to the antiwar demonstrations organized in the country by the Young leadership, whose principal base was the Warsaw Workers Committee. The ability of the socialist parties to organize May Day demonstrations in Warsaw, Radom, Piotrków, Łódź, and Suwałki in the face of strong police countermeasures emboldened the Warsaw PPS leadership to turn to public demonstrations against the war as a means of mobilizing opinion behind the party. The first such demonstrations, in the late spring and early summer in Warsaw, were hardly formidable displays of antigovernment sentiment. Involving as few as thirty or forty participants, they were easily dispersed by the police and resulted in numerous arrests, prompting a rival Social Democratic leader to refer to the PPS activity in this period as "comical."[41]

The PPS demonstrations did, however, begin to gather momentum, stimulated by the unbroken string of Russian military defeats in the Far Eastern war and succeeding rounds of mobilization in various parts of the Kingdom. By early July, the demonstrators were arming themselves with rocks, clubs, and bottles, and by late July, "fighters" from the PPS self-defense circles began to make their appearance at scenes of organized protest.[42] Dispersing the demonstrations without resorting to arms consequently became more difficult. Clashes between protesters and police and the creation of victims of "tsarist brutality" among the former were the inevitable and, to the PPS leadership, most desirable results. By mid-September the move-

40. For more on the adventures of Piłsudski and Dmowski in Tokyo, see Pobóg-Malinowski, *Józef Piłsudski*, pp. 249–250, and his *Narodowa Demokracja, 1887–1918: Fakty i dokumenty* (Warsaw, 1933), pp. 259–268; see also Wacław Jędrzejewicz, *Piłsudski: A Life for Poland* (New York, 1982), pp. 34–36; Andrzej Micewski, *Roman Dmowski* (Warsaw, 1971), pp. 91–94; and Alvin Marcus Fountain, *Roman Dmowski: Party, Tactics, Ideology, 1895–1907* (Boulder, 1980), pp. 115–139.

41. CA PZPR, AM 25/1, Zespół Feliksa Dzierżyńskiego, "Social-Patriotic Demonstrations," July 1904.

42. AGAD KGGW 2383, Report of the Warsaw Superintendent of Police on events in the week of July 10–17, 1904.

ment had spread from Warsaw to Łódź, where in one incident, demon-strators attacked the residence of the superintendent of police.[43]

The official announcement of a new round of mobilization of reservists on October 22 effectively shifted the antiwar movement into higher gear. In the last week of October, relatively large demonstrations involving as many as five hundred participants occurred at several locations in Warsaw, as well as in Łódź, Zawiercie, and Częstochowa,[44] almost all of them ac-companied by violent clashes between police and demonstrators. By this time, the Old Guard had adopted the antiwar movement as its own cause and transferred the émigré headquarters of the party from London to Kraków to be closer to the action. The Bund, followed by the SDKPiL, abandoned their preoccupation with strikes and began organizing demon-strations of their own or in cooperation with the Warsaw and Łódź PPS committees. For their part, the Social Democrats no longer found the an-tiwar movement laughable and now sought to steal some of the credit. The party's main organ, *Czerwony Sztandar* (Red Banner), went so far as to claim that a Social Democratic demonstration against mobilization on Oc-tober 30 "was undoubtedly the largest and most successful of all workers' demonstrations that Warsaw has seen in recent months."[45]

Then came the tragic debacle on Grzybowski Square, the misguided attempt of the PPS to ignite a general revolt by provoking a massacre. Although the plan misfired, the movement against the war and mobilization could no longer be contained. From mid-November to mid-January, anti-war demonstrations were practically an everyday occurrence. The state played its prescribed role by calling up reservists in twenty-eight counties in the Kingdom just before Christmas. Warsaw remained the center of the movement, followed by Łódź and Radom, but demonstrations were also organized in the smaller cities of Kalisz, Pabianice, and Częstochowa and in the industrialized gmina of Ćmielów in Radom Province. Shortly after the incident on Grzybowski Square, the PPS reportedly spent several thou-sand rubles on arms and ammunition for its "fighters" in Łódź and Ra-dom.[46] Not surprisingly, violence erupted in both cities during the winter holidays, as police and demonstrators clashed.[47] Meanwhile, assassination attempts were made on policemen, gendarmes, and soldiers in Łódź, Częs-

---

43. Pawel Korzec, ed., *Źródła do dziejów rewolucji 1905–1907 w okręgu łódzkim,* vol. 1, pt. 1 (Warsaw, 1957), pp. 345–347.
44. Ibid., pp. 355–357; Rappaport, *Narastanie rewolucji,* pp. 642–644, 646–649, 655–656.
45. *Czerwony Sztandar,* no. 21 (October 1904).
46. AGAD KGGW 2384, Report of the SDPA to the WGG, December 14 (27), 1904.
47. Korzec, *Źródła do dziejów rewolucji* I (1): 373–374; Rappaport, *Narastanie rewolucji,* p. 703.

tochowa, and Ćmielów. In a sign of things to come, bombs exploded in Łódź on January 15 during an exchange of fire between armed PPS demonstrators and police.[48] To the Russian bureaucracy in the Kingdom, the situation had already, by the end of November, become critical enough for the Warsaw govenor-general to seek authorization from the Minstry of Internal Affairs to proclaim a state of "intensified security" in Warsaw, Warsaw County, and all of Piotrków Province.[49]

The antiwar movement of 1904 did not lead directly to the Revolution of 1905, but it certainly helped prepare the ground. By bringing people of different social backgrounds into the streets, where they frequently came face to face with the forces of state repression for the first time, the movement contributed to the creation of an atmosphere charged with confrontation. The spilling of blood in these encounters served to inflame passions, if not to the extent desired by the movement's organizers, then at least to the point where they could be employed for political mobilization. More than any other form of popular protest or expression of social unrest in 1904, the antiwar movement visibly dramatized a situation that was rapidly approaching a state of crisis.

### Economic Dislocation and Labor Unrest

The economic impact of the war on the Kingdom, though less spectacular than the political, was nevertheless of equal consequence and indeed nourished the growing sentiment against the Russian government and its war in the Far East. Agriculture, to be sure, was not directly affected by the war, and farm prices continued their slow recovery from the collapse of the last quarter of the nineteenth century. The agrarian economy had other afflictions in 1904, namely, drought and a poor harvest. The war, of course, affected the family income of conscripted peasants and farm laborers, but agriculture in general did not suffer a labor shortage thanks to rural overpopulation. The average annual wage of farm laborers actually declined, from twenty-two rubles and 10.8 bushels of rye in 1900 to twenty rubles and nine bushels of rye in 1904.[50]

The Kingdom's industrial economy, however, was thrown into a tailspin

48. AGAD KGGW 2385, Report of the SDPA to the WGG, January 4 (17), 1905.
49. Rappaport, *Narastanie rewolucji,* pp. 684–688.
50. Irena Pietrzak-Pawłowska, "Depresja ekonomiczna w Królestwie Polskim i elementy kryzysu rewolucyjnego 1904 r.," *Przegląd Historyczny* 46, 1–2 (1955): 14; see also Krzysztof Groniowski, *Robotnicy rolni w Królestwie Polskim, 1871–1914* (Warsaw, 1977), p. 69.

by the war. The outbreak of hostilities in the Far East could not have come
at a worse time. The Kingdom's industry was just beginning to rebound
from the general European slump of the first years of the twentieth century,
and the war abruptly interrupted the recovery process. The financial burden
of the war, resulting in higher taxes, rents, and industrial prices, was sufficient to discourage investment. In Warsaw, private investors withdrew
thirty million marks from local banks and looked for less risky opportunities outside the country. Foreign banks likewise withdrew their reserves
from banks in the Kingdom. Suddenly, there was a shortage of capital, and
credit became more expensive, especially as the state competed for funds
to finance its military effort. Interest rates increased by only 1 percent in
state banks but soared by 10 percent in private banks. The subsequent
decline in investment did not, however, affect Polish industry uniformly.
The war initially stimulated investment in mining, metal, metallurgical, and
other military-related industries, but this expansion came largely at the
expense of peacetime production. Overall, the total value of industrial production in the Kingdom declined already by 30–40 percent by the summer
of 1904.[51]

The textile industry was especially affected by adverse wartime conditions. Not only did investment dry up, but sales took a nosedive. The textile
industry's dependence on Russian and eastern markets now came fully to
light against the backdrop of the war's disruption of normal economic
activity. The mobilization of the empire's weak railroad network for military purposes created chaos in the transportation system, making it difficult, if not impossible, for Polish goods to reach traditional eastern clients.
Consequently, five months into the war, the "export" of textile products
from Łódź fell by 20 percent, from Częstochowa by 55 percent. Related
industries, such as haberdashery and shoemaking, suffered from the ripple
effects and experienced sharp declines in sales ranging from 27 to 35
percent.[52]

Textile industrialists and factory owners responded predictably by saving
on labor costs. In Łódź, the larger factories initially sought to keep all
employees on the payroll, but this could be accomplished only by reductions in hours and wages. In a survey of 210 factories and plants employing
sixty thousand workers in the spring of 1904, state inspectors discovered

51. Pietrzak-Pawłowska, "Depresja ekonomiczna," pp. 6–8.
52. Ibid., p. 7; see also Stanisław Kalabiński and Feliks Tych, *Czwarte powstanie czy
pierwsza rewolucja: Lata 1905–1907 na ziemiach polskich,* 2d ed. (Warsaw, 1976), pp.
16–17.

that hours had been reduced on the average by 25 percent and that half the labor force had experienced a decline in earnings.[53] By the summer, the situation in Łódź had become much worse. In an expanded survey of 350 factories and plants employing seventy-five thousand workers, 25 percent reported that operations had been reduced to only three days a week.[54] In Piotrków Province as a whole, approximately half of the 910 firms sending statistical data to the Factory Inspectorate were operating on a part-time basis.[55]

Meanwhile, unemployment began to be a mass phenomenon. At first, unemployment was confined to the smaller factories, artisanal shops, and cottage industries dependent on the larger textile firms for their orders. Already by March, 479 of 1,225 weavers in Pabianice, whose only source of orders were the great firms of Łódź, were completely without work.[56] A similar situation existed in nearby Zduńska Wola in Kalisz Province, where only 900 of 2,000 weavers had sufficient orders from Łódź to continue working on their handlooms.[57] By the middle of May, 4,000 were fully unemployed in the Łódź industrial region, which left at least 10,000 persons in affected families without means of sustaining themselves. By contrast, in the mining and metallurgical region of southern Piotrków Province, the local economy remained relatively unaffected by the war, and there were no reported changes in employment patterns, working hours, or wages.[58]

As the crisis deepened during the summer, unemployment spread from the smaller shops and cottages into the large factories. Although the principal victims remained the handweavers, who worked at home on their own looms, by July, forty-two larger factories in Łódź had laid off 1,280 workers, and the remainder had their hours drastically reduced.[59] In the Łódź region alone, 10,000 workers were unemployed by the middle of August, leaving 25,000 persons without any source of income. Those who remained at their jobs experienced an average decline in earnings of more than 30 percent.[60] Again, by way of contrast, the condition of workers

53. AGAD KGGW 2382, Piotrków Governor to the WGG, May 7 (20), 1904.
54. Ibid., July 15 (28), 1904.
55. Korzec, Źródła do dziejów rewolucji 1 (1): 154–156.
56. Ibid., pp. 76–77.
57. Ibid., pp. 77–78.
58. AGAD KGGW 2382, Report of the Piotrków Governor to the Department of Police, May 7 (20), 1904.
59. Korzec, Źródła do dziejów rewolucji 1 (1): 109–113.
60. AGAD KGGW 2382, Piotrków Governor to the WGG, August 11 (24), 1904.

employed in the mining and metallurgical industries remained "relatively satisfactory," although even here reductions occurred periodically as a result of insufficient orders.[61]

Before the crisis bottomed out in the late fall, officials estimated that more than 75 percent of the workers in Piotrków Province were in "a difficult material situation" as a result of unemployment or part-time employment, which had brought about a decline in family incomes averaging 50 percent.[62] Mining and metallurgy, moreover, no longer remained immune. The war's initial stimulation of the Kingdom's heavy industry drew a significant number of unemployed workers from other parts of the country to the Dąbrowa Basin. The area's traditional labor shortage, particularly in mining, quickly gave way to a labor surplus, enabling firms to reduce wages. Once Russian military orders declined in the second half of 1904, heavy industry began to experience its own sales crisis, primarily as a result of the transportation bottleneck that limited access to Russian markets. As in the textile industry, declining sales led to layoffs and reduced working hours. Although the Dąbrowa Basin remained a picture of health in comparison with the Łódź region, unemployment and partial employment nevertheless affected 30 percent of the labor force by the autumn of 1904.[63]

The Kingdom's industry, of course, was not confined to Piotrków Province, nor was the industrial crisis. In Warsaw, unemployment already affected 30,000 people, mainly textile workers and their families, by midsummer.[64] As the crisis spread to Warsaw's metal industry in the second half of 1904, working hours were cut back, leading to a decline in wages averaging 20 percent. At the peak of the crisis, some 120,000 inhabitants of Warsaw were suffering from the impact of unemployment and reduced employment in industry, which affected some 60 percent of the city's industrial labor force. Official statistics did not embrace the city's small artisans and craftsmen, most of whom were Jewish. Yet evidence that 20,000 Warsaw Jews were receiving relief from community philanthropic institutions by the summer of 1904 suggests that many Jewish tradesmen had experienced a significant decline in income. Numerous artisans were forced to close their shops altogether. In the immediate environs of Warsaw, many of the small breweries, distilleries, and brickyards that provided employment to neighboring peasants were also driven out of business.[65]

---

61. Ibid., July 15 (28), 1904.
62. Korzec, *Źródła do dziejów rewolucji* 1 (1): 142–147.
63. Pietrzak-Pawłowska, "Depresja ekonomiczna," pp. 24–25.
64. AGAD KGGW 2382, Report of the Warsaw Section of the Society for the Support of Russian Industry and Trade, July 24 (August 6), 1904.
65. Pietrzak-Pawłowska, "Depresja ekonomiczna," pp. 16–20.

Distribution of flour in Warsaw. (Muzeum Niepodległości 24639)

Outside of Piotrków and Warsaw provinces, the industrial crisis had considerably less impact on local economies. In Radom Province, a thousand workers had been laid off by the summer, but since the majority consisted of small peasant landowners, many were able to support themselves by returning to traditional agricultural pursuits. Local officials were concerned, however, that more serious problems could arise once work in the fields came to an end.[66] A similar situation existed in Łomża Province, where employment in industry was largely a side occupation for peasant smallholders and not a principal source of income.[67] In Lublin Province, unemployment was confined to artisans and unskilled laborers. Although workers' hours were reduced slightly in the small factories of the province, the resulting decline in wages was considered "insignificant."[68]

Even so, throughout the Kingdom of Poland, unemployment and partial

---

66. AGAD KGGW 2382, Radom Governor to the Department of Police, August 26 (September 8), 1904.
67. AGAD KGGW 2382, Łomża Governor to the Department of Police, June 26 (July 9), 1904.
68. AGAD KGGW 2382, Lublin Governor to the WGG, August 31 (September 12) and November 17 (30), 1904.

employment affected close to one-third of all those who derived, or were dependent on, income from industry and trade, approximately 350,000 people.[69] Never before in the history of Polish industry had unemployment been so severe as in the autumn of 1904. To make matters worse, the industrial crisis coincided with a sharp rise in prices for basic foodstuffs, the major expenditure in working-class budgets.[70] In Łódź the price of potatoes doubled by the spring.[71] During the course of 1904, price increases for beef, bacon, butter, milk, eggs, and cabbage ranged from 25 percent to 150 percent. Meanwhile, apartment rents and the price of clothing, also important items in workers' budgets, increased on the average by 25 percent.[72] Hence even those workers who were fortunate enough to maintain full-time employment during the crisis nevertheless experienced a decline in their real earnings.

For the most part, the state proved incapable of organizing relief for those most adversely affected by the crisis. In Lublin Province, where unemployment was less widespread and where agricultural pursuits served as a safety valve, the state's relief efforts were moderately successful. There, the provincial governor established a relief committee consisting of government officials and private citizens which created a job information and placement office, provided basic goods at low prices with the help of private philanthropy, and opened up shelters and soup kitchens for unemployed workers and artisans.[73]

In Piotrków Province, though, the dimensions of the crisis continually outran the government's efforts to organize relief. In May, Karl Miller, the Piotrków governor, sought and received permission to transfer sixteen thousand rubles from the Łódź city administration to Christian and Jewish philanthropic organizations for distribution among the families of the unemployed. Despite the subsidy, the funds of these organizations were exhausted within two months.[74] Miller then made a series of more far-reaching proposals and recommendations, some of which were quite radical in the context of prevailing Russian bureaucratic attitudes. In July,

69. Kalabiński and Tych, *Czwarte powstanie czy pierwsza rewolucja*, pp. 16–17.
70. In an average Warsaw working-class household of four members, food purchases could easily consume half to two-thirds of a family's income; see Żarnowska, *Robotnicy Warszawy*, pp. 114–115.
71. AGAD KGGW 2382, Piotrków Governor to the Department of Police, May 7 (20), 1904.
72. Pietrzak-Pawłowska, "Depresja ekonomiczna," p. 27.
73. AGAD KGGW 2382, Lublin Governor to the WGG, August 31 (September 13) and November 17 (30), 1904.
74. Korzec, *Źródła do dziejów rewolucji* 1 (1): 97–98, 119–125.

he proposed that the factory and plant owners of Piotrków Province carry the financial burden of improved and better organized relief efforts. Miller also argued for the creation of a permanent unemployment relief fund under the auspices of the State Bank to help secure the workers' existence in future times of crisis.[75] Unfortunately, Miller's advice went unheeded, and he was subsequently forced to plead for the placement of orders for army uniforms with Łódź industrialists as well as the issuing of passports and railroad tickets free-of-charge to the unemployed so that they might work abroad. Finally, at the end of September, the Piotrków governor's office, recognizing the failure of its various efforts to provide relief, requested permission to deport twenty-five hundred "permanently unemployed" workers from Łódź to their places of birth.[76]

The effects of the industrial depression, coupled with inflation and the state's inability to organize relief where it counted—in the major urban and industrial areas—were bound to generate labor unrest. In part, that unrest also resulted from what historian Richard Lewis has termed "a crisis of rising expectations."[77] Workers' real wages had risen steadily in the 1890s, aided by an increasingly offensive-minded strike movement that drew up to 10 percent of the industrial labor force. Wages then plummeted sharply during the European depression of 1900–1903, but recovery in the second half of 1903 and early 1904 generated hope among the workers that a return to normal economic conditions would result in an improvement in their standard of living. Workers' expectations are reflected in the escalating number of strikes (twenty in 1903 compared with six in 1902), almost all of which resulted in at least some concessions from management.[78] The momentum of the strike movement initially carried forward into the first months of 1904. At the end of January, 580 textile workers struck at five factories in Tomaszów Mazowiecki in Piotrków Province, effectively bringing the local economy to a standstill. Within a week, management at all five factories agreed to raise piece rates in a compromise acceptable to their employees. Throughout the strike, provincial authorities reported that the workers remained "calm" and "peaceful," thus obviating a resort to extraordinary police measures.[79]

75. AGAD KGGW 2382, Piotrków Governor to the WGG, July 15 (28), 1904.
76. AGAD KGGW 2382, Piotrków Governor to the WGG, August 11 (24) and August 12 (25), 1904; Korzec, *Źródła do dziejów rewolucji* 1 (1): 142–147.
77. Richard D. Lewis, "The Labor Movement in Russian Poland in the Revolution of 1905–1907" (Ph.D. diss., University of California, Berkeley, 1971), p. 75.
78. Ignacy Orzechowski and Aleksander Kochański, *Zarys dziejów ruchu zawodowego w Królestwie Polskim, 1905–1918* (Warsaw, 1964), pp. 41–51.
79. AGAD KGGW 2221, Report of the SDPA to the WGG, January 20 (February 3), 1904; Korzec, *Źródła do dziejów rewolucji* 1 (1): 303–312.

The workers' hopes, as well as their quiet and confident demeanor, were shattered by the Russo-Japanese War. The ensuing industrial depression quickly becalmed the strike movement. Faced with unemployment and reduced wages, workers found themselves with no choice but to give up their efforts to improve their living standards. The few strikes that did occur during the remainder of 1904 were by necessity defensive in nature, aimed at maintaining wages at their prewar level or preventing their drastic decline. Employers, for their part, could and did threaten to close their factories and plants if workers resisted the reductions. This proved a most effective bargaining tool.

The one major strike of 1904 occurred in the Warsaw construction industry, one of the few oases of economic activity unaffected by the war. The seasonal nature of employment in the industry determined the timing of the strike; the desire to keep up with inflation, its purpose. Already, at the beginning of the construction season in April, bricklayers struck at several building sites in Warsaw, but after ten days they had achieved only minor wage increases, and these were soon eroded by rising prices.[80] The relatively high demand for skilled construction workers and the need to complete already initiated projects prompted a second three-week strike at the end of the summer. This time the bricklayers demanded a substantial wage increase, from the existing fifteen kopecks per hour, as well as a nine-hour working day. Their lesser demands included immediate and direct payment of wages at work sites, the construction of shelters to protect workers from the elements, and a two-week advance warning of layoffs.[81] In contrast to the April strike, the strike of August–September was joined by carpenters, painters, and other construction workers—at its peak, thirty-five hundred workers—halting construction at 121 building sites.[82]

The nearly general strike in the Warsaw construction industry achieved few of its goals, and workers again had to satisfy themselves with minor wage concessions. But the Warsaw construction strike was important in that it displayed for the first time many of the characteristics that would become common to the labor movement in 1905. First, socialist parties played a principal role in organizing and spreading the strike, a role to which they were not particularly accustomed. At the majority of striking construction sites, for example, workers' demands followed those set forth in proclamations of the PPS-Proletariat. As the strike continued, workers

---

80. AGAD KGGW 2336, Warsaw Governor to the WGG, April 14 (27), 1904; see also Kiepurska, *Warszawa w rewolucji*, p. 62.
81. AGAD KGGW 2336, Report of the SDPA to the WGG, August 9 (22), 1904.
82. Ibid., August 17 (30), 1904.

looked to both the PPS-Proletariat and the SDKPiL to represent their interests, and four delegates from each party joined the bricklayers' strike
committee.[83] Second, the strike was accompanied by a good deal of violence. In the April strike, workers who did not join had been threatened
with beatings. In August and September, that threat was carried out, leading
to the charge by employers that the strike was the work of a minority who
terrorized an otherwise peaceful and contented majority.[84] Although the
employers' claim was surely an exaggeration designed to bring about state
intervention, rioting did erupt in the Warsaw suburb of Praga on September
10, when rock-throwing strikers attacked those who remained on the job,
inflicting several minor head injuries.[85] Finally, the workers took their demands into the streets, holding public meetings and demonstrations numbering up to five hundred in Praga, Mokotów, Wola, and Śródmieście. In
the first week of the strike, these crowds dispersed peacefully; but as the
strike continued into September, they began to resist police demands, leading to the arrest of dozens of construction workers.[86]

Workers in the Warsaw construction industry may have been able to
demonstrate their dissatisfaction through a general strike, but most of the
labor force resorted to other means. From Piotrków Province, in particular,
came reports of a turbulent and ''ugly'' mood spreading among the proletariat. That mood found graphic expression, for instance, in May when
a crowd of more than five thousand in the Łódź suburb of Chojny attempted to lynch a factory watchman suspected of beating a young boy to
death. Several Cossacks were injured as they tried to forestall vigilante
justice.[87] In Warsaw on June 13, a fire at a pharmacy on Grzybowska Street
drew a crowd of several thousand working-class spectators, which in turn
attracted the police, who were greeted with taunts and then a hail of rocks.
The crowd dispersed only when confronted with salvos fired by a company
of Cossacks. Two civilians were killed and six injured in the brawl, which
also left twenty-two policemen, nine gendarmes, and four Cossacks with
serious wounds. A similar clash occurred nine days later, when police tried
to disperse workers who had gathered to watch a fire at a pub on Worona

83. Ibid., August 16 (29), 1904; see also Kiepurska, *Warszawa w rewolucji*, pp. 62–63. For
the SDKPiL's version of its involvement in the strike, see *Czerwony Sztandar*, no. 20 (September 1904).
84. AGAD KGGW 2336, Warsaw Bricklayers' Guild to the Warsaw Magistrate, September
7 (20), 1904.
85. Rappaport, *Narastanie rewolucji*, pp. 618–619.
86. AGAD KGGW 2336, Warsaw Superintendent of Police to the WGG, August 24 (September 6), 1904.
87. AGAD KGGW 2346, Piotrków Governor to the WGG, May 12 (25), 1904.

"Street Demonstration." Contemporary drawing by Witold Wojtkiewicz, 1905.
(Muzeum Niepodległości 35860)


Street.[88] The growing number and size of these disturbances, which por-
tended "major disorders," led four provincial governors to request the
dispatch of additional troops to reinforce local garrisons. Already back in
May, the Piotrków governor's shopping list had included two battalions of
infantry, a company of cavalry, and two companies of Cossacks.[89]

Officials in urban areas also reported a rising tide of crime, fights, and
public drunkenness, which they attributed to the demoralizing effects of a
sharp decline in workers' living standards. The crime rate in Łódź doubled
in comparison with 1903, primarily as a result of an increase of thefts and
robberies related to food.[90] By autumn larceny had reached such proportions that several Łódź industrialists appealed directly to the Ministry of
Internal Affairs to take stronger measures to defend the property and security of "law-abiding citizens."[91] Local authorities, meanwhile, sought to
identify and remove from factory centers unemployed workers suspected

88. AGAD KGGW 2383, Report of the SDPA to the WGG, June 1 (14), 1904, and Warsaw
Superintendent of Police to the WGG, June 13 (26), 1904.
89. AGAD KGGW 2346, Piotrków Governor to the WGG, May 12 (25), 1904.
90. Korzec, Źródła do dziejów rewolucji I (I): 142–147.
91. AGAD KGGW 2382, Piotrków Governor to the WGG, September 25 (October 8), 1904.

of criminal activity or deemed guilty of disturbing the peace as a result of riotous or drunken behavior.[92]

In the eyes of the Russian authorities, labor unrest in the Kingdom assumed its most dangerous proportions in the autumn, as a result of workers' increasing participation in the political demonstrations organized by the socialist parties, especially in the antiwar movement headed by the PPS. The May Day demonstrations of 1904, by the very fact of their occurrence in several cities in the face of strong preventive police measures, provided the authorities with an initial warning. This achievement, unprecedented in the annals of Polish socialism, could not be immediately exploited, however. The PPS antiwar demonstrations of the late spring and early summer, for example, still consisted largely of party activists and student sympathizers. Similarly, of fifty-six persons arrested in a Warsaw funeral demonstration organized by the SDKPiL in May, thirty-four were students or former students, and only two could be classified as workers.[93]

The antiwar movement nevertheless proved a most effective vehicle for directing labor unrest into desired political channels. After the mobilization of reservists in October, the dozens of demonstrators turned into hundreds, and by December, thousands. Authorities pointed the finger at the growing influence of socialist propaganda among the workers; but it did not take party newspapers like the PPS's *Robotnik* or the SDKPiL's *Czerwony Sztandar* to convince a textile mill hand that the Russo-Japanese War was a direct cause of his current misery. Moreover, the socialists had not brought the workers into the streets; they were already there, unemployed or working limited hours, angry and at times intoxicated, agitated first by the forced abandonment of their expectations and then by the drastic decline in their living standards. They were itching for a fight. While the PPS bojowcy, armed with revolvers and Brownings, began turning up at demonstrations, the workers brought their own ''cold'' weapons—knives, bottles, rocks, and clubs. The very appearance of such weapons, commonplace by the late fall, marked the confluence of social with political protest. For the imperial authorities, it was to prove a most dangerous combination.

### The Student Movement

Students played a prominent role, as already mentioned, in the early phases of the antiwar and antigovernment movement of 1904. Long alien-

---

92. AGAD KGGW 2382, WGG to the Minister of Internal Affairs, September 19 (October 2), 1904.
93. AGAD KGGW 2337, Warsaw Superintendent of Police to the WGG, May 1 (14), 1904.

ated by the inflexibility and discrimination of the russified system prevailing in institutions of secondary and higher education, many students had found refuge in "secret" self-education circles where they discussed prohibited literary, philosophical, and historical topics. Many of the "secret" circles dated from the 1890s—their appearance coinciding with the emergence of the nationalist and socialist movements. From the beginning, the new ideologies of what would develop into mass movements were fashionable among students, perhaps because they provided the self-education circles with a forum for debate of contemporary issues and a sense of political direction. By 1904, nationalist and socialist student organizations were competing and sometimes cooperating with one another in all of the country's institutions of higher education and in many secondary schools as well. As a consequence, students were the most politicized social group in Polish society on the eve of the Russo-Japanese War.

Meanwhile, disturbances in the schools had become almost usual in the first years of the twentieth century. In Lublin, the self-education circles at the boys' gymnasium were sufficiently strong to coordinate successful boycotts of concerts, balls, literary evenings, and other activities organized by the school authorities. Their activities culminated in "disorders" in the spring of 1902 during the singing of the Russian national anthem.[94] Gymnasium students in Łomża and Płock, also in 1902, responded to official observances of the fiftieth anniversary of Gogol's death by boycotting the ceremonies and disrupting classes. In the latter case, the incident led to the expulsion of forty students.[95] The most widespread action of these years, however, occurred in the ethnically mixed eastern counties of Siedlce and Lublin provinces, where nationalist youth organized a series of actions in 1902 and 1903 protesting the arbitrary introduction of Russian as the language of religious instruction. Despite expulsions and other countermeasures, the authorities were forced to restore Polish for the study of religion in eight secondary schools.[96]

A proliferation of self-education circles followed, accompanied by the penetration of nationalist and "progressive" (liberal and socialist) influences. By 1904, underground student circles of various political stripes existed at almost all institutions of higher and secondary education in Warsaw, and the Society for Secret Instruction, created in 1894 by Cecylja

94. Bogdan Nowroczyński, ed., *Nasza walka o szkołę polską, 1901–1917: Opracowania, wspomnienia, dokumenty*, vol. 1 (Warsaw, 1932), pp. 461–466.
95. Ibid., pp. 405–410, 429.
96. Ibid., pp. 414–417, 421–429; see also Urszula Głowacka-Maksymiuk, *Gubernia siedlecka w latach rewolucji, 1905–1907* (Warsaw, 1985), p. 57.

Śniegocka, provided illegal Polish language instruction for two thousand Warsaw children of elementary school age.[97] Conspiratorial organizations and underground activity had also become widespread in the provinces but varied widely in size and significance. The "secret" library shared by nationalist and progressive student groups in the Piotrków secondary schools, for instance, held three thousand volumes.[98] By contrast, the "progressive" self-education circle in the Kielce Boys' Gymnasium, strongly influenced by the PPS, consisted of forty students and possessed a library containing only four hundred volumes.[99]

The competition of political organizations active among student youth intensified greatly during the course of 1904. As already mentioned, the Union of Polish Youth, better known as "Zet," was closely tied to the nationalist movement. In the first years of the twentieth century, Zet succeeded in creating conspiratorial groups among Polish university students and, through a satellite organization called Przyszłość (The Future), among Polish students in the secondary schools as well. The Union of Socialist Youth, on the other hand, was created in 1902 and brought together student members and sympathizers of the PPS, SDKPiL, Bund, and PPS-Proletariat. Whereas nationalist youth groups were ethnically exclusive and limited membership to students of Polish nationality, "progressive" and socialist groups (which were frequently synonymous) contained both Polish and Jewish students. Both nationalist and socialist youth groups cooperated in mutual-aid organizations (e.g., at the Warsaw Polytechnical Institute) and sent delegates to the Central Circle, which represented all shades of opinion among secondary school youth in Warsaw. Student solidarity was fragile, however, and competition among political organizations could just as easily result in the fragmentation and polarization of student opinion. Political rivalry between nationalist and socialist youth groups, for example, brought about the breakup of the mutual-aid organization at Warsaw University by 1899. Sharp divisions between nationalist and socialist student sympathizers also prevailed in several secondary schools in Warsaw and Łódź.

Nevertheless, student opposition to the Russian educational system became both more organized and more politicized in 1904, and the level of student unrest, as measured in official documents, grew appreciably. The Warsaw Polytechnical Institute became the scene of repeated incidents dur-

97. Helena Ceysingerówna, "Tajne nauczanie w Warszawie, 1894–1906," *Niepodległość* 2 (April–September 1930): 95–103.
98. Nowroczyński, *Nasza walka o szkołę polską* 1: 372.
99. Ibid., p. 397.

ing the course of the year, beginning with the already-mentioned walkout of Polish and Jewish students eleven days after the outbreak of hostilities in the Far East. A few months later, efforts to organize a demonstration at the institute on the anniversary of the Polish Constitution of May 3 resulted in the arrest of thirty students.[100] Students from the institute, as well as from Warsaw University, figured prominently among those arrested and sentenced for "active participation" in the Grzybowski Square demonstration of November 13.[101] Exactly one month later, forty-nine students were arrested for participating in a demonstration that celebrated the recent assassination of Viacheslav Plehve, the Russian minister of Internal Affairs. This particular "disorder" resulted in the closing of the institute four days before the end of the semester.[102]

The Institute of Agriculture and Forestry in Puławy was another center of unrest in 1904, this despite its overwhelming proportion of Russian students. In fact, many of the young Russians were actively involved in or sympathized with the socialist and radical movements, and collaboration with like-minded Polish colleagues had been established in 1899. The ground was therefore fertile at the Puławy Institute for organizational activity of an "internationalist" flavor carried out primarily by the SDKPiL. In fact, the entire Southern Committee of the SDKPiL consisted of students from the Puławy Institute, and its influence, although confined at the time within the institute, was nonetheless considerable. The Southern Committee, moreover, maintained contacts with and supported the activity of the Military Revolutionary Organization of the Russian Social Democratic Workers Party, which, in turn, was active among the soldiers of the Russian garrison at Puławy.[103] Consequently, as early as March 1904, authorities feared a student strike at the institute and blamed the activity of the Southern Committee.[104] Although a strike did not occur in the spring as expected, unrest at the Puławy Institute remained high. In the middle of March, six students were arrested and subsequently fined for "disturbing the peace." Two months later, windows were broken at the homes of the institute's inspector and three of its professors.[105]

A series of incidents at the boys' gymnasium in Radom, leading to the

100. Rappaport, *Narastanie rewolucji,* pp. 525–526.
101. APW WGZŻ 934.
102. AGAD KGGW 2384, Warsaw Superintendent of Police to the WGG, December 2 (15), 1904.
103. Robert Blobaum, *Feliks Dzierżyński and the SDKPiL: A Study of the Origins of Polish Communism* (Boulder, 1984), p. 128.
104. AGAD KGGW 2219, Report of the SDPA to the WGG, February 20 (March 4), 1904.
105. Ibid., April 13 (26) and May 10 (23), 1904.

expulsion of eighty students during the spring semester of 1904, well il-lustrates the tensions prevailing in the secondary schools. On February 4, students from the upper forms walked out of the gymnasium after de-manding the dismissal of a teacher who had "illegally" prohibited the reading of the morning prayer in Polish. The gymnasium's director, though refusing to remove the teacher, promised to look into the matter upon the return of the students to classes.[106] No action, however, was taken against the teacher, and on March 6, nineteen students from the fifth form walked out of his class. They were followed by dozens of colleagues from the sixth, seventh, and eighth forms, all of whom were expelled.[107] Despite the expulsions, the students remained defiant. On May 3, about a hundred gymnasium students sang the forbidden hymn "Boże coś Polskę" (God preserve Poland) in a Radom church and then marched down the city's main thoroughfare.[108] The climax occurred on the night of June 1–2, when an explosion from a homemade bomb rocked the quarters of the gymna-sium's inspector. Although the police failed to come up with direct evi-dence, they immediately and justifiably suspected the involvement of recently expelled students.[109]

During the course of 1904, walkouts, closings, and mass expulsions of students also took place at the E. Święciński Technical School in Warsaw, the Mariampol Boys' Gymnasium in Suwałki Province, and the Mariampol Teachers Seminary. By the end of the year, rumors of a nationwide student strike were rife. Zet began making preparations for student meetings at Warsaw University and the Polytechnical Institute. At the same time, the possibility of a strike in the secondary schools was openly debated at a congress of nationalist students in December. In anticipation of a strike, student organizations from three secondary schools in Kalisz formed a committee to direct the action once it occurred. Similarly, representatives of nationalist and "progressive" youth groups in Piotrków met to discuss preparations for a strike despite the lack of instructions from Warsaw. Also in December, students at the Sosnowiec Real School were told by a del-egate to the Central Circle in Warsaw to expect "some sort of action" at the beginning of the new year. In the words of a former student of the Kielce Boys Gymnasium, "nobody was surprised" once the call for a nationwide school strike finally materialized the following January.[110]

106. Ibid., February 23 (March 7), 1904.
107. Ibid., March 12 (25), 1904.
108. AGAD KGGW 2282, Radom Governor to the WGG, April 30 (May 5), 1904.
109. AGAD KGGW 2219, Radom Governor to the WGG, June 4 (17), 1904.
110. Nowroczyński, *Nasza walka o szkołę polską* 1: 132–133, 274, 376, 383, 391, 398.

## Stirrings in the Countryside

Compared with factory centers and academic institutions, the Polish countryside remained relatively quiet for most of 1904. There was no organized antiwar movement in the villages, only sporadic and isolated incidents of resistance to conscription and wartime taxation. To the peasantry, the disruption of sales of the Kingdom's industrial goods in Russian markets had little meaning, and questions relating to "imperialist expansionism" even less. Overall, the Polish peasantry remained indifferent to the war; only a few peasants hoped for a Japanese victory or saw some advantage for the "Polish cause" in a Russian defeat. Indeed most peasants did not yet recognize the existence of a "Polish cause."

Those who did, however, became increasingly active, especially toward the end of the year. The awakening of national consciousness among certain segments of rural peasant society was a long, drawn-out process that extended back to the 1880s and the first postemancipation generation of Polish peasants. As mentioned in the first chapter, this generation, unlike the previous one, did not perceive the tsar as its benefactor or the land it owned as "a gift." Meanwhile, it increasingly perceived the Russian bureaucracy as an alien and external force usurping statutory rights of local self-government. That bureaucracy's arbitrary introduction of the Russian language into the conduct of communal affairs, its interference in communal elections and meetings, and the pressures it applied to force members of communal assemblies to act in a prescribed way—all led to declining peasant participation in local political processes clearly manipulated from the outside.

The principal contact between peasants and the Russian state, however, occurred during encounters of the former with the rural police, or Land Guard. The Land Guard appeared at the scene of almost every local dispute, whether between peasant neighbors or between entire villages and nearby estate owners, and made its presence felt at every meeting of communal assemblies. The Land Guard was a completely alien force. Although statistical information on its composition is available only for Lublin Province, it serves as a representative example for the entire Kingdom. Of the 388 men employed in the Lublin Land Guard in 1904, 359 were classified as "Orthodox," that is, Russian, whereas only 5.5 percent were Roman Catholics born inside the Kingdom, and most of these served in the town of Lublin rather than in the countryside.[111]

---

111. APL KGL 1905:64.

Finally, the system of elementary education in the countryside, which in the 1880s increasingly substituted Russian for Polish as the language of instruction, was not only alien to peasant society but also woefully inadequate in pedagogic terms. In 1904, there were 2,977 elementary schools funded by organs of communual self-government, or one school for every 3,105 inhabitants. Or put another way, 32 children for every 1,000 inhabitants in the Polish countryside were enrolled in an elementary school in 1904. By comparison, 42.9 children for every 1,000 inhabitants attended elementary schools in the rest of European Russia. In Great Britain, Germany, and the United States the ratios stood at 160, 190, and 230 per 1,000 respectively. Moreover, of the small minority of children receiving primary education, 92.5 percent were enrolled in one-class elementary schools and completed their "education" after three years of study. At the most, they picked up rudimentary reading and writing skills, and these were not in their native language. Small wonder then that illiteracy continued to afflict three out of every four Polish peasants in the first years of the twentieth century. [112]

Individual peasants and groups of peasants responded to their growing sense of alienation from the Russian regime and its local bureaucratic and police representatives in various ways. One was to create their own social organizations, such as volunteer fire departments, which, with the permission of the authorities, could serve the interests of village communities without undermining those of the Russian state. In many localities, a volunteer fire department was often the only such social organization in existence. Even the authorities recognized the need for volunteer firemen. Until World War I, almost all buildings in the Polish countryside were constructed of wood and other flammable materials, and losses from fires ran into the millions of rubles each year. Consequently, provincial governors in consultation with the Ministry of Internal Affairs approved the creation of 128 associations of volunteer firemen by 1900. For practical reasons, Polish was the language of command in the volunteer organizations, which also possessed their own biweekly Polish-language publication. In time, the firemen's associations came to play an important integrative role in their communities through the promotion of social, educational, and cultural activities. Equally important, dedication to public service earned the firemen sympathy, respect, and authority in their com-

---

112. Zenon Kmiecik, *Ruch oświatowy na wsi: Królestwo Polskie, 1905–1914* (Warsaw, 1963), pp. 11–12; Edmund Staszyński, *Polityka oświatowa caratu w Królestwie Polskim* (Warsaw, 1968), pp. 88–89.

munities.[113] State officials, for their part, became alarmed at the proliferation of the firemen's associations and increasingly suspicious of their range
of activities, which, in the words of the Siedlce governor, translated into
"agitation" and "a failure to carry out the obligations for which [they]
were constituted."[114]

Participation in volunteer firemen's associations was a legal circumvention of externally imposed Russian institutions in the countryside and permitted the cultivation of Polish language and customs. Another, even more
important awakener of national consciousness in rural areas was the widespread involvement of peasants in illegal Polish-language reading and writing courses. In 1901, a special commission created by the Warsaw
governor-general reported that one-third of the rural population had received or was currently receiving secret instruction in the Polish language.[115] In Siedlce Province in 1904, there was one underground school
for every two public elementary schools.[116] In Radom Province, where the
state network was even weaker, the authorities uncovered and suppressed
more than two hundred secret schools in the years immediately before the
revolution.[117]

Inasmuch as secret instruction often had a moral-religious flavor, the
didactic achievements of the underground schools were not particularly
impressive by modern secular standards. Nevertheless, maintenance of the
secret schools and the hiring of teachers required forms of collective social
organization that raised the national consciousness of a substantial section
of the peasantry. Most secret courses were held in buildings belonging to
the local Catholic parish or in peasant cottages and were conducted by
church organists, semiliterate village women, ex-soldiers and reservists,
and employees of local manors, as well as by fired and retired teachers
from the state schools. Some clandestine teachers traveled from cottage to
cottage and from village to village to hold their courses. Covert instruction
was also aided by the young intelligentsia, particularly students from Warsaw and Puławy during vacations. An average of slightly more than ten
pupils, usually a mixed group of boys and girls, attended an underground
school, where they studied Konrad Proszyński's Polish primer (the so-
called Promyk grammar) or a Polish-language catechism. After 1900,

113. On the history of the volunteer firemen's associations, see Józef Ryszard Szaflik, *Dzieje ochotniczych straży pożarnych* (Warsaw, 1985).
114. AGAD KGGW 2472, Siedlce Governor to the WGG, October 14 (27), 1904.
115. Helena Brodowska, *Ruch chłopski po uwłaszczeniu w Królestwie Polskim, 1864–1904* (Warsaw, 1967), p. 255.
116. Głowacka-Maksymiuk, *Gubernia siedlecka w latach rewolucji*, pp. 44–47.
117. Brodowska, *Ruch chłopski*, pp. 248–251.

teaching in the secret schools carried the risk of a three-hundred-ruble fine and three months in jail. Parents of participating children could also be subjected to stiff fines or up to two weeks in jail.

The Society for National Education, known by its popular Polish acronym as TON, played an important role in the spread of secret instruction in rural areas. Founded in 1899, TON functioned as a satellite organization of the Endecja in the countryside. By 1904, six thousand peasant members participated in two hundred cells of TON, many of which were located in the Kingdom's northern and eastern provinces.[118] As TON took over and enlarged the network of secret schools, it gave the underground educational movement in the countryside a far greater sense of organization and political purpose.

A logical extension of TON's underground educational activities in the Polish countryside was its agitation for the polonization of the institutions of communal self-government. *Polak* (The Pole), a Kraków-based Endecja publication aimed at the peasantry and distributed by the TON cells in the Kingdom, began popularizing the slogan of "gmina action" in the autumn of 1904. Conceived as activity legally conducted and restricted initially to demands for Polish language, gmina action eventually embraced about one hundred communes by the end of the year. The center of the movement was in Płock and Warsaw provinces, where forty-one gmina assemblies passed resolutions drafted in Polish instead of Russian, an action justified on the basis of the statutes of 1864 that provided for communal self-government.[119] At several other meetings, moreover, the right of the assemblies to use the Polish language in their resolutions was at least asserted, if not actually exercised.

Almost all this activity occurred at the end of 1904. The uniformity of the gmina assembly resolutions points to an organized movement among the peasants in which TON and *Polak* played significant inspirational roles. The movement's strength, however, was in its indigenous roots. In the words of the Lublin governor, agitation for the Polish language was "conducted by persons well known to the local population and enjoying its trust"—that is, presumably, by persons like the volunteer firemen.[120] Such agitation took a variety of forms, especially earlier in the year. In early March, for example, peasants from the gmina of Niemce in Lublin Prov-

---

118. The history of TON in the years immediately before the revolution is documented by Tadeusz Wolsza, "Towarzystwo Oświaty Narodowej, 1899–1905," *Kwartalnik Historyczny* 89, 2 (1987): 71–96.
119. *Polak* no. 2 (February 1905): 28.
120. Stanisław Kalabiński and Feliks Tych, eds., *Walki chłopów Królestwa Polskiego w rewolucji 1905–1907*, vol. 1 (Warsaw, 1958), pp. 133–134.

ince refused to tax themselves for the capital repair of two primary schools so long as instruction was in the Russian language. As a result, four local "agitators" were placed under "open" police surveillance (a type of house arrest).[121] In another protest action during the summer, several Russian road and directional signs in the communes of Dzierzkowice and Urzędów, also in Lublin Province, were covered with homemade Polish equivalents.[122] At the end of the summer, the mayor of the gmina of Łuków in Siedlce Province was dismissed from his office and placed under police surveillance after demanding that the minutes and resolutions of the gmina assembly be written in Polish.[123]

The rising tide of peasant protest against the russification of local institutions that were supposedly created to serve peasant interests was the most visible form of unrest in rural areas in 1904. Once it assumed the character of an organized movement, it also began to attract the serious attention of the Russian authorities. Other sources of potential agrarian unrest were considerably less alarming by comparison: ongoing disputes over easement rights, a rising rural crime rate, the steady deterioration in the living standards of agrarian laborers, and the mounting pressures of overpopulation. Yet these too, along with gmina action, would help define the contours of the coming revolution in the Polish countryside.

At the end of 1904, leading provincial officials clearly anticipated the outbreak of "major disorders" in the Kingdom of Poland and requested that the machinery for emergency rule, long in place, be set in motion as part of a preemptive strategy. Not only was the expression of political and social discontent among different strata of society becoming more bold and demonstrative, but it was also becoming more efficiently organized. Signs of oppositional activity began to appear as well among such previously reticent social and occupational groups as teachers and the Catholic clergy. Furthermore, the various underground parties by now were emerging from their conspiratorial shells in an effort to direct that unrest into desired political channels and, in the process, were reaping dividends in the form of increased memberships.

Even conservatives who had previously urged society to reconcile itself to Russian rule could no longer ignore that rule's deleterious impact, nor the dramatic shift in popular attitudes during the course of 1904. At the end of December, Count Władysław Tyszkiewicz, a longtime "concilia-

121. Rappaport, *Narastanie rewolucji*, pp. 479–480.
122. Ibid., pp. 584–585.
123. Ibid., p. 618.

tionist'' and president of the Warsaw branch of the Society for the Support of Russian Industry and Trade, delivered a "memorial" signed by twenty-three prominent members of the Polish elite to the minister of Internal Affairs, urging the government to implement immediate reforms to prevent a further escalation of the crisis. Citing a litany of sins perpetrated by the Russian bureaucracy in the Kingdom, Tyszkiewicz claimed that Russian rule had led to widespread uncertainty regarding the future, to a weakening of the public and "entrepreneurial" spirit—in short, to "a general demoralization of society." To prevent even greater disasters, Tyszkiewicz called for the granting of rights to Poles equal to those shared by other subjects of the tsar; the return of the Polish language to the Kingdom's schools, courts, and administration; the employment of Poles in state and public institutions; the realization and strict observance of statutes providing for local self-government; the granting of religious freedom to the Uniate population; and the restoration of full rights to the Roman Catholic Church.[124]

Whether the adoption of these measures would have been enough to avert a revolution is difficult to say; in any event, Tyszkiewicz's memorial had little impact on St. Petersburg's way of thinking. As 1904 gave way to 1905, the central government remained determined to rule the Kingdom according to the familiar methods of repression. Instead of timely concessions and reforms, the tsarist autocracy preferred to rely on police force, the emergency powers vested in the Warsaw governor-general, and the presence of a large body of troops—time-tested devices that had, after all, kept the Kingdom subdued for more than forty years. Within a few weeks of the receipt of the Tyszkiewicz memorial, however, events would convince the central government, if not its provincial agents, that the efficacy of repressive measures alone had just about run its course.

124. AGAD AB, druk 220.

# The Emergence of
# the Labor Movement

Beginning with Bloody Sunday, the infamous massacre of working-class demonstrators in St. Petersburg on January 22, industrial labor played an undeniably significant role in the Revolution of 1905 in European Russia. The outrage after Bloody Sunday, expressed in massive strikes and demonstrations throughout the empire, indeed became the spark that ignited Russia's subsequent bourgeois-democratic revolution. In October, Russian workers intervened directly in that revolution by means of a statewide general strike to force a recalcitrant autocracy to accede to the demands of a temporarily united political opposition for democratic freedoms and a constitutional restructuring of the old political order. Between January and October, however, Russian industrial workers remained relatively quiet, if not entirely neutral, in the struggle between the principal combatants, the autocracy and its liberal opponents. By the end of the year, and especially after the ill-fated Moscow uprising, the Russian proletariat had played out its collective historical role, at least as far as this revolution was concerned. Although more than mere spectators, Russian workers were largely offstage in the revolutionary drama of 1905 save for two brief but exciting appearances.

In the Kingdom of Poland, however, the industrial labor movement played a far more central role in the revolution. Without the industrial workers, it is hard to conceive of a "Polish revolution" worthy of the name. The revolt of the industrial workers in late January and early February gave other independent social and political movements their cue. Unlike their Russian counterparts, industrial workers in Poland refused to leave the stage to other actors between January and October. They maintained their position, moreover, throughout 1906 and into the first months of 1907, until finally removed by a crushing defeat in a dramatic confrontation with management in Łódź known as the "Great Lockout." In the meantime, the labor movement in the Kingdom became politicized and organized to a degree unknown elsewhere in the Russian Empire. Simply put, the revolution's initiation of the era of mass politics and the consequent transformation of Polish political culture would not have occurred without the active participation and involvement of the Kingdom's working class.

Statistical data clearly illustrate the engagement of the Kingdom's proletariat in the revolution, especially when compared with workers in the rest of the empire. According to Laura Engelstein's study of Moscow workers in 1905, the great "general" strikes of January and October involved only 20 percent of the labor force.[1] By contrast, 93.2 percent of the industrial workers in Russian Poland participated in the strike movement in 1905. In the same year, one-third of all strikes in the Russian Empire occurred in the Kingdom of Poland, and the proportion was even greater in 1906 (42 percent of all strikes).[2] Piotrków Province alone supplied 37.5 percent of all striking textile workers in the empire in 1905, and 57.6 percent in 1906.[3] Similarly, the May Day general strike in Warsaw in 1905 accounted for 40 percent of all participants in that strike in the entire Russian state.[4]

Trade union organization in Russian Poland also far outpaced the rest of the empire. At the turn of 1906–1907, some 20 percent of the labor force in the Kingdom had been organized, compared with only 5 percent in Russia. In fact, industrial labor was more organized in Russian Poland at this time than in Austria, Belgium, and France.[5] A high percentage of trade union members were also active in political organizations. In Warsaw at the end of 1906, the trade union movement embraced thirty-two thousand workers; of these twenty thousand belonged to a political party.[6] The

1. Laura Engelstein, *Moscow, 1905: Working-Class Organization and Political Conflict* (Stanford, 1982), pp. 64, 109.
2. Anna Żarnowska, "Próba analizy ruchu strajkowego w Królestwie Polskim w dobie rewolucji 1905–1907," *Przegląd Historyczny* 56, 3 (1965): 433.
3. Władysław Lech Karwacki, *Łódzka organizacja Polskiej Partii Socjalistycznej-Lewicy, 1906–1918* (Łódź, 1964), p. 77.
4. Żarnowska, "Próba analizy," p. 443.
5. Władysław Lech Karwacki, *Związki zawodowe i stowarzyszenia pracodawców w Łodzi* (Łódź, 1972), pp. 54–60; see also Stanisław Kalabiński and Feliks Tych, *Czwarte powstanie czy pierwsza rewolucja: Lata 1905–1907 na ziemiach polskich,* 2d ed. (Warsaw, 1976), p. 444.
6. Anna Żarnowska, *Robotnicy Warszawy na przełomie XIX i XX wieku* (Warsaw, 1985), pp. 241–244.

formation of workers' cooperatives, the rapid growth of reading rooms and libraries, and a general striving to expand educational opportunities—though more difficult to measure statistically—provide additional evidence of a genuine political and cultural awakening among a large section of the Kingdom's working-class population.[7]

Although the politicization and general cultural advance of industrial workers must be counted among the positive achievements of this period, the revolution also encouraged recourse to violent solutions on the shop floor, lack of tolerance for opposing views, polarization of working-class opinion, and eventually a disastrous particularism that resulted from the workers' political inexperience and the absence of democratic traditions. If the emergence of the labor movement was truly the locomotive of the revolution in the Kingdom, its imperfect construction as well as popular disillusionment with its would-be political engineers from the intelligentsia eventually facilitated the efforts of the imperial bureaucracy to derail the entire train.

### The January-February General Strike

The response of workers in Russian Poland to events in St. Petersburg needed no political prompting. The initiative for the subsequent general strike, spreading from Łódź and Warsaw to provincial industrial centers, came from the workers themselves. Both the government and the opposition political parties in the Kingdom were caught completely off-guard by the workers' action. To be sure, police authorities in Warsaw took preventive measures to defend banks, governmental institutions, and power plants in anticipation of "disturbances" after Bloody Sunday, but these measures were conceived more with political terrorists than industrial workers in mind.[8] In the event, they proved totally inadequate. Meanwhile, the SDKPiL rejected proposals by the Bund and the PPS immediately after Bloody Sunday to form an intraparty strike commission in Warsaw.[9] As the socialist parties haggled among themselves and prepared independent

7. On the cultural and educational aspirations of industrial workers, see Władysław Lech Karwacki, "Teatr dla robotników przed 1914 r.," *Polska Klasa Robotnicza: Studia Historyczne* 7 (1976): 159–216, and Jadwiga Krajewska, "Z dziejów oświaty robotniczej: Biblioteki robotnicze w Królestwie Polskim w latach 1870–1914," *Polska Klasa Robotnicza: Studia Historyczne* 3 (1973): 180–209.
8. Stanislaw Kalabiński, ed., *Carat i klasy posiadające w walce z rewolucją 1905–1907 w Królestwie Polskim: Materiały archiwalne* (Warsaw, 1956), pp. 4–6.
9. Halina Kiepurska, *Warszawa w rewolucji 1905–1907* (Warsaw, 1974), p. 82.

appeals for a protest strike, the workers acted on their own. The parties' role in the initiation of the strike was therefore extremely limited. The very news of Bloody Sunday and the Petersburg strike reached the Kingdom's industrial labor force more by way of standard press accounts and government warnings than as a result of party agitation.[10]

The general strike, moreover, began not in Warsaw, where the socialist discussions and "planning" had occurred, but in Łódź. At the end of 1904, the city's textile industry experienced a slight upturn when a few of the larger firms received new state orders.[11] Within weeks, workers in the affected factories sought to recoup wages lost or reduced earlier in the year. On the eve of Bloody Sunday, the SDKPiL organized a strike of four hundred workers at the Karol Steinert factory that soon spread to the great mills and factories of Ludwik Geyer. By January 26, six thousand workers from eight Łódź factories had walked off the job, demanding an eight-hour workday and a minimum hourly wage of fifteen kopecks.[12] Within forty-eight hours the strike became general, embracing twenty-three thousand workers on the twenty-seventh, and all of the city's factories and shops together with one hundred thousand workers and employees by the morning of the twenty-eighth.[13]

From Łódź, the general strike spread quickly to the city's satellite textile towns of Zgierz, Pabianice, and Tomaszów as well as Zduńska Wola in Kalisz Province. In the latter case, authorities attributed the strike to the influence of events in Łódź rather than to local causes.[14] Perhaps for this reason, the government proclaimed a state of emergency on January 30 that extended beyond the Łódź industrial region to all of Piotrków Province.[15] This move did not, however, prevent the general strike during the first week of February from embracing Częstochowa and the Dąbrowa Basin, where it continued well after most workers in Łódź had returned to their jobs.

In Warsaw, the general strike began in the Wola district, where work was suspended in many factories and mills on the morning of January 27. On that day, a clash on the corner of Chłodna and Wronia streets between

10. APŁ KGP 1515(1), Chief of the Piotrków Provincial Gendarmes to the Piotrków Governor, January 14 (27), 1905.

11. Paweł Korzec, ed., Źródła do dziejów rewolucji 1905–1907 w okręgu łódzkim, vol. 1, pt. 1 (Warsaw, 1957), pp. 154–156.

12. APŁ KGP 1515 (1), Chief of the Piotrków Provincial Gendarmes to the Piotrków Governor, January 14 (27), 1905.

13. AGAD KGGW 2494, Report of the SDPA to the WGG, February 8 (21), 1905.

14. Korzec, Źródła do dziejów rewolucji 1(1): 516–519.

15. APŁ KGP 1517, Proclamation of the Piotrków Governor, January 17 (30), 1905.

police and gendarmes and a crowd of a thousand workers immediately set a more violent tone for the strike in Warsaw.[16] As crowds of roaming workers spread the strike from factory to factory, "street disorders" and rioting frequently followed in their wake. The Wola district not only concentrated a large percentage of the city's factory workers but provided asylum to many criminal elements as well. Hence the crowds of striking workers were accompanied by professional thieves, hooligans, vandals, and street urchins, who took advantage of the prevailing confusion to destroy street lanterns and to loot private shops and state-owned alcohol stores. Already, on the first day of the strike, police made sixty-nine arrests.[17]

As the strike spread from Wola to other industrial districts of the city on January 28, the rioting, looting, and violent confrontations with the police also became general. On this, the most alarming day of the Warsaw "disorders," one alcohol store after another was robbed, and dozens of shops were ransacked. The crowd, moreover, responded to police intervention with armed opposition as makeshift barricades went up on the corner of Wronia and Grzybowska streets. Police made 157 arrests in the rioting, which left nine dead and thirteen seriously injured.[18] On the next day, "only" thirty private shops and stores were looted, thanks to the reinforcement of police by troops. In the process, however, more than forty persons were killed and several dozen more wounded by soldiers firing into the crowd.[19] After the proclamation of a state of emergency on January 30, city life began to return to normal, although the strike continued with full force. Altogether, sixty-five persons lost their lives and more than seven hundred were arrested on a variety of charges.[20]

As the authorities restored order in Warsaw, the strike spread to plants and factories throughout Warsaw County. Short-lived strikes were also reported in sugar refineries in Błonie, Kutno, Włocławek, Łowicz, and Gostynin counties. Many of these strikes, according to county officials,

---

16. AGAD KGGW 2488, Warsaw Superintendent of Police to the WGG, January 14 (27), 1905.
17. Kalabiński, *Carat i klasy posiadające*, pp. 7–8; see also Elżbieta Kaczyńska, "Tłum i margines społeczny w wydarzeniach rewolucyjnych: Królestwo Polskie, 1904–1907," *Dzieje Najnowsze* 15, 1–2 (1983): 221–230.
18. AGAD KGGW 2488, Warsaw Superintendent of Police to the WGG, January 29 (February 11), 1905.
19. AGAD KGGW 2488, Chief of the Warsaw Okhrana to the Department of Police, January 16 (29), 1905. On January 30, the Warsaw Strike Committee of the PPS called on workers to use all possible means at their disposal to prevent further rioting; AGAD AB, druki ulotne 43.
20. AGAD KGGW 2488, Warsaw Superintendent of Police to the WGG, January 24 (February 6), 1905.

were accompanied by incidents of coercion usually aimed at local Jewish shopkeepers and small merchants. In Pruszków a crowd of workers forced the teacher of the local primary school to dismiss fifty-seven children from classes.[21]

Massive strikes were also reported at the end of January and the first week of February in Kalisz and Radom provinces. The general strike in Kalisz Province involved approximately ten thousand workers, the vast majority of them employed by textile firms in Ozorków, Kalisz, and Zduńska Wola. These strikes were not accompanied by rioting, so the use of troops proved unnecessary. The authorities, however, took no chances, and the province was placed under a state of emergency on February 5. By February 6, half of the workers had returned to their jobs in Kalisz and Ozorków, while negotiations in the smaller factories promised a quick end to the strike. The weavers of Zduńska Wola, having synchronized their demands with those of the Łódź textile workers, waited until the sixteenth before settling with management.[22]

In Radom the strike took in all the city's factories and workshops together with three thousand workers. As in Warsaw, crowds of strikers spread the walkout from factory to factory, leading to similarly violent confrontations with local authorities attempting to restore order. On February 2, a crowd succeeded in closing the city's electric power station. "Disorders" inevitably followed the blackout. On February 3, troops fired into a "riotous mob," leaving fourteen dead and fifty wounded.[23] Before the authorities could proclaim a state of emergency in the province, twenty-five more were killed on February 4, when troops opened fire on a crowd of a thousand workers attempting to close the nearby railroad station of Skarżysko.[24] Elsewhere in Radom Province, the strike at the Ostrowiec Mining Company in the Holy Cross Mountains, the scene of an anti-Semitic pogrom the previous year, followed a peaceful course and ended on February 8.

In Częstochowa, the strike began on February 3, when a crowd of a hundred workers armed with clubs and knives broke into the Gantke factory, forcing the plant to close. By the next day the strike in Częstochowa was general and began to spread to firms throughout the county. In Raków,

21. AGAD KGGW 2488, Reports of the SDPA to the WGG, January 20 (February 2) and January 26 (February 8), 1905.
22. AGAD KGGW 2506, Reports of the SDPA to the WGG, January 27 (February 9) and February 15 (28), 1905.
23. Jan Boniecki, "Rewolucja 1905–1907 roku w Radomiu," *Biuletyn Kwartalny Radomskiego Towarzystwa Naukowego* 11, supplement (1974): 22–25.
24. AGAD KGGW 2518, Report of the SDPA to the WGG, January 23 (February 5), 1905.

two thousand employees of the Częstochowa Mining Company struck on February 6. Nearly five thousand workers participated in the strike in the Częstochowa region.[25] Uncharacteristically, the workers spreading the strike resorted to violent threats at only one factory. Bloodshed was also avoided when a crowd of six thousand gathered near the Stradom factory to formulate strike demands.[26]

In the Dąbrowa Basin, events took a considerably more dangerous turn. The strike there began on February 1 among boilermakers at the Fintzer and Gamper factory of Sosnowiec. On the same day, a crowd of several hundred disrupted work at mines owned by the Saturn Company. By February 3 the strike had spread to steel mills and coal mines throughout the region. Authorities later attributed the expansion to the agitation of students from the Dąbrowa School of Mines.[27] Governor Artsimovich of Piotrków took immediate alarm and for good reason. The miners' strike, if not settled quickly, could leave many factories in the Kingdom without sufficient coal and force them to close. Moreover, sharp conflict between strikers and those wishing to work was evident from the beginning, creating a situation where a minor incident could provoke a wave of violence. Finally, the governor believed that county administrative and police officials were underestimating the situation in the basin, especially the threat that striking miners posed to unprotected stores of explosive materials. When crowds of up to twenty thousand appeared in Sosnowiec and Dąbrowa, Artsimovich took all available military reserves from the Częstochowa region and sent an urgent request to Warsaw for a significant and immediate increase in troop strength.[28]

In the event, Artsimovich's efforts failed to prevent the worst tragedy of the January-February general strike. On February 9, a large crowd of striking workers crashed the gates of the Katarzyna steel mill in Sosnowiec, where management had attempted to resume production with the help of scab labor. Anticipating trouble, two companies of infantry were stationed at the mill. When shots rang out from the crowd, the panic-stricken soldiers responded with three salvos that dispersed the strikers but also took the lives of thirty-three workers. Subsequently, funerals for the victims of the

---

25. AGAD KGGW 2494, Report of the SDPA to the WGG, February 8 (21), 1905; APŁ KGP 1517, Chief of Częstochowa County to the Piotrków Governor, January 24 (February 6), 1905.
26. APŁ KGP 1517, Częstochowa Chief of Police to the Piotrków Governor, January 27 (February 9), 1905.
27. APŁ KGP 1516, Chief of the Piotrków Provincial Gendarmes to the Department of Police, March 12 (25), 1905.
28. APŁ KGP 1516, Piotrków Governor to the WGG, January 24 (February 6), 1905.

Katarzyna massacre turned into major demonstrations in the streets of So-snowiec, which authorities blamed on the local clergy's failure to follow prescribed processional routes.

At the same time, more than four hundred pounds of dynamite disappeared from stores belonging to the Kazimierz mine, one of the largest in the region, putting both owners and the authorities on notice that striking coal miners now possessed a formidable weapon of their own to prevent a return to work.[29] As late as March 1, only the mines owned by the Saturn Company had resumed operations. Shortly thereafter, the general strike came to an end in the Dąbrowa Basin, though its conclusion came weeks after workers in Łódź and Warsaw had returned to their jobs. The Piotrków governor credited the length of the strike to the workers' determination and, somewhat mistakenly, to socialist and nationalist agitation. Nevertheless, he submitted Będzin County administrative and police officials to a scathing criticism for their inactivity during the strike, particularly for their failure to offer mediation between labor and management, which might have led to earlier settlements and avoided considerable bloodshed.[30]

Elsewhere, the strike was far less imposing. In Lublin, twelve hundred workers walked out on January 31 but returned to work by February 6.[31] The Kielce governor reported "no sign of a labor movement" in his province and therefore requested that factories and plants in the region be exempted from posting government appeals to the workers.[32] The same could be said for Łomża and Suwałki provinces. The general strike spread to Płock, thanks to the arrival of a crowd of two hundred workers from adjacent Warsaw Province, but ended soon after their departure.[33] In the towns of Siedlce Province, Jewish journeymen initiated short-lived strikes, often lasting less than twenty-four hours. The mere appearance of troops in these towns proved sufficient to maintain order. A more serious strike occurred at the Elżbietów sugar factory in Sokołów County, where a settlement was not reached until the end of February.[34]

Workers' demands during the general strike varied widely from region to region, from industry to industry, and indeed from factory to factory,

---

29. Ibid., January 27 (February 9), 1905; AGAD KGGW 2494, Report of the SDPA to the WGG, February 8 (21), 1905; Kalabiński, *Carat i klasy posiadające*, pp. 41–42.
30. APŁ KGP 1515 (2), Piotrków Governor to the WGG, February 16 (March 1), 1905.
31. AGAD KGGW 2513, Report of the SDPA to the WGG, February 10 (23), 1905; see also Alicja Wójcik, *Ruch robotniczy na Lubelszczyźnie* (Lublin, 1984), p. 45.
32. AGAD KGGW 2508, Kielce Governor to the WGG, January 14 (27), 1905.
33. AGAD KGGW 2516, Report of the SDPA to the WGG, January 22 (February 4), 1905.
34. AGAD KGGW 2525, Siedlce Governor to the WGG, January 25 (February 7), February 8 (21), and February 20 (March 5), 1905.

highlighting the absence of advance planning. In many Warsaw factories, workers walked out without making any sort of demands whatsoever.[35] Not only was there nothing to negotiate, but there was no one with whom to negotiate. In such cases, management as well as the government, represented by the factory inspectors, encouraged workers to elect delegations. Even then, workers' initial demands tended to be general and excessive. From the socialist movement they borrowed the slogans of the eight-hour working day and a fifteen-kopeck hourly minimum wage, not to mention a host of political postulates to which they really did not attach any particular importance.

Eventually, however, the workers' strike demands became quite specific, focusing on their immediate concerns and reflecting local conditions. At the Krusche and Ender textile mill in Pabianice, the workers' delegates presented a list of eight demands which expressed, among other things, their desire to form a trade union, to participate in the hiring of foremen, to have direct control over the factory sickness fund, to expand the factory school, to establish a retirement fund, and to extend the provision of medical care to their families.[36] Workers employed by the Saturn Mining Company in the Dąbrowa Basin demanded the construction of a washroom, a school, and a library; free housing heated by coal and wood supplied by the company; free midwife care; and female doctors for the medical examination of women employees.[37] Delegates representing the two thousand employees of the Częstochowa Mining Company in Raków presented eleven demands, which became uniform for all striking crews in the region. These included the payment of 50 percent of lost wages in the event of illness, the establishment of a school, recognition of the workers' "deputation" as a permanent body for the conduct of future negotiations with management, and the provision of five minutes to wash up at the end of each workday.[38] Workers from the Elżbietów sugar beet manufacturing plant in Siedlce province demanded subsidies for those not housed by the factory as well as the right to graze one cow each on company property.[39]

Strikers' demands also displayed important similarities beyond the usual

---

35. Kalabiński, *Carat i klasy posiadające*, pp. 18–20.
36. APŁ KGP 1515 (1), Director of the Krusche and Ender firm to the Chief of Łask County, January 21 (February 3), 1905. For a general study of the provision of medical care in the factories, see Zdzisław Leszczyński, *Zagrożenia zawodowe a medycyna fabryczna na ziemiach polskich na przełomie XIX i XX w.* (Warsaw, 1986).
37. APW WWO 23, Copy of demands dated February 9 (22), 1905.
38. APŁ KGP 1517, Chief of Częstochowa County to the Piotrków Governor, January 24 (February 6), 1905.
39. AGAD KGGW 2525, Siedlce Governor to the WGG, February 8 (21), 1905.

postulates of shorter working hours and increased wages. In almost every instance, workers demanded the establishment of a school for their children or the expansion and improvement of existing facilities. They also demanded the dismissal of particularly hated company officials and supervisors. At Elżbietów the workers' list of those to be fired included a deputy director, a technician, and a deputy foreman. At the Częstochowa Mining Company, several engineers were mentioned by name. The employees of Saturn went one step further, calling for the unconditional dismissal of administrative personnel whenever demanded. Workers also insisted that company officials and supervisors respect their personal dignity, which entailed abandoning the use of the informal second person "ty" in addressing the workers and eliminating searches of employees leaving the factory, plant, or mine. Workers also demanded the elimination or reform of the prevailing and abusive system of fines as well as direct control over sickness funds, to which they contributed but had no voice in distributing.

Whatever the workers' demands, the government had no uniform policy for dealing with the strikes. In Warsaw, authorities mainly concentrated on preserving or restoring order in the streets. Baron Nolken, the Warsaw superintendent of police, issued appeals to the workers to return to their "daily occupations" while attempting to convince them that their needs would be satisfied by the emperor's promise to establish a special labor commission in St. Petersburg. These appeals were also coupled with warnings that all means, including military force, would be used to maintain public order and security. Nolken also warned that the full force of the law would be applied against those workers who, by use of coercion and threats, prevented others from entering the factories.[40] At the same time, the government, through its factory inspectors, assisted the negotiations in Warsaw by encouraging the formation of factory delegations. The inspectors, however, did not play a particularly visible role once discussions between labor and management actually ensued.

In the Łódź region the authorities, led by the Piotrków governor, Artsimovich, were far more active. From the first days of the strike, Artsimovich moved quickly and resolutely to maintain order. All alcohol stores in Łódź were closed, and the electric power station was placed under military protection. Five new regiments of infantry and six squadrons of cavalry immediately strengthened the local garrison.[41] Łódź thus avoided the major rioting that rocked Warsaw and Radom. With the proclamation of a

40. APW ZOW 1078, Proclamations of the Warsaw Superintendent of Police, January 14 (27), January 20 (February 2), and February 1 (14), 1905.
41. AGAD KGGW 2494, Report of the SDPA to the WGG, February 8 (21), 1905.

state of emergency in Piotrków Province on January 30, Artsimovich appealed to Łódź workers to end the general strike. He also sought the assistance of the Catholic clergy in this matter.[42] The Piotrków governor, nevertheless, sympathized with some of the workers' economic demands. By holding continuous discussions with representatives of the leading Łódź industrialists, he undoubtedly prevented a massive lockout on February 6, thus opening the way to a negotiated settlement four days later.[43]

Elsewhere in the province, Artsimovich was less successful. Although only six persons died in minor clashes with police and troops in Łódź proper during the general strike, twelve were killed in Łódź County. Artsimovich roundly criticized county administrative and police officials for losing their composure and even called for legal and disciplinary measures against the captain of the Land Guard who ''needlessly fired into the crowd.'' A similar situation existed in the Dąbrowa Basin, where a lack of discipline and insubordination characterized the behavior of local officials. As a result, the general strike in the basin continued well into March, when it finally ended, thanks to the active mediation of provincial as opposed to county authorities.[44]

Workers' gains during the January–February general strike also varied widely. According to Stanisław Kalabiński and Feliks Tych, the strike forced employers to concede wage increases averaging 10–15 percent and a reduction in the workday by one hour.[45] In Warsaw, a nine-hour day was achieved in the larger factories.[46] In Łódź, eighteen leading firms employing three-quarters of the city's labor force agreed to a ten-hour workday and wage increases ranging from 5 percent for employees at the top of the wage scale to 15 percent for those at the bottom. Firms in Tomaszów and Zduńska Wola, whose employees modeled their demands on those of the Łódź workers, followed the lead of the Łódź industrialists. Individual firms in the Łódź region also agreed to certain specific demands of their employees. The board of directors of the Karol Scheibler Company conceded, for example, medical care for the families of workers, the provision of female doctors for women employees, an end to searches of female employees by male supervisors, an increase in the number of classes at the

---

42. Korzec, *Źródła do dziejów rewolucji* I (1): 420–421, 428.

43. Kazimierz Badziak, ''Burżuazja łódzka w rewolucji 1905–1907,'' in *Rewolucja 1905–1907 w Łodzi i okręgu,* ed. Barbara Wachowska (Łódź, 1975), pp. 57–58.

44. APŁ KGP 1515 (2), Piotrków Governor to the WGG, February 16 (March 1), 1905; Korzec, *Źródła do dziejów rewolucji* I (1): 520–528.

45. Kalabiński and Tych, *Czwarte powstanie czy pierwsza rewolucja,* pp. 118–119.

46. Żarnowska, *Robotnicy Warszawy,* p. 136.

factory school, a decrease in rents for factory dwellings, and an elected delegation of workers to meet with management once a week.[47]

In the Częstochowa region, a negotiating cartel of twenty-two employers agreed to recognize workers' delegations, eliminate searches of employees, respect the workers' personal dignity, establish schools, improve access to medical care, and allow five minutes for washing up at the end of the workday—this in addition to wage and hour concessions.[48] At the Elżbie-tów sugar refinery, a settlement was reached that reduced the workday by one hour, provided a 10 percent wage increase, and restricted searches. The refinery also promised to open a school, provide ten *puds* (three hundred sixty pounds) of firewood to each worker annually, respect the workers' dignity, and not fire any employees because of their involvement in the strike.[49]

In all of these negotiated settlements, the workers had demanded considerably more concessions, and their limited gains left many dissatisfied. Disenchantment increased as inflation quickly began to nullify the effect of the wage hikes. Outside the large factories in the major industrial regions, workers had yet to win any concessions (though Elżbietów was an exception). Not all workers, moreover, participated in the general strike. Those who did not included the approximately eight thousand workers employed by the textile industry in Żyrardów, not to mention white-collar employees and the tens of thousands who labored in small enterprises and artisan shops. As winter gave way to spring, massive labor unrest continued to plague the Kingdom's industrial economy.

## Expansion of the Labor Movement

The workers' efforts to improve their material condition during the January–February general strike won the support of elements of educated society cutting across ideological and party lines. Naturally the radical intelligentsia at the head of the parties in the socialist movement was ec-static. The socialists tended to view the strike as a confirmation of their various programs as well as an excellent starting point for future political

---

47. Korzec, *Źródła do dziejów rewolucji* 1 (1):455–457, 485–488; see also Kazimierz Bad-ziak and Paweł Samuś, "Ruch strajkowy robotników przemysłowych w Łodzi w 1905 r.," in Wachowska, *Rewolucja 1905–1907,* pp. 95–97.
48. APŁ KGP 1517, Chief of Częstochowa County to the Piotrków Governor, January 24 (February 6), 1905.
49. AGAD KGGW 2525, Siedlce Governor to the WGG, February 20 (March 5), 1905.

action. The socialist press praised the "heroism" of the working class
while it downplayed or justified the looting and violence that accompanied
the general strike. The socialist intellectuals were not alone in their ide-
alization of the "working masses," whose cause also moved the liberal
and self-styled "progressive" intelligentsia. In Warsaw, the Committee for
Aid to the Strikers was set up under the patronage of *Kuźnica* (The Forge),
a popular liberal journal.[50] Sympathy for the workers' social and economic
goals also came from the Endecja. In Łódź the nationalists appealed directly to industrialists and factory owners to reduce working hours, increase
wages, insure workers against old age and illness, and provide working-
class children with educational opportunities.[51]

The support and sympathy of educated public opinion during the general
strike played an important role in confirming the workers' conviction that
their demands were just. Moreover, the mediating efforts by administrative
and police officials in January and February seemed to condone the workers' resort to illegal methods of collective action. Both factors combined
to produce a morally and psychologically favorable climate for the continuation and extension of the strike movement in the early spring.

Immediate issues of wages and working conditions, however, remained
the motivating force of that movement, given the considerable dissatisfaction with the settlements that ended the general strike, leaving so many
questions important to the workers entirely unresolved. In Łódź the agreement carefully mediated by Governor Artsimovich nearly came unglued
over the issue of payment of wages during the time of the strike. In fact
Artsimovich was forced to publish a public denial that he had ordered
factory owners to make such payments.[52] Even so, many workers still remained unconvinced. From February 15 through 22, half of the city's industrial labor force struck over the issue.[53] This time, Artsimovich backed
the industrialists because he considered the workers' demand "illegal." He
even went so far as to request an administrative order from the Warsaw
governor-general forbidding industrialists from paying workers for time
lost during the general strike.[54] Faced with such unyielding opposition, the
workers withdrew their demand and returned to the mills on February 23.

Meanwhile, in Warsaw Province, a strike finally broke out in the textile

50. Halina Kiepurska, *Inteligencja zawodowa Warszawy, 1905–1907* (Warsaw, 1967), p. 74.
51. APŁ KGP 1515 (1), Appeal of the Regional Circle of the National Democratic Party,
January 1905.
52. AGAD KGGW 2494, as recorded in the government-sponsored *Lodzinskii Listok*, no.
18 (January 29/February 11, 1905).
53. Badziak and Samuś, "Ruch strajkowy," pp. 96–97.
54. Korzec, *Źródła do dziejów rewolucji* I (1): 481–482.

industry of Żyrardów on February 6. The timing and nature of that strike indicate that nationalist influences among the workers were not inconsiderable. Socialist appeals to Żyrardów workers to participate in the general strike had failed in January and may, in fact, have been frustrated by nationalist counteragitation. This did not mean, however, that the nationalist movement was unsympathetic to workers' grievances, and once the walkout occurred in Żyrardów, the Endejca moved quickly to form a committee under its auspices to provide material assistance for the striking workers.[55] As had been the case elsewhere, management at the huge Żyrardów Manufacturing Company invited its employees to elect two workers from each section to form a delegation for negotiations. In addition to wage concessions, workers demanded that courses in the factory schools of Żyrardów be conducted in the Polish language—another indication of nationalist influences. The Żyrardów management, of course, had no authority over the language issue. Regardless, the strike continued until March 21, when workers accepted the wage concessions offered five weeks earlier.[56]

Nationalist influences also may have been involved in strikes at various sugar beet refineries in Kutno County, where workers' demands likewise included instruction in Polish at factory schools. Such demands were absent, however, during the successful three-day strike of 270 workers at the Łyszkowicki sugar beet plant in Łowicz County.[57]

In Warsaw and its industrial suburbs, new economic strikes occurred at the end of February as a result of workers' dissatisfaction with earlier concessions. Most were short-lived; at Gerlach and Pulst, the largest firm involved, the strike lasted only one day. The strikes at gasworks in Wola and Czyste and at brickyards in Mokotów and Pruszków were somewhat more protracted, but by mid-March all strikes in the towns and settlements of Warsaw County had ended. The walkouts were accompanied by sporadic incidents of violence against strikebreakers. In Wola, for example, an employee who had continued working at the gasworks during the strike was brutally murdered shortly after its conclusion.[58]

The expansion of the labor movement in February and March also embraced railroad personnel and white-collar employees, mainly in the War-

55. AGAD KGGW 2500, Report of the SDPA to the WGG, February 14 (27), 1905.
56. AGAD KGGW 2500, Warsaw Governor to the WGG, February 4 (17), 1905, and 2501, Warsaw Governor to the WGG, March 9 (22), 1905.
57. AGAD KGGW 2500, Warsaw Governor to the WGG, February 19 (March 4), 1905, and Report of SDPA to the WGG, February 21 (March 6), 1905.
58. AGAD KGGW 2500, Warsaw Governor to the WGG, February 12 (25), February 16 (March 1), February 22 (March 7), and March 3 (16), 1905; and 2501, Report of the SDPA to the WGG, March 20 (April 2), 1905.

saw and Łódź regions. A brief statewide strike of railwaymen came to an abrupt end when all state-owned railroads, including the Vistula line in the Kingdom, were "militarized" (i.e., placed under martial law) on February 24. The strike continued, however, at the repair shops and passenger stations of the privately owned Warsaw–Vienna Railroad until a settlement was reached. The concessions won by the Warsaw–Vienna employees spurred white-collar personnel in the banking, pharmaceutical, and insurance industries to present economic demands. Though bank employees extracted concessions without resorting to a walkout, pharmaceutical workers struck for three days in successful support of their demands. But the collective action of employees at the state-owned Russia Insurance Company failed to win any concessions. Postal and telegraph workers, likewise employed by the state and intimidated by threats of mass firings, failed to present any demands at all in the spring.[59]

Radom Province was another important center of the strike movement of the early spring, particularly in Opatów, Opoczno, and Końskie counties, where workers in heavy industry had failed to participate in the January–February general strikes. During the last days of February and the first days of March, hundreds of workers from four metal factories in Opoczno and Końskie counties struck for higher wages. In the Ostrowiec region, a partial strike of two hundred miners quickly spread to the nearby Bodzechów steel mill, where it was accompanied by incidents of vandalism at the home of the millowner and at the state vodka store. More than one hundred workers also struck at the Stelman iron foundry near Radom. As elsewhere, managerial concessions to wage demands brought a quick end to these strikes. The Bodzechów strike, which continued to the end of March, proved an exception.[60]

From Radom Province the spring strikes spilled over into northern Kielce Province, which the governor a month earlier had characterized as an oasis of labor tranquillity. At the Suchedniów iron foundry north of Kielce, a settlement negotiated in early February fell apart when the foundry's six hundred workers raised new wage and hour demands in line with concessions won by workers in Radom Province. In this instance, however, management refused to budge, and when workers failed to return to their

59. Paweł Korzec, *Walki rewolucyjne w Łodzi i okręgu łódzkim w latach 1905–1907* (Warsaw, 1956), pp. 84, 120–121; Kiepurska, *Inteligencja zawodowa Warszawy*, pp. 79–88, 94, 100.
60. AGAD KGGW 2518, Reports of the SDPA to the WGG, February 15 (28), February 18 (March 3), February 19 (March 4), February 28 (March 13), and March 13 (26), 1905.

jobs after many threats, the foundry was closed.[61] Even more serious was the spread of the strike movement from the Dąbrowa Basin into the eastern part of the province, especially Olkusz County. Already on February 9 a crowd of two hundred broke into a wire factory at Sławków and dispersed its employees. Of the six arrested in the incident, five were workers from Będzin. Events in the Dąbrowa Basin also may have provided inspiration for the March strikes at the Moess and Klucze paper factories, both located in Olkusz County, where workers ousted company officials and demanded the dismissal of others. Meanwhile, an armed band of fifteen, reportedly formed of young workers from the Będzin region, attacked the administrative offices of at least three factories in Olkusz County.[62]

In Siedlce Province, individual strikes occurred in several sugar refineries, breweries, and glass factories in February. These strikes assumed greater importance by the end of the month, however, when they expanded to incorporate farm workers. The close relationship between rural proletarians and agrarian farmhands was best illustrated in Sokołów County, where a negotiated settlement to the prolonged strike at the Elżbietów sugar refinery was not reached until February 27. During their holdout, one hundred workers from Elżbietów appeared on February 21 on the nearby Ruchna estate belonging to Count Lubieński and persuaded his laborers to leave their jobs and join them as they proceeded to other industrial plants and estates in the county. Within a week, agrarian strikes hit twenty-seven estates in Sokołów County and would soon spill over into neighboring counties and provinces (a phenomenon I take up in the next chapter).[63]

### The Escalation of Labor Violence and the Łódź Uprising

The expansion of the labor movement by the numerous economic strikes of the early spring, like the January–February general strike, was accompanied by a resort to force and coercion on the part of striking workers. In the vast majority of cases, the threat of physical violence was aimed at fellow workers, particularly strikebreakers who refused to leave their jobs

---

61. AGAD KGGW 2508, Kielce Governor to the WGG, February 8 (21), 1905, and Report of the SDPA to the WGG, February 22 (March 7) and March 1 (14), 1905.
62. AGAD KGGW 2508, Kielce Governor to the WGG, January 28 (February 10), March 1 (14), March 9 (22), and March 15 (28), 1905.
63. AGAD KGGW 2525, Report of the SDPA to the WGG, February 12 (25), 1905; see also Urszula Głowacka-Maksymiuk, *Gubernia siedlecka w latach rewolucji, 1905–1907* (Warsaw, 1985), pp. 68–69.

and scabs hired by management during the course of a strike. Such incidents were sufficiently widespread for the Warsaw governor-general to issue a special decree on March 4, which warned of administrative sentences of up to three months in jail and maximum fines of five hundred rubles for those found guilty of using coercive means to disrupt trade and commerce or the operations of industrial firms.[64] Physical assaults on managerial personnel, however, were rare in the first three months of 1905.

During the next three months the situation changed radically. Particularly in the Łódź region and in the Dąbrowa Basin, tensions between workers and lower-level administrative personnel, engineers, and foremen—many of whom were German—were evident well before the revolution. During the January–February general strike, workers' demands in many cases included the dismissal of supervisors and company officials. Management generally refused to consider such demands, with the result that subsequent settlements failed to resolve a fundamental issue of industrial-labor relations, namely, relations on the shop floor.

Workers in the Dąbrowa Basin were the first to take matters into their own hands, exercising what became known as "factory constitutionalism" (a prototype of workers' self-management) by brute force. No sooner had the general strike in the region ended than police reported a series of "unceremonious ousters" of foremen, directors, engineers, and supervisors from the factories and mines. Complaining that the breakdown of labor discipline had slowed production and resulted in enormous losses, industrialists threatened to shut down unless the government took measures to protect managerial and supervisory personnel. The Piotrków governor tried to mollify entrepreneurs with promises of "strong action" against perpetrators of violence; for example, five workers from the Czeladź mine were sentenced to several months in jail for throwing out their supervisor. At the same time, the governor ordered factory inspectors in the region to take a more active role in mediating disputes.[65]

Somewhat later, during the second half of May, a rash of similar incidents occurred in the Łódź region in conjunction with strikes in smaller enterprises that then spread to some of the larger factories by the end of the month. On May 19, workers of the S. Czamański Company threw the head foreman into the street, a fate shared shortly thereafter by the supervisors of two other factories. At the main factory belonging to the giant

---

64. AGAD KGGW 2495, Binding Decree of the WGG, February 19 (March 4), 1905.
65. AGAD KGGW 2495, Piotrków Governor to the WGG, March 3 (16), 1905, and 2496, Piotrków Governor to the WGG, April 25 (May 8), 1905; APŁ KGP 1515 (2), Chief of the Piotrków Provincial Gendarmes to the Department of Police, March 12 (25), 1905.

Karol Scheibler Company, the director and two foremen were expelled on May 29. There were also several cases of factory owners themselves being forcibly escorted to the gates of their plants.[66] As in the Dąbrowa Basin, some Łódź industrialists complained to the Piotrków governor about the impotence of the local police as they appealed for greater protection of their persons and property. That spring, many of Łódź's wealthier inhabitants together with subjects of foreign states left the city from fear of "terrorist acts."[67]

The first in a series of occupation strikes and employer lockouts coincided with the increasingly tense situation in Łódź. Five hundred workers employed by the Łódź Thread Manufacturing Company in the industrial suburb of Widzew, who had failed to win any concessions during the general strike, struck a second time on April 7 after the breakdown of nearly a month of negotiations with management. The latter responded by announcing the closing of the factory. More than half the workers, however, remained at the factory to stage a sit-in, despite the arrival of a team of factory inspectors sent by the Piotrków governor to mediate the conflict. The inspectors were taken hostage overnight. Only the arrival of troops convinced the workers to release the inspectors and leave the factory. Yet the conflict with management remained unresolved, and on April 26 the factory was closed for an unspecified period—this despite the angry admonishments of Governor Artsimovich, who accused the company's administration of complete intransigence and "morally reprehensible" behavior. Indeed, company officials not only refused to recognize delegates elected by the workers for the conduct of negotiations but also declined a meeting with representatives of the Factory Inspectorate.[68] Consequently, the factory did not reopen until mid-July.

The brief occupation strike at the Łódź Thread Manufacturing Company undoubtedly influenced workers at the much larger Heinzel and Kunitzer firm, also located in Widzew. On April 11, nearly two thousand workers from the company's weaving mill struck on behalf of their unrealized demands of January and February. Two hundred of them then occupied the factory. Although the weavers were poorly prepared for such action and lacked provisions, they held out for two days, only giving in when troops surrounded the mill as the government moved to prevent such collective

66. Badziak and Samuś, "Ruch strajkowy," p. 102.
67. Kalabiński, *Carat i klasy posiadające*, p. 170; Korzec, *Źródła do dziejów rewolucji* 1 (2): 28–34.
68. APŁ KGP 1515 (2), Piotrków Governor to the Management of the Łódź Thread Manufacturing Company, April 9 (22), 1905; Kalabiński, *Carat i klasy posiadające*, pp. 116–120; Badziak and Samuś, "Ruch strajkowy," pp. 97–99.

action from spreading even further. State intervention, regardless of its intention, again worked to the benefit of management, which closed the mill on April 19. In the case of Heinzel and Kunitzer, the subsequent lockout lasted until the middle of May.[69]

Although the use of troops to maintain order in the Łódź region was accomplished without resorting to violence, workers were clearly angered by the presence of military units at or near the factories. Already, at the end of March, more than three thousand weavers from the I. K. Poznański Company struck to demand the removal of troops from factory grounds.[70] The interventions in Widzew further inflamed workers' passions against the government, despite Artsimovich's behind-the-scenes efforts on their behalf. The hostility of the workers, in turn, caused the authorities concern over the morale of the soldiers posted at the factories. At the end of April, acting on Artsimovich's advice, the government began a regular rotation of these units, but this did nothing to alleviate working-class resentment toward the authorities.[71]

Such resentment soon spilled over into violent confrontations. The international workers' holiday of May 1, preceded by weeks of intensive agitation on the part of the socialist parties, provided the occasion for the clashes. Duly forewarned, the authorities took precautionary measures. The Piotrków governor ordered the closing of all state vodka outlets and private drinking establishments well in advance of the holiday. Moreover, forty "agitators" were arrested in Łódź, Pabianice, and Częstochowa in a co-ordinated police action on April 28.[72] On the same day, the acting Warsaw superintendent of police informed his city's inhabitants in the legal dailies of his intention to resort to military force if necessary to prevent May Day disturbances.[73]

Regardless, the authorities' measures failed to head off the anticipated disorders. In Częstochowa's industrial suburb of Raków, the preventive arrest of sixteen socialist agitators actually proved counterproductive when, on April 29, a crowd of six thousand workers from three factories demonstrated to demand the release of these "political prisoners." In the sub-

69. Badziak and Samuś, "Ruch strajkowy," p. 99; Kalabiński, *Carat i klasy posiadające*, pp. 131–134.
70. Korzec, *Źródła do dziejów rewolucji* 1 (2): 8–10.
71. Ibid., pp. 38–42.
72. APŁ KGP 1515 (2), Piotrków Governor to the County Chiefs and the Łódź Superintendent of Police, April 7 (20), 1905, and Chief of the Piotrków Provincial Gendarmes to the Department of Police, April 22 (May 4), 1905.
73. Kalabiński, *Carat i klasy posiadające*, pp. 155–158.

sequent melee with dragoons sent to the scene, two demonstrators were killed.[74] In Łódź, although less than half of the factory labor force actually observed May Day by quitting work, police and military units broke up some twenty-seven demonstrations during the course of the day. In five reported instances there was an exchange of fire that led to the loss of six lives. Two days later, thirteen more were wounded, mainly from revolver shots, during rioting that accompanied the funeral of one of the victims.[75] In Kalisz, the May Day holiday was celebrated by a Mass at St. Wojciech's parish church, followed by a procession with patriotic and religious songs. Yet despite the admonitions of the parish priest, clashes between the police and crowds of workers were not avoided and resulted in a woman's death. Her funeral occurred without incident, perhaps because the police maintained a low profile and entrusted the preservation of order to the city fire department.[76]

The worst incident of violence, however, took place in Warsaw. Here the May Day strike was indeed general, forcing all plants, factories, shops, and commercial institutions in the city to suspend operations. By ten in the morning, groups of workers had brought a halt to all street traffic. Both the PPS and the Bund, having satisfied themselves with such a display, heeded well-publicized police warnings and refrained from attempts to mount street demonstrations. The SDKPiL, however, proved more impulsive when its local leadership decided to test the authorities' resolve. Although the demonstration and march of two thousand inspired by the Social Democrats was far from imposing, once it reached Jerusalem Boulevard, it met with disaster. In the subsequent "massacre," or exchange of fire with police and troops, twenty-six were killed and thirty-four hospitalized with serious wounds.[77] Forty-five arrests were also made. Five persons were killed later in the day, including two women who happened to be on Marszałkowska Street when a bomb exploded near a Cossack patrol. Subse-

74. AGAD KGGW 2495, Chief of Częstochowa County to the Piotrków Governor, April 16 (29), 1905, and 2496, Report of the SDPA to the WGG, April 25 (May 8), 1905.
75. APŁ KGP 1515 (3), Piotrków Governor to the WGG, May 11 (24), 1905; AGAD KGGW 2496, Report of the SDPA to the WGG, April 25 (May 8), 1905; Korzec, Źródła do dziejów rewolucji I (2): 61–74.
76. AGAD KGGW 2506, Kalisz Governor to the WGG, April 19 (May 2) and April 21 (May 4), 1905.
77. AGAD KGGW 2491, Acting Warsaw Superintendent of Police to the WGG, April 19 (May 2), 1905. The SDKPiL, anxious to gain publicity for its cause, immediately inflated the size of the demonstration (to 20,000) as well as the number of "massacre" victims (to 50 dead and 100 wounded); see the account published in the party's underground newspaper, Z Pola Walki, no. 8 (May 7, 1905).

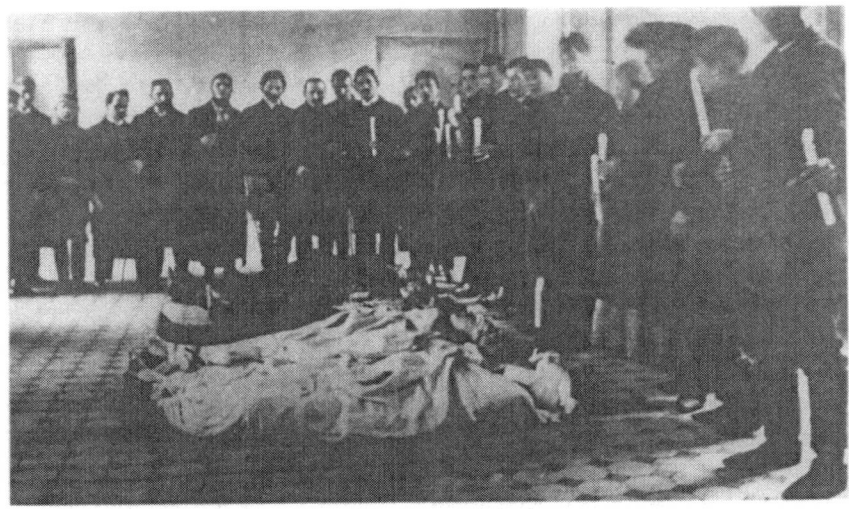

Mourning the victims of the May Day Massacre in Warsaw, 1905. (Personal collection)

quently, police were able to identify twenty-five of the thirty-one victims; of these, nearly half were women, half were teenagers, and almost all were Roman Catholics.[78]

Elsewhere in Warsaw Province only 31 percent of the labor force struck on May 1.[79] Conspicuously uninvolved, as they had been during the January–February general strike, were the eight thousand workers of Żyrardów. But workers from the Sochewka paper mill and the Sanniki sugar beet refinery in Gostynin County did quit work on May Day, and in Grójec County three hundred shoemakers from the settlement of Mogielnica observed the holiday by attending a mass meeting wearing red neckties. In neither case was the public order disturbed. By contrast, a crowd of one thousand Jewish demonstrators in Kaluszyn, Nowominsk County, dispersed only when dragoons fired shots into the air.[80]

Indeed, outside of Warsaw, Łódź, and Częstochowa, May Day strikes

78. APW ZOW 1079, Undated materials compiled by the office of the Warsaw Superintendent of Police.
79. Stanisław Kalabiński, "Ruch strajkowy robotników przemysłowych Warszawy i gubernii warszawskiej w okresie najwyższego jego natężenia: Próba analizy statystycznej lat 1905–1906 (Część I: Rok 1905)," *Polska Klasa Robotnicza: Studia Historyczne* 4 (1973): 85.
80. AGAD KGGW 2502, Report of the SDPA to the WGG, April 20 (May 3), 1905, and Warsaw Governor to the WGG, April 21 and 22 (May 4 and 5), 1905.

and demonstrations were isolated and sporadic. The holiday passed without major incident in Łomża, Płock, Lublin, Kielce, Siedlce, and Suwałki provinces, despite brief strikes by mainly Jewish artisans and craftsmen. The Dąbrowa Basin also remained relatively quiet in early May, the reason for which police attributed to the coincidental break in instruction at the Dąbrowa School of Mines and the resulting temporary absence of nonresident students.[81] Radom Province also escaped major disorders, despite a general strike in the provincial capital and sizable demonstrations in the towns of Wierzbnik and Ostrowiec. In the latter instance, the Opatów County chief was called to account by the Radom governor for "actually permitting" a demonstration involving a crowd of eight thousand to occur.[82] The Wierzbnik demonstration, too, had subsequent repercussions when, several days after the event, a crowd of three thousand workers forced the chief of the provincial gendarmes and a deputy prosecutor to leave the gmina administration building, where they were compiling evidence against the May Day "organizers."[83]

As spring gave way to summer, working-class violence took an even more elemental turn. Vigilante actions against gangsters, thieves, and prostitution rings, beginning in Warsaw and subsequently spreading to other urban and industrial centers, threatened to assume the form of a mass movement at the end of May. Already in early January, an alarming increase in cases of armed robbery, criminal assault, and public displays of prostitution was reported in the Warsaw industrial suburbs of Koło, Wola, and Czyste.[84] The breakdown of public order during the massive strikes and demonstrations of the first five months of 1905 gave an even freer rein to criminal elements who lived side-by-side with and preyed on the working-class population. The forces of the urban police, when not bribed by criminal organizations, were nevertheless too few in number and too ill-equipped to offer effective protection to persons and property in working-class neighborhoods—this especially at a time of acute social unrest, when their primary attention was naturally focused elsewhere.

The breakdown of law and order, however, also enabled small groups

81. APŁ KGP 1515 (2), Chief of the Piotrków Provincial Gendarmes to the Department of Police, April 22 (May 5), 1905.
82. AGAD KGGW 2519, Director of the Chancellory of the WGG to the Radom Governor, May 26 (June 8), 1905, and Chief of Opatów County to the Radom Governor, June 25 (July 8), 1905.
83. AGAD KGGW 2519, Report of the SDPA to the WGG, May 11 (24), 1905.
84. AGAD KGGW 314, Internal memorandum of the Chancellory of the WGG, December 25 (January 7), 1905; APW ZOW 1079, Internal memorandum of the Office of the Warsaw Superintendent of Police, July 25 (August 7), 1905.

and sometimes crowds of workers to take the law into their own hands. From the middle of May to the end of July, biweekly informational compilations on "extraordinary incidents and events" drawn up by the Warsaw governor's office invariably included the discovery of several new corpses of "professional thieves" either riddled with bullets or beaten to death.[85] Three days of rioting directed against brothels at the end of May proved even more indicative of the fury of working-class vigilantism in Warsaw. Beginning in the Jewish quarter on May 24 and then spreading to Christian neighborhoods the next day, crowds of workers attacked pimps, prostitutes, and houses of ill repute throughout the city. More than a hundred apartments were ransacked, with damages estimated at two hundred thousand rubles. Five persons were killed on the spot, ten others suffered fatal injuries, and forty-two were hospitalized as a result of the rampage, which was brought to a halt only when troops were brought in to restore order and, ironically, to protect the criminals.[86]

The Warsaw vigilantes, despite denunciations of their activities by the SDKPiL and PPS, soon found imitators in other industrial working-class centers. The SDKPiL condemned the riots as "the blind acts of an unconscious crowd"; the PPS tried to direct the movement toward a different symbol of the workers' social denigration—alcoholism and the state monopoly stores.[87] The Bund, however, supported the vigilante actions as popular attempts to build a new proletarian morality and actively worked to spread the attacks on criminal and prostitution rings to Łódź and the Dąbrowa Basin.[88] Elsewhere, the movement, which frequently adopted the forms and features of pogroms, remained of purely local inspiration. In Sieradz (Kalisz Province), after the theft of a necklace from a religious icon in mid-June, four "well-known" thieves were beaten by a crowd of five hundred and hospitalized. Shortly thereafter, workers of both sexes in Ostrowiec carried out an action that resulted in the beatings of several local prostitutes.[89]

The vigilante movement coincided with a new, even sharper upsurge in

85. AGAD KGGW 342.
86. Kiepurska, *Warszawa w rewolucji*, pp. 173–175; Richard D. Lewis, "The Labor Movement in Russian Poland in the Revolution of 1905–1907" (Ph.D. diss., University of California, Berkeley, 1971), pp. 146–147.
87. AGAD AB, druk 249, Leaflet of the Warsaw Committee of the SDKPiL, May 1905; Korzec, *Walki rewolucyjne*, pp. 116–117; Lewis, "Labor Movement," pp. 146–147.
88. AGAD KGGW 2496, Report of the SDPA to the WGG, May 21 (June 3), 1905.
89. AGAD KGGW 2507, Report of the SDPA to the WGG, June 9 (22), 1905, and 2519, Radom Governor to the WGG, June 21 (July 4), 1905.

social tensions. In Warsaw, the factory owner Gustaw Nejmanowicz was murdered on Leszno Street on May 25.[90] From the Częstochowa suburbs of Raków and Bleszno came reports of factory administrators "completely terrorized" by the workers.[91] Attacks on police and troops also became commonplace, and this was only partially attributable to organized terrorist activities. For example, the ambush of two Cossacks in Pabianice by four men armed with revolvers in early June was undoubtedly the work of the PPS fighting organization. But the murder of the gendarme Primachenko on June 12 in the village of Łagiewniki in Łódź County resulted from an incident with an angry crowd of working-class demonstrators.[92]

The escalation of violence against the background of heightened social tensions and labor unrest was bound to lead to the tragedy for which Łódź provided the unfortunate stage. As previously noted, the January–February general strike in Łódź was much more peaceful than in Warsaw, thanks to the timely intervention of Piotrkow governor Artsimovich. May Day, too, had been relatively calm. Nevertheless, the several deaths that had resulted from the minor clashes of police and troops with crowds on May 1 and again on May 3 left the city in an ugly mood. Shortly thereafter, police reported the defiant singing of the prohibited Polish national hymn "Boże coś Polskę" every day in Łódź churches.[93]

Such incidents of defiance toward the authorities were accompanied by a new rash of economic strikes. Beginning in small and medium-sized factories in the middle of May, and subsequently spreading to the great firms of Scheibler, Grohman, Silberstein, and Steinert by the end of the month, the strike wave in Łódź assumed what the authorities termed "epidemic proportions."[94] As before, coercion accompanied the walkouts. Fighting among workers preceded the strike at the Scheibler factory on May 26; the intervention of Cossacks in turn provoked rioting that left one worker dead and two injured.[95] Elsewhere, workers destroyed machines and blocked entrance gates to stop operations at their plants. By such

90. AGAD KGGW 350, Report of the Warsaw Superintendent of Police, second half of May 1905.
91. AGAD KGGW 2496, Report of the SDPA to the WGG, May 21 (June 3), 1905.
92. APŁ KGP 518, Piotrków Governor to the WGG, May 28 (June 10), 1905, and Director of the Chancellory of the WGG to the Piotrków Governor, June 9 (22), 1905.
93. APŁ KGP 1515 (3), Chief of the Piotrków Provincial Gendarmes to the Department of Police, May 2 (15), 1905.
94. AGAD KGGW 2496, Report of the SDPA to the WGG, May 21 (June 3), 1905; Korzec, *Walki rewolucyjne*, pp. 127–129.
95. AGAD KGGW 2496, Report of the SDPA to the WGG, May 16 (29), 1905.

means, the number of workers on strike in Łódź reached eighteen thousand
by the beginning of June and thereafter fluctuated between eight thousand
and twelve thousand until June 20.[96]

The Łódź strike epidemic of the late spring and early summer was also
characterized by several factory occupations. As had occurred in April,
military units were then sent to remove the workers from the plants or
posted on factory grounds to maintain order. This ignited what became
known as the "struggle for the factories," in which workers sought to
block the entrance of troops into the plants or to force their ouster. Occasionally, the results of this "struggle" bordered on comedy, as at Heinzel
and Kunitzer, where workers attacked a dozen Cossacks while they were
bathing and forced them to flee the factory completely naked.[97] The attacks
on troops and police posted at the factories, coinciding as they did with a
new wave of expulsions of foremen and managerial personnel, caused the
Piotrków governor to make an urgent appeal to Warsaw for additional
regiments of dragoons and infantry. Once those arrived, lockouts took place
at Heinzel and Kunitzer on June 2 and at Scheibler on June 11.[98]

Meanwhile, the number of working-class victims of the "struggle for
the factories" mounted steadily. On May 28, ten thousand Christian workers participated in the funeral of one of those killed at Scheibler; a second
demonstration of three thousand Jewish workers occurred the next day.
Both were peaceful, which influenced the local authorities to permit a third
demonstration involving four thousand Jewish workers on June 14. In hindsight, they were to regret their decision; for on June 18, police and Cossacks had to be called in to break up an "illegal" political demonstration
that resulted in the deaths of five Christian and two Jewish workers. The
SDKPiL and Bund responded by organizing a funeral demonstration for
June 20, an action subsequently joined by the PPS. Thirty thousand turned
up for the protest, accompanied by fourteen red flags, the shouting of
revolutionary slogans, and speeches by party agitators.

The situation soon became unmanageable, thanks in part to bungling by
the authorities. The sheer size of the June 20 demonstration sowed confusion among police and army units, who failed to cooperate when the
crowd broke through the cordons that had been erected. Worse still, it
became known that police had absconded with the bodies of the two Jewish
workers killed on June 18 and secretly buried them. This action, designed
to forestall yet another funeral demonstration, backfired completely. On

96. Korzec, *Źródła do dziejów rewolucji* I (2): 105, 114–115, 144–147, 151–152.
97. AGAD KGGW 2496, Piotrków Governor to the WGG, June 11 (24), 1905.
98. Ibid., May 19 (June 1), 1905; Korzec, *Walki rewolucyjne*, p. 133.

June 21, the authorities met an even larger demonstration of outraged workers which was dispersed only when a company of Cossacks fired directly into the crowd.[99]

The rioting that day resulted in more than thirty casualties. The next morning, the first makeshift barricades went up in the Jewish quarter, unprompted by the socialist parties, who were preoccupied in haggling over whether to call a general protest strike for June 23. Despite the opposition of the PPS, this general strike did take place as factories shut down throughout the city; but by then, a spontaneous revolt was already in full swing. The appearance of barricades also surprised the authorities. Again, police and army units failed to cooperate. Troops dispatched to aid police remained passive in the absence of precise instructions from the latter. Nor were the police prepared by their training to put down a modern urban insurrection, and the situation in Łódź was the first of its kind in the history of the Russian Empire. Consequently, workers armed mainly with nothing more than bricks and rocks successfully defended their positions in light street fighting on the twenty-second. Encouraged by these results, workers from other parts of the city constructed barricaded positions of their own, more than one hundred in all by the morning of the twenty-third.[100] Meanwhile, gas lanterns were destroyed and state vodka stores ransacked in the wholesale rioting that accompanied the breakdown of order in the city.

On the twenty-third, however, the authorities acted with far more resolve. Governor Artsimovich moved quickly to strengthen the forces of the Łódź garrison to twenty thousand men, to allow military commanders to act on their own initiative, and to obtain a decree from the tsar proclaiming a state of martial law in Łódź and Łódź County.[101] The first two measures proved immediately decisive. Six regiments of infantry and several regiments each of cavalry, dragoons, and Cossacks were now thrown into the fray, and at the cost of some four hundred casualties (only three of whom were soldiers or police), order was restored by the morning of June 24. The next day, the Warsaw governor-general entrusted the implementation and execution of the emergency provisions of martial law to Lt. Gen. Nicholas Shuttleworth of the First Cavalry Corps.[102]

99. AGAD KGGW 2496, Chief of the Piotrków Provincial Gendarmes to the SDPA, June 19 (July 2), 1905; Korzec, *Źródła do dziejów rewolucji* 1 (2): 230–233, and *Walki rewolucyjne*, pp. 134–138.
100. Korzec, *Źródła do dziejów rewolucji* 1 (2):236–237, 252–263; *Z Pola Walki*, no. 10 (June 30, 1905); Korzec, *Walki rewolucyjne*, pp. 140–144; Władysław Lech Karwacki, *Łódź w latach rewolucji, 1905–1907* (Łódź, 1975), pp. 62–64.
101. Korzec, *Źródła do dziejów rewolucji* 1 (2): 239.
102. Ibid., pp. 242–246; Karwacki, *Łódź w latach rewolucji*, pp. 67–69.

During the course of the fighting in Łódź, some twenty thousand people fled the city, many of them Jews who feared a pogrom in the aftermath of the disturbances. Indeed the heaviest fighting had occurred in the Jewish quarter; of 151 killed on the street barricades and subsequently identified by police, more than half were Jews.[103]

The Łódź Uprising was the bloodiest single episode of the 1905 Revolution in Russian Poland. Preceded by sharp tensions in the factories and mounting violence in the streets, the social unrest had been exacerbated by the poorly conceived and inconsequential measures of the authorities, who were then compelled to take severe, repressive action. The ill-fated revolt also marked a transition in the newly emergent labor movement. Henceforth the influence of the socialist parties began to penetrate the movement sufficiently to give it a more organized character. Coercion and violence were not thereby eliminated as a result; they simply assumed less anarchic forms. In the meantime, Łódź, which had provided the setting for the most elemental passions of disorderly crowds of workers, would remain under martial law until the beginning of December.

### The Politicization of the Labor Movement

At the beginning of 1905, the underground political parties of the socialist movement exercised only a slight influence on the industrial workers, whom they considered their principal constituency. Although some headway had been made in 1904 through the antiwar and antimobilization movements, the PPS, SDKPiL, PPS-Proletariat, and Jewish Bund could claim at most an aggregate total of a few thousand active working-class members in the industrial centers of Russian Poland. Most of these, moreover, were concentrated in Warsaw, and only the PPS could boast of actually functioning organizations outside the capital. Although socialist influences no doubt extended somewhat beyond the minuscule percentage of dues-paying, organized members, that range remained strictly limited nonetheless.

In addition, two of these parties, the SDKPiL and Bund, recruited the majority of their supporters from artisanal rather than factory labor, although many of the former were affected, if not incorporated, by the factory system. The support of the PPS-Proletariat was even more confined, a problem it never surmounted and which would doom that party to ex-

---

103. AGAD KGGW 2496, Chief of the Piotrków Provincial Gendarmes to the SDPA, June 17 (30) and June 19 (July 2), 1905; Korzec, *Źródła do dziejów rewolucji* 1 (2): 263–286.

tinction by the end of the year. For its part, the PPS had only just begun to organize cells inside the factories. The socialist parties at the outbreak of the revolution essentially remained conspiratorial organizations dominated by radical intellectuals, a far cry from the mass working-class parties of western Europe which they took as their model.

Such organizations could hardly have had much of an impact on events during the first few months of 1905. Moreover, as a result of the intense competition between them, they either failed or refused to cooperate and coordinate their actions except in a few localized instances. The January–February general strike thus occurred with their participation rather than under their leadership. Indeed, the socialist parties could only react to the largely spontaneous outburst of working-class discontent. The socialist slogan of the eight-hour working day, to be sure, did appear in strike demands, but it was also the first to be abandoned once workers entered direct negotiations with management. And, although the socialist parties issued inflammatory appeals in an effort to spread the strike and encouraged the use of coercion to enforce working-class "solidarity," they tried just as frequently to restrain the crowd behavior of workers over which they ultimately had little control; hence their warnings of "tsarist provocations," their admonitions against looting, and their insistence on maintaining "proletarian discipline."

The January–February general strike, nevertheless, left behind a "legal" organizational tool, in the form of factory delegations, which proved crucial to the subsequent penetration of the labor movement by socialist influences. Created primarily at the behest of management or local government officials for the conduct of negotiations during the general strike, many workers' delegations remained intact once a settlement had been reached, particularly in the larger industrial firms. Frequently, their continued existence formed part of such settlements. Government guarantees of immunity from arrest and prosecution to delegation members, at least during the course of negotiations, imbued the delegations with a quasi-legal status, as did the absence of official measures to dissolve them afterward. Although the government still refused to recognize the right of workers to associate in trade unions, the factory delegations were permitted to become a kind of limited substitute. Where they existed, the delegations were thus able to represent workers' interests in disputes with management throughout most of 1905, that is, until their replacement by legal trade unions conceded in the October Manifesto.

The socialist parties, especially the PPS and SDKPiL, were quick to take advantage of the window of opportunity for open activity provided by the factory delegations. Initially, the parties targeted delegation members, who enjoyed obvious authority among fellow workers, for recruitment into the ranks. When successfully recruited, delegates received instruction in the methods of agitation in order to recruit others. As socialist influences in the factories thereby expanded, the parties sought to have their own members elected to the delegations. The socialist parties also tended to pick up support during strikes, when the factory delegations transformed themselves into ad hoc strike committees. According to Kalabiński, 78 percent of the economic strikes of 1905 in the Warsaw industrial region ended in concessions to the workers' demands.[104] The relative success of the strikes could not but work in favor of the socialist parties, whose members on the factory delegations were often the loudest proponents of a strike action. As a result, the authority originally enjoyed by the factory delegations among workers was gradually and partially transferred to the PPS and SDKPiL.

Naturally, competition between these two organizations for influence and control over the workers' delegations became fierce. The PPS or SDKPiL, once having gained a majority within a particular factory delegation, would then strive to monopolize its membership. Consequently, struggles over political turf inside the factories were frequently resolved by the threat or use of physical violence, especially once the "working-class" parties recruited more authentic factory workers, whose traditional method of persuasion was the closed fist. Supporters of the minority party, especially if they engaged in irreconcilable opposition, often found themselves removed from the factory or banned from entering it by fellow workers.

The extent of this expansion of socialist influences among industrial workers through the infiltration of factory delegations became clear only in the late spring and summer. All the socialist parties invested considerable effort in agitation for a general political strike on May 1. In Warsaw, their traditional base, that goal was largely achieved, although it was accompanied by the tragedy of the already-mentioned "massacre." Outside of the capital, however, May Day demonstrated the limited range and effect of socialist agitational and organizational activity. In industrial centers such as Łódź and Radom, the May Day action did not nearly reach the proportions of a general strike and barely elicited a response at all from workers in the Dąbrowa Basin and Żyrardów.

The labor movement, therefore, continued to maintain its predominantly "wildcat" and apolitical character well into the early summer, through the Łódź Uprising. Meanwhile, the socialist parties concentrated on building

---

104. Kalabiński, "Ruch strajkowy, 1905," p. 43.

up their organizations outside of Warsaw, with Łódź and the Dąbrowa Basin assuming special priority. The fighting in Łódź, though unanticipated, was nevertheless preceded by large funeral demonstrations and mass meetings in the factories organized by the socialists. Once the barricades went up, the socialist parties found it impossible to remain on the sidelines. The PPS, which tried to prevent the popular revolt from occurring in the first place, nonetheless threw its local fighting organization into the fray once the fighting began. Consequently, PPS fighters accounted for more than one-third of those killed in the Łódź Uprising.[105]

The bloody events in Łódź also provided the socialist parties an opportunity to test their strength in other industrial regions by exploiting working-class solidarity with the Łódź insurgents. Although the parties failed to synchronize their calls for a general political strike in the Warsaw region, some 64 percent of the industrial labor force walked off the job between June 24 and June 26 to protest the authorities' strong repressive actions in Łódź. In Warsaw itself, the sympathy strike was accompanied by demonstrations, minor skirmishes with police and troops, the construction of makeshift barricades, and the arrest of 689 persons. Warsaw's "June Days," however, never threatened to turn into the violent outburst of crowd passions that had occurred in Łódź. On June 27, workers returned to their factories and calm returned to the streets.[106]

The relative success of the general protest strike in Warsaw encouraged the socialist parties, which now began to coordinate their efforts, to call for similar strikes in industrial centers throughout the Kingdom. Set for June 28, the response from workers was far from universal. Yet the results were more impressive than they had been eight weeks earlier during the May Day action. In Częstochowa, where the situation most resembled that of Łódź, the strike was general. All factories and plants in nearby Zawiercie also closed as a result of the strike. The response from workers in the Dąbrowa Basin, however, had to be even more encouraging to the socialist parties. As late as May 1, the socialists had shown little organizational clout in the basin; now, under the impetus of the Łódź events, the parties nearly succeeded in bringing about a general strike. One-day protest strikes were also reported in Lublin and several towns and industrial settlements of Siedlce Province.[107]

105. Jerzy Pająk, *Organizacje bojowe partii politycznych w Królestwie Polskim, 1904–1911* (Warsaw, 1985), p. 63.
106. Kalabiński, "Ruch strajkowy, 1905," p. 85; Kiepurska, *Warszawa w rewolucji,* pp. 175–177.
107. AGAD KGGW 2496, Chief of the Piotrków Provincial Gendarmes to the SDPA, June 17 (30) and June 18 (July 1), 1905; APŁ KGP 1514, Chief of Będzin County to the Piotrków

This is not to say that the socialists had captured the labor movement, but the parties were quickly learning how to capitalize on popular initiatives and actions for their own political purposes. In Częstochowa, for example, unplanned factory takeovers and a funeral demonstration involving ten thousand participants certainly abetted the calling of the political protest strike in solidarity with the Łódź workers and helped ensure its success.[108]

In the Dąbrowa Basin, the solidarity strike with Łódź was followed by the arbitrary introduction by the workers themselves of the eight-hour working day in several mines throughout the region. Tensions in the basin were further exacerbated when, at the end of July, the administration of the giant Huta Bankowa steel mill responded to the workers' expulsion of the deputy director with a lockout. Solidarity strikes in support of the workers of Huta Bankowa occurred at Fitzner and Gamper as well as the Jan, Reden, Flora, and Mortimer mines. Only at this point did the SDKPiL and PPS try, unsuccessfully, to transform the uncoordinated actions in individual factories and mines into an organized general strike for the eight-hour working day. The failure of this general strike, however, encouraged employers in the region to take stern countermeasures for restoring labor discipline. The lockout at Huta Bankowa ended on August 16 with the complete victory of management and the firing of more than four hundred workers. By the end of the month, as many as two thousand miners who had insisted on working eight-hour shifts were also fired and then blacklisted from employment in the region. Subsequent efforts by the socialist parties to revive the eight-hour movement, understandably, met with little response.[109]

Ironically, though the socialist parties failed to mobilize labor in support of general economic postulates like the eight-hour working day, they were achieving increasing success in inspiring workers to political protest. The principal occasion after the Łódź solidarity strikes was the announcement on August 19 of election procedures for a consultative assembly, or state

---

Governor, June 21 (July 4), 1905; Korzec, *Źródła do dziejów rewolucji* I (2): 307–308, 310–314, 319–322; Kalabiński, *Carat i klasy posiadające*, pp. 216–217; Głowacka-Maksymiuk, *Gubernia siedlecka*, p. 97; Wójcik, *Ruch robotniczy*, p. 63.

108. AGAD KGGW 2496, Chief of the Piotrków Provincial Gendarmes to the SDPA, June 18 (July 1), 1905; Korzec, *Źródła do dziejów rewolucji* I (2): 307–308.

109. AGAD KGGW 2497, Piotrków Governor to the WGG, July 7 (20) and July 14 (27), 1905, and Report of the SDPA to the WGG, July 19 (August 1), 1905; see also Adam Kałuża, "Z dziejów walk masowych proletariatu Zagłębia Dąbrowskiego w 1905 r. o 8-godzinny dzień pracy i inne postulaty," *Polska Klasa Robotnicza: Studia Historyczne* 3 (1972): 229–258.

duma, conceded by the tsar in February. The project had taken shape under the direction of A. G. Bulygin, the minister of Internal Affairs, and although it assured the peasantry considerable representation in a complex system of indirect voting in separate estates, it sharply restricted suffrage in urban areas by property and other qualifications, with the result that industrial workers were virtually disenfranchised. Throughout the empire, radical and revolutionary organizations called for an "active boycott" of the forthcoming "comedy of elections," and the socialist parties in Russian Poland were no exception. In the event, a one-day general strike in protest of the Bulygin Duma project was called for August 21.

In the Warsaw region, over twenty-one thousand workers responded to the socialist appeals, which provided the Warsaw governor-general sufficient justification to request and receive the tsar's approval for the imposition of martial law in the city and county. In Łódź, seventeen thousand workers struck, and although the political protest action was far from general, it was nevertheless impressive for a city under martial law and for a labor movement still trying to pick up the pieces after the abortive uprising. In Pabianice, ten thousand quit work on August 21, although the police claimed that the strikers were "unaware of the reasons for the strike" and were being "misled by agitators."[110] Strikes were also reported in four large and fourteen smaller factories in the Częstochowa region. Altogether, nearly half of all industrial workers throughout the empire who participated in the protest strike against the Bulygin Duma were employed in the Kingdom of Poland.[111]

The greatest display of socialist influences among industrial workers occurred during the statewide general strike of October-November, which culminated in the major political concessions contained in the October Manifesto. Although the general strike of October, like that of January, began in the Kingdom with little forewarning and no organized preparation, the socialist parties were in a far better position this time to manipulate working-class voluntarism. In stark contrast to events in January, the October general strike did not spread from factory to factory by undisciplined crowds of roaming workers. Instead, once work stopped in the depots and repair shops of the Kingdom as part of the Russian railroad strike, the walkout spread mainly by means of the socialist press and organized po-

110. Korzec, *Źródła do dziejów rewolucji* 1 (2): 414–416.
111. AGAD KGGW 2498, Piotrków Governor to the WGG, August 13 (26) and August 17 (30), 1905, and Report of the SDPA to the WGG, August 17 (30), 1905. See also Żarnowska, "Próba analizy," p. 443; Kiepurska, *Warszawa w rewolucji,* pp. 184–185; Kalabiński, "Ruch strajkowy, 1905," p. 85; and Lewis, "Labor Movement," pp. 213–220.

litical agitation. The role of crowds was largely confined to spreading the
strike to outlying areas of an industrial region where socialist influences
had yet to penetrate.[112] Separate groups of workers did appear in the streets,
with the aim of disrupting public transportation, and strike solidarity was
often enforced by coercive means, but these actions too had an organized
character. In the latter case, revolver-wielding militants from the fighting
and self-defense organizations of the socialist parties played a key role in
persuading the insufficiently ''class-conscious'' segment of the proletariat
to join the strike.

Already, by October 27, the strike was general in Warsaw and Łódź,
but workers had walked out without making any demands, and the socialist
parties were slow in defining the political goals of the movement. Only
with the proclamation of the October Manifesto on the thirtieth did these
parties respond with specific political demands. On November 2, a mass
meeting at the Warsaw Philharmonia, attended by four thousand and dominated by speakers from the PPS, SDKPiL, and Bund, resolved to continue
the general strike until martial law was lifted in Warsaw and Łódź and a
blanket amnesty granted all political prisoners. The parties also resolved
to continue revolutionary work aimed at the overthrow of the tsarist government, the convocation of a constituent assembly, the achievement of
complete equality for the Jews, and the introduction of Polish in schools,
courts, and other public institutions.[113]

The mass meeting at the Warsaw Philharmonia took place during the
''days of freedom'' in the Kingdom, a period confined to the first ten days
of November, when government authority, as well as law and order, nearly
collapsed. The socialist parties, though able to organize a continuation of
the general strike and to bring thousands of working-class demonstrators
into the streets in support of their political goals, still found it difficult, if
not impossible, to control the actions of the crowds once they formed. In
Kalisz, for example, a crowd of demonstrators appeared in front of the city
jail on November 1 to demand the release of political prisoners. When it
became clear that the intimidated prison guards would offer no resistance,
the crowd stormed the jail and ten inmates escaped.[114] No casualties were
reported in Kalisz, but when a similar incident occurred in front of the
Warsaw magistrate's office on Theater Square later that evening, troops

112. AGAD KGGW 2504, Report of the SDPA to the WGG, October 18 (31), 1905.
113. AGAD KGGW 2493, Report of the SDPA to the WGG, October 24 (November 6), 1905.
114. AGAD KGGW 2507, Report of the SDPA to the WGG, October 24 (November 6), 1905.

fired several broadsides into the surging crowd, killing forty-four besiegers in yet another massacre.[115]

Meanwhile, the "days of freedom" bordered on complete anarchy in Częstochowa and the Dąbrowa Basin. The commander of the Częstochowa garrison reported that the crowd took control of the city on November 3 and was arming itself with weapons smuggled in from Austria. In an appeal to the population of the city the next day, he threatened to crush all "revolutionary disturbances" with military force, although privately he believed that only martial law would do the job.[116] In the cities and towns of the Dąbrowa Basin, the police disappeared entirely from the streets and, in some cases, were actually disarmed by groups of workers. Troop strength in the region was sufficient only for the defense of dynamite stores located near the mines.[117] The socialist parties tried to fill the local power vacuum by creating an interparty committee of public safety as well as a citizens' militia. To purchase arms for the militia, representatives of the socialist parties demanded large sums of money from factory and mine owners, frequently resorting to threats against their lives and property. The terrorized industrialists frantically petitioned the Warsaw governor-general, requesting that he appeal to imperial Germany for military assistance to crush the "Polish insurrection."[118] Such desperate action proved unnecessary. With the introduction of martial law throughout the Kingdom of Poland on November 10, government forces quickly regained control of the situation, and the ten-day "Basin Republic" came to an end.

The general strike, however, continued in all industrial centers of the country well after the introduction of martial law. Its motivating force was no longer the political goals of the socialist parties but the economic demand of the workers for full payment of wages for the time of the strike up to and including October 30, the day of the October Manifesto. In Łódź, the textile magnate I. K. Poznański voluntarily offered his workers such payment on October 31. This led to similar demands throughout the Łódź textile industry, which were frequently accompanied by threats of violence and the destruction of property.[119] Hence, long after

115. Kalabiński, *Carat i klasy posiadające*, pp. 315–320; Kiepurska, *Warszawa w rewolucji*, pp. 201–202.
116. AGAD KGGW 2499, Commander of the Częstochowa Garrison to the Chief of the Piotrków Okhrana, October 23 (November 5), 1905; Kalabiński, *Carat i klasy posiadające*, p. 300.
117. Kalabiński, *Carat i klasy posiadające*, p. 305.
118. AGAD KGGW 2498, Petition of Factory Owners of the Sosnowiec-Dąbrowa Region, October 26 (November 8), 1905.
119. AGAD KGGW 2499, Provisional Governor-General of Łódź and Łódź County to the Director of the Chancellory of the WGG, October 27 (November 9), 1905.

Russian workers had returned to their jobs, the general strike continued in full force in most parts of the Kingdom. Only when striking railwaymen returned to their jobs on November 16—and this after considerable pressure from their Russian counterparts—did the strike actually abate. In Łódź the number of striking workers fell precipitously, from a peak of 65,523 on November 18 to 9,501 on November 20. In the Kazimierz, Renard, and Feliks mines in the Dąbrowa Basin, workers held out until the end of November in an unsuccessful effort to receive wages for the earlier, "political" phase of the general strike.[120]

With lost wages for the October–November strike the common experience of the vast majority of industrial workers, any future socialist appeals for participation in a political strike were bound to meet with hesitation and reluctance on the part of the workers, if not their outright opposition. Indeed organized opposition within the working class to the socialist movement's "strike mania" rapidly gathered momentum after the October Manifesto. Workers earlier coerced into striking or satisfied by the October Manifesto concessions allowing the workers' right of association now found a willing means of articulation in the National Workers' Union (Narodowy Związek Robotniczy—NZR). The NZR had been created during the Łódź Uprising in June 1905 as a satellite organization of the National League to spread nationalist propaganda among Polish workers and artisans and to combat the "harmful" and "alien" influences of the socialist movement. In industrial-labor relations, the NZR assumed a reformist stance, offering conditional support to economic strikes; but it emphatically opposed political strikes, particularly those that linked the labor movement in Poland to supranational, or Russian, revolutionary goals. Before the October Manifesto, the NZR enjoyed the support of only a small minority of workers, but it rapidly expanded its ranks in subsequent months, eventually rising to twenty-three thousand members by the autumn of 1906.[121]

The opposition of the NZR to the socialist movement and political strikes was also shared by the Association of Christian Workers (Stowarzyszenie Robotników Chrześcijańskich—SRCh), legally recognized by the tsarist government in 1906. The SRCh, organized by clerical social activists in Warsaw, Łódź, Częstochowa, and the Dąbrowa Basin on the basis of Leo XIII's papal encyclical *Rerum Novarum* of 1893, was formed specif-

---

120. AGAD KGGW 2493, Report of the SDPA to the WGG, November 4 (17), 1905; Korzec, *Źródła do dziejów rewolucji* I (2):461–467; Kalabiński, *Carat i klasy posiadające*, p. 364.
121. On the history of the NZR, see Teresa Monasterska, *Narodowy Związek Robotniczy, 1905–1920* (Warsaw, 1973).

ically to paralyze socialist influences among industrial and artisanal labor. At the same time, the SRCh sought to alleviate working-class poverty by concentrating on educational and cultural activity while promoting mutual assistance and the cooperative movement. The SRCh, once legal recognition was granted, like the NZR, succeeded in organizing more than twenty thousand workers.[122]

With such organized and, in the case of the NZR, sometimes armed opposition in place, workers' support for political strikes quickly began to waver. Already in December during the ill-fated Moscow uprising, the appeals of the socialist parties in the Kingdom for yet another general strike in support of the Moscow insurgents met with a limited response. In Łódź, more than 80 percent of the industrial labor force participated in the December strike, but in Warsaw, until now the pride of socialist organizational efforts, fewer than half walked out. Less than a month later, the socialist parties called for a one-day general strike on January 22 to observe the anniversary of Bloody Sunday. Again, the response of Łódź industrial workers far exceeded that of workers from the Warsaw region. In general, the December and January strikes in the Kingdom drew less than half the number of those who had participated in the October-November general strike.[123] With the exception of a one-day strike in observance of May Day, workers' participation in political strikes continued to decline throughout Russian Poland in 1906.

Nationalist and clerical counteragitation obviously played a major role in breaking the political strikes called by the socialist parties. So, too, did the repressive measures that accompanied the imposition of martial law. More important, however, was the genuine desire of workers to take advantage of a concrete political concession in the October Manifesto which affected them most, namely, the right of free association in trade unions. For most workers, trade union organization now assumed priority over the political goals of convening a constituent assembly or restoring autonomy to the Kingdom of Poland. By throwing their organizations into trade union activity, the socialist parties showed their recognition of this reality as they sought to maintain their political influence among industrial workers. And, so long as the socialist trade unions effectively represented and defended workers' economic interests, this influence was partially preserved.

---

122. On the SRCh, see Aleksander Wóycicki, *Chrześcijański ruch robotniczy w Polsce* (Poznań, 1921).
123. Żarnowska, "Próba analizy," p. 440; Lewis, "Labor Movement," p. 266; Stanisław Kalabiński, "Ruch strajkowy robotników przemysłowych Warszawy i gubernii warszawskiej w okresie najwyższego jego natężenia: Próba analizy statystycznej lat 1905–1906 (Część II: 1906)," *Polska Klasa Robotnicza: Studia Historyczne* 5 (1973): 87.

## The Trade Union Movement

Until the autumn of 1905, the officially tolerated factory delegations, which had come into existence at the beginning of the year, represented workers' interests in disputes and negotiations with management. As mentioned earlier, during the course of 1905, many of these delegations had fallen under the control or influence of one or more of the socialist parties. Although the parties often succeeded in monopolizing the membership of any number of these quasi-legal institutions, each delegation remained a separate entity with its area of jurisdiction confined to a particular factory or plant, or sometimes only to a particular section of an industrial enterprise. In other words, there were no interfactory delegations, and whatever coordination did exist during the course of a strike usually came from ad hoc committees created by the socialist parties. Still, these strike committees, especially when they functioned as arenas for the competing parties, frequently failed to cooperate with one another. Hence the vast majority of economic strikes of 1905, despite the involvement of socialist parties in them, had a local, even wildcat, character quite in line with the predominantly spontaneous nature of the labor movement during this period.

At the peak of the October general strike, the SDKPiL transformed the factory delegations under its exclusive control into "factory unions" that continued to function as individual strike committees. Like the factory delegations, these "unions" were too atomized to be a basis for authentic trade unions, and they too disappeared once the October Manifesto conceded the right of collective association. Then, without waiting for appropriate legislation and taking advantage of the chaotic "days of freedom" in early November, the socialist parties actively, but independently, began to create trade unions under their political auspices. These organizations, however, were just as quickly driven underground by the imposition of martial law.

It would take until the middle of March 1906 for the government to make good on its promise to allow the right of association when it provided the legal structure for trade union organization through the issuing of a set of "provisional regulations." While these regulations created a framework for the legal registration of unions and associations, they also contained stipulations that severely restricted trade union activity. State employees were prohibited from forming organizations that concerned themselves with wages and working conditions. Their right of association was limited to collective participation in bodies that dealt with mutual assistance, self-help, and educational-cultural activities. As for employees of private enterprise, supraindustrial unions and associations were prohibited, and those

legally permitted and organized in individual industries found that their
territorial range could not extend beyond provincial boundaries. Although
these unions could engage in collective bargaining activities on behalf of
their memberships, strikes remained an illegal form of collective action, as
did the creation of strike funds. All the unions were also prohibited from
engaging in political activity and from maintaining any affiliation with
political organizations that harbored "criminal intentions." The state reserved for itself the right to suspend all unions and associations that acted
contrary to the "provisional regulations," to their own written and legally
recognized statutes, or that threatened "the peace or public security."[124]

The revolutionary socialist parties were the obvious targets of the pro-
hibitions on unions "conceived for political aims." Such parties now had
to make a fundamental choice between legality and continued underground
union organization. In Russia, all of them, including Lenin's Bolsheviks,
eventually opted for the possibilities afforded by legal or "nonparty" union
activity, although they remained determined to exercise at least an indirect
influence on the trade union movement. In Poland the SDKPiL, Bund, and
PPS initially maintained their illegal "party" union organizations. The PPS
and Bund experienced a change of heart, however, when they realized that
underground union activity limited both the size and effectiveness of organizations they hoped would have a mass character.[125] They subsequently
encouraged party activists to support, join, and help organize "nonparty"
trade unions. The SDKPiL alone held out, preserving a direct link between
its political and trade union organizations, and therefore the illegality and
conspiratorial nature of both. Indeed, the SDKPiL took the principle of
*partyjność* (party spirit) to the extreme of requiring all party members to
join Social Democratic trade unions while restricting membership in the
latter to those who had joined the party.

In the first months after the March "provisional regulations," this strategy gave the SDKPiL certain advantages as the "nonparty" unions went
through the laborious bureaucratic process of legal registration with the
authorities. In a report on the activities of "groups and unions" from April
through October 1906, the Okhrana ascribed the main influence on the
emerging trade union movement to the SDKPiL.[126] Social Democratic primacy, however, was short-lived; it ended with the legal registration by the

124. APW ZOW 454, "Provisional Regulations on Unions and Associations," as published
in *Warszawska Gazeta Policyjna*, March 18 (31), 1906.
125. The case for nonparty unions and for the open rather than conspiratorial conduct of
their activities was made by the PPS activist Bernard Szapiro in a twenty-four-page brochure,
"Związki zawodowe robotnicze"; AGAD AB, druk 217.
126. APW WWO 41.

end of the year of most of the "nonparty" trade unions supported by the PPS and Bund. Moreover, the socialist trade unions, whether "party" or "nonparty," faced stiff competition from "Polish" trade unions sponsored by the nationalist movement. These unions, with membership restricted to Catholic Poles, eventually organized 50,000 members (33,500 in the textile industry), or approximately half the total combined membership of the various socialist trade unions.[127] The Association of Christian Workers made no effort to form a union organization of its own, and as a consequence many of its members joined the "Polish" trade unions. The SRCh did, however, take the lead in other areas such as cultural-educational work, the creation of mutual assistance funds, the provision of job-placement services and free medical assistance, the establishment of savings and loan institutions, and above all, in the promotion of a cooperative movement among consumers and small producers. By 1907, nine cooperative stores in Warsaw and eight in Łódź were in operation after receiving start-up capital from the SRCh.[128]

As mentioned at the beginning of this chapter, trade union organization in the Kingdom embraced 20 percent of the industrial labor force at its peak at the end of 1906 and the first months of 1907, compared with 5 percent for the rest of European Russia. In the leading industrial regions of Łódź and Warsaw, that percentage was considerably higher. In Łódź sixty-six legal unions and ten illegal (Social Democratic) unions were active in 1907 with a combined total membership of more than eighty-five thousand. Of the city's industrial labor force, 50 percent had been organized, including three-quarters of all textile workers (the corresponding figure for textile workers in European Russia was 3.9 percent). In Warsaw, as many as fifty thousand workers were unionized, including more than half the employees of the city's key metal industry.[129]

This achievement over the course of a single year could not, however, be sustained. Repressive measures, carefully reserved for the authorities' use in the "provisional regulations" of March 1906, in time struck all the unions, beginning with those of the illegal, "party" variety organized by the SDKPiL. At the end of 1907, the authorities moved against the "nonparty" unions supported by the PPS and the Bund, which were deemed guilty of violating the spirit of the "provisional regulations" by virtue of

---

127. Monasterska, *Narodowy Związek Robotniczy*, pp. 63–64; Ignacy Orzechowski and Aleksander Kochański, *Zarys dziejów ruchu zawodowego w Królestwie Polskim, 1905–1918* (Warsaw, 1964), pp. 127–137; Karwacki, *Związki zawodowe*, pp. 80–90.
128. Wóycicki, *Chrześcijański ruch robotniczy w Polsce*, p. 136.
129. Karwacki, *Związki zawodowe*, pp. 107–118; Żarnowska, *Robotnicy Warszawy*, pp. 242–244.

their transparent political associations. The most devastating blows came in December with the suspension of all branches of the Union of Metal Workers in the Kingdom of Poland, as well as the Textile Workers' Union in Łódź and Łódź County, the two largest unions associated with the PPS.[130] A month earlier, George Skalon, the Warsaw governor-general, had forbidden entrance into the factories "to persons not employed by them and, particularly, to delegates of all associations and unions."[131]

Taken together, the effect of these measures reduced the range of union activity dramatically. Already, by the end of 1907, trade union membership among textile workers in Łódź had declined by 60 percent from the peak level of mid-1907. During the course of 1908, the "Polish" trade unions, which had remained strictly apolitical vis-à-vis the state authorities if not their socialist competitors, experienced a precipitious decline in membership, a fate shared by the Christian associations in 1909.

The repressive measures of the authorities, however, were only one factor in the rapid decline of the trade union movement in Russian Poland. Equally important was a new economic slump beginning in early 1907 and lasting until the end of the decade. A reduction in orders and a surplus of labor gave employers an opportunity to take the offensive against organized workers and regain some of the ground lost in 1905. Lockouts became increasingly commonplace and effective during the course of 1906. The most dramatic example of this counteroffensive was the Great Lockout in the Łódź textile industry during the first three months of 1907, which nearly broke the back of the socialist unions then and there.[132] Unable to defend workers' interests against the aggressive acts of the employers, the unions gradually saw their support evaporate.

Whatever the reasons for the collapse of the trade union movement in Russian Poland, the unions did not have sufficient time during their brief heyday from mid-1906 to mid-1907 to redirect indigenous labor protest into organized channels. To be sure, there were fewer wildcat strikes during this period than during the relative labor anarchy that prevailed in 1905. Still, many economic strikes retained a localized, voluntaristic character that could not be checked by union organizations. Strikes continued to occur in individual enterprises or in sections of a plant over the firing of a fellow worker, the actions of a single foreman, the hiring of workers of

130. APW ZOW 827, Director of the Chancellory of the WGG to the Warsaw Superintendent of Police, December 8 (21), 1907; Karwacki, *Związki zawodowe*, pp. 135–141.
131. APK TGGK 7, Proclamation of the WGG, November 4 (17), 1907.
132. See Richard D. Lewis, "Labor-Management Conflict in Russian Poland: The Łódź Lockout of 1906–1907," *East European Quarterly* 7 (January 1974): 413–434.

Workers from the Karol Scheibler Mills in Łódź after the Proclamation of the Great Lockout, December 1906. (Muzeum Niepodległości 38006)

another nationality or religion, and a host of other particular reasons. Violence remained a principal means of settling disputes, both with lower-level management and among workers themselves.

Moreover, membership in a trade union did not translate into a rock-hard allegiance, political or otherwise. Even in the strictly "party" trade unions organized by the SDKPiL, only half of the estimated thirty thousand recruited members actually paid their dues in 1907, and the proportion was considerably less the subsequent year, and this despite a fall in membership by nearly half.[133] As for the "nonparty" trade unions influenced by the PPS and the Bund, the period of their legal activity was cruelly short, averaging from six months to a year; only a few of them survived into the next decade. Many of the legally registered "Polish" unions were also suspended, especially those that discussed the possibility of organizing or participating in a strike action. As a result, membership in the trade unions was extremely fluid. Workers would move from one union to another, and especially in the first year of the provisional regulations, their loyalties frequently went to the union, whether legal or illegal, "party" or "non-

133. Orzechowski and Kochański, *Zarys dziejów ruchu zawodowego*, pp. 182–190.

party," socialist or nationalist, that best defended their immediate economic interests. Toward the end of 1907 and in early 1908, considerable movement occurred from the outlawed socialist organizations to the safer haven of still-legal "Polish" unions and Christian associations. When, toward the end of the decade, none of these organizations proved capable of defending labor's interests against management's counteroffensive, most workers dropped out of the organized labor movement altogether.

The trade union movement in Russian Poland, after an initial flurry of enthusiastic activity and feverish organization, never really had time to consolidate. As a consequence, the labor movement as a whole, born in the chaotic conditions of 1905, never fully matured. Had the authorities permitted greater latitude to trade union activity and, in particular, recognized the right of privately employed workers to strike, much of the lingering anomic unrest in the labor movement would have been gradually eliminated. A higher degree of stability and cooperation in labor-management relations would also have been achieved over time. Instead, the constant threat of suspension and delegalization, and the all-too-frequent realization of that threat, created conditions of flux in the labor movement and served in the end to promote the continuation of instability in industrial-labor relations. This outcome was not immediately apparent to employers savoring their victory after the Great Łódź Lockout, but in the first years of the next decade, when economic conditions improved and labor unrest resurfaced in unstructured and voluntaristic forms, many industrialists bemoaned the absence of organized bodies and institutions representing workers with whom they might conduct orderly negotiations.

Yet the labor movement had achieved some significant gains. For most workers, the revolution brought improvements in both wages and working conditions which survived, at least partially, the postrevolutionary period. Of the approximately 150,000 workers who joined political parties of all tendencies during the course of the revolution, the vast majority became participants in the political process for the first time. Not only did this mark the beginning of a new era of mass politics, but it also did much to promote political literacy among tens of thousands of workers who could now distinguish the nuances dividing the political parties and make more rational, clearer choices between them. The revolution also removed legal barriers to participation in "nonpolitical" organizations that responded to the workers' educational, cultural, and professional aspirations. Thus the labor movement in Russian Poland, though not permitted to reach maturity, was not still-born either. In the years after the revolution, it resembled more the perpetual adolescent, experienced enough to know how to act in collective defense of its interests but lacking the wisdom to tolerate opposing views, to reject rash actions and violent solutions to immediate problems, and, most important, to appreciate the stabilizing virtues of democratic processes and institutions.

# THE REVOLUTION IN
# THE COUNTRYSIDE

In contrast to the revolt among urban industrial workers in 1905, with its point of departure clearly marked by the January–February general strike, it is far more difficult to pinpoint the outbreak of revolution in the Polish countryside. On the one hand, although a wave of agrarian strikes swept large areas of rural Poland in the spring of 1905, farm workers were seeking higher wages and improved conditions from landowners—hardly revolutionary demands. The strike movement among farm laborers, moreover, was generally peaceful, and once authorities intervened or employers made concessions (or both), the agrarian strikes quickly ended. "Gmina action," on the other hand, which had already begun to assume the form of a mass movement toward the end of 1904, continued to gain momentum in the first months of 1905. Aided and abetted organizationally by nationalist-inspired agitation and publications, the movement retained a strictly "legalistic" character. Gradually, however, the movement assumed more revolutionary forms, especially when early-summer government concessions on the language and school issues failed to satisfy rural society. By autumn, a majority of gmina assemblies were in open revolt against the government, expressing their alienation in a flood of increasingly radical resolutions. No longer content merely to limit the arbitrary exercise of state authority by the Russian bureaucracy, rural inhabitants now sought to replace it with locally derived, popular Polish authority.

To a considerable extent, the growing assertiveness of the gmina movement, its radicalization, and its departure from the cautious and legalistic methods set by the Endecja coincided with the near breakdown of Russian state authority in the Polish countryside. It would take several months of martial law before a semblance of that control could be restored in the

spring of 1906. In the meantime, the paralysis that struck Russian administration and police at the local level had profound consequences that extended beyond the state's inability to check the activities of unruly gmina
assemblies. Villagers frequently took the law into their own hands, whether
in resolving property and easement rights (servitudes) disputes or in carrying out vigilante justice against real and suspected thieves. The breakdown of state authority also facilitated a violent turn in long-standing
ethnic and religious animosities, particularly in the eastern counties of Russian Poland. Worse still from the government's point of view, the countryside provided a safe haven, indeed a supporting base, for the terrorist
activities of "revolutionary" bands. Small wonder, then, that reports of
local officials in the last months of 1905 and the first months of 1906
spoke, in alarming terms, of rural anarchy and insurgency.

Revolution, most assuredly, came to the Polish countryside. That it failed
to assume the Russian form of a wave of violence against the manors,
though of great moment to latter-day Marxist historians,[1] was immaterial
to Russian bureaucrats and police on the scene in 1905 and 1906. In plead-
ing his case with the Ministry of Internal Affairs for introducing martial
law throughout the Kingdom of Poland in November 1905, Warsaw
governor-general George Skalon placed special emphasis on the disaffec-
tion of the peasantry, the stratum of Polish society the government had
long considered most amenable to Russian rule.[2] It was therefore in the
countryside that the government suffered its most serious setback. Its forty-
year operating policy in the Kingdom of Poland, based on a presumption
of eternal peasant gratitude and loyalty to the throne for state-sponsored
emancipation, had now become completely useless. Instead, it would take
extraordinary means of repression afforded by martial law and emergency
rule to bring an end to the revolution in rural Poland.

### Agrarian Strikes

Although it is difficult to find anything revolutionary in the agrarian
strikes of the spring of 1905, they nevertheless assumed the form of a
purely self-generated mass movement. As already mentioned, the full-time
farm worker, or ordynariusz, stood at the bottom of the social and eco-

---

1. See esp. Stanisław Kalabiński and Feliks Tych, *Czwarte powstanie czy pierwsza rewolucja: Lata 1905–1907 na ziemiach polskich,* 2d ed. (Warsaw, 1976), pp. 155, 530.
2. Stanisław Kalabiński, ed., *Carat i klasy posiadające w walce z rewolucją 1905–1907 w
Królestwie Polskim: Materiały archiwalne* (Warsaw, 1956), pp. 302–303.

nomic order in Russian Poland and endured wretched working and living conditions. Moreover, no political party, including the socialist organizations, paid much attention to farm workers before 1905. In contrast to their activities among other social groups, the parties made no attempt to organize farm workers in defense of their economic interests or to mobilize them for political purposes. Leadership for a movement therefore had to come from the agricultural workers themselves.

The inspiration for the strikes came from several sources. There was the already-noted decline in wages paid to farm workers in money and kind during the first years of the twentieth century despite the general recovery of agriculture from the agrarian crisis of the preceding decades. The January–February strike of industrial workers, particularly when joined by employees of sugar refineries located in the countryside, also influenced agrarian workers, sometimes directly. Indeed, the first strikes can be traced to the action of employees of the Elżbietów sugar refinery in Sokołów County of Siedlce Province. On February 21, approximately one hundred workers from Elżbietów appeared on the nearby Ruchna estate belonging to Count Lubieński, where they persuaded farmhands to leave their jobs and join them as they proceeded to neighboring estates.[3] By February 27, the date the Elżbietów workers settled with refinery management, twenty-seven estates in Sokołów County had been struck.[4]

The slow, contradictory, and equivocal response of estate owners and government officials to the strikes also played an important role, if not in their inspiration, then in their rapid expansion. As the strikes spread from Sokołów to Węgrów County, landowners provided the crowd of striking workers with lodging, bread, kiełbasa, money, and even horses and wagons as it roamed from estate to estate. Not a single landowner in either county turned to the authorities for help. On the Ceranów estate, according to police reports, farm workers were even permitted to hold a dance in the manor kitchen. When the Land Guard arrived, the proprietor himself turned the rural police away, informing them that "the county chief has no right to interfere with the workers on his estate and that the workers will return to their jobs when it pleases him and them."[5] The conciliatory attitude of landowners in Sokołów and Węgrow counties and their willing concessions to the strikers' economic demands undoubtedly contributed to the spread of the strike to six estates in Konstantynów County, where, however,

3. AGAD KGGW 2525, Report of the SDPA to the WGG, February 12 (25), 1905.
4. Urszula Głowacka-Maksymiuk, *Gubernia siedlecka w latach rewolucji, 1905–1907* (Warsaw, 1985), pp. 68–69.
5. AGAD KGGW 2525, Report of the SDPA to the WGG, February 12 (25), 1905.

the atmosphere, was less festive. The landowner Zaborowski refused the crowd's demand for money, and, as a result, his son was taken hostage. For the first time, troops were dispatched to the scene. The mere news of their approach together with the intervention of the Huszlew parish priest provided sufficient argument for the crowd to disperse and release the younger Zaborowski.[6]

By that time, the movement had already spread to Lublin Province, where it acquired even greater momentum. Here the estate owners proved far more recalcitrant, the crowds more coercive, and local authorities less prepared to intervene effectively, especially where the conflict pitted Orthodox workers against Catholic employers. Before March ended, 358 agrarian strikes had been recorded in eight counties of Lublin Province, compared with 129 strikes in Siedlce Province, the original center of the movement, and 573 for the entire Kingdom.[7] Only in Nowa-Aleksandria (Puławy) County, where individual proprietors expressed quick agreement to meet workers' demands provided that other estates followed suit, could landowners be accused by authorities of abetting the strike movement's expansion.[8] By contrast, panic-stricken landowners in ethnically mixed Krasnystaw, Hrubieszów, and Zamość counties preferred to appeal to authorities for military protection against the crowds rather than negotiate workers' demands.[9] In Chełm County a dozen Polish landowners telegrammed the acting Lublin governor to complain bitterly about the inactivity of the authorities, which, in their opinion, encouraged roaming bands of Orthodox (mainly Ukrainian) workers to make threats, demand money, and force a suspension of work on local estates.[10]

Toward the end of March, the authorities finally began to take active measures, prompted by the pressure of landowners and the threat to public order posed by the swelling size of the crowds. Immediately upon receipt of the landowners' petitions and complaints, the Lublin governor issued a proclamation warning that attacks on the property of the landed class, as well as the making of demands accompanied by coercion and threats, would be tried by courts-martial.[11] Simultaneously, he demanded that

6. AGAD KGGW 2525, Siedlce Governor to the WGG, February 26 (March 11), 1905.

7. Krzysztof Groniowski, *Robotnicy rolni w Królestwie Polskim, 1871–1914* (Warsaw, 1977), pp. 195–196; Albin Koprukowniak, *Ruchy rewolucyjne na wsi lubelskiej w latach 1905–1907* (Lublin, 1967), p. 57.

8. Stanisław Kalabiński and Feliks Tych, eds., *Walki chłopów Królestwa Polskiego w rewolucji 1905–1907*, vol. 1 (Warsaw, 1958), pp. 151–152.

9. AGAD KGGW 2513, Telegrams of the Minister of Internal Affairs to the WGG, March 7 (20) and March 21 (April 3), 1905.

10. Kalabiński, *Carat i klasy posiadające*, pp. 88–89.

11. APL KGL 1905:120, Proclamation of the Lublin Governor, March 8 (21), 1905.

county officials use armed force to disperse the crowds and arrest "agitators."[12] To assist them, several companies of Cossacks were then dispatched to Chełm, Krasnystaw, and Lubartów counties, where the use of infantry had earlier proved ineffective against the crowds.[13] Smaller units were also sent to Zamość and Hrubieszów counties.

As in Siedlce Province, the authorities' employment of military force brought the agrarian strike movement to a rapid halt. By the time a company of Don Cossacks was dispatched to a dozen estates in Chełm County in the last days of March, the disturbances had already ended and farm workers had returned to the fields.[14] Elsewhere the crowds dispersed without resistance when faced with military force. The arrest of approximately five hundred "agitators," "organizers," and "active personal participants" also served to pacify the farm workers in Lublin Province.[15] The subsequent sentencing of those arrested, however, was relatively lenient. In Krasnystaw County, for example, of the 121 arrested during the spring strikes, the authorities sentenced 34 to a mere five days in jail and placed the remainder under police surveillance.[16]

Nieszawa, Kutno, and Włocławek counties of Warsaw Province, together with adjacent Koło County in Kalisz Province, formed the third major center of the agrarian strike movement of the early spring. Wages paid farm workers in this region, especially in comparison with Siedlce and Lublin provinces, were relatively high. The strikes in Włocławek County, for example, occurred on "model estates" where workers' conditions were reputed to be the best in the Kingdom.[17] As in Lublin and Siedlce provinces, the strikes were spread by impulsively formed crowds of two to five hundred workers which dispersed immediately, however, when confronted by military force.[18] The one exception, and the only tragedy of the strike movement, took place at the Łanięta estate in Kutno County and resulted in twelve deaths. According to subsequent testimony of the owner of Łanięta, Marian Kiniorski, the farm workers did not understand the demand to disperse, made in Russian, by the captain of the county Land Guard; instead they believed that he had called them to gather around him. As the crowd pressed in, the captain ordered the troops to fire.[19]

12. Kalabiński, *Carat i klasy posiadające,* pp. 88–89.
13. Kalabiński and Tych, *Walki chłopów* 1:177–178, 208–213.
14. Ibid., pp. 198–199.
15. Groniowski, *Robotnicy rolni,* pp. 198–201.
16. APL KGL 1905:250, Directive of the Lublin Governor, September 11 (24), 1905.
17. Kalabiński and Tych, *Walki chłopów* 1:828.
18. AGAD KGGW 2501, Warsaw Governor to the WGG, March 4 (17) and March 7 (20), 1905, and 2506, Kalisz Governor to the WGG, March 10 (23), 1905.
19. AGAD KGGW 2501, Petition of Marian Kiniorski to the WGG, March 18 (31), 1905.

Striking farm workers from Gostynin County, Warsaw Province. (Muzeum Niepodległości 38082)

Despite the resort to repression, the authorities were not entirely unsympathetic to the plight of farm workers. Ethnic and religious considerations
partially informed official attitudes, particularly in the eastern counties of
Lublin and Siedlce provinces where Orthodox peasants, many of them
former Uniates, labored for Polish proprietors. The pitiful condition of
agrarian laborers and the purely economic nature of their demands also
impressed authorities. As soon as the strikes ended in Zamość and Krasnystaw counties, for example, local authorities expressed the opinion that
most of the farm workers' demands were justified and encouraged gmina
officials to take up the matter with landowners.[20] Such views seemed to
pervade upper levels of the bureaucracy as well. Later in the summer when
farmhands at the Piaski Wielkie estate in Lublin County struck, the Lublin
governor himself labored hard to budge landowner Józef Drecki toward
concessions, justifying his intervention by the fact that the conditions of
Drecki's workers were far worse than on neighboring estates.[21]

. Elsewhere in the Kingdom, provincial officials sought to persuade landowners to raise the standard of living of their workers as a preventive
measure. Such methods were particularly successful in Łomża Province,
where the only strike of the spring was a one-day walkout by seven work-

20. Kalabiński and Tych, *Walki chłopów* 1: 190–191; APL KGL 1905:79/2, Chief of Krasnystaw County to the Lublin Governor, March 18 (31), 1905.
21. AGAD KGGW 2514, Lublin Governor to the WGG, July 13 (26), 1905.

ers on an estate in Mazowieck County.[22] Indeed, for all of April, reports of agrarian strikes came from only three counties of the Kingdom.[23] The movement then flared up again in May in the western counties of Warsaw Province, the northern (Lithuanian) part of Suwałki Province, and two counties of Płock Province. In June and July, agrarian strikes were largely confined to the Lithuanian counties of Suwałki Province. In November, the strike movement returned to the western part of Warsaw Province, affecting estates that had not improved workers' conditions in the spring and summer. Never again, however, would the agrarian strike movement achieve the size and degree of success of the spring, when the vast majority of all agricultural strikes in 1905 occurred.

In the course of the year, agricultural strikes took place in forty-one of the Kingdom's eighty-four counties, affecting some 740 estates.[24] According to one estimate, strikes occurred on approximately half the Kingdom's 1,300 large estates, that is, those larger than 1,400 acres.[25] At least 600 of these estates were located in Lublin, Siedlce, and Warsaw provinces, the centers of the spring strike movement. Smaller estates employing but a few workers, more typical of the rest of Russian Poland, were largely unaffected by the strikes.

Crowd behavior and workers' demands during the agrarian strikes followed similar general patterns, although with some interesting variations. Everywhere the strikes occurred, they spread like a contagion as groups of workers roamed from estate to estate, gathering up new strikers in crowds that changed in size and composition as they went. In Krasnystaw and Zamość counties of Lublin Province, farm workers participated in the initiation of six strikes before returning to their own estates. In Koło and Nieszawa counties of central Poland, workers returned home after initiating four strikes.[26] Through such rotational shifts, sufficient manpower was secured for spreading the strike to the next estate. A few workers, however, always remained behind to take care of the livestock.

The crowds, though generally peaceful, were not entirely nonviolent. Actual physical attacks on landowners or destruction of manorial property were extremely rare. More commonplace were threats aimed at extracting from owners small amounts of money and food, and sometimes

22. AGAD KGGW 2510, Łomża Governor to the WGG, March 11 (24), 1905; Kalabiński and Tych, *Walki chłopów* 1: 427–429.
23. Groniowski, *Robotnicy rolni*, pp. 201–202.
24. Jan Borkowski, *Chłopi polscy w dobie kapitalizmu* (Warsaw, 1981), p. 95.
25. Richard D. Lewis, "Revolution in the Countryside: Russian Poland, 1905–1906," *Carl Beck Papers in Russian and East European Studies* 506 (1986): 30.
26. Ibid.; AGAD KGGW 2506, Kalisz Governor to the WGG, March 10 (23), 1905.

lodging, to sustain the crowd as it moved on to other estates. As most proprietors readily accepted these demands, the threats were seldom carried out. When they were, the usual consequence was a few broken windows. More frequently, estate officials were coerced into joining the crowd or leaving the estate. The crowd also administered beatings to workers who refused to strike. The coercion and violence that accompanied the agrarian strikes, however, paled in comparison with that perpetrated by crowds of industrial workers. Moreover, although the rural police in their small numbers usually proved insufficient to disperse the crowds of striking farm workers, there were no instances of resistance to military armed force.[27]

Strikers naturally sought improvements in monetary wages and in the size of the *ordynaria,* the payments many of them received in kind. Farm workers in Siedlce Province claimed that the tsar himself supported their demands for doubling their wages and ordynaria as well as for a nine-hour working day.[28] In Lublin County, striking farm workers uniformly demanded wage increases from twenty to thirty rubles, the local annual norm, to forty rubles, as well an increase in ordynaria from twelve to sixteen bushels of grain.[29] In the Lithuanian counties of Suwałki Province, workers demanded a 50 percent increase in wages and in-kind payments.[30] Other demands frequently included the right to pasture two cows instead of one and larger plots for growing potatoes.

Less frequent were demands for separate living quarters for each family and the elimination of the relatively widespread *posyłka* system, which required a full-time farm worker to maintain a temporary workhand at his own expense. Usually, one of the worker's grown children performed this function, but if he lacked such, the worker was obliged to feed and lodge a helper, for which he received compensation in kind.[31] Other demands were uniquely specific. In the Siedlce region, workers demanded the return of money collected from fines earlier levied against them by their employers.[32] In Lublin County, workers demanded the construction of day-care facilities for their young children. One proprietor,

27. For acts of crowd coercion during the agrarian strikes, see Jan Molenda, "Przemoc grupowa w masowych wystąpieniach chłopów i robotników rolnych w Królestwie Polskim na przełomie XIX–XX wieku," in *Przemoc zbiorowa, ruch masowy, rewolucja,* ed. Elżbieta Kaczyńska and Zbigniew Rykowski (Warsaw, 1990), pp. 143–145.

28. Kalabiński and Tych, *Walki chłopów* 1: 669–670.

29. AGAD KGGW 2513, Report of the SDPA to the WGG, March 9 (22), 1905.

30. Groniowski, *Robotnicy rolni,* p. 201.

31. Lewis, "Revolution in the Countryside," pp. 30–31; Groniowski, *Robotnicy rolni,* p. 261.

32. AGAD KGGW 2525, Siedlce Governor to the WGG, March 17 (30), 1905.

the owner of Jakubowice Muranowe, actually agreed to this demand, providing two separate rooms and adult supervision for 120 children under eleven years of age.[33]

Generally, owners agreed to make concessions on wages, in-kind payments, and land usage but ignored the other demands. These concessions, however, were usually enough to satisfy farm workers, who ended their strikes after a few days. In most cases, local employers concerted their response to workers' demands. In Sokołów County of Siedlce Province, where the strike movement began, the landowners met within days of the initial strikes and agreed on a 25 percent increase in wages and a 15 percent increase in ordynaria.[34] Similarly, in Warsaw Province, landowners agreed to a modest improvement in workers' conditions without benefit of state mediation or pressure. In Lublin Province, where owners were most recalcitrant, the state, after using military force to disperse the crowds, successfully influenced most employers to make concessions.

The agrarian strike movement of 1905 thus resulted in a qualified victory for the farm workers as it brought economic improvements to the poorest stratum of the rural population. This was remarkable for a movement that recruited its own leaders and relied on its own internal organizational impetus. Socialist and populist groups were slow to recognize the political possibilities in the agrarian strike movement, whereas the Roman Catholic Church and the National Democrats denounced the striking crowds, although the latter did try to persuade employers to make voluntary concessions. The landowning peasantry, moreover, was generally indifferent to the farm workers' cause.[35] The strike movement succeeded in the first months of 1905, however, primarily because the authorities and landowners had been taken by surprise. In the spring of 1906, when farm workers struck again, this time with the external organizational support of the PPS, both the authorities and the large landed proprietors were themselves better prepared and organized to suppress the strikes and resist workers' demands.

## Gmina Action

Whereas the movement among farm workers was largely spontaneous and devoid of political goals, the movement for communal self-government

33. Kalabiński and Tych, *Walki chłopów* 1: 268–269.
34. AGAD KGGW 2525, Siedlce Governor to the WGG, February 25 (March 5), 1905.
35. There were, however, some notable exceptions: e.g., peasants from Opatów County in Radom Province refused to quarter dragoons sent to quell agrarian strikes; Kalabiński and Tych, *Walki chłopów* 1: 607–608.

in the Polish countryside had an entirely different character, at least until the autumn of 1905. By the end of 1904, more than one hundred gmina assemblies had passed resolutions calling for the introduction of Polish into local administrative, educational, and judicial institutions. At least thirty others approved similar resolutions during their winter meetings, which concluded in January. Thus, even before the outbreak of the January–February industrial general strike and the revolt of student youth against the Russian educational system, slightly over 10 percent of the 1,291 gmina assemblies in the Kingdom of Poland had initiated "gmina action." Already a mass movement, gmina action would affect at least two-thirds of all rural communes by the end of the year. In the process, however, the movement underwent several significant changes that transformed it into a revolutionary force.

In its initial phase, from the spring of 1904 to early 1905, the movement evolved under the close scrutiny of the nationalist movement with its emphasis on gradualism, legal methods of struggle, and the language issue. The first assemblies were therefore advised to limit their action to a refusal to sign Russian-language protocols of their meetings and to the drafting of Polish-language protocols in their place, which included resolutions asserting the statutory right to use the native language in the conduct of gmina affairs. The anticipated rejection of these demands by county and provincial officials would then be appealed to a higher authority. The politically cautious, procedurally legal strategy recommended to the peasants in the issues of *Polak* and by TON activists was designed to calm the nerves of those who feared government retribution.[36] The use of Polish in gmina business also made practical sense to peasants, many of whom could not understand the reading of Russian-language protocols that awaited their signature.

As the movement evolved in the course of 1904, however, the proponents of gmina action discovered that a principal obstacle lay within the local communities themselves in the form of opposition from gmina officials, particularly the pisarz (the clerk appointed by the county chief) and the wójt (the mayor elected by the assembly but confirmed in office by the state administration). Frequently, the pisarz would refuse the assembly's demand that he draft a Polish-language protocol, or the wójt would refuse to sign such a protocol and enter it into the official record. Peasant supporters of gmina action responded simply by refusing to affix their signatures to a Russian-language protocol of the assembly's resolutions, an action that could temporarily paralyze local "self-government."

---

36. Tadeusz Wolsza, *Narodowa Demokracja wobec chłopów w latach 1887–1914: Programy, polityka, działalność* (Warsaw, 1992), pp. 162–163.

By the end of 1904, *Polak* began to advise assemblies to take a more aggressive posture in dealing with recalcitrant gmina officials: namely, to dismiss the pisarz from the local administration if he refused to draft the desired protocol and resolutions, to demand that the wójt and plenipotentiaries (*pełnomocnicy*) arrange for the election of a new pisarz, and to entrust the drafting of the protocol and resolutions to a person selected by the assembly.[37] The opposition of the wójt could be circumvented by emphasizing the role of other elected gmina officials, especially the candidate mayor, the plenipotentiaries, and the village elders (*sołtysy*).[38] Though the emphasis still remained on orderly procedure and peaceful methods, the tactical shift at the end of 1904 imparted to the gmina action movement a new goal in addition to mere polonization: the reform of local self-government by making officials truly responsible to the gmina assembly as the highest source of communal authority.

The state administration was slow to comprehend the potential challenge this posed to its own authority in the Polish countryside. At the end of 1904 and in early 1905, Russian officials continued the traditional policy of refusing to confirm the election of persons of doubtful loyalty to gmina offices and of pressuring those deemed loyal to conform to government dictates. Protocols drafted in the Polish language were simply rejected, as were resolutions demanding the use of Polish in gmina administration. Frequently, county chiefs would reconvene the assemblies and appear personally with members of the Land Guard to inform the peasants of the "illegality" of their action. Where intimidation and threats failed to suffice, certain county officials resorted to deception, warning gmina assemblies that their actions could lead to a restoration of serfdom.[39] Such methods were only partially effective, especially because actual punitive action was mild and aimed at individual "agitators" rather than the collective. For example, fourteen peasants from Lublin County were fined ten rubles each in mid-January 1905 for "agitation against the state language" at their gmina assembly meetings. Nine months later, however, local authorities had yet to collect the fines, fearing that forceful methods could lead to popular disturbances.[40]

There is little evidence to suggest that the industrial general strike of January–February either stimulated or radicalized the gmina movement, with the possible exception of gminy located in or adjacent to industrial

---

37. Ibid., p. 211.
38. Lewis, "Revolution in the Countryside," p. 13.
39. Kalabiński and Tych, *Walki chłopów* 1: 64, 117–118.
40. APL KGL 1905:59, Chief of Lublin County to the Lublin Governor, September 13 (26), 1905.

centers. The student strike at institutions of higher and secondary education, however, did have a galvanizing effect on gmina action and led to the first departure of the popular movement from the tactical norms prescribed by the Endecja. Although the demand for the polonization of elementary schools had been included in the resolutions of gmina assemblies, a boycott of the Russian system of primary education was neither recommended nor, it appears, even contemplated by nationalist politicians. The National Democratic leadership, moreover, did not initially support the student strikes and was in the process of policy readjustment when the movement against the russified schools spread to the countryside. Initiative therefore devolved to local activists not waiting for instructions from above and, more important, to the peasants themselves.

In the early spring, the movement from below against the Russian primary school was particularly strong in Płock and Łomża provinces, where thirty-two and twenty-three communal assemblies, respectively, had already taken up gmina action.[41] Documentary evidence reveals a common pattern to these incidents. A crowd of peasants would appear at a village school, demand instruction in Polish, and then remove their children from the school when refused. As a result, instruction was temporarily disrupted at dozens of elementary schools. In a few cases, sympathetic teachers accepted parental demands and began conducting lessons in Polish; others actually encouraged the peasants to act.[42] The peasants, however, were not always steadfast in their boycott action. For example, peasants from the village of Świelice in Łomża Province removed their children from the primary school on March 8, only to permit them to return a few days later.[43] At the Sobótka primary school in Łęczyca County (Kalisz Province), parents backed away from their initial demand for the exclusive use of Polish, informing the teacher that they would allow their children to return to the school if instruction in Russian were limited to three days a week.[44]

The methods of peasant protest against the Russian school, moreover, remained moderate. Violence was rare and limited to vandalism and destruction of portraits of the imperial family.[45] Most village communities

41. Kalabiński and Tych, *Walki chłopów* 1: 561–564; AGAD KGGW 2510, Report of the SDPA to the WGG, February 28 (March 13), 1905.
42. AGAD KGGW 2500, Report of SDPA to the WGG, February 23 (March 8), 1905, and 2510, Łomża Governor to the WGG, March 17 (30), 1905; APŁ KGP 1519, Chief of the Piotrków Provincial Gendarmes to the Piotrków Governor, February 24 (March 9), 1905.
43. AGAD KGGW 2510, Łomża Governor to the WGG, March 2 (15), 1905.
44. AGAD KGGW 2506, Report of the SDPA to the WGG, March 10 (23), 1905.
45. APW WGZŻ 1028, SDPA to the Chief of the Warsaw Provincial Gendarmes, February 28 (March 13), 1905.

involved in the movement at this stage simply stopped sending their children to school. Occasionally, peasants would refuse to a pay a teacher's salary or make capital repairs at a school as long as Russian remained the language of instruction.[46] Such was the extent of peasant boldness. More typical was the timid action of peasants from four villages in Miechów County in Kielce Province who permitted their children to remain in school but sent them without their Russian textbooks.[47]

Timid or not, peasant action against the Russian primary school system in the countryside coincided with a growing diversification and assertiveness of rural protest. With the next quarterly gmina assembly meetings scheduled for March and April, government officials began searching for more effective repressive measures. In anticipation of a new round of "illegal" assembly demands, the Łomża governor requested the authority to sentence administratively gmina action "agitators" as well as those who attempted to interrupt instruction at state schools.[48] To these and other appeals, the acting Warsaw governor-general Podgorodnikov responded with a proclamation on March 7 "in the aim of preserving order in the countryside." It warned that those guilty of violating laws regulating peasant self-government at gmina and village assembly meetings could be subject to administrative fines of five hundred rubles and sentenced to three months in jail under Article 15 of the statutes of "intensified security."[49]

Because repressive measures remained targeted at individual "agitators" rather than entire communities, they failed to intimidate the peasants and deter gmina action. Within days of Podgorodnikov's proclamation, the Kalisz governor reported that the gmina movement was gaining strength everywhere in his province. In Słupca County, for example, Polish language demands were made by seven more gmina assemblies; in addition, several of them refused to assign local funds to support families of reservists.[50] Several other assemblies in Kalisz Province simply refused to sign Russian-language protocols, thereby, among other things, holding up the distribution of the local tax burden.[51] Similarly, in Warsaw Province, several

46. AGAD KGGW 2525, Siedlce Governor to the WGG, January 27 (February 9), 1905; APŁ KGP 1519, Chief of the Piotrków Provincial Gendarmes to the Piotrków Governor, February 24 (March 9), 1905.
47. AGAD KGGW 2508, Kielce Governor to the WGG, March 6 (19), 1905.
48. AGAD KGGW 2510, Łomża Governor to the WGG, February 14 (27), 1905.
49. APŁ KGP 1518.
50. AGAD KGGW 2506, Kalisz Governor to the WGG, February 26 (March 11), 1905, and Report of the SDPA to the WGG, March 2 (15), 1905.
51. AGAD KGGW 2506, Kalisz Governor to the Minister of Internal Affairs, April 2 (15), 1905.

assemblies refused to confirm obligatory expenditures or authorize village elders to draw up tax-distribution lists. Moreover, crowds of peasants in Warsaw Province continued to withdraw their children from the primary schools, forcing many of them to close.[52] In Łomża Province, assembly demands reflected the trend toward diversification and local initiative. Some stuck to the traditional demand of introducing Polish into gmina administration; others extended language demands to the public schools. Several refused to pay for further obligatory subscriptions to *Oświata* (Enlightenment), a Polish-language government publication aimed at the peasantry, and a few joined in the nascent tax revolt.[53]

The unexpected response of Polish rural communities to Podgorodnikov's proclamation, as well as the ineffectiveness of the new repressive measures, led the authorities to a consideration of limited concessions. Although there were a few calls from county administrators for the outright suspension of gmina assembly meetings,[54] most leading officials in the Kingdom, and St. Petersburg as well, continued to cling to the delusion that the mass of Polish peasants constituted a basically loyal social and political force. The Warsaw governor-general, although he believed that a serious threat to Russian authority in the countryside now existed, placed the blame on the pernicious effect of nationalist propaganda.[55] Authorities also tended to identify their traditional nemeses, the Polish nobility and the Catholic clergy, along with the urban-based intelligentsia, as the principal leaders of gmina action.[56] Such notions, however, did not square with reality. The clergy's involvement was limited to those parts of Kalisz and Piotrków provinces which came within the ecclesiastical jurisdiction of Bishop Stanisław Zdzitowiecki of Kujawy-Kalisz, the sole episcopal supporter of clerical participation in gmina affairs.[57] The participation of urban-based intellectuals in gmina action was even less noteworthy. Among the "outsiders," a good deal of nationalist agitation in the countryside was conducted by local landowners who doubled as activists for TON and its successor organizations. Nevertheless, the szlachta provided

---

52. Kalabiński and Tych, *Walki chłopów* 1: 866–867.
53. Ibid., pp. 427–429; AGAD KGGW 2510, Report of the SDPA to the WGG, February 28 (March 13), 1905.
54. Kalabiński and Tych, *Walki chłopów* 1: 251–255.
55. AGAD KGGW 2501, WGG to the Minister of Internal Affairs, March 7 (20), 1905.
56. AGAD KGGW 2506, Kalisz Governor to the Ministry of Internal Affairs, April 2 (15), 1905, and 2510, Report of the SDPA to the WGG, February 28 (March 13), 1905; APL KGL 1905:59, Director of the Chancellory of the WGG to the Lublin Governor, April 4 (17), 1905; Kalabiński and Tych, *Walki chłopów* 1: 892–894.
57. Robert Blobaum, "The Revolution of 1905–1907 and the Crisis of Polish Catholicism," *Slavic Review* 47, 4 (1988): 674–675, 682.

only a minority of community leaders for gmina action. The majority of the activists were peasant assembly members and lower-ranking peasant officeholders.[58]

In any event, the government's perceptions of reality led to an attempt to undermine "outside agitation" through a series of limited concessions. These included certain provisions specifically aimed at Poles in the Edict of Religious Toleration of April 30 and the limited language concessions contained in the June 19 decision of the Committee of Ministers confirmed by the tsar. Neither measure, however, satisfied peasant aspirations or neutralized the gmina movement. Quite the contrary, their ultimate effect was to encourage an escalation of peasant demands as well as bolder, more arbitrary action in their behalf.

The Edict of Toleration, often considered in the literature as a concession designed for the sole purpose of winning the cooperation of the Roman Catholic episcopate in combating the revolutionary movement, was also aimed at the church's peasant parishioners. To begin, the provision of the edict recognizing the right of the tsar's Orthodox subjects to convert to other Christian denominations affected hundreds of thousands of former Uniate peasants residing in the eastern counties of Suwałki, Lublin, and Siedlce provinces (the latter two comprising the so-called Chełm region), who could now voluntarily join the Roman Catholic Church. Equally important, the edict permitted religious instruction in the native language of the students enrolled in public schools, thus meeting at least one demand that had appeared in many gmina assembly resolutions.

Whatever the state's intentions, the main impact of the edict was to further erode Russian authority in the countryside. Before the spring of 1905, Polish nationalist and religious agitation had made considerable inroads among the ethnically Byelorussian and Ukrainian Uniates. In Siedlce Province, where Catholic religious fanaticism was especially strong among the peasantry and where draft evasion was particularly widespread, rumors abounded that the pope had blessed the Japanese in their war with Russia. Peasants also constructed several roadside shrines and crosses without official permission in what the state considered to be Russian Orthodox communes.[59] In Augustów County of Suwałki Province, former Uniates stopped sending their children to the state primary schools.[60] Organized gmina action in these provinces, however, had yet to take firm root.

---

58. For an attempt to aggregate data on local leadership, see Lewis, "Revolution in the Countryside," pp. 12–16.
59. AGAD KGGW 2525, Siedlce Governor to the WGG, January 27 (February 9), 1905.
60. AGAD KGGW 2522, Suwałki Governor to the WGG, April 2 (15), 1905.

The Edict of Toleration unintentionally transformed the nature of resistance in the ethnically mixed eastern counties and stimulated their gmina assemblies to act far more aggressively than their counterparts in the Kingdom's north-central and western provinces, where the movement had originated. After massive conversions to Catholicism in gminy populated by Uniates in Lublin Province, assemblies elected only Catholics to administrative positions. Such action forced Orthodox mayors, plenipotentiaries, and elders either to convert or to lose office.[61] In Siedlce Province religious tensions flowed outside the gmina assemblies. Catholics and Uniates used physical coercion against Orthodox believers resisting conversion, and crowds reclaimed by force former Uniate churches that had been turned over to the Orthodox Church a generation earlier. In a couple of instances, troops had to be sent to defend Orthodox monasteries from menacing Catholic and Uniate crowds.[62] Such incidents were sufficient in number by the beginning of June to prompt a special proclamation from the Warsaw governor-general, who warned that violations of the religious rights of the Orthodox minority would be punished to the full extent of the law.[63] The authorities also refused to confirm the election of converted mayors in "Orthodox" gminy and removed Catholics from office in those gminy that had excluded Orthodox peasants from participating in the electoral process. Far more severe repressive measures, however, would prove necessary to contain the ethnic and religious strife in the region.[64]

Meanwhile, peasants elsewhere in the Kingdom were unimpressed—as the polonization movement gathered momentum—by the edict's provision permitting religious instruction in the native language. By the early summer of 1905, 245 gmina assemblies in the Kingdom, some 20 percent of the total, had passed resolutions demanding the introduction of Polish in village schools and courts as well as local administration.[65] Such a level of gmina action proved sufficient to force further concessions from the state in the form of the Decision of the Committee of Ministers of June 19.

By virtue of this legislation, the government adopted the principle of bilingualism in gmina administration.[66] Henceforth all gmina books, cor-

---

61. APL KGL 1905:18, WGG to the Lublin Governor, August 26 (September 8), 1905.
62. AGAD KGGW 2525, Siedlce Governor to the WGG, April 26 (May 9), 1905.
63. APL KGL 1905:18, Proclamation of the WGG, May 20 (June 2), 1905.
64. For a more detailed treatment of these issues, see Robert Blobaum, "Toleration and Ethno-Religious Strife: The Struggle between Catholics and Orthodox Christians in the Chełm Region of Russian Poland, 1904–1906," *Polish Review* 35, 2 (1990): 111–124.
65. Zenon Kmiecik, *Ruch oświatowy na wsi: Królestwo Polskie, 1905–1914* (Warsaw, 1963), p. 15.
66. AGAD KGGW 2621, Decision of the Committee of Ministers, June 6 (19), 1905.

respondence, and protocols could be kept in Polish in addition to Russian. The government also promised in the future to hire only bilingual people for job vacancies in the commissariats of peasant affairs and to end discrimination based on nationality or religion in state approval of land transactions. As to the future, the government announced that the State Council was considering the introduction of zemstvo institutions and justices of the peace into the Kingdom, two of Alexander II's "Great Reforms" long denied Russian Poland.

In education, the government reconfirmed the right of Catholics to religious instruction in the native language of the pupils while permitting the Catholic clergy a virtual monopoly on such instruction. More important, the government permitted the use of Polish for the study of arithmetic and the native grammar in state primary schools. The government was more generous to private schools, which were now allowed to use Polish as the language of instruction for all subjects except Russian grammar, history, and geography, all of which remained compulsory subjects. The latter concession, however, affected very few peasants.

None of these provisions applied to the "Russian" gminy of Lublin and Siedlce provinces (the so-called Chełm region) or to the Lithuanian counties of Suwałki Province, where Russian remained the sole language of administration and educational instruction. In the former, such restrictions foreshadowed the separation of the Chełm region from the Kingdom of Poland in the postrevolutionary period; in the short term they served to exacerbate already tense ethnic and religious relations among a mixed population. Fearing that a wave of Catholic "pogroms" against the Orthodox population was imminent, the Siedlce governor pleaded, albeit unsuccessfully, for the introduction of martial law in his province already that summer.[67]

In northern Suwałki Province, Kawalaria, Mariampol, Władysławów, and Wyłkowyszki counties were almost exclusively inhabited by Lithuanian peasants. The failure to extend the language concessions contained in the ministerial decision to these counties acted as spur to the Lithuanian national movement. Even before June, signs of unrest in the Lithuanian gminy had appeared in the form of agrarian strikes and the resolutions of a couple of gmina assemblies containing language demands on the Polish model.[68] After the June decision, gmina action became largely a Lithuanian

67. AGAD KGGW 2584, Minister of Internal Affairs to the WGG, August 19 (September 1), 1905.
68. AGAD KGGW 2522, Suwałki Governor to the WGG, April 2 (15), 1905, and Report of the SDPA to the WGG, April 29 (May 12), 1905.

movement in Suwałki Province. That movement also became far more politically radicalized than its Polish counterpart, thanks largely to successful agitation conducted by the Lithuanian Social Democratic Party (LSDP). The demands contained in the July 8 resolutions of the Leśnictwo gmina assembly in Władysławów County, for example, called not only for equal rights for Lithuanians and the lithuanization of local government agencies and public schools but also for freedom of religion, the introduction of zemstvo institutions, total gmina control over local expenditures, the establishment of a system of universal primary education at state expense, the reestablishment of a university at Vilnius, the elimination of certain taxes, a ban on "Lithuanian" timber exports, and the expansion of Jewish residence rights.[69] The national movement among Lithuanian peasants, moreover, was aimed not only at the Russian bureaucracy. Peasants interrupted homilies of Catholic priests, almost uniformly Poles, who were unsupportive of Lithuanian national demands; and a wave of strikes of farm workers against Polish landowners, encouraged by the LSDP, engulfed three of the four Lithuanian counties in July.[70]

In the rest of the Kingdom of Poland, thousands of peasants interpreted the government's concessions as a license to express their emerging national consciousness. For example, the provision in the Edict of Toleration permitting Catholic religious processions spawned various illegal phenomena. In several provinces, volunteer firemen met and accompanied such processions in their uniforms; soon they were joined by peasants wearing distinctive local and regional costumes, headware, and emblems and carrying Polish banners—all this in violation of an imperial ukase of 1876. On such occasions, local music ensembles, formed under the auspices of the volunteer fire departments, often played the forbidden "God Preserve Poland." To prevent the religious processions from turning into national demonstrations, the Warsaw governor-general instructed provincial authorities to punish violations of the ban on Polish national costumes with harsh administrative sentences.[71]

Neither concessions nor repression, however, could slow the escalation of the movement against the government in the Polish countryside. In Łomża and Płock provinces, gmina assemblies responded to the language concessions of June by calling for a boycott of state-sold alcohol and tobacco products. The Łyse gmina assembly in Kolno County (Łomża Prov-

69. Kalabiński and Tych, *Walki chłopów* 1: 783–786.
70. AGAD KGGW 2523, Suwałki Governor to the WGG, June 11 (24), June 26 (July 9), June 27 (July 10), and July 18 (31), 1905.
71. AGAD KGGW 2577, Circular of the WGG to Provincial Governors, June 17 (30), 1905.

ince) even resolved to levy fines on those who failed to adhere to the popular ban on drinking and smoking.[72] In Mława, Ciechanów, and Przasnysz countries (Płock Province), peasants attended "congresses" disguised as picnics and hosted by local landowners to discuss temperance and "other methods of struggle" against the government.[73] From Warsaw Province as well came reports that the concessions of June were having little impact, except to encourage gminy to strive for the complete elimination of Russian from the conduct of local affairs.[74]

The National Democrats, too, sensed the growing militancy among the peasantry. The leadership of the Endecja had been surprised by the extent of popular antipathy to the Russian educational system and only belatedly endorsed the spontaneous action of peasant communities which had closed numerous village elementary schools in the spring. In an attempt to regain the initiative over gmina action, the Endecja, through the still-influential periodical *Polak,* now instructed peasants to go to the schools at the beginning of the academic year and demand instruction exclusively in Polish. If teachers refused, parents were to remove their children from the premises and place them in "secret schools." The Endecja also encouraged gminy to assert their right to control and supervise village schools in assembly resolutions, including the right to hire and fire teachers.[75]

With the battle lines thus drawn, the quarterly gmina assembly meetings scheduled for July and August became the most crucial test of peasant attitudes toward the concessions of June. In Łomża Province, where gmina action had struck deep roots, assemblies again went beyond the recommendations of *Polak.* The Długoborz assembly, for example, refused to construct two new schools with state assistance until Polish became the exclusive language of instruction. The Kubra assembly went even further, annulling its resolution of the previous year to build a new school "because it would not satisfy the needs of our children."[76] Villagers of Wojciechów in Chełm County of Lublin Province resolved not to pay the school tax because "we don't need Russian schools."[77] Members of the Krzeczonów gmina assembly in Lublin County expressed their dissatisfaction with the June concessions by refusing to attend the meeting convened by the au-

72. AGAD KGGW 2511, Report of SDPA to the WGG, June 21 (July 4), 1905.
73. AGAD KGGW 2517, Płock Governor to the WGG, June 22 (July 5), 1905, and Report of the SDPA to the WGG, June 22 (July 5), 1905.
74. Kalabiński and Tych, *Walki chłopów* 1: 912–913.
75. Wolsza, *Narodowa Demokracja wobec chłopów,* pp. 163–164.
76. AGAD KGGW 2511, Report of the SDPA to the WGG, September 13 (26), 1905, and 2512, Łomża Governor to the WGG, October 8 (21), 1905.
77. AGAD KGGW 2514, Report of SDPA to the WGG, August 30 (September 12), 1905.

A gmina assembly meeting. Contemporary drawing by Stanisław Masłowski, 1906.
(Muzeum Niepodległości 35869)

thorities on August 7. This did not stop them, however, from sending a petition to "President" Sergei Witte, listing their grievances and demands.[78] In Piotrków Province, several gmina assemblies passed resolutions a second time reconfirming and expanding earlier language demands.[79]

Gmina action thus continued to move into new terrain. Similarly, the opening of the schools in September led to the spread of the popular movement against them despite the state's concessions on bilingualism. According to the Warsaw governor, "disturbances" occurred wherever subjects were instructed in Russian.[80] Similar reports came from Płock and Łomża provinces, where the movement against the schools had begun the previous spring. Peasants also forced the closing of schools, for the first time, in Piotrków, Kielce, and Radom provinces. Usually, parents disrupted lessons simply by removing their children from the school, the form of action

78. Ibid., July 25 (August 7), 1905; APL KGL 1905:59, Chief of Lublin County to the Lublin Governor, July 27 (August 9), 1905.
79. APŁ KGP 1521, List of gmina assemblies that passed Polish-language resolutions, compiled in mid-October, 1905.
80. AGAD KGGW 2504, Warsaw Governor to the WGG, September 25 (October 9), 1905.

recommended by *Polak,* but in one instance an explosion from a petard disrupted instruction at the Błaszki primary school in Kalisz Province.[81]

Meanwhile, as the school boycott intensified in the countryside, "secret instruction" proliferated. In fact, during the course of the revolution, the authorities would uncover more than three hundred illegal schools, and this was only a fraction of the total.[82] For example, the nineteen-year-old peasant Antoni Malczewski, whose own education was limited, nevertheless organized an underground school on an estate in Płonsk County (Warsaw Province), where children of both sexes between the ages of eight and fourteen received instruction in Polish grammar and religion for a tuition of thirty kopecks.[83] Twenty children received similar instruction in the home of the peasant Ignacy Zieliński in the village of Dolsznów in Lublin County.[84]

By the time of the October Manifesto, gmina action had been taken in one-third of all communes in the Kingdom of Poland, but the most intensive stage of its development was yet to come. The expansion of the movement before the October Manifesto had been gradual and, for the most part, remained nonviolent. Resistance to the government, however, took increasingly active and aggressive forms. The growing arbitrariness of peasant behavior through gmina action, encouraged by the progressive decline of government authority in countryside, also spilled over into other areas of rural life. Whereas the gmina movement was shaped by a significant degree of political organization, however, certain other collective actions of peasant communities—namely, trespassing and vigilantism— defied organization and control from the outside.

## Servitudes

Disputes in the Polish countryside over servitudes, or peasant easement rights, had a much longer history than gmina action, extending back to the emancipation legislation of the 1860s. The gradual liquidation of private servitudes over the course of two generations, accomplished through negotiated agreements and state intervention, had nevertheless left some village communities dissatisfied. Peasants frequently resorted to litigation,

81. AGAD KGGW 2507, Kalisz Governor to the WGG, September 9 (22), 1905.
82. Borkowski, *Chłopy polscy w dobie kapitalizmu,* p. 118.
83. APW WGZŻ 1730, Chief of the Warsaw Provincial Gendarmes to the SDPA and the Superintendent of the Warsaw School Directorate, March 22 (April 4), 1906.
84. APL KGL 1905:25, Chief of the Lublin Provincial Gendarmes to the Lublin Governor, December 7 (20), 1905.

sometimes lasting several years, only to receive what they considered unjust decisions. Regarding easement rights on state-owned property, peasants enjoyed no legal recourse whatsoever. Where the state continued to permit peasants to cut timber, gather firewood, graze livestock, and fish, it now charged fees. Peasants again felt cheated, especially when these fees were increased in the first years of the twentieth century.

The most bitter disputes revolved around peasant access to private and state forests. Because of rising lumber prices and the increasing scarcity of timber, estate owners were particularly eager to liquidate forest servitudes. For similar reasons, the state sought to expand profitable timber exports while simultaneously limiting peasant access. The liquidation of private servitudes and the restrictive forest conservation policies of the state affected not only peasant felling of timber in commercial and state forests but also the pasturing of peasant livestock and the gathering of firewood.[85]

Although the number of servitude-related disputes increased at the beginning of the century, peasants could do little but turn to the courts or petition the authorities, forms of collective action that had failed to produce the desired results. The gradual breakdown of Russian state authority in the countryside in 1905, however, encouraged peasants to take more aggressive action in defense of their economic interests, action mainly in the form of massive illegal trespassing incidents involving entire villages. Believing that the woods and meadows in dispute were rightfully theirs and essential to their survival, peasants also resisted forest guards, the rural police, and state officials who tried to halt their illegal felling, pasturing, and gathering operations.

In the course of 1905, illegal trespassing and servitude-related disturbances occurred in 189 of 1,287 gminy, or 14.7 percent of the total, peaking in the last three months of the year.[86] The peasants had various sources of inspiration for taking illegal and forceful action. The governor of Piotrków Province, where some of the first incidents occurred, believed that peasants derived their example from industrial workers "who gained desired results by illegal means."[87] Similarly, villagers of Czarna in Radom County reportedly began cutting down trees and resisting state forest guards under the leadership of the artisan Michał Wierzbicki, who sought

85. Krzysztof Groniowski, *Kwestia agrarna w Królestwie Polskim, 1871–1914* (Warsaw, 1966), p. 136.
86. Borkowski, *Chłopy polscy w dobie kapitalizmu,* p. 96; Lewis, "Revolution in the Countryside," p. 26.
87. AGAD KGGW 2495, Piotrków Governor to the WGG, March 1 (14), 1905; Paweł Korzec, ed., *Źródła do dziejów rewolucji 1905–1907 w okręgu łódzkim,* vol. 1, pt. 1 (Warsaw, 1957), pp. 547–550.

asylum with his rural relatives after his participation in the "disorders" in Radom.[88] In nearby Iłża County, peasants invoked the name of the emperor in claiming that the disputed forest land belonged to them.[89] Peasants who illegally felled timber near Przasnysz in Płock Province, with damages estimated at seven thousand rubles, were apparently persuaded in their action by soldiers returning from service in the central Russian provinces, where, according to the soldiers, "even the old ladies are chopping."[90]

Peasants also had long memories, basing their claims to easements on ancestral rights. Illegal peasant grazing on the Kłomnice estate in Noworadomsk County (Piotrków Province) was only the most recent episode in a twenty-year dispute.[91] Peasants from the gmina of Szumowo in Łomża County, led by a candidate sołtys, justified their illegal trespassing and felling of timber in the state forest with the argument that "the land belonged to our fathers."[92] State forest rangers in Wieluń County (Kalisz Province), in attempting to remove trespassing villagers from Dzietrzyniki, were told by resisting peasants that this part of the forest had been "stolen" from their ancestors and that they were only reclaiming what was rightfully theirs.[93]

Ambiguities in government policy also played a role in encouraging illegal peasant behavior. As an economic concession to assist the rural economy, the Ministry of Agriculture and State Domains decided in the late spring to permit peasants to pasture livestock in specially designated areas of state forests where grazing did not harm young growth. The concession, instead of being greeted by peasant gratitude, was immediately misconstrued as a license for free, unrestricted access to state forests. For example, six hundred peasants from the villages of Wilków and Psary in Kielce County took the ministry's decision to mean that they now had the right to graze two cows each in the nearby state forest. The villagers, armed with clubs and scythes, could not be persuaded that they had been misinformed. Subsequently, the Land Guard arrested one of the peasant leaders, but a crowd liberated him from the gmina jail. Finally the Land Guard, this time assisted by dragoons, arrested sixteen peasants involved in the storming of the jail and other acts of resistance to the authorities.[94]

88. Kalabiński and Tych, *Walki chłopów* 1: 605–607.
89. AGAD KGGW 2518, Radom Governor to the WGG, January 30 (February 12), 1905.
90. AGAD KGGW 2517, Płock Governor to the WGG, December 7 (20), 1905.
91. Kalabiński and Tych, *Walki chłopów* 1: 506.
92. AGAD KGGW 2510, Łomża Governor to the WGG, March 2 (15), 1905.
93. AGAD KGGW 2506, Kalisz Governor to the WGG, April 25 (March 8), 1905.
94. AGAD KGGW 2509, Kielce Governor to the WGG, June 9 (22), June 21 (July 4), and June 25 (July 8), 1905.

The Szydłowiec state forest, spanning parts of three counties in Radom Province, provided the setting for a similar chain of incidents. Conflict between dozens of villages and state authorities began in mid-May when the state raised its fee for pasturing livestock from nine to forty kopecks per head. Peasants were given until June 2 to pay the new fee or remove their livestock. But when they learned from various newspapers about the government's concessions on access to state forests, the peasants refused to pay any fee and violently resisted the attempts of rangers and the Land Guard to halt their operations. Eventually, after several weeks of illegal grazing and felling, a "flying detachment" of Cossacks successfully dislodged the trespassing villagers. Arrest warrants were issued for twenty-four "main agitators," who subsequently received jail sentences ranging from one week to two months, a mild punishment considering that the Radom governor had recommended their exile from the Kingdom.[95]

The greatest number of trespassing incidents resulting from misinterpretations of government concessions occurred in the Spała imperial forest, one of the tsar's favorite hunting grounds, which spanned large parts of Piotrków and Radom provinces. After the ministry's decision, peasants from 130 villages arbitrarily grazed their livestock and, to a lesser extent, cut down timber in the forest. Peasants, defending what they considered their legitimate rights, resisted efforts to remove them with clubs and axes. As the tsar was personally concerned, the minister of Internal Affairs took charge, ordering the dispatch of four squadrons of cavalry to stop the trespassing, arrest the leaders, and sequester the peasants' livestock.[96] Peasants in Opoczno County (Radom Province) continued to graze their cattle in Spała, however, until disease rather than troops forced them to remove their livestock.[97]

The government's inconsistent application of repressive measures in response to the trespassing incidents added to the confusion. Generally, resort to military force came quickly when the peasants continued to trespass on state property and resisted forest guards and rural police. On private estates, however, the government tried to rely on mediation and other political means to end disputes. Some officials proved less than sympathetic to complaining landowners. The chief of Noworadomsk County (Piotrków Province), for example, refused to intervene on behalf of the landowner Ziółkowski, who "grossly exaggerated" an incident of illegal grazing on

---

95. AGAD KGGW 2519, Radom Governor to the WGG, June 13 (26), June 14 (27), and July 3 (16), 1905; Kalabiński and Tych, *Walki chłopów*, 1: 626–627, 631, 638–644.
96. AGAD KGGW 2519, Minister of Internal Affairs to the WGG, June 8 (21), 1905.
97. Kalabiński and Tych, *Walki chłopów*, 1: 634–635.

A servitudes dispute. Contemporary drawing by M. Kościelniak, 1905. (Muzeum Niepodległości 24539)

his estate.[98] The Piotrków governor, who requested several squadrons of cavalry to end trespassing in the Spała imperial forest, restricted his intervention in incidents on private estates to dispatching county officials and peasant commissars to the scene, where they were to resolve matters "without the spilling of blood."[99] Sometimes, the peasants' use of force against estate officials compelled the state to intervene, particularly on the 250,000 acres of forests owned by the Zamoyski estates in Lublin and Siedlce provinces, where some 148 villages engaged in illegal logging and pasturing. Even then, provincial authorities subsequently tried to persuade Count Zamoyski to drop his lawsuits against the offending peasants.[100]

Peasants often asserted their claim to easement rights by denying access to others. In July, peasants from the village of Prusy in Stopnica County (Kielce Province), led by their elder, refused to permit agricultural workers employed by a neighboring estate to graze livestock on a parcel of disputed land.[101] More frequently, they interfered with the operations of logging

98. Ibid., pp. 501–502.
99. Ibid., pp. 516–517; Korzec, Źródła do dziejów rewolucji 1 (1): 562–564.
100. Lewis, "Revolution in the Countryside," p. 27; APL KGL 1906:155, Lublin Governor to Count Konstanty Zamoyski, August 30 (September 12), 1906.
101. AGAD KGGW 2509, Kielce Governor to the WGG, July 16 (29), 1905.

firms in forests belonging to private estates. One of the more famous incidents occurred in a forest owned by Count Zamoyski in Biłgoraj County
(Lublin Province) which had been leased to the A. Franke Lumber Company. At the end of March, twenty peasants appeared at the site and demanded a halt to logging operations. When the lumberjacks refused, a
crowd of fifty peasants arrived the next day, confiscated the logging equipment, and drove the Franke workers from the forest.[102] Peasant opposition
to logging operations also made its way into gmina assembly resolutions.
For example, the Wyszków gmina assembly (Warsaw Province) at its quarterly meeting in late December demanded not only unlimited access to
state forests but an end to all timber exports as well.[103]

Although peasant assertion of easement rights sometimes merged with
gmina action, servitudes disputes were more likely to promote class antag-
onisms in rural society and thereby undermine the polonization movement.
The Endecja, the main political force behind gmina action, came out
strongly against illegal peasant trespassing, claiming that the agrarian disputes were fanned by ''subversives'' and provided the Russian government
a pretext for employing military force.[104] Such appeals to national solidarity, however, were largely ineffective among peasants convinced of the
legitimacy of their claims. The Kalisz governor reported that although
gmina action was widespread in his province, in economic matters peasants
were ''looking after their own interests.''[105] In Radzyń County (Siedlce
Province) peasants met with landowners on the Milianów estate, where the
latter tried to win them over to the idea of gmina action. The peasants
began to leave, however, when told that this did not mean they could fell
timber and graze cattle on private estates.[106] Likewise, nationalist agitation
made little headway in Zamość County (Lublin Province), the scene of
some of the more bitter servitudes disputes.[107]

Disputes over land use in rural society, moreover, were not confined to
peasants and noble landowners, even though they certainly represented the
vast majority of cases. In Tomaszów County (Lublin Province) the neigh-

102. APL KGL 1905:120, Chief of Biłgoraj County to the Lublin Governor, March 31 (April
13), 1905.
103. APW WGZŻ 1711, Protocol of the Wyszków Gmina Assembly Meeting, December
15 (28), 1905.
104. APW WGZŻ 1747, Appeal of the National Democratic Organization in Opatów, November 1905.
105. AGAD KGGW 2507, Kalisz Governor to the WGG, October 29 (November 11), 1905.
106. AGAD KGGW 2526, Report of the SDPA to the WGG, September 2 (15), 1905.
107. AGAD KGGW 2515, Provisional Governor-General of Lublin Province to the WGG,
November 18 (December 1), 1905.

boring Catholic and Orthodox villages of Nabróż and Radków, respectively, had their long-standing dispute over common land referred to the gmina court. When the court found in favor of the latter, the Catholic peasants vented their dissatisfaction with the decision by attacking the victors.[108] In Radom Province, factory workers from Ostrowiec intervened on behalf of tenant farmers in a dispute over common land with peasant proprietors from the village of Godzielin. In this instance, only the timely mediation of Opatów County officials prevented a violent confrontation.[109] The Jewish community of Międzyrzec in Siedlce Province illegally gathered wood on an estate, of the same name, where it claimed servitude rights. Police arrested ten community leaders, and when a crowd of one thousand Jews attempted to free them, it had to be dispersed by military force. Similarly, the Jewish inhabitants of Węgrów, also in Siedlce Province, in their property dispute with the owners of local flour mills, were responsible for eight thousand rubles in damages resulting from trespassing incidents at the end of May.[110]

In all these incidents, more extreme manifestations of rural class conflict—namely, actual peasant land seizures and attacks on individual nobles and their property—were indeed rare, particularly in comparison with the central Russian provinces. Overall, there were only fourteen cases of peasant land seizure in the Kingdom of Poland during the revolution; of these, half took place in Lublin Province.[111] Where they did occur, they were based almost entirely on disputes over access and compensation, rather than ownership. In March, 150 peasants attacked the manor of Józef Klemensowski, owner of the Celejów estate in Lublin Province, after he refused to turn over eight morgs (approximately eleven acres) of land in exchange for lost servitudes.[112] Similarly, villagers from Skurcza in Gawrolin County (Siedlce Province) arbitrarily seized sixty morgs (eighty acres) of land long disputed with the owner of the Wilga estate.[113] In fact, only one documented land seizure was not related to servitudes; in Częstochowa County, four hundred peasants seized two morgs of land from the Mykanów estate for the construction of a chapel.[114]

108. APL KGL 1906:91, Chief of the Lublin Provincial Gendarmes to the Lublin Governor, January 14 (27), 1906.
109. Kalabiński and Tych, Walki chłopów 1: 619–620.
110. AGAD KGGW 2525, Report of the SDPA to the WGG, March 21 (April 3), 1905, and 2526, Report of the SDPA to the WGG, May 23 (June 5), 1905.
111. Lewis, "Revolution in the Countryside," p. 28.
112. Kalabiński and Tych, Walki chłopów 1: 136–137.
113. AGAD KGGW 2526, Siedlce Governor to the WGG, July 28 (August 10), 1905.
114. AGAD KGGW 2498, Report of the SDPA to the WGG, September 17 (30), 1905.

In disputes over easement rights on private and state property, peasants generally engaged in willful acts of civil disobedience. Open violation of property rights, most often coupled with resistance until confronted by superior force, characterized peasant behavior. Peasants considered their clearly illegal behavior legitimate, based on just claims and rights recently lost. Only in rare instances did they allow their hunger for additional land to extend beyond those claims and perceived rights. Peasant action may have been arbitrary, even lawless, in the effort to defend or recapture easement rights, but it knew certain limits. The vigilante movement in the countryside, in contrast, recognized almost no legal boundaries as peasants took the law into their own hands.

### Rural Vigilantism

Peasant reliance on the instrumentalities of popular justice in Russian Poland, of course, long predated the first decade of the twentieth century. As in other cultures, popular justice, or *samosąd* (literally, self-justice), among the Polish peasantry had multiple applications: to enforce compliance with locally established mores, to punish petty theft and other property transgressions involving members of the local community, or to protect the village from threats posed by "outsiders."[115] When dealing with their own members, village communities relied on traditional forms of ritualized public humiliation, rather than outright violence, to prevent future violations of customary standards or recognized property rights. Violence was usually reserved for "outsiders" who themselves had committed an act of violence against individual villagers or were believed to constitute a danger to the community as a whole. Peasants resorted to popular justice because it was "natural" but also because they believed it to be a more effective deterrent than a regular legal system that had yet to take deep root in the countryside.

What distinguished popular justice during the revolution in Russian Poland was a dramatic upsurge in violent vigilante actions directed at criminal elements and resulting in scores of fatalities. Like the cases involving illegal peasant trespassing, the number of violent incidents of samosąd began to escalate in the spring of 1905 and peaked during the last three months of the year. Unlike the mass trespassing incidents, which declined dramatically after the implementation of martial law at the end of 1905, vi-

---

115. Cf. Stephen P. Frank, "Popular Justice, Community, and Culture among the Russian Peasantry, 1870–1900," *Russian Review* 46 (1987): 239–265.

gilantism remained a relatively widespread phenomenon in the Polish countryside throughout 1906 and well into 1907. It also appears to have had greater range. During a two-year period from May 1905 to May 1907, twenty-eight counties in nine provinces reported incidents of violent vigilantism.[116] Yet vigilantism, like illegal peasant trespassing, was hardly a unified and organized mass movement, as village communities responded individually to local stimuli. For example, in Siedlce Province vigilante activity was confined to the summer months of 1905; in Płock Province, peasant samosądy peaked in the early autumn of 1906. In Lublin and Warsaw provinces, in contrast, vigilantism was a more or less constant feature of the entire period.

Systematic scholarly analysis of peasant samosądy during the revolution is nonexistent. Nevertheless, it is not particularly difficult to determine the causes of the dramatic increase. First, as mentioned, the efficacy of popular justice was deeply rooted in village tradition. Second, though official statistics are not especially reliable, they do denote a sharp increase in rural crime rates at the turn of the century, partly from the general increase in population, partly from the deterioration of the rural police as a crime deterrent. Exceedingly overburdened, understaffed, and poorly paid, the Land Guard found it difficult to cope with organized bands of criminals who cooperated in extensive networks, engaged in armed robbery over large areas, and lived in their own heavily guarded settlements. Demoralized elements of the Land Guard, moreover, frequently found it in their interest, physical or financial, to turn a blind eye, allowing the criminal to work without fear of capture. A populist pamphlet of the era no doubt expressed peasant perceptions: "We all know full well that our police are pals of the thieves. If something is stolen and the injured party turns to the police, they either will not make an effort to investigate, or they only pretend to investigate—of course, in such a way that they do not find the guilty party."[117]

Peasants lived in constant fear of these gangs, as reporting their activities frequently invited revenge. Yet the gangs also inspired a burning hatred among their victims; for the theft of a peasant's horse or livestock could bring economic ruin to a household. With the gradual decline, then near collapse, of Russian authority in the Polish countryside over the course of

---

116. These figures are based on data collected by the author from Polish central and provincial archives; unfortunately, because documentary sources refer both to specific incidents and to "several" or "a number" of vigilante actions in a given locality, more elaborate quantification is rendered impossible.
117. Quoted by Lewis, "Revolution in the Countryside," p. 22.

1905, coupled with the preoccupation of the police with combating political agitation, social disturbances, and the like, criminal elements took advantage of the situation to increase their parasitic activities. Yet the breakdown in government authority also eliminated the most important barrier to the peasants' ridding their communities of the gangs of armed robbers and horse thieves through their own action. The result was a wave of mob violence in the countryside unprecedented in the postemancipation era.

The rural vigilante movement began in the late spring of 1905 in Piotrków and Siedlce provinces. In early June, peasants from the village of Śrock in Piotrków County, after attending morning Mass, broke into the gmina jail and beat two thieves to death.[118] Six weeks later, the body of the locally notorious Józef Woszczak turned up near the village of Dobroń in Łask County. In this case, the thief had been apprehended by the peasants themselves during an attempted armed robbery.[119]

In Łuków County of Siedlce Province, groups of peasant vigilantes killed four thieves and administered severe beatings to two others in mid-June. Seven criminals, fearing similar action against themselves, voluntarily turned themselves in to local authorities. This attempt to escape popular justice failed, however, when a crowd of forty broke into the county jail.[120] Similarly, in Radzyń County, five thieves were beaten to death in early July; of the five, only one had actually been convicted of a crime.[121]

All of this paled in comparison with the scale of vigilantism in Włodawa County, the scene of a recent crime wave and where a number of gmina assemblies had complained bitterly that the authorities were not taking sufficient action. The theft of church money and valuables in the town of Włodawa on July 15 served as the trigger: the incident incited a crowd of two hundred Christians, who were then joined by Jewish teenagers, to hunt down the suspects. Three "well-known" thieves were caught and beaten, another drowned in a pond, and five others turned themselves in.[122] The movement then spread to surrounding villages, where crowds of peasants, numbering up to a thousand, set off in search of known and suspected thieves. Alarmed by the size of the crowds, the Włodawa County chief issued a circular forbidding samosądy and warning peasants that they would be punished if they continued their violent action. Instead, he invited

---

118. AGAD KGGW 348, Piotrków Governor to the WGG, June 4 (17), 1905.
119. Ibid., July 14 (27), 1905.
120. AGAD KGGW 341, Siedlce Governor to the WGG, June 14 (27), 1905, and 2526, Report of the SDPA to the WGG, June 13 (26), 1905.
121. AGAD KGGW 2526, Siedlce Governor to the WGG, June 25 (July 8), 1905.
122. Ibid., July 20 (August 2), 1905, and 341, Report of the SDPA to the WGG, July 23 (August 5), 1905.

peasants to report the criminals to the authorities. At the same time, the Siedlce governor sent urgent appeals to both the Catholic and Orthodox clergy to denounce vigilantism in their homilies. Not that clerical influence always deterred the peasants. One priest who interfered with a vigilante action after Mass in Kriwowerba was told, "If you defend a thief, you too are a thief." The crowd went on to murder six criminals.[123]

Most crowds, although they failed to disperse, nevertheless rounded up dozens of thieves and escorted them to county officials in Włodawa. Between August 7 and August 9 alone, peasants deposited fifty-two thieves in the county jail. Claiming that "they want[ed] to be able to sleep at night without fear of being robbed," the peasants warned the county chief that they would kill his prisoners if they were released.[124]

The story, unfortunately, does not have a happy ending. To prevent the anger of the population from falling on the police, the county chief detained the thieves for several weeks. Formal charges could not be brought against many of them, however, and the chief eventually ordered their release. Some villages then tried a different tack. For example, the inhabitants of Dubeczno petitioned the Siedlce governor to exile eleven thieves from their midst. Because eight had not been formally charged with a crime, only three of the named persons were deported from the province. Meanwhile, the criminals took their revenge. Shortly after the Siedlce governor proclaimed an end to samosądy in Włodawa County, the homes of peasants from Chmelew and Lubicin were set ablaze by arsonists in retaliation for the villages' participation in the vigilante movement.[125]

In the autumn, the center of the movement shifted to Warsaw and Lublin provinces. Beginning with a samosąd carried out by thirty peasants in the gmina of Łukowiec in Nowomińsk County in early September, the movement in Warsaw Province soon ranged over six counties.[126] In Warsaw County, peasant samosądy followed on the heels of and may have been inspired by a wave of working-class attacks on criminal gangs in Warsaw's industrial suburbs.[127] In Płońsk County, inhabitants from several villages

123. AGAD KGGW 2526, Report of the SDPA to the WGG, August 17 (30), 1905, and Siedlce Governor to the WGG, August 26 (September 8), 1905.
124. AGAD KGGW 2526, Reports of the SDPA to the WGG, August 1 (14) and August 4 (17), 1905, and Siedlce Governor to the WGG, August 2 (15), 1905; and 341, Siedlce Governor to the WGG, August 17 (30), 1905.
125. AGAD KGGW 2526, Siedlce Governor to the WGG, September 12 (25), 1905; 2527, Siedlce Governor to the WGG, October 7 (20), 1905; and 341, Report of the SDPA to the WGG, September 21 (October 4), 1905.
126. AGAD KGGW 2503, Warsaw Governor to the WGG, August 27 (September 9), 1905.
127. AGAD KGGW 342, Warsaw Governor to the WGG, October 12 (25), 1905.

went on a rampage against criminals in late October, leaving five victims in their wake.[128] A distinguishing feature of the vigilante movement in Warsaw Province, especially in the months after the October Manifesto, was the attempt to institutionalize popular justice as an alternative to the regular legal system. The gmina of Belsk in Grójec County resolved to form its own police and claimed that if the authorities released a criminal, "he will then be brought before the people's court."[129] Peasant courts and committees to prosecute criminals were also set up in the gminy of Radecznica, Wola Bogłowska, and Przybyszew.[130]

In Lublin Province, peasant vigilantism swept over seven counties, beginning in areas that were predominantly Polish in November and December and then spreading to the largely Ukrainian communities of Chełm and Zamość counties in the first months of 1906. In Lublin County, one of the few places where the agrarian section of the PPS wielded some influence in the countryside, vigilante assaults on settlements inhabited by criminals were reportedly inspired by socialist agitation.[131] If so, they provide the only cases of external involvement and organization. Dozens of peasants were arrested in these incidents, but punishment was relatively light. For example, fourteen peasants from the colony of Borzechów, the scene of a particularly violent samosąd, were sentenced to one-month jail sentences for their active leadership of a vigilante mob of two hundred.[132] The contagion of popular justice also spread to the Jewish communities scattered in small towns throughout the province. In Chełm a crowd of Jews captured sixteen local thieves and held them in a prayer house until they agreed to return the stolen goods; those who refused were administered severe beatings before the authorities could intervene.[133]

Violent samosądy were also reported in Kielce, Radom, Łomża, and Suwałki provinces in the last three months of 1905. In Iłża County (Radom Province), crowds of as many of five hundred peasants tried to eliminate criminals in the area. Dragoons stopped one of these crowds near Lipsko on November 16. When the frenzied mob refused to disperse, the soldiers

128. Ibid., November 8 (21), 1905.
129. AGAD KGGW 2505, Warsaw Governor to the WGG, December 28, 1905 (January 10, 1906).
130. Lewis, "Revolution in the Countryside," pp. 23–24.
131. AGAD KGGW 2515, Report of the SDPA to the WGG, November 16 (29), 1905, and Lublin Governor to the WGG, December 4 (17), 1905.
132. AGAD KGGW 2515, Provisional Governor-General of Lublin Province to the WGG, December 30, 1905 (January 12, 1906); APL KGL 1905:178/2, Chief of Lublin County to the Lublin Governor, December 10 (23), 1905.
133. AGAD KGGW 2515, Report of SDPA to the WGG, December 22, 1905 (January 4, 1906).

fired, mortally wounding six peasants.[134] In Suwałki Province, vigilantism was largely a Lithuanian movement. The most violent incident occurred in Mariampol County, where Lithuanian peasants waged a running battle with criminal arsons. On the night of December 14–15, a crowd pummeled seven thieves, who later died from their injuries. In this instance, the authorities were not inclined toward leniency; nine members of the crowd were arrested and charged with murder.[135]

Armed robbers and horse thieves were the overwhelming majority but not the only targets of peasant vigilantism. In May 1905, Stanisław Torka, a forest guard on the Kruszyn estate in Noworadomsk County (Piotrków Province) shot and killed the peasant Ewa Cesielska while she was illegally gathering firewood. A crowd of four hundred peasants then descended on Kruszyn, intending to carry out vigilante justice. Although stopped by estate officials and members of the Land Guard, the crowd gave them a week to turn over Torka, threatening to pillage the estate if refused. The incident ended when Torka fled before the peasants' deadline expired.[136] In January 1906, the body of a state forest ranger was found in the village of Borki in Końskie County (Radom Province). His death was apparently the work of peasant vigilantes who retaliated against the guard's behavior during recent trespassing incidents.[137] In addition to forest guards, hated members of the rural police, soldiers who had displayed excessive brutality in dealing with the local population, and gmina officials who cooperated with the execution of repressive measures all figured among the victims of peasant samosądy.

Vigilantism, although it peaked in the last months of 1905, was the most persistent of the agrarian movements. New waves of peasant violence against thieves were reported in Płock, Kielce, and Warsaw provinces in the summer of 1906 and in Lublin and Radom provinces during the winter of 1906–1907. The mere restoration of formal state authority in the countryside was not enough to eliminate the popular resort to samosądy. Only with the dramatic increase in the size of the Land Guard in subsequent years, coupled with an improvement in the material condition of the police,

---

134. AGAD KGGW 2520, Report of the SDPA to the WGG, November 15 (28), 1905, and Provisional Governor-General of Radom Province to the WGG, November 18 (December 1), 1905.

135. AGAD KGGW 2524, Suwałki Governor to the WGG, December 3 (16), 1905.

136. AGAD KGGW 2496, Report of the SDPA to the WGG, May 17 (30), 1905; APŁ KGP 515, Chief of the Piotrków Provincial Gendarmes to the Piotrków Governor, May 13 (26), 1905; Korzec, *Źródła do dziejów rewolucji* 1 (1): 587–588.

137. AGAD KGGW 517, Report of the Radom Governor's Office for the second half of January 1906.

were the authorities able to check the expanding rate of rural crime as well as the spontaneous and violently reactive response of its peasant victims. Well before then, however, when rural vigilantism was reaching its peak at the end of 1905, it merged with other movements in the Polish countryside, both organized and spontaneous, to create a situation that many high-ranking state officials in the Kingdom characterized as "complete anarchy."

### Rural Poland after the October Manifesto

The October Manifesto, with its promise of constitutional guarantees of basic civil freedoms along with a generally elected legislative assembly, also encouraged hopes for the restoration of an autonomous Kingdom of Poland. Rural Poland, the principal stage of the movement for home rule through gmina action, therefore greeted the manifesto of October 30 with genuine enthusiasm, even gratitude. The manifesto was officially proclaimed to the population during church services on Sunday, November 5, and was followed by large but peaceful demonstrations in hundreds of small towns dotting the Polish countryside. Throughout Russian Poland these national processions adhered to a fairly common pattern, indicative of a high degree of organization. They were almost exclusively initiated by National Democratic activists and sympathizers, whether landowners in Nowomińsk County (Warsaw Province), physicians in Pułtusk County (also Warsaw Province), Catholic clergy in Kalisz Province, or volunteer firemen in Ciechanów County (Płock Province).[138] Members from all walks of rural society participated in the colorful processions, which were headed by the clergy and accompanied by the orchestras of volunteer fire departments intoning "Boże coś Polskę." The volunteer firemen also assumed responsibility for preserving order. After an expression of thanks to the tsar for the new "freedoms," the crowds dispersed to their homes, which were then illuminated by candles. The only incidents of violence occurred later that night and involved the vandalism of unlit homes, usually belonging to local Russian administrative and police officials. In the town of Turek (Kalisz Province), for example, a stockbroker, a tax assessor, a no-

---

138. AGAD KGGW 2504, Warsaw Governor to the WGG, November 15 (28), 1905; 2505, Warsaw Governor to the WGG, November 22 (December 5), 1905; 2507, Kalisz Governor to the WGG, October 29 (November 11), 1905; and 2517, Report of the SDPA to the WGG, November 3 (16), 1905.

tary, a treasury official, and a postal-telegraph official, all Russians, had their windows smashed.[139]

Despite the peaceful and celebratory mood of early November, rural society did not patiently await the implementation of the new "freedoms." Encouraged by nationalist propaganda and widespread reports in the Polish press of imminent political autonomy, peasants wasted little time in stepping up their attacks on the most visible symbols of foreign rule. The destruction of Russian-language road, street, and building signs now assumed epidemic proportions in parts of Warsaw, Łomża, Lublin, Suwałki, and Siedlce provinces.[140] Elementary schools, another traditional target of rural discontent, also came under increasing popular assault. In Warsaw Province alone, sixty-six primary schools were closed in early November because of attacks on schools and teachers, boycotts by pupils and parents, or the refusal of gmina assemblies to meet contracted obligations.[141] Peasants in Iłża County (Radom Province) added state vodka stores and local government buildings to their list of "Russian" targets.[142]

In this atmosphere charged with expectations of home rule, gmina action now assumed the proportions of a tidal wave. In the three months following the October Manifesto, more than four hundred communal assemblies joined the movement for the complete polonization of rural administrative, educational, and judicial institutions. Although gmina action continued to follow orderly procedural forms, the diversity and assertive nature of the assembly resolutions point to the movement's growing popularization and radicalization. In Nieszawa County (Warsaw Province) all gmina assemblies resolved in early November to withhold funding for village schools until Polish became the exclusive language of instruction.[143] Some assemblies, like that in Lubanie, further resolved not to pay the salary of the village school teacher, to forbid the presence of members of the Land Guard at assembly meetings, and to replace bilingual road and building signs with their Polish equivalents.[144] The Czemiernik gmina assembly (Lubartów County, Lublin Province) went further: in addition to demanding

139. AGAD KGGW 2507, Report of the SDPA to the WGG, October 29 (November 11), 1905.

140. AGAD KGGW 2504, Warsaw Governor to the WGG, October 25 (November 7), 1905; 2512, Report of the SDPA to the WGG, November 18 (December 1), 1905; 2515, Report of the SDPA to the WGG, November 1 (14), 1905; 2524, Report of the SDPA to the WGG, December 5 (18), 1905; and 2527, Report of the SDPA to the WGG, November 16 (29), 1905.

141. Michal Szulkin, Strajk szkolny 1905 roku (Wrocław, 1959), pp. 151–152.

142. AGAD KGGW 2520, Report of the SDPA to the WGG, November 4 (17), 1905.

143. AGAD KGGW 2504, Warsaw Governor to the WGG, November 1 (14), 1905.

144. AGAD KGGW 2504, Report of the SDPA to the WGG, November 9 (22), 1905.

the polonization of local institutions and the barring of police functionaries from assembly meetings, it resolved to prepare the official gmina seal in Polish, to remove the settlement of disputes between peasants from the jurisdiction of peasant commissars, and to resist the implementation of administrative fines and sentences.[145]

According to the governor of Piotrków Province, gmina action gathered particular strength in those parts of his province where local community officials, namely mayors and clerks, joined the movement.[146] Indeed, as Richard Lewis has pointed out for the country as a whole, the expanded role of gmina administrators in this intense phase of the movement represented a most dramatic change in local leadership patterns.[147] Earlier viewed as "lackeys" of the Russian government because of their refusal to support or cooperate with the implementation of "illegal" assembly resolutions, mayors and clerks had lost a good deal of their authority. Some had actually been removed from office by their constituents; others had been subjected to violent physical attacks. For example, the pisarz of Ćmielów gmina (Radom Province), a well-known opponent of gmina action, was murdered on September 22.[148] The escalation of such incidents, together with the desire to maintain their positions and salaries, prompted the defection, especially after the October Manifesto, of increasing numbers of community officials to the side of the government's opponents.

The steady erosion of this former base of support in the Polish countryside, coupled with the perception that the revolutionary movement was making ever-deeper inroads among a previously apolitical peasantry, contributed to the government's decision of November 10 to extend martial law from the Warsaw and Łódź industrial regions to all of Russian Poland. But whereas military rule helped to pacify urban areas as the great general strike came to an end, it did little to restore immediate order to the villages. Concentrating its main effort in the cities, the state lacked the manpower and resources to reestablish its authority, quickly and effectively, in the countryside. To be sure, "binding" decrees were issued by the Warsaw governor-general as well as by the "temporary" provincial military governors. The local population was made liable for all property damage incurred as a result of attacks on public and state institutions; those who resisted payment could be subjected to fines of up to three thousand rubles

145. APL KGL 1905:194.
146. APŁ KGP 1521, Piotrków Governor to the WGG, January 25 (February 7), 1906.
147. Lewis, "Revolution in the Countryside," p. 15.
148. AGAD KGGW 2519, Report of the SDPA to the WGG, September 19 (October 2), 1905.

or to three months in jail.[149] In Radom Province, rural communities were made responsible for the defense of telegraph lines, railroad tracks, and bridges and financially liable for all damages to state property "regardless of the circumstances."[150]

Yet the attacks on state institutions and property continued, and efforts to collect fines from rural communities met with open resistance. In Opatów County (Radom Province), not only did rural residents refuse to defend state property, but they began actively to resist tax collection, a phenomenon that quickly spread to other parts of the province.[151] Without the means of enforcement, the state's attempt to impose martial law in rural Poland only served to exacerbate existing tensions. In Kielce Province, relatively quiet thus far according to its governor, martial law immediately transformed an "abnormal" relationship between the population and the authorities to one of "open hatred" of the former for the latter.[152] Likewise in Łomża Province, the genuine gratitude to the tsar displayed in early November quickly dissipated after the proclamation of martial law.[153]

The decision to lift martial law at the end of November, made after a mere eighteen days in force, that is, before it had made any real impact, also proved ill-advised. Again, as in early November, small towns became the scene of large Polish patriotic demonstrations. In the meantime a clear shift had occurred in popular attitudes. The largely peasant crowds now claimed victory, which is how they interpreted the lifting of martial law, and, unwilling to wait for further concessions from above, they began to seize its fruits from below. The next three weeks, from December 1 to December 22 (the date when martial law was reimposed), marked the peak of the revolution in the countryside.

During these three weeks, state power virtually collapsed as rural communities defiantly substituted "Polish" for "Russian" authority. In Płonsk and Kutno counties of Warsaw Province, gmina correspondence was conducted exclusively in Polish, whereas in the remaining counties of the province, peasants signed only the Polish text of assembly protocols.[154] In Mława County (Płock Province), one of the original centers of gmina

---

149. APŁ KGP 1518, Decree of the WGG, October 16 (29), 1905.
150. AGAD KGGW 2520, Proclamations of Provisional Governor-General of Radom Province, November 4 (17) and November 6 (19), 1905.
151. AGAD KGGW 2520, Provisional Governor-General of Radom Province to the WGG, November 9 (22), 1905.
152. AGAD KGGW 2509, Kielce Governor to the WGG, November 7 (20), 1905.
153. AGAD KGGW 2512, Report of the SDPA to the WGG, December 10 (23), 1905.
154. AGAD KGGW 2505, Warsaw Governor to the WGG, November 24 (December 7), 1905.

action, twenty-five mayors and clerks appeared before the county chief
without their Russian badges and submitted only Polish versions of their
assemblies' resolutions. Earlier they had agreed to resign en masse if the
authorities removed any of their number from office.[155] Similarly, twenty-
four gmina court officials from the first circuit of Płock Province collectively resolved to conduct legal proceedings and correspond with the
authorities exclusively in the Polish language.[156] The arbitrary and exclusive use of Polish also extended to the village schools throughout the Kingdom. Teachers who refused to abide by gmina decisions were summarily
dismissed and their schools closed. In Garwolin County (Siedlce Province),
the teachers themselves resolved to conduct lessons solely in Polish at their
local congress of December 10.[157]

Gmina assemblies, moreover, asserted the right to elect all local officials,
either in community resolutions or through direct action. For example, in
Koło County (Kalisz Province), all gmina clerks appointed by the county
chief were removed from office and replaced by newly elected ones.[158]
Other rural communities sought to democratize local government by eliminating property qualifications for participation in assembly meetings. During this period, many assemblies, such as the one in Izbica (Krasnystaw
County, Lublin Province), permitted those without voting rights to participate in its meetings, in blatant disregard of the warnings of county and
police officials who were also in attendance.[159] A late-December resolution
of the Wyszków gmina assembly (Pułtusk County, Warsaw Province) extended the vote to all inhabitants of the commune, including one hundred
people who had attended the meeting illegally and affixed their signatures
to its protocol.[160]

The democratization of gmina action at the end of 1905 indicated the
growing appeal of populist, and to a lesser extent, socialist propaganda in
the villages. Three PPS agitators, for example, attended the aforementioned

---

155. AGAD KGGW 2515, Resolutions of the Congress of Gmina Mayors and Clerks of
Mława County, November 29 (December 12) 1905, and 2517, Report of SDPA to the WGG,
December 16 (29), 1905.
156. AGAD KGGW 2517, Telegram of the Provisional Governor-General of Płock Province
to the WGG, December 11 (24), 1905, and Senior President of the Warsaw District Court
to the WGG, December 16 (29), 1905.
157. AGAD KGGW 2527, Siedlce Governor to the WGG, December 3 (16), 1905.
158. AGAD KGGW 2507, Kalisz Governor to the WGG, December 10 (23), 1905.
159. APL KGL 1905:267/2, Chief of the Lublin Provincial Gendarmes to the Lublin Governor, December 31, 1905 (January 13, 1906).
160. APW WGZŻ 1836, Resolutions of the Wyszków Gmina Assembly of December 15
(28), 1905.

Wyszków assembly meeting.[161] Populist influences, however, were making even greater inroads. In November, an appeal of the Polish People's Union (Polski Związek Ludowy—PZL) had called upon peasants to demand the convocation of a national legislature in Warsaw, equal voting rights for all community members, radical tax reform, and a limitation of the military service of the Kingdom's residents to their own country, all of which now found their way into the resolutions of several gmina assemblies.[162] Inspired by the success of this agitation, the PZL went even further in December, encouraging peasants not to pay taxes or provide recruits. It also called upon community officials to refrain from dealing with the Russian government until demands for "our own national government" had been satisfied.[163]

Such propaganda harmonized with the radical and exceedingly anarchic inclinations of the peasants themselves. The peasant tax revolt, which had begun in Radom Province in early November, spread quickly to several other provinces after the lifting of martial law. Some assemblies resolved not to pay specific taxes; others sanctioned nonpayment of all taxes. Government efforts to collect encountered violent resistance. Tax collectors were chased from the villages; local officials assisting in tax collection were physically assaulted; and county officials were prohibited from auditing community records. To break the resistance of Siemień gmina (Radzyń County) to tax collection, the Siedlce governor ordered the sequestering of peasant livestock, which was then sold at government auction.[164] Local inhabitants responded, however, by boycotting the auction. In Opatów County (Radom Province), where the tax revolt eventually involved ten gminy, the use of Cossacks to collect taxes, though temporarily successful, deprived towns in this mixed rural-industrial region of adequate troop strength.[165]

Similarly, in Opatów County, conscripts from eleven gminy refused induction into the army.[166] At the settlement of Grodzisk (Błonie County, Warsaw Province), a crowd of peasants prevented recruits from reporting for military service. Troops sent to restore order then clashed with local

161. APW WGZŻ 2484, Report of the Chief of the Warsaw Provincial Gendarmes, September 20 (October 3), 1906.
162. AGAD KGGW 2505, Appeal of the PZL, November 1905.
163. AGAD KGGW 2517, Płock Governor to the WGG, December 10 (23), 1905.
164. AGAD KGGW 2527, Siedlce Governor to the WGG, December 1 (14), 1905.
165. Kalabiński, *Carat i klasy posiadające,* pp. 388, 410.
166. AGAD KGGW 2520, Provisional Governor-General of Radom Province to the WGG, December 24, 1905 (January 6, 1906).

residents, leaving two dead in a bloody melee.[167] Throughout the Kingdom, gmina assemblies passed resolutions calling on local recruits to refuse military service. As a result of this widespread popular resistance to conscription, according to one account, the authorities were able to mobilize in the Kingdom in 1905 only 70 percent of those called up for military service.[168]

Rural communities frequently coupled their refusal to provide recruits for the tsar's army with resolutions that renounced their obligation to provide supplies (usually in the form of food and lodging) for the Land Guard and provincial gendarmes. In its resolution, the Kościelnice gmina assembly (Turek County, Kalisz Province) justified its refusal to subsidize the rural police "because the Land Guard is not necessary."[169] The Otwock assembly (Nowomińsk County, Warsaw Province) went even further, resolving to remove the Land Guard from the gmina and to replace it with a popular guard formed from local inhabitants.[170] Throughout Siedlce Province, where a branch of the monarchist and ultranationalist Union of the Russian People had recently announced its existence, crowds of peasants mustered in arms (mainly hunting weapons) to defend their communities from the rumored arrival of "Black Hundreds."[171] The formation of popular militias and self-defense forces in the countryside coincided, moreover, with the already mentioned creation of "people's courts" to administer popular justice and defend village communities from rural crime.

As peasants formed their own indigenous institutions, attacks on Russian state institutions continued to escalate. In Warsaw Province, post offices, vodka retail outlets, and local administrative offices provided the principal targets of crowds that numbered in the several hundreds. One such crowd ransacked gmina administration offices in Rudzienko, ousted the local mayor and clerk, and destroyed deeds and documents in the chancellory.[172] Rioting in the settlement of Białobrzegi (Radom Province) resulted in damages to state property in the amount of almost two thousand rubles as local residents "failed to take any measures to stop the looting and aid po-

167. AGAD KGGW 2505, Warsaw Vice-Governor to the WGG, December 2 (15), 1905, and Warsaw Governor to the WGG, December 17 (30), 1905.
168. Borkowski, *Chłopi polscy w dobie kapitalizmu*, p. 118.
169. AGAD KGGW 2507, Report of the SDPA to the WGG, November 30 (December 13), 1905.
170. APW WGZŻ 1724, Chief of the Gendarmes of Warsaw, Nowomińsk, and Radzymin counties to the Chief of the Warsaw Provincial Gendarmes, January 5 (18), 1906.
171. AGAD KGGW 2527, Siedlce Governor to the WGG, November 29 (December 12), 1905; Provisional Governor-General of Siedlce Province to the WGG, December 23 and 26, 1905 (January 4 and 7, 1906).
172. AGAD KGGW 2505, Warsaw Governor to the WGG, December 19, 1905 (January 1, 1906).

lice."[173] In the four Lithuanian countries of Suwałki Province, incidents of arson against state institutions became so widespread as to convince St. Petersburg to approve provincial requests for a localized reintroduction of martial law already on December 17.[174]

Crowd violence, moreover, did not confine itself to institutions. Gmina assemblies in Lithuanian Suwałki openly threatened police officials and gendarmes with death if they even appeared in their communities. Consequently, all twenty-four members of the Land Guard in Wyłkowyszki County were transferred to the county seat out of concern for their lives.[175] Similarly, members of the rural police in Gostynin County (Warsaw Province) and Koło County (Kalisz Province) asked to be either transferred or relieved of their duties because of threats against their lives.[176] A dramatic increase in attacks on the rural police, "even on their quarters at night," totally "terrorized" and "paralyzed" the Land Guard in Kielce Province, according to its governor.[177] Likewise in Łomża Province, those members of the Land Guard who resided among the population, few in number and poorly armed, found themselves "in an impossible situation" and were "in daily fear for their lives."[178]

Everywhere the precarious condition of the Land Guard inspired alarming reports from provincial officials bemoaning anarchy, chaos, and the collapse of civil administration. Equally alarmed were the National Democrats, who feared losing control over events in the countryside to peasant spontaneity and political rivals. Already in November, the Endecja warned against "excesses" of rural violence fanned by "subversives" which only served to provide the Russian government with a pretext for military intervention.[179] By December, the Endecja was reduced to using the argument that it would be much worse under German rule, which would be the inevitable result if the peasants listened to "the socialists."[180] The truth of the matter, however, was that by the beginning of winter, appeals for calm behavior, regardless of the quarter from which they came, could

173. AGAD KGGW 2521, Radom Governor to the WGG, February 22 (March 7), 1906.
174. AGAD KGGW 2524, Circular of the Suwałki Governor to County Chiefs, December 3 (16), 1905; and 2584, WGG to the Minister of Internal Affairs, December 2 (15), 1905.
175. AGAD KGGW 2524, Report of the SDPA to the WGG, December 5 (18), 1905.
176. AGAD KGGW 2505, Warsaw Vice-Governor to the WGG, December 3 (16), 1905; and 2507, Report of the SDPA to the WGG, December 30, 1905 (January 12, 1906).
177. AGAD KGGW 2509, Kielce Governor to the WGG, November 7 (20), 1905.
178. AGAD KGGW 2512, Provisional Governor-General of Łomża Province to the WGG, December 21, 1905 (January 3, 1906).
179. APW WGZŻ 1747, Appeal of the National Democratic Organization in Opatów, November 1905.
180. AGAD KGGW 2505, Warsaw Governor to the WGG, December 14 (27), 1905.

not hope to restore order in a situation where organized state authority had seemingly evaporated. To reestablish that authority, the Russian government reintroduced martial law to the entire Kingdom on December 22.

In the course of 1905, revolution indeed came to the Polish countryside. Though not marked by violent social upheavals of peasants against the landed class, the revolt nevertheless resulted in a displacement, albeit temporary, of Russian authority from rural Poland. The creation of an alternative authority by popular forces from below to fill the vacuum left by the temporary abandonment of the countryside by Russian officials, nevertheless, failed to happen. To be sure, for the first time in its history, the peasantry of Russian Poland became actively engaged in political life. As a consequence of its inexperience, however, that engagement became absorbed more in the elimination of existing institutions than in their replacement by viable alternatives that could withstand a reassertion of state power. Makeshift people's courts could not substitute for a regular system of justice, nor could ''secret instruction'' be mistaken for a system of education. Popular guards and militias likewise failed to take the place of a regular police and army. Russian military rule, once it was applied with far greater seriousness of purpose, easily swept these ad hoc popular institutions away.

Yet restoring order in the Polish countryside proved no easy task, despite the severity of martial law after December 22. In some provinces, the process lasted months, elsewhere years. In the meantime, gmina assemblies continued to pass illegal resolutions; armed bands continued to attack state institutions; rural police and county officials remained targets of assassins; educational institutions remained closed; and vigilantism continued to claim victims among the criminal element. Eventually, through a massive injection of additional personnel and resources, the Russian government succeeded in arresting the upheaval that had engulfed the Polish countryside by the end of 1905. It never succeeded, however, in fully reestablishing the institutional authority of the state over the rural population.

# THE STRUGGLE OVER
# EDUCATION

Already on the eve of the Russo-Japanese War, students in the Kingdom's institutions of higher and secondary education formed the most politicized social group in the country. Although divided by ideological differences, party sympathies, and ethnicity, students had been prepared by established traditions of self-organization and political protest for the role of an avantgarde in the antiwar and antimobilization movements of 1904. Incidents inside the schools multiplied, and by the end of the year rumors of a nationwide student strike were rife.

Preparations for some sort of broad student action were still in the planning stage, however, when industrial workers preempted them with their own massive general strike. The sudden emergence of a mass, though politically inchoate, labor movement galvanized the students at the end of January, particularly in Warsaw. Within weeks, students strikes had spread throughout the country, fanned by political agitation, varying degrees of parental sympathy, and government bungling. The perseverance of the students, coupled with mounting strike-associated violence, led to minor concessions in the spring and summer. The political unacceptability of these concessions, which were both too little and too late, transformed the student strikes into a nationwide popular boycott of state educational institutions at all levels in the fall.

Despite even greater government concessions, the boycott continued into 1906 and beyond. By that time, however, the struggle over education had long ceased to be merely a bipolar affair between Polish society and the Russian state over the language of instruction, curricula, and faculty appointments. As the "Muscovite" educational model declined in the face of popular rejection, competing "Catholic," "national," and "progressive'' models emerged to fill the vacuum. In the end, the inability of the Polish actors to reach a compromise with each other played into the hands of the resilient Russian authorities and doomed or undermined all the Polish alternatives. By the eve of the Great War, the state's revamped system, though no longer the tool of russification it once was, had been restored as the main instrument for educating the Kingdom's young generation.

## The Warsaw Epicenter

On January 28, as the general strike of industrial workers moved into high gear, meetings involving hundreds of students convened at Warsaw University and the Polytechnical Institute. At both institutions the organizational impetus came from the more radical student groups, who used existing mutual-aid associations to mobilize their colleagues. Zjednoczenie (Unity), the student self-help organization at the Polytechnical Institute, was formed in 1898, shortly after the opening of the institute. Unlike its counterpart at Warsaw University, Zjednoczenie did not split into nationalist and socialist wings.[1] Consequently, 850 of the institute's 1,169 enrolled students answered Zjednoczenie's call to convene at eleven in the morning of the twenty-eighth, led by a core of approximately 200 activists roughly divided between the nationalist youth organization Zet and the Union of Socialist Youth.[2] A police cordon quickly surrounded the institute, as students debated until five o'clock the next morning the wording of a resolution to be presented to the school's director. By that time, their number had dwindled to 300. These, too, departed when the director refused to meet with their elected delegates, who were to deliver a compromise resolution containing demands for both the ''nationalization'' and ''democratization'' of the institute. Anticipating a strike, the director temporarily suspended classes and closed the school until order could be restored.[3]

The restoration of ''order'' proved elusive, however, as the student revolt spread to other institutions. At the end of February the Polytechnical Institute's Pedagogic Council, by a majority of thirteen to four, voted to

---

1. Bogdan Nowroczyński, ed., *Nasza walka o szkołę polską, 1901–1917: Opracowania, wspomnienia, dokumenty,* vol. 1 (Warsaw, 1932), pp. 259–274.
2. AGAD KGGW 2581, Report of the Director of the Warsaw Polytechnical Institute to the Institute's Pedagogic Council, February 11 (24), 1905.
3. AGAD KGGW 2488, Director of the Warsaw Polytechnical Institute to the SDPA, January 16 (29), 1905.

close the institute for the remainder of the semester.[4] Ironically, the closing of the institute brought an end to Zjednoczenie as well. When the institute reopened for the fall semester (this too proved temporary), the ideological gulf between nationalist and socialist student sympathizers could no longer be bridged by common interests. Coexistence in a mutual-aid organization, particularly in the charged political atmosphere of September and October, had become unthinkable.

At Warsaw University, where the nationalist Pomoc Bratnia (Fraternal Aid) competed with the socialist Spójnia (Union), such coexistence had ended already in 1899 over the issue of solidarity with the strikes and protest actions of Russian students of that year. Although Pomoc Bratnia remained the larger of the two mutual-aid organizations, it was Spójnia that initiated the meeting of students at the university on January 28. Inability to agree on a common set of resolutions and demands in advance of the gathering led to a nationalist boycott.[5] Consequently, only 432 of the 1,661 enrolled students attended the socialist-sponsored meeting. This minority resolved to strike if its demands for polonization and democratization of the university were not met. The students then dispersed without incident on the arrival of the police, whose subsequent investigation turned up vandalized portraits of the tsar and a few littered appeals printed by the Warsaw committee of the Bund.[6]

Only later would the nationalist students join the strike at Warsaw University. Their position may have been confused somewhat by the attitude of their elders in the National League and the Endecja. Though vocal proponents of the polonization of the country's public educational system, the political leaders of the nationalist movement opposed strikes as a matter of principle. The rapid spread of the student strike to Warsaw's secondary schools, however, led to a change of heart. Already on January 28, pupils at the Real School, followed by their counterparts at the Rontaler School of Commerce, the Second, Fourth and Fifth Boys' gymnasia, and the Second Girls' Gymnasium, walked out of their classes.[7] Although political

4. AGAD KGGW 2581, Protocol of the Pedagogic Council of the Warsaw Polytechnical Institute, February 15 (28), 1905.
5. Nowroczyński, *Nasza walka o szkołę polską* 1: 241; see also Edmund Staszyński, *Polityka oświatowa caratu w Królestwie Polskim: Od powstania styczniowego do I wojny światowej* (Warsaw, 1968), pp. 126–130.
6. APW WGZŻ 1010, Chief of the Warsaw Okhrana to the Chief of the Warsaw Provincial Gendarmes, January 27 (February 9), 1905.
7. Staszyński, *Polityka oświatowa*, pp. 131–135; Nowroczyński, *Nasza walka o szkołę polską* 1:293–340, 345–348; Stanisław Kalabinski, ed., *Carat i klasy posiadające w walce z rewolucją 1905–1907 w Królestwie Polskim: Materiały archiwalne* (Warsaw, 1956), pp. 11–13.

initiative for this largely unplanned turn of events seemed to rest with the Union of Socialist Youth, many students who sympathized with the nationalist movement joined in the strikes and participated in the work of ad hoc committees created to draft student demands. These strike committees, in turn, sent representatives to a Circle of Delegates, set up in early February to coordinate the student movement in Warsaw's secondary schools.[8] It was at this point that the Endecja decided to accept the student strikes as a fait accompli and to give the movement a "national" character by attempting to take over its leadership, beginning with the Circle of Delegates. At the same time, the Endecja created a special organization, the Union for the Nationalization of the Schools (Związek Unarodowienie Szkół), to counter the influence of the "progressive," that is, liberal and socialist, Circle of Educators (Koło Wychowawców), the only organization among adults to come out immediately in support of the student strike movement.[9]

Before that movement could spread even further, however, Curator Aleksandr N. Schwartz of the Warsaw Educational District ordered the closing of all Warsaw schools for the duration of the workers' general strike. This preventive action served only to give the student movement an opportunity to organize itself more efficiently, as the Circle of Delegates, now roughly balanced between socialist and nationalist sympathizers, hammered out a compromise set of demands for the thirty-six schools it came to represent. Once factories and plants in Warsaw resumed operations, Schwartz attempted a gradual and selective reopening of the city's secondary schools beginning on February 8. The curator's strategy backfired miserably. At the Rontaler School and at the Third, Fourth, and Fifth Boys' gymnasia, a majority of the students boycotted classes. At the Fourth Girls' Gymnasium, Jewish students joined their Catholic colleagues, mainly from the fifth, sixth, and seventh forms, in a walkout that forced the closing of the school.[10] As a result, Schwartz again suspended instruction in all Warsaw secondary schools on February 11 and turned to punitive measures. The authorities ordered the arrest of twenty-five student activists, mainly on the charge that they had prevented others from attending classes.[11] At the Fifth Boys' Gymnasium, school authorities expelled fifty-three students

8. Nowroczyński, *Nasza walka o szkołę polską* 1: 274–283.

9. Stanislaw Kozicki, *Historia Ligi Narodowej: Okres 1887–1907* (London, 1964), pp. 247–250; Halina Kiepurska, *Inteligencja zawodowa Warszawy* (Warsaw, 1967), pp. 102–104.

10. Nowroczyński, *Nasza walka o szkołę polską* 1:348–354; AGAD KGGW 2488, Report of the SDPA to the WGG, January 29 (February 11), 1905.

11. Michał Szulkin, *Strajk szkolny 1905 roku* (Wrocław, 1959), pp. 61–64.

identified as strike leaders. Similar action was taken at the Fourth Girls' Gymnasium.[12]

The repressive measures were aimed as much at parental and adult opinion as at the student "troublemakers." In the first weeks of the Warsaw school strike, that opinion had not been particularly sympathetic to the students. Conservative groups as well as the Roman Catholic episcopate opposed the student walkouts in no uncertain terms; the majority of parents and guardians, although they may have sympathized with certain goals of the strike, nevertheless opposed the students' methods.[13] Given this relatively favorable climate of opinion, Schwartz scheduled a meeting with concerned "parents" for February 19 at the Warsaw Museum of Industry and Agriculture. With the walkouts spreading to the provinces, the curator obviously hoped to gain from the meeting a resolution condemning the strikes and thereby exert parental pressure on the students to return to classes. The endorsement of the student strikes by the Endecja, however, did much to frustrate the curator's plans. Some fifteen hundred prominent citizens and parents turned up for the meeting with Schwartz, and although the majority remained ambivalent toward the strike, they approved a resolution demanding Polish as the language of instruction in the Kingdom's schools.[14]

This resolution, although a blow to the authorities, appeared as a betrayal to certain student leaders, especially given that the older generation had remained silent on other issues affecting the schools. Even students who belonged to organizations connected with the nationalist movement had concerns that went beyond the mere polonization of the schools. In the Circle of Delegates they had agreed to support "progressive" demands for placing the public schools under the control of "society" and for an end to restrictions and discrimination in admissions policy. Socialist and liberal student leaders, of course, had more far-reaching demands, including coeducation, freedom of assembly and speech in the schools, the establishment of universal primary education at public expense, and an end to compulsory religious instruction.[15] Despite these differences, which more

---

12. Nowroczyński, *Nasza walka o szkołę polską* 1: 336–337, 354.
13. Kiepurska, *Inteligencja zawodowa Warszawy*, p. 104; Staszyński, *Polityka oświatowa,* pp. 153–154.
14. AGAD AB, XIX-10. An excellent account of the public meeting with Schwartz was published by the liberal newspaper *Iskra,* no. 6 (February 19, 1905). See also Kiepurska, *Inteligencja zawodowa Warszawy*, pp. 105–107; Szulkin, *Strajk szkolny 1905 roku,* pp. 66–67; and Staszyński, *Polityka oświatowa,* pp. 149–150.
15. For a comparison of nationalist and "progressive" postulates as presented in the debates of the Warsaw Circle of Delegates, see Staszyński, *Polityka oświatowa,* pp. 143–145.

than once threatened student solidarity, the central committee of the Circle of Delegates considered it necessary to reaffirm its original strike demands in a public appeal of February 26. The appeal reminded adults that youth were fighting not only for Polish schools but also for a more "democratic" system of education; the statement also served to prevent a break with Jewish students, who had joined the walkout in considerable numbers.[16]

Curator Schwartz, meanwhile, chose to ignore the parental resolution altogether and went ahead with his plan to reopen the Warsaw middle schools on February 20. This time, striking students appeared at the schools, forming patrols to dissuade and prevent others from attending. Violent incidents, accompanied by numerous arrests, occurred at the Real School, the Fifth Boys' Gymnasium, and the Second Girls' Gymnasium.[17] At the Third Boys' Gymnasium, only sixty pupils out of a student body of more than three hundred attended classes.[18] Where Poles were in a minority of the student body, as in the Sixth Boys' Gymnasium, their action took the form of a simple walkout. The strike also spread beyond the middle schools to private schools, vocational Sunday schools attended by young artisans, and schools of commerce. At the Seven-Class Preparatory School at 61 Grzybowska Street, twelve-year-old boys led the first walkout of Polish pupils from a city primary school.[19] After a week of violent confrontations, further arrests, and ever-declining attendance, Schwartz was forced to suspend instruction once again.

The schools would remain closed for an entire month, as the authorities prepared a new wave of expulsions. For example, the Pedagogic Council of the Real School immediately decided to expel thirty-two students, two of them on "wolves' tickets," which prohibited their reenrollment in any of the empire's middle schools. A few weeks later, 361 others were expelled from the Real School "for nonpayment of tuition." After the authorities decided to reopen the schools on March 21 regardless of the number of participating students, another 107 were expelled from the Real School for nonattendance.[20] Before the spring semester had ended, 1,945 students had been expelled from the Warsaw boys' gymnasia alone.[21]

The mass and indiscriminate expulsions, coupled with the curator's decision to ignore the parental resolution of February 19, turned public

16. Nowroczyński, *Nasza walka o szkołę polską* 1: 283–292.
17. Ibid., pp. 314–315, 330–337, 343–345; AGAD KGGW 2489, Report of the Warsaw Superintendent of Police to the WGG, February 8 (21), 1905.
18. Nowroczyński, *Nasza walka o szkołę polską* 1: 348–351.
19. Ibid., pp. 365–369.
20. Ibid., pp. 315–317.
21. Staszyński, *Polityka oświatowa*, p. 166.

opinion decisively against the authorities. Only conservative groups remained opposed to the student action, but now even they considered it necessary to circumvent the unresponsive Schwartz and the educational bureaucracy in the Kingdom and to turn directly to St. Petersburg for a resolution of the school crisis. On March 9, a petition with thirty thousand signatures was handed over to Sergei Witte and the Committee of Ministers requesting the reestablishment of Polish schools in the Kingdom.[22] Meanwhile, the shift in public opinion had abetted the spread of the school strike to the provinces, a development that would force the central authorities to entertain seriously the idea of concessions.

## The School Strike in the Provinces

In the first week of February, the student strike began to spread rapidly from Warsaw to the outlying provinces. As early as February 4, Warsaw governor-general Chertkov wired the Ministry of Internal Affairs with the alarming information that instruction had been suspended at almost all the country's middle schools, prompted by student walkouts over Polish language demands and preventive closings.[23] A few days after Chertkov's telegram, gymnasia in Biała, Płock, and Włocławek joined the list.[24]

Already on January 30, the Lublin Boys' Gymnasium had suspended classes. There, students struck not in solidarity with the Warsaw student movement and Polish language demands but as a result of an incident within the school.[25] Provincial authorities soon found good reason, however, to keep the school closed. At the nearby Institute of Agriculture and Forestry in Puławy, long a hotbed of student unrest, a majority of the students voted on February 3 to strike for the remainder of the academic year.[26] Meanwhile, a Zet delegate arrived in Lublin from Warsaw to help organize walkouts and prepare student petitions in the middle schools. To preempt a strike at the Lublin Girls' Gymnasium, the governor ordered its closing, along with all other schools in the city, on February 3. The schools reopened in Lublin on February 8, but two days later, more than one hundred girls walked out of the gymnasium after demanding Polish as the

---

22. Ibid., p. 152.
23. AGAD KGGW 2488, Telegram of the WGG to the Ministry of Internal Affairs, January 22 (February 4), 1905.
24. Staszyński, *Polityka oświatowa*, pp. 135–136.
25. AGAD KGGW 2513, Report of the SDPA to the WGG, January 20 (February 2), 1905; Nowroczyński, *Nasza walka o szkołę polską* 1: 471–472.
26. AGAD KGGW 2513, Report of the SDPA to the WGG, January 24 (February 6), 1905.

language of instruction as well as the introduction of Polish literature into the curriculum.[27]

As in Warsaw, parents in Lublin Province initially opposed the actions of their progeny. At the Hrubieszów Boys' Progymnasium, a student walkout collapsed after a couple of days as a result of active parental intervention against the strike.[28] At the same time, a parental committee formed to negotiate with school authorities at the Lublin Boys' Gymnasium, thus deliberately undermining a recently formed student strike committee. The gulf separating the generations seemed unbridgeable to Mieczysław Skrzetuski, a student leader at the gymnasium: "Fathers and sons: these were two separate worlds. Unable to understand each other, they fought each other instead. The older generation spoke of constructive work, about positions and wealth. On the other hand, we were the 'madmen' [szalency] of that time, nurtured in the underground and on the romanticism of our great poets. We wanted to fight; we had no concern for our careers or for personal success."[29] Soon after meeting with the parents, the authorities decided to reopen the school on February 21 after a selective expulsion of twenty-eight students distinguished by their active role in the strike. In this case, however, the young people held firm as a majority continued to boycott classes. Their number increased after a bomb exploded on school grounds the evening of March 5. By the end of the month, the authorities had expelled more than two hundred male and female students from Lublin's middle schools, nine of them on "wolves' tickets."[30]

In Łomża, by contrast, parents stood strongly behind student demands. Łomża Province, as already noted, was an early center of the gmina action movement and its advocacy of the polonization of local administration and institutions, including the schools. As elsewhere, however, initiative for the strike in the Łomża middle schools belonged to the students themselves, and they moved into action after the arrival of a delegate from Warsaw.[31] On February 3, a majority of the students from the sixth, seventh, and eighth forms walked out of the Boys' Gymnasium. The gates were then closed by the school's administration to prevent the departure of pupils from the lower forms. The striking students subsequently forced the closing of the Łomża Girls' Gymnasium, where a partial walkout had already oc-

27. Ibid., February 10 (23), 1905.
28. Ibid., February 19 (March 4), 1905.
29. Nowroczyński, *Nasza walka o szkołę polską* 1: 469.
30. Ibid., pp. 475–477; AGAD KGGW 2501, Report of the SDPA to the WGG, March 10 (23), 1905.
31. Nowroczyński, *Nasza walka o szkołę polską* 1: 405–414.

curred, before returning to their own school. Fearful of a violent incident, the director closed the gymnasium.[32]

In an attempt to exert pressure on parents and guardians to intervene in the strike, school authorities in Łomża soon announced their decision to expel all students who failed to return to classes by February 14. This plan was undermined, however, when Curator Schwartz ordered a blanket closing of all middle schools under the jurisdiction of the Warsaw Educational District until February 20. The respite gave both students and parents an opportunity to plot further action. When instruction resumed in Łomża on that date, only a small minority of Catholic and Jewish students (thirty-three out of four hundred) attended class at the Boys' Gymnasium. By contrast, only ten Orthodox and Lutheran students (out of 115) joined the strike. Similar ratios prevailed at the Girls' Gymnasium. The next day, the percentage of Catholic pupils attending classes at the two middle schools dropped even lower.[33]

Meanwhile, hundreds of parents, including several employed by the state administration, sent a petition to the Ministry of Education in St. Petersburg in which they expressed their support of student demands for instruction in the Polish language, for Polish teachers and administrative personnel, and for a curriculum that included Polish language and history as its main subjects.[34] Both students and parents subsequently held firm to these demands, despite the immediate expulsion of twenty-nine male and fifty female students for "active participation" in the school "disorders."

Parental support also proved crucial to the success of the strike in the Kalisz middle schools. Here police reports went so far as to blame the strike on the hostile attitude of parents toward school authorities.[35] Equally important in this case was a student solidarity that crossed ethnic and religious boundaries. The written demands presented at the Kalisz Boys' Gymnasium on February 7, which placed equal weight on the goals of polonization and democratization, included the signatures of several Russian students from the upper forms as well as nearly all of the school's Jewish students. Consequently the walkouts left only eighteen students at the Boys' Gymnasium, twelve at the Girls' Gymnasium, and one student at the Kalisz Real School.[36] In March, the strike spread to the Łęczyca

32. AGAD KGGW 2510, Łomża Governor to the WGG, January 23 (February 5), 1905.
33. Ibid., February 10 (23), 1905.
34. AGAD KGGW 2510, Report of the SDPA to the WGG, February 15 (28), 1905.
35. AGAD KGGW 2506, Report of the SDPA to the WGG, February 3 (16), 1905.
36. Ibid., February 4 (17), 1905.

Teachers Seminary and the Koło School of Commerce, although at the latter, Jewish students refused to join in a walkout over exclusively "Polish-national" demands.[37]

The authorities eventually reopened all the above-mentioned schools in Kalisz Province at the end of March, even though only a small minority of enrolled students attended. In the event, the resumption of instruction was accompanied by a good deal of violence and vandalism aimed at "strike-breaking" students and their parents. On April 10, for example, a bomb was planted at the Real School. Although the bomb failed to explode, the incident nevertheless had the anticipated effect on attendance.[38]

In Łódź and its satellite towns of Zgierz and Pabianice, the Piotrków governor, on his own authority, immediately closed all schools in a preventive measure connected to the outbreak of the workers' general strike. Student declarations and walkouts in this textile industrial region were thus delayed until the end of February. Even then, only a minority of the students, almost exclusively Poles, joined in the strike, as ethnic diversity and divisions (German, Jewish, and Russian students generally outnumbered their Polish counterparts in Łódź) undermined student solidarity.[39] In such a setting, the otherwise typical demand for Polish-language instruction, even when coupled with "democratization," was more likely to draw opposition than support.

In contrast, the provincial capital of Piotrków, untouched by either labor unrest or the governor's preventive action, became the scene of major student disturbances that closed the boys and girls' gymnasia as well as the Alexander Academy, an elite six-year elementary school. Unlike in Łódź, a substantial number of Germans and Jews joined the majority of Polish students in a walkout marked by both vandalism against school property and "terror" against the parents of "strike-breaking" students. In the latter instance, this amounted to throwing ink bottles through apart-

37. AGAD KGGW 2506, Kalisz Governor to the WGG, March 9 (22), 1905. The petition of students at the Łęczyca Teachers Seminary, however, went beyond demands for instruction in the Polish language and called for an end to discrimination on admissions, freedom of speech and assembly, and the liquidation of the school authorities' extracurricular supervisory and disciplinary powers; see Paweł Korzec, ed., *Źródła do dziejów rewolucji 1905–1907 w okręgu łódzkim*, vol. 1, pt. 1 (Warsaw, 1957), pp. 630–631.

38. AGAD KGGW 2506, Kalisz Governor to the WGG, April 1 (14), 1905, and 2507, Report of the Kalisz Governor to the Emperor, mid-May 1905; Nowroczyński, *Nasza walka o szkołę polską* 1: 391–397.

39. AGAD KGGW 2494, Piotrków Governor to the WGG, January 25 (February 7), 1905; APŁ KGP 1515 (2), Declaration of Students at the Łódź Boys' Gymnasium, February 14 (27), 1905, and Report of the Director of the Łódź Girls' Gymnasium, February 17 (March 2), 1905; Nowroczyński, *Nasza walka o szkołę polską* 1: 456–461.

ment windows. The school authorities, however, acted swiftly, and by February 3, they had already expelled 257 from the Boys' Gymnasium, 186 from the Girls' Gymnasium (including thirty-three Jews specially noted by the school's director), and 137 from the Alexander Academy.[40]

As already noted, the preventive actions taken by the authorities, particularly the blanket closing of all middle schools on February 7 by Curator Schwartz, proved mostly counterproductive. Indeed the curator's decision drew loud protests from certain provincial administrative quarters. For example, the Suwałki governor expressed his disagreement with Schwartz directly to the Warsaw governor-general over the closing of the Suwałki Boys' Gymnasium, "inasmuch as no disorders have occurred there."[41] He was successful in getting the school reopened on February 16, an event marked nonetheless by a petition and walkout of 117 Polish students. As nonstriking Russians, Lithuanians, and Jews constituted the majority of the student body, however, the gymnasium remained open. The Suwałki governor also opposed the expulsion of the striking Poles as premature, with an eye to allowing parents and guardians a chance to encourage a return to classes. The governor's prudence, which contrasted starkly with the hasty administrative reaction elsewhere, reduced the number of student strikers by one-fourth within days of the original walkout.[42]

Meanwhile the rash action of the central school authorities undermined the efforts of the Siedlce governor to end a walkout at the Siedlce Boys' Gymnasium. Here, 150 Polish students had presented a petition to the school's director and left classes on February 3. After a conference between the governor and parents employed by the state administration, however, sixty students quickly returned, leaving only ninety to face potential expulsion. The decision of February 7 to close all middle schools without exception thus angered the governor because "it plays into the hands of the Polish party."[43] Two weeks later, the governor's fears were confirmed. The reopening of the gymnasium of February 20 was met with a much larger walkout as some Jewish students joined their Polish colleagues, whose demands now linked polonization with democratization. Ultimately,

40. AGAD KGGW 2494, Report of the SDPA to the WGG, February 8 (21), 1905; APŁ KGP 1517, Captain of the Piotrków County Land Guard to the Piotrków Governor, January 19 (February 1), 1905; Korzec, Źródła do dziejów rewolucji 1 (1): 602–607; Nowroczyński, Nasza walka o szkołę polską 1: 369–381.
41. AGAD KGGW 2522, Suwałki Governor to the WGG, January 25 (February 7), 1905.
42. AGAD KGGW 345, Report of the Suwałki Governor's Office on Events in the Province for the first half of February 1905, and 2522, Suwałki Governor to the WGG, February 3 (16) and February 5 (18), 1905.
43. AGAD KGGW 2525, Siedlce Governor to the WGG, January 27 (February 9), 1905.

205 students were expelled from the Siedlce Boys' Gymnasium instead of the ninety earlier anticipated, a sizable group that quickly became a major disruptive force in the provincial capital.[44]

The blanket closures of February 7 thus resulted in a radicalization of student demands, the growing sympathy of parents for the school strikes, and the increased involvement of non-Catholic and especially Jewish students in the movement against the state system. The decision of Curator Schwartz to renew instruction in all secondary schools on February 20, regardless of the number of students in attendance, now turned many institutions into battlegrounds. Especially those Catholic students who continued to attend classes were frequently subjected to violent threats and outright physical assault from their coreligionists. In Warsaw these students eventually required police or military escorts, whose protection reduced, but did not end, the attacks against them.[45] Unguarded facilities and the homes of school officials were also targeted, although the damage usually remained confined to broken glass, more the consequence of well-aimed rocks than crudely devised bombs. When police and troops began patrolling the schools and surrounding areas, parents of ''strike-breaking'' students became the principal targets. County officials in Warsaw Province and in Częstochowa reported receiving daily complaints from parents victimized by ''terrorist'' acts that in essence, consisted of vandalism of their property.[46]

In many provincial centers, striking or expelled students were considered by local authorities to be not only a public nuisance but a threat to the social order. Expelled gymnasium students played a conspicuous role in local public disturbances in Siedlce, compelling provincial officials to force their removal from the city to their places of residence.[47] In Sochaczew (Warsaw Province), striking students mixed with and agitated among local inhabitants; in Płock they appeared prominently in the town's first May I demonstration. Such incidents prompted the Warsaw governor to opine that nowhere else in the empire was student antipathy toward the government as strong as in Russian Poland.[48]

---

44. Ibid., March 6 (19) and March 8 (21), 1905.
45. AGAD KGGW 2490, Acting Warsaw Superintendent of Police to the Chancellory of the WGG, May 18 (31), 1905.
46. AGAD KGGW 2500, Warsaw Governor to WGG, February 18 (March 3), 1905; APŁ KGP 1519, Director of the Częstochowa Boys' Gymnasium to the Piotrków Governor, February 26 (March 11), 1905.
47. AGAD KGGW 2525, Siedlce Governor to WGG, March 6 (19), 1905.
48. AGAD KGGW 2501, Warsaw Governor to the WGG, March 22 (April 4), 1905, and 2516, Report of the SDPA to the WGG, April 25 (May 8), 1905.

## The Student Strikes: An Analytic Balance Sheet

According to contemporary Polish press accounts, some 25,000 students participated in the school strikes of the late winter and spring of 1905. Such claims are only partially confirmed by the available statistical evidence. From the Central State Historical Archive in Leningrad, the historian Edmund Staszyński retrieved a report by Curator Schwartz drafted in late June which contains incomplete data on the strike in twenty-seven state secondary schools. According to this report, only 4,479 (37.2 percent) of the 12,039 students enrolled in the twenty-seven schools on January 1, 1905, continued to attend classes at the end of the school year in June. The level of student attendance ranged from 4.9 percent at the Warsaw Third Boys' Gymnasium to 75.4 percent at the Łódź Boys' Gymnasium, the latter owing to the low percentage of Polish students enrolled in the school.[49]

The data in the curator's report, although valuable for the schools named therein, cover fewer than half of the gymnasia and progymnasia in the Kingdom and slightly more than half of the total number of students enrolled in these institutions. None of the girls' gymnasia outside of Warsaw are represented in the curator's report, nor are any of the Kingdom's twenty-four schools of commerce that came under the jurisdiction of the Ministry of Finance. Yet according to reports of provincial and county officials, students at many of these institutions also proclaimed strikes and walked out of their classes. If the curator's sample is representative and the 62.8 percent level of strike participation is applied to the 17,000 students and pupils unaccounted for in his report, a total estimate of 18,116 striking secondary school students is the result. To be sure, this figure does not include striking students from institutions of higher education, the artisanal trade schools, and the few primary schools that participated in the spring strike. Nevertheless, the 25,000 students cited in press accounts appears a somewhat exaggerated number; it is more likely that approximately 20,000 students of all ranks participated in the strike at this stage.

In January 1905, approximately 17,000 Catholic students (i.e., Poles and a sprinkling of Lithuanians from Suwałki Province) were enrolled in the Kingdom's secondary schools, and from their number came the majority of striking students. Yet not all Polish students participated in the strike action during the first half of 1905, for which there is sufficient evidence in the numerous reports of violent threats and attacks against "strike-

49. Staszyński, *Polityka oświatowa*, p. 168.

breakers." The parents of many of these nonparticipating and subsequently ostracized students were employed at various lower levels in the state administration, which could and did provide the authorities significant leverage in any number of instances. This, however, was not the only determinant of Polish participation in the strike. In report after report, the initiative for strike actions in the gymnasia was assigned primarily to students in the fifth, sixth, and seventh forms. Conspicuously absent, particularly in the boys' gymnasia, are students from the eighth, or graduating, form. For example, only seventeen of the 257 students expelled from the Piotrków Boys' Gymnasium came from the eighth form.[50] These older students, near the end of their studies, obviously had a good deal to lose from their participation in the strike, including future matriculation at a university. Among their less career-minded female counterparts who, as mentioned, were denied access to higher education in any case, such factors were of considerably less concern.

Jewish students also participated in the school strike movement, especially in the girls' gymnasia, where no ceiling existed on Jewish enrollment (a 10 percent maximum applied in the boys' gymnasia). In any case, Jewish participation was naturally higher in those strikes where student demands went beyond polonization and emphasized issues of discrimination based on nationality and religion. Yet here, too, other considerations came into play. In Kielce, a group of Jewish students expelled from the boys' gymnasium formed the Committee of Jewish Youth, which through acts of coercion and vandalism sought to enforce strike solidarity among their coreligionists. In a confrontation at the entrance to the gymnasium, Jewish students still attending the school told the committee that they were "Russian," not "Polish" Jews, and that for them the strike was irrelevant.[51] Such divisions among Jewish youths, between students whose families had resided in Poland for generations and the children of the recent wave of Jewish migration from Russia (the so-called Litwaks), undoubtedly influenced the nature of Jewish participation in the school strikes, especially outside the major urban areas.

Nevertheless, the role of Jewish students in the school strike was of far greater proportional significance than that of Russian students, the sons and daughters of state officials and Orthodox clergy who constituted 20 percent of the student body in the boys' gymnasia and 33 percent in the girls' gymnasia. Despite later efforts by officially approved historians in the Po-

---

50. APŁ KGP 1517, List of Students Expelled from the Piotrków Boys' Gymnasium, dated January 21 (February 3), 1905.
51. AGAD KGGW 2508, Report of the SDPA to the WGG, March 28 (April 10), 1905.

lish People's Republic to highlight the participation of Russian students in the school strike,[52] the documentary evidence points to only individual cases, which can hardly be taken as representative.

Regardless of the number, age, and nationality of the student strikers, it is clear that their actions resulted from their own initiative and organization. Both interwar and postwar historiography, a good deal of which is of partisan political inspiration in the first place, has wrongly assigned credit for the initiation of the strikes and whatever success they enjoyed to nationalist, "progressive," or socialist groups active among the student youth, depending, of course, on one's political point of view. Although a sizable minority of the students was indeed highly politicized, such politicization could and did result in the movement's fragmentation rather than in the kind of solidarity necessary to a strike's success. And while individual students connected or sympathetic to the nationalist and socialist movements jockeyed for positions on strike committees or were dispatched to agitate students at other schools, this involvement hardly translates into a leading role for the political organizations. Instead of initiating the strikes as a vanguard, the politically organized among the students reacted to a situation that their own carefully laid and competing plans and preparations had not foreseen.

In reality, most of the participants in the school strike movement were not bound by rock-hard political allegiances; had they been, it is probable that the movement would have collapsed of innumerable factional splits. Student solidarity was cemented instead by ties of friendship, shared experience, and of course, peer pressure, which together transcended political divisions. These ties, in turn, were fostered by the long-standing traditions of secret instruction, especially in the self-education circles and mutual-aid organizations, and by the socializing effects of the schools themselves. Other agents of socialization, namely, parents and custodians, played a major—and often overlooked—role in the strikes. Parental attitudes, whether in support or opposition, frequently proved crucial to the outcome of a given strike.

Adult opinion, initially ill-disposed to the students' strike action, completely shifted over the course of the spring. The curator's clumsy attempts to manipulate parents and custodians without giving consideration to their views and the subsequent heavy-handed methods of various authorities in dealing with the strike, especially the mass expulsions of students, turned adult opinion first in the direction of ambivalence and then toward support

52. E.g., see Szulkin, *Strajk szkolny 1905 roku*, pp. 160–167.

of the student movement. To the authorities, it was the "moderate" opinion of adult society rather than "radical" student demands that ultimately
counted. Having once ignored that opinion at considerable cost, the regime
prepared to abandon futile repressive measures for the enticement of concessions. These concessions, however, proved too little and came too late
to prevent the struggle over public education from entering a second phase,
in which the striking students gave way to a much broader social movement.

## The Failure of Concessions

The first government concession to public opinion on educational issues,
and the only one during the course of the spring strike, came as an after-
thought to the state's religious reform, which culminated in the Edict of
Toleration of April 30, 1905. Most important to this chapter is Point 14 of
the edict, which permitted the use of Polish as the language of Catholic
religious instruction in all state schools while entrusting that instruction
exclusively to the Catholic clergy.

This concession, of major significance to the Catholic episcopate, was
expected to have an impact on Polish public opinion as well. In Prussian
Poland, where the language of religious instruction was a major issue between state and society, such a gratuitous gesture might well have fore-
stalled a subsequent wave of school strikes in 1906 and 1907.[53] In
revolutionized Russian Poland, however, it only served to exacerbate popular dissatisfaction with the church's stance in relation to the existing
school strikes. From the beginning, the Catholic hierarchy and a majority
of the lower clergy in the Kingdom had greeted the student strike movement with hostility. The conservative *Przegląd Katolicki* (Catholic Review), expressing the views of the episcopate, condemned specific student
demands and especially the idea of coeducation as contrary not only to
Christian morality but, incredibly, "to Jewish morality as well."[54] Local
clergy in Olkusz County (Kielce Province) went so far as to betray student
plans for a walkout at the Olkusz Trade School to the authorities.[55] Priests

---

53. See John J. Kulczycki, *School Strikes in Prussian Poland, 1901–1907: The Struggle
over Bilingual Education* (Boulder, 1981).
54. "Słowko do naszych reformatorów," *Przegląd Katolicki*, no. 6 (February 9, 1905):
89–90.
55. AGAD KGGW 2508, Kielce Governor to the WGG, January 28 (February 10), 1905.

like Father Biernacki, who protested the expulsion of one hundred Catholic students from the Biała Boys' Gymnasium (Siedlce Province) by refusing to continue in his position as a teacher of religion at the school, were few.[56]

The church naturally accepted Point 14 of the edict with gratitude to the state and prayers for the tsar. With its own narrow interests now satisfied, the episcopate launched a new campaign against the student strikes. In a pastoral letter to Polish parents and guardians in early June, Warsaw archbishop Wincenty Popiel, while admitting that "the present school system does not fulfill the spiritual and national needs of our children," nevertheless denounced the prolonged absence from school, which in his view promoted only laziness, demoralization, and the lack of civic virtue. "Your conscience and heart will tell you," the archbishop concluded, "that a bad school is better than no school at all."[57]

The archbishop's letter was met with public outrage. Nationalists joined liberals and socialists in vilifying him.[58] By this time, however, even the government had come to the realization that more concessions were necessary. In the countryside, an increasing number of gmina assemblies had demanded the polonization of village schools, and some communities had already taken action by removing their children from the schools. The specter of a nationwide boycott of the state primary school system coupled with the hostile reaction to the archbishop's letter forced the government to announce additional measures in the summer in the hope of opening the new academic year peacefully.

The state's concessions, however, proved too minor. On June 19, the Committee of Ministers issued a decree, confirmed by the tsar on July 22, which permitted the use of Polish for the instruction of arithmetic in primary schools and made possible the creation of a lectureship in Polish language and a chair in Polish literature at Warsaw University. It also conceded the exclusive use of Polish as the instructional language for Polish grammar lessons in state primary and secondary schools and held out the prospect for future private schools where Polish would become the medium of instruction for most subjects.[59] Even so, the limitation of Polish language study to two hours per week in the state middle schools remained unchanged, as did the ban on informal conversation in Polish inside the

56. AGAD KGGW 2527, Siedlce Governor to the WGG, February 26 (March 11), 1905.
57. AGAD AB, druk 257, Pastoral letter of the Archbishop of Warsaw to Polish Parents, June 10, 1905.
58. E.g., APW WGZŻ 1711, Appeal of the National Workers' Union of August 1905.
59. AGAD KGGW 2621, Decision of the Committee of Ministers, June 6 (19), 1905.

schools. And although study of Polish grammar was now introduced into
the uniform curriculum of the teachers seminaries for the first time, Russian
remained the language of instruction for this new subject as well.[60]

For a moment the state's concessions, insignificant as they were, coupled
with parental fears of another lost school year, stirred up considerable
controversy over the efficacy of continuing social action against the Russian schools, especially among the Warsaw intelligentsia. Nonetheless, all
the major political parties and organized groupings, with the exception of
the conservative *ugodowcy* (conciliationists), came out in favor of continuing the school strikes. The central committee of the National League, in
an appeal of August 1, called for an "absolute boycott" of the Russian
school system and the simultaneous organization of "secret" Polish
schools.[61] For their part, the socialist parties continued to demand both the
democratization and the polonization of public education and to sanction
the resort to violence against "strike-breaking" students and parents.

Influential voices, however, came out against continuation of the strike
into the new school year, including those belonging to two leading Warsaw
historians, Szymon Askenazy and Tadeusz Korzon. Askenazy, in particular, claimed that the school strikes were antidemocratic because only the
wealthy had resort to private instruction. These men were joined by the
lawyer Adolf Pepłowski, who at the February 19 public meeting with Curator Schwartz had done much to frustrate the efforts of the authorities to
pit adult society against the striking students. From Kraków, the novelist
Bolesław Prus entered the fray, deriding Askenazy, Pepłowski, and other
opponents of the strike as "legitimists." Meetings of lawyers, engineers,
and railroad employees passed motions, often after heated debate, in favor
of continuing the boycott.[62]

Although the majority of adult opinion favored the boycott, ultimately,
and for the last time, the fate of continued action against the Russian
schools rested with the students. Members of the Warsaw Circle of Delegates and the countrywide Central Organization of Middle School Youth
met during the summer and reaffirmed their decision to continue the strike.
With the onset of the new school year, these organizations then ceased to
exist, as many of their members left the Kingdom to pursue their educa-
tions, and others threw themselves into the whirlwind of party politics.[63]

60. Staszyński, *Polityka oświatowa*, pp. 75–83, 170.
61. AGAD AB, druki ulotne 148.
62. See Halina Kiepurska, *Warszawa w rewolucji 1905–1907* (Warsaw, 1974), pp. 128–
133, as well as her *Inteligencja zawodowa Warszawy*, pp. 166–171.
63. Nowroczynski, *Nasza walka o szkołę polską* 1: 282–283.

Similarly, the nationalist and socialist mutual-aid organizations at Warsaw University reacted to the administration's attempts to reopen the university by resolving at a joint meeting on October 7 to boycott the institution until its polonization. They then voted to dissolve themselves.[64] Shortly thereafter, students at the Polytechnical Institute, where it all began, passed the briefly worded resolution: "The strike continues."[65]

The continuation of the student strike or (to put it more accurately at this phase) school boycott into the new academic year and its rapid spread to both urban and rural elementary schools forced the government to make its most significant concession on educational issues. An imperial rescript of October 14, as foreseen in the Ministry of Education's administrative decree of June 19, agreed to the use of Polish as the medium of instruction in private schools for all subjects with the exception of compulsory courses in Russian language, history, and geography. At the same time, Aleksandr Schwartz was relieved of his duties as curator of the Warsaw educational district and transferred to Moscow. His departure was followed by that of many teachers, mainly Russians, whose positions were taken up by Poles.

For an increasingly radicalized society, the tsar's rescript represented, at best, a partial victory, one that was acceptable to conservatives and some moderates but fell far short of the more commonly shared goal of a Polish public school system. Many striking students and their parents did not possess the means to afford a private education. Students at the secondary level often came from privileged backgrounds, but the elementary schools, most of which existed in the vast Polish countryside, were populated mainly by pupils from the lower classes. Hence, despite the concessions of October 14, the boycott of the elementary schools intensified, especially in rural Poland.

The peak of the movement against the state educational system coincided with the events of late October and early November and the accompanying chaos and anarchy that threatened to overwhelm the government. As the October general strike moved into high gear, the authorities moved quickly to close the three institutions of higher education in Warsaw—the Polytechnical Institute on October 27, the Veterinary Institute on October 28, and Warsaw University on November 2.[66] The Puławy Institute of Agriculture and Forestry remained open until November 11 and the proc-

---

64. Ibid., p. 249.
65. Kiepurska, *Warszawa w rewolucji*, p. 133.
66. AGAD KGGW 2581, WGG to the Minister of Finance, October 14 (27), 1905, WGG to the Minister of Education, October 15 (28), 1905, and Curator of the Warsaw Educational District to the WGG, October 21 (November 3), 1905.

lamation of martial law. In the meantime, students from the institute led crowds that attempted to agitate troops from the nearby garrison and organized mass meetings attended by several thousand local residents. Once the authorities got around to ordering an indefinite suspension of instruction at the Puławy Institute, the order was accompanied by the immediate arrest of four students and two professors.[67]

The period was also marked by increasingly violent attacks on those public primary and middle schools that had continued instruction. Club-wielding crowds sacked the Lipno Teachers Seminary as well as secondary schools in Kielce and Kalisz.[68] Similar "disorders" also interrupted instruction in the Łódź primary schools and in several towns of Płock Province. In Łomża the homes of parents who continued to send their children to the "Muscovite" schools now became constant targets for petards, projectiles, and other small explosives.[69]

Throughout the country, individuals and groups, taking advantage of the temporary paralysis of the state administration, began to take matters into their own hands. On November 6, a meeting of Polish teachers, many of them members of the Endecja's Union for the Nationalization of the Schools, resolved to conduct lessons exclusively in Polish in all Warsaw city schools. This prompted the closing of all Warsaw schools for a week. Upon renewal of instruction, gangs of armed students visited several schools, threatening Russian teachers with death if they failed to leave the city. Pupils were then escorted to schools where both the teachers and the language of instruction were Polish.[70] In Łódź, citizens elected their own "school council," which, in turn, passed resolutions making Polish the language of instruction.[71] Throughout the countryside, peasant "school so-

---

67. APL KGL 1905:250, Chief of Nowa-Aleksandrya County to the Lublin Governor, October 21 (November 3), 1905; AGAD KGGW 2515, Chief of Nowa-Aleksandrya County to the Commander of the Warsaw Military District, October 20 (November 2), 1905, and Reports of SDPA to the WGG, October 13 (26), October 28 (November 11), and November 11 (24), 1905.

68. AGAD KGGW 2507, Curator of the Warsaw Educational District to the WGG, October 26 (November 8), 1905, 2509, Report of the SDPA to the WGG, October 25 (November 7), 1905, and 2517, Report of the SDPA to the WGG, October 31 (November 13), 1905.

69. AGAD KGGW 2512, Report of the SDPA to the WGG, September 30 (October 13), 1905, and Łomża Governor to the WGG, October 14 (27), 1905; and 2517, Płock Governor to the WGG, October 31 (November 13), 1905; APŁ KGP 1519, Piotrków Governor to the Łódź Chief of Police, January 8 (21), 1906.

70. AGAD KGGW 2493, Report of the Warsaw Superintendent of Police, October 25 (November 7), 1905, Curator of the Warsaw Educational District to the WGG, October 24 (November 6), 1905, and Report of the Inspector of Warsaw City Schools, November 8 (21), 1905; see also Kiepurska, Inteligencja zawodowa Warszawy, pp. 242–243.

71. Eugenia Podgórska, Szkolnictwo elementarne w Łodzi w latach 1808–1914 (Łódź, 1966), pp. 132–133.

cieties'' arbitrarily dismissed teachers who refused to cooperate in replacing Russian with Polish as the instructional language.

None of this, however, moved the government to further concessions beyond the provisions of the imperial rescript of October 14. Meanwhile, the emergency powers of martial law helped arrest and then bring an end to attempts to polonize the public school system. The crackdown fell on all those who had actively participated in the polonization movement. One hundred forty-two teachers who had arbitrarily replaced Russian with Polish as the medium of instruction were dismissed from their positions.[72] Expelled students were forbidden from wearing their school uniforms; those who remained enrolled were prohibited from frequenting restaurants, cafés, dairy bars, and confectionaries, and they were subjected to strict curfews. Violations of these martial law decrees carried stiff fines and prison terms (three thousand rubles and/or three months), and liability extended to parents and guardians of the offenders.[73] Instruction at Warsaw University, the Polytechnical and Veterinary institutes, the Institute of Agriculture and Forestry in Puławy, and the Dąbrowa School of Mines remained suspended indefinitely as higher education in the Kingdom ceased to function for the next several years.

The struggle to polonize the system of public education thus came to an end in early 1906, despite lingering protests. Yet even martial law could not force society to send its youth to the state-run schools, partially bilingualized by the reforms of June and October. As the boycott continued, it became clear that as far as educational issues were concerned, martial law had brought about a stalemate. To avoid the loss of an entire generation of students and pupils, society now turned to legally permitted activity, the creation of private schools and other educational institutions, as foreseen in the October imperial rescript, where Polish could function as the principal language of instruction. The initial success of the private Polish schools and the perceived necessity to compete with them in turn compelled the state first to make its last concessions to bilingualism, then to move against the private schools. Unfortunately, this important achievement of the revolution could not be sustained in subsequent years, as internal divisions over the purpose and curriculum of the private Polish

72. Zenon Kmiecik, *Ruch oświatowy na wsi: Królestwo Polskie, 1905–1914* (Warsaw, 1963), p. 21.
73. AGAD KGGW 2512, Proclamation of the Provisional Governor-General of Łomża Province, November 8 (21), 1905, and 2520, Binding Decree of Provisional Governor-General of Radom Province, November 13 (26), 1905; APŁ KGP 1549, Binding Decree of the Provisional Governor-General of Piotrków Province, December 19, 1905 (January 1, 1906).

schools abetted the plans of key government officials to suppress them entirely.

## The Polska Macierz Szkolna and Other Educational Initiatives

During the school strikes and boycott of 1905, underground institutions of secret instruction, a long-established weapon of popular resistance to russification, provided an alternative educational experience for many students and pupils engaged in the movement against the state schools. At the end of April 1905, the "progressive" Circle of Educators collaborated with its nationalist counterpart, the Union for the Nationalization of the Schools, in the organization of the Polska Macierz Szkolna (Polish Motherland Schools) to institutionalize and coordinate the activities of the secret study circles. A majority of these circles, particularly in the provinces, quickly came under the influence of proponents of the Endecja, a natural development given the long experience in secret instruction of the pronationalist TON organization. By early 1906 the Polska Macierz Szkolna had organized a network of seventy-seven circles (twenty in Warsaw), a sufficient base for the subsequent development of a legally recognized private Polish school system.[74]

Legalization, however, proved a slow process. Although the October rescript permitted the creation of private Polish schools, educational organizations had to await the March 1906 law on unions and associations before they could apply for registration with the authorities. Although the Polska Macierz Szkolna circles immediately submitted their organizational statutes to the provincial governors for approval, months followed before actual confirmation. The Warsaw governor, for example, withheld his agreement to the registration of eighteen of the circles in Warsaw until the end of August.[75] Further, the private schools sponsored by the organization were required to submit for official approval their curricula and the number of hours of instruction planned for each subject before the beginning of the school year, as the state sought to ensure provisions for the teaching of Russian language, history, and geography. The authorities also reserved for themselves the right to confirm teachers appointed by the Polska Macierz Szkolna.

74. Kmiecik, *Ruch oświatowy na wsi,* pp. 29–30.
75. APW ZOW 625, Warsaw Governor to the Warsaw Superintendent of Police, August 12 (25), 1906. In Łódź, the first Polska Macierz Szkolna school was already operational in April 1906; see Podgórska, *Szkolnictwo elementarne,* pp. 140–141.

Emblem of the Polska Macierz Szkolna, 1907. (Muzeum Niepodległości 24850)

Meanwhile, the character and goals of the private Polish schools had become a matter of considerable public controversy. The circles, though treated individually by the state, were not in fact autonomous units; they were subordinated to a main directorate that in turn was dominated by proponents of the Endecja. *Gazeta Polska* (The Polish Gazette), the main organ of the National Democratic Party in the Kingdom, considered the propagation of "Christian culture and love of country" to be the main task of the Polska Macierz Szkolna.[76] The rigorous but conservative program of instruction worked out by the organization's Department of Popular Education for the private elementary schools quickly drew fire from "progressive" educational activists associated with the liberal and socialist movements who had long called for an end to compulsory religious instruction. "Progressives" also protested enrollment practices that discriminated on the basis of sex, religion, and nationality.

Nevertheless, because the Polska Macierz Szkolna had much broader curricula and therefore represented an improvement over the Russian state

76. Kmiecik, *Ruch oświatowy na wsi*, p. 38.

schools, most "progressives" continued to support the Polish organization simultaneously directing their energies to other educational enterprises, especially the Association of Courses for Adult Illiterates established by Stefania Sempołowska and the University for All created by the eminent sociologist Ludwik Krzywicki. At the same time, the socialist parties and associated trade unions sponsored lectures, readings, libraries, and other cultural-educational activities for their members.[77] While these programs focused on the urban working class, a group of Lublin intellectuals led by the writer Stefan Żeromski formed the Society for the Spread of Education, better known as Światło (The Light), to reduce illiteracy among the peasantry. These left-wing initiatives, however, were not connected to each other and could only offer a limited alternative to the Polska Macierz Szkolna, which eventually engaged in similar activities. For example, the evening and weekend courses of its Uniwersytet Ludowy (People's University) were designed to rival those of Krzywicki's University for All.

If the Polska Macierz schools were insufficiently secular and modern for the "progressives," they proved far too secular and "modernist" for the Kingdom's Roman Catholic episcopate. Shortly after the October imperial rescript, the conservative Catholic press began its campaign for a Polish school system based on "Christian principles," claiming that the not-yet-legalized Polska Macierz schools had already become "a seedbed of moral anarchy."[78] The following February, a pastoral letter of the Polish bishops reiterated the church's demand for a private school system "not positivist and materialist, but true and Catholic."[79] Throughout the summer the episcopate maintained its pressure on the Polska Macierz Szkolna to adopt a clear "Catholic" direction while blaming the organization's failings in this regard on the Endecja. Yet despite its considerable misgivings, as a new school year rapidly approached, the episcopate not only decided to tolerate the new schools but encouraged the participation of parish clergy in their local administrative circles.[80]

Having surmounted these many obstacles, the Polska Macierz Szkolna

---

77. See Jadwiga Krajewska, "Z dziejow oświaty robotniczej: Biblioteki robotnicze w Królestwie Polskim w latach 1870–1914," *Polska Klasa Robotnicza: Studia Historyczne* 5 (1973): 191, 207; and Władysław Lech Karwacki, *Związki zawodowe i stowarzyszenia pracodawców w Łodzi* (Łódź, 1972), pp. 286–311.

78. "Co warta jest szkoła obecnie niby już 'polska,' " *Przegląd Katolicki,* no. 47 (November 23, 1905): 729–732.

79. *Przegląd Katolicki* no. 11 (March 15, 1906):146–148, and no. 12 (March 22, 1906): 166–170. See also Roman Dzwonkowski, *Listy społeczne biskupów polskich, 1891–1918* (Paris, 1974), pp. 106–107.

80. ADK AK OA-2/13, Stefan Zwierowicz, Bishop of Sandomierz, to the Diocesan Clergy, October 1, 1906.

An adult literacy course at the Rudzki Factory in Warsaw. (Muzeum Niepodległości 35811)

opened the new school year with 680 registered schools enrolling approximately seventy thousand students. By any measure, this was a considerable
achievement, although serious problems and gaps remained. The main emphasis had been the organization of elementary schools; consequently only
six middle schools were registered with the authorities in 1906. The network was particularly strong in Warsaw and Lublin provinces, weakest in
Suwałki Province, with its large Lithuanian population, and nonexistent in
the Chełm region of Siedlce and Lublin provinces, an area of mixed population where the establishment of private Polish schools was prohibited.[81]

The organizational success of the Polska Macierz Szkolna nevertheless
compelled the state to undertake one last reform of the Kingdom's public
schools. In an attempt to head off popular support for the organization, the
Ministry of Education in early March 1906 informed Vladimir Belaev, the
new curator of the Warsaw educational district, that all subjects in the one-
class elementary schools could be taught in Polish (or Lithuanian in the
northern counties of Suwałki Province), with the exception of Russian,

---

81. Staszyński, *Polityka oświatowa*, p. 202; Kmiecik, *Ruch oświatowy na wsi*, pp. 31–33.

which remained an obligatory subject.[82] By this not-inconsiderable concession, the state elementary school ceased to be a tool of russification.
The government obviously felt less pressed in the area of secondary education, where the Polska Macierz Szkolna had yet to create a viable alternative. Nevertheless, the state began to permit the employment of Polish
faculty in mathematics and the classical languages, and it lifted the long-
standing ban on informal conversation in Polish on school grounds.[83]

Despite these concessions, the popular boycott of the state schools held
firm, and support for the Polska Macierz Szkolna continued to grow. By
1907, there were some 781 circles grouping 116,341 members. Before the
opening of the 1907–1908 academic year, these circles presented to the
authorities requests to approve 1,247 schools, which included many new
middle schools. This was a significant expansion over the previous year.
The government, however, approved only 681 schools, one more than the
year before, an ominous sign for the nascent private Polish school system.[84]
Moreover, state educational authorities, beginning in September 1907, required all one-class elementary schools, including those operated by the
Polska Macierz Szkolna, to offer Russian language instruction a minimum
of fourteen hours per week. This unwelcome interference in the curricula
of the private schools invited evasion and circumvention by the instructors
and inevitable conflict with the state.

Meanwhile, the Catholic Church renewed its attacks on the new school
organization. In the autumn of 1906, many lower clergy had responded
enthusiastically to the opportunity to participate in the work of the Polska
Macierz Szkolna. In half of their circles in the countryside, priests held
key administrative positions. Even if religion were not an obligatory subject in these schools, such a level of clerical participation assured an important place for religious studies in the curriculum. To say the least, the
new school system's authorities gave the clergy much freedom of action,
and many priests became ardent supporters of these private Polish schools.
Yet the conservative Catholic press reminded its readers that "the church
is not represented by priests, even in the thousands, but only by the bishops,
the successors of the apostles."[85]

Before the 1906–1907 academic year was over, it became clear that the
Polish bishops would be satisfied with nothing less than complete episcopal
supervision of the Polska Macierz Szkolna, including its teachers, text-

82. Podgórska, *Szkolnictwo elementarne*, p. 134.
83. Staszyński, *Polityka oświatowa*, pp. 75, 237–238.
84. Kmiecik, *Ruch oświatowy na wsi*, p. 37.
85. "Spraw Kościelnych," *Przegląd Katolicki*, no. 46 (November 15, 1906): 705–708.

books, and methods of instruction. In the first months of 1907, *Przegląd Katolicki* renewed its campaign against the "pantheistic" Endecja as a prelude to attacks on the organization as a "non-Catholic" institution, attributing what it called its "areligious, pagan, and liberal" character to nationalist tutelage. If the private schools system were truly "Catholic," it intimated, the bishops would be represented on its main directorate.[86] By June the episcopate presented three nonnegotiable demands to the Polska Macierz Szkolna. In addition to representation of the episcopate on the main directorate, the bishops demanded that all its institutions be guided in a "Catholic spirit" (as opposed to a nondenominational "Christian spirit") and that clerical teachers of religion occupy a preeminent position among the faculty, which would enable them to guarantee the "Catholic direction" of the schools. If its demands were not met, the episcopate threatened, it would "forbid the clergy and the faithful any involvement in the Polska Macierz Szkolna as a faithless and, therefore, dangerous institution."[87]

The main directorate, although it continued its efforts to convince the episcopate that it was not "anticlerical," rejected the bishops' attempt to confer upon its schools an exclusively Catholic religious character. Claiming that "the most fundamental issues of the church were at stake" in the matter of the national, albeit private, school system, the episcopate effectively declared war, triggering a conflict for which it held the "narrow nationalism" of the Endecja directly responsible.[88] Those clergy and prominent lay Catholics who defended Polska Macierz Szkolna, or tried to soften the attacks against it, were themselves subjected to strident polemical abuse. For example, Cecylia Plater-Zyberkówna, founder of both the Catholic Society of Friends of Youth and the Catholic Women's Union, was branded "a nymph of the modernists" by Catholic conservatives for her support of the private school system.[89] Meanwhile, clerical supporters of the motherland schools were accused of religious indifference and false patriotism. In any event, moderate Catholics and reformist clergy were unable to prevent the church boycott of the Polska Macierz Szkolna that marked the opening of the 1907–1908 academic year.

---

86. Ks. dr. Wł. Namiotko, "Polska Macierz Szkolna," *Przegląd Katolicki,* no. 10 (March 7, 1907): 149–153.
87. ADK AK OA-2/13, Administrator of Kielce Diocese, Ks. Franciszek Brudzyński, to the Diocesan Clergy, June 15, 1907.
88. Ks. Charszewski, "Kościół a Polska Macierz Szkolna," *Przegląd Katolicki,* no. 20 (May 16, 1907): 317–318, and no. 21 (May 23, 1907): 328–330.
89. Ryszard Bender, *Społeczne inicjatywy chrześcijańskie w Królestwie Polskim, 1905–1918* (Lublin, 1978), pp. 119–120.

The organization might have survived the boycott of the Catholic Church had it not been for state action against it. In the middle of June 1907, Warsaw governor-general George Skalon ordered the closing of all Polska Macierz schools in Ostrów County (Łomża Province) and the dissolution of the county circle because of its "antigovernment tendencies and activity." At issue was the circle's projected use of Polish patriotic illustrations in geography and history textbooks.[90] The main directorate protested Skalon's decision, which, it argued, would deny hundreds of children all possible educational opportunity.[91] By mid-November the Polska Macierz Szkolna had successfully petitioned the Łomża governor, whose recommendation to reopen the Ostrów County private schools was accepted by the Warsaw governor-general.[92]

Despite the successful resolution of its conflict with the state in Ostrów County, Polska Macierz Szkolna was obviously anticipating a more general crackdown. Already in April 1907, the main directorate had called upon its circles in the countryside to organize a parallel network of underground schools and to train teachers specifically for the tasks of secret instruction. The authorities, too, prepared for such a contingency, compiling precise information on both the registered and the secret motherland schools, including the courses, lecturers, and thirteen locations of the Uniwersytet Ludowy. Between August and December, the authorities were thus able to uncover and dissolve hundreds of secret schools in Łomża, Siedlce, Warsaw, and Lublin provinces.[93]

It was therefore not surprising that within less than a month after the reopening of Polska Macierz schools in Ostrów County, the Warsaw governor-general issued a directive closing all these schools in the Kingdom of Poland. Skalon cited three reasons for his decision: Polska Macierz Szkolna had encouraged "narrow-nationalistic particularism" in its educational activities among the masses; it had violated legal provisions regarding Russian language instruction; and its leadership had fallen into the hands of "Polish separatists."[94] In this single stroke, the most significant educational achievement of the revolution came to an ignominious end.

90. AGAD KGGW 719, WGG to the Acting Governor of Łomża Province, June 3 (16), 1907.
91. AGAD KGGW 719 Petition of the Main Directorate of the Polska Macierz Szkolna to the WGG, September 10 (23), 1907.
92. AGAD KGGW 719, Łomża Governor to the WGG, November 1 (14), 1907.
93. Kmiecik, *Ruch oświatowy na wsi,* p. 43; APW ZOW 625, Lists compiled by the Office of the Warsaw Superintendent of Police, September 27 (October 3), 1907, and October 27 (November 9), 1907.
94. APW ZOW 625, Directive of the WGG, December 1 (14), 1907.

The Polska Macierz Szkolna went down with a whimper, not a bang. The socialist press protested the closing, but not too loudly. With the subsequent suppression in mid-1908 of the Association of Courses for Adult Illiterates and the University for All, accompanied by the arrests of Stefania Sempołowska, Stefan Żeromski, and other "progressive" educational and cultural activists, the SDKPiL even withdrew its support for a continuation of the boycott of the state schools, referring to such action as a "demonstration of impotence."[95] Within three years, the Union of Socialist Youth followed suit. At the other end of the political spectrum, the episcopate blamed the closing of the Polska Macierz Szkolna on the Endecja and on its "monopolistic" attitudes, which had "enslaved" the private Polish schools.[96] Meanwhile, parish circles of the newly formed conservative Catholic Union energetically entered the field of educational activity while seeking ways to transfer the defunct organization's funds to schools dedicated to "spreading education in the Catholic spirit."[97] The authorities, however, were to apply strict limits to even this activity in subsequent years.

Yet even the nationalist movement failed to mount any kind of significant protest against the delegalization of the private school system. The Polish Circle in the Third State Duma, although dominated by the Endecja, had been reduced substantially in size by Prime Minister Stolypin's arbitrary revisions of the electoral law. Thus weakened and disoriented, the Polish Circle did not even attempt an interpellation of the government over the suppression of the Polska Macierz Szkolna.[98] The Endecja's subsequent turn toward conciliation of the government, punctuated only by occasional criticism of Russian policies in the Kingdom, would lead to its own abandonment of the boycott of the state schools in 1911.

Such apparent public apathy toward the fate of the motherland schools further encouraged the government to retreat from other concessions made in 1905 and 1906. Beginning in 1908, state educational authorities required that teachers of Russian language, history, and geography be of Russian nationality in those private Polish schools that survived the dissolution of the Polska Macierz Szkolna. A year later, the state required that diplomas

---

95. Janusz Żarnowski, "Z dziejów strajku szkolnego 1905 r.," *Przegląd Historyczny* 46, 1–2 (1955): 211–212.
96. "Zamknięcie Polskiej Macierzy Szkolnej," *Przegląd Katolicki*, no. 51 (December 19, 1907): 812–813.
97. Bender, *Społeczne inicjatywy*, p. 102; Kmiecik, *Ruch oświatowy na wsi*, pp. 53–54.
98. Zygmunt Łukawski, *Koło Polskie w rosyjskiej dumie państwowej w latach 1906–1909* (Wrocław, 1967), pp. 123–139.

for students completing studies in the private elementary schools be written in Russian. In the public elementary schools, starting with the 1908–1909 academic year, the state required the teaching of arithmetic in both Polish and Russian, which in turn ended the employment prospects of teachers not fluent in the state language. In addition, Russian primers were re-introduced in public elementary schools after November 1908.[99]

The state continued to underfund public education in the Kingdom in the meantime. The increase in the number of village schools from 2,977 in 1904 to 3,662 in 1912 was far more the result of gmina initiatives than of the insignificant increase in state outlays for elementary education. That increase, moreover, failed miserably to satisfy existing needs. In Radom Province, the public schools could accommodate only 20 percent of estimated demand for elementary education. Consequently, in 1911, only twenty-five children per thousand inhabitants attended state primary schools in the Kingdom, compared with 129.7 per thousand in "impoverished" and "backward" Austrian Galicja.[100]

The private Polish schools could pick up only some of the slack. On the eve of the Great War, eight hundred private elementary schools enrolling seventy thousand pupils had survived the state's repressive policies, but they accommodated only 18 percent of all elementary school pupils. The situation was drastically different in the middle schools. Public secondary education still served as a tool of russification and continued to receive far more generous levels of state funding. Popular opinion, however, remained hostile toward the state middle schools, and the people effectively continued to boycott them despite the abandonment of such action by key political parties and organizations. Consequently, by 1914, the 191 private middle schools and schools of commerce had come to play a dominant role in secondary education in the Kingdom, enrolling 38,000 pupils, compared with the 23,500 enrolled in state institutions.[101]

In effect, the crisis of education in Russian Poland continued after the revolution, but this does not mean that positive change had not resulted from the events of 1905 and 1906. The state elementary schools in the Kingdom, though not significantly expanded, had nevertheless been transformed into partially polonized institutions that differed little from their

---

99. Podgórska, *Szkolnictwo elementarne*, pp. 141, 151–152; Staszyński, *Polityka oświatowa*, p. 229.
100. Staszyński, *Polityka oświatowa*, pp. 239–240; Kmiecik, *Ruch oświatowy na wsi*, pp. 80–82.
101. Staszyński, *Polityka oświatowa*, pp. 207–209. For an excellent study of Warsaw's private secondary schools, see Jolanta Niklewska, *Prywatne szkoły średnie w Warszawie, 1905–1915* (Warsaw, 1987).

private Polish counterparts. Also as a consequence of the revolution, the Polish language made its way into the state secondary schools, schools of commerce, and teachers seminaries, although not to the extent that they could effectively compete with the legally permitted private schools. Although a Polish school system, represented by the aborted Polska Macierz Szkolna, withered on the vine, the blows struck against russification as state educational policy were substantial indeed.

Most significant, the revolution sparked an unprecedented popular awareness of and interest in education, a consciousness made manifest by workers living in the slum district of Bałuty in Łódź, when in mid-1906 they decided to tax themselves in order to create five new elementary schools so long as Polish served as the language of instruction.[102] So long as the University for All and the Uniwersytet Ludowy remained legally registered institutions, tens of thousands who otherwise would have had no opportunity to continue their education enrolled in evening and weekend courses in both town and countryside. Before it was suspended, the Association of Courses for Adult Illiterates provided remedial learning to thousands of industrial workers. Such popular enthusiasm survived the above-mentioned institutions, all of them suppressed by 1908. Between 1912 and 1914, more than a thousand new village schools were created by local, communal initiative with no effective help from the state. On the eve of the World War I, twenty gminy in Kielce Province alone passed resolutions calling for a system of universal primary education.[103] These and many other examples of a new cultural consciousness support the conclusion that the revolution had not only stirred broad social passions and emotions but also encouraged the popular mind to strive for satisfaction of that most basic of human intellectual needs—the need to learn.

102. Podgórska, *Szkolnictwo elementarne*, p. 135.
103. Kmiecik, *Ruch oświatowy na wsi*, p. 95.

# THE TRANSFORMATION OF POLITICAL CULTURE

Polish politics during the Revolution of 1905 has traditionally been presented as a conflict of competing ideologies, parties, and personalities—that is, as political history. The struggle between nationalism and socialism (between realism and idealism, for a more contemporary cast of mind),[1] between the National Democratic Party and the Polish Socialist Party, between Roman Dmowski and Jozef Piłsudski—such is the material for the conventional "textbook" rendition of Polish politics during the revolution. A slightly more sophisticated political history would mention loyalism, populism, and "international socialism" as other competing though less attractive ideologies; the Party of Polish Realists, the Polish People's Union, and the Social Democracy of the Kingdom of Poland and Lithuania as parties of at least temporary significance; and perhaps Erazm Piltz, Stefan Brzeziński, and Rosa Luxemburg as political personalities worthy of more than just passing attention. Yet regardless of the number of ideologies, parties, and actors historians have placed on this stage, the historiographic backdrop of politics interpreted politically has overwhelmed the literature.[2] Unfortunately, far too many historians have also succumbed to

---

1. See Adam Bromke, *Poland's Politics: Idealism versus Realism* (Cambridge, Mass., 1967), and *The Meaning and Uses of Polish History* (Boulder, 1987).
2. The most eloquent rejection of the traditional historiographic emphasis on the role of political parties during the revolution is Elżbieta Kaczyńska, "Tłum i margines społeczny w wydarzeniach rewolucyjnych: Krolestwo Polskie, 1904–1907," *Dzieje Najnowsze* 15, 1–2 (1983): 221–230. Similarly, Paweł Samuś, *Dzieje SDKPiL w Łodzi, 1893–1918* (Łódź, 1984), consciously de-emphasizes political personalities, tactics, and ideology to provide a brilliantly researched sociologic dissection of a single local political organization.

the temptation or, what is worse, have been pressured to take sides and pronounce judgments on the basis of partisan political considerations.[3]

This chapter concerns the politics of the revolutionary era not as political history, but as integrative social history. A conscious de-emphasis on the role of political parties, ideologies, and personalities puts them in a more balanced historical perspective without denying the political significance of the revolution; for that significance can be properly appreciated only in its social context, in the totality of social experiences of the revolutionary years. From this larger perspective, the most striking political development of the revolution was that of popular political participation, reflected in the emergence and rapid growth of organizations claiming to represent the interests of mass constituencies. The resulting democratization of Polish political culture is indeed a development so profound that one may dare label it revolutionary. It is this genuinely popular aspect of the Revolution of 1905 that most clearly distinguishes it from the previous gentry-led movements and insurrections. Though the seeds of this transformation may have been sown decades earlier, it was the Revolution of 1905 that brought forth the harvest of change. As a consequence, the largest and most important territory of partitioned Poland entered the modern political era, the era of mass politics.

An emphasis on the political debut of the "mass" nation rather than on the political parties whose growth embodied that process is thereby justified. The principal significance of the political parties is that they served as conduits for popular participation and, in the process, were themselves transformed as organizational structures evolved to accommodate new mass constituencies. The conduct of politics also changed under popular pressure. Politics, to the extent that the changing conditions of Russian rule allowed, became more open and less conspiratorial, more representative and less elitist—in a word, more democratic. Democratization of political life, however, was also accompanied by vulgar forms of discourse and physical forms of action, by radicalization, polarization, fragmentation, and violence. Such phenomena tended to cut across party lines as politics ceased to be the preserve of a gentry and intelligentsia elite and began to serve as a tool for realizing popular aspirations.

---

3. Stanisław Kalabiński, *Antynarodowa polityka endecji w rewolucji 1905–1907* (Warsaw, 1955), is a prominent example of the politically partisan historical writing of the communist era in Poland. Władysław Pobóg-Malinowski, *Narodowa Demokracja, 1887–1918: Fakty i dokumenty* (Warsaw, 1933), though of a different era and political perspective (i.e., of the Piłsudski camp), is hardly less tendentious.

## The National Democrats

By the beginning of the revolution, the nationalist movement, or Endecja, had already attained the status of a mass movement. That status, however, had been achieved not so much through the agency of the National Democratic political party, from which the movement took its name, but through the existence of several agencies, including the party, all of which revolved in different orbits around the conspiratorial National League.

Unlike its satellite organizations, the National League throughout its history was a rather narrow and elitist group; within the Kingdom of Poland its membership numbered only three hundred, drawn primarily from the propertied classes and professional intelligentsia. Within the league, effective power rested in the hands of a five-man central committee, led by Roman Dmowski, and in the offices of the Kraków-based *Przegląd Wszechpolski* (All-Polish Review), edited by Dmowski and J. L. Popławski. By contrast, organizations affiliated with the league, especially the Society for National Education (TON) with some six thousand members, opened their ranks to popular participation in both town and countryside. The organizational model of satellite organizations, ''open'' to mass participation, revolving around a closed conspiratorial center (the composition of the central committee of the league did not change between 1896 and 1905), produced an inevitable tension between the popular democratism embodied by the former and the paternalistic democratism pursued by the latter. Thus arose a paramount question that was never truly resolved: Would the *lud* (people) be the basis of the movement's ''national policy'' or merely its tool?

This fundamental contradiction of the Endecja—of a movement consciously based on the participation of the *lud,* on the one hand, but headed by an elite that distrusted popular initiative, on the other—remained submerged before 1905. The Endecja was far from being a centralized political machine, and the ties binding organizations like Zet or TON to the league were far more elastic than is usually assumed. This organizational slackness, necessitated by prerevolutionary conditions of political activity and however distasteful to the movement's leadership, nevertheless served to maintain an impressive degree of unity within the movement as a whole.

The revolution, by creating new and unprecedented opportunities both for the ''national policy'' of the leadership and for popular initiatives ''from below,'' presented the Endecja with an immediate organizational crisis. Its first victim was TON, the most genuinely popular nationalist organization in the Kingdom. TON's primary activity was in the countryside, where it had played a significant role in the first phase of the gmina action movement. But the illegal actions initiated by TON were soon subsumed by the active participation and involvement of the peasants themselves, and their demands only partially coincided with those of "national policy" as conceived by Dmowski and his colleagues in the league. Many TON village circles became caught up in the wave of popular enthusiasm, and by summer, the Endecja's presumed leadership over the gmina action movement was largely fictitious.

The nationalist leadership's effort to regain influence in the Polish countryside began with an effort to assert central control over TON's mass organization. This was most easily accomplished by the dissolution of TON, effected in June 1905, and the placing of its village circles under the direct jurisdiction of commissars appointed by the National League. This proved a transitional measure before the absorption of the rural TON circles into a new, more centralized Organizacja Narodowa (National Organization) more responsive to the directives of the Endecja leadership.[4] Simultaneously, TON's urban circles, then numbering as many as three thousand working-class members, were transformed into the Narodowy Związek Robotniczy (NZR—National Workers Union). Its first five-man main directorate included two members of the National League, Czesław Sobolewski and Gustav Simon. The other three members came from the Jan Kiliński Union, a vanguard of the Zet organization centered in the Warsaw Polytechnical Institute.[5]

The dissolution of TON and its replacement by two entirely new organizations had been preceded by changes within the league organization itself. In the pages of *Przegląd Wzechpolski* and elsewhere, Roman Dmowski responded to the new situation and opportunities created by the revolution with arguments and justifications for a strong, efficient, centralized organization to guide a unified nation in the struggle for the realization of Polish "national interests" within a weakening Russian Empire.[6] In line with such thinking, the league's home committee in the Kingdom was expanded to include new people, primarily representing propertied elements that far preferred the Endecja conception of controlled change from above to unrestrained revolution from below. In turn, the home committee created a new, smaller executive headed by Dmowski. The Kingdom

---

4. Tadeusz Wolsza, "Towarzystwo Oświaty Narodowej, 1899–1905," *Kwartalnik Historyczny* 94, 2 (1987): 95–96.
5. Teresa Monasterska, *Narodowy Związek Robotniczy, 1905–1920* (Warsaw, 1973), pp. 28–34.
6. See esp. "Nasze cele i nasze drogi" and "Podstawy polityki polskiej," in Roman Dmowski, *Wybór pism* (Warsaw, 1990), pp. 121–130 and 147–152, respectively.

itself was divided into five regions, each responsible to one of the members on the executive committee, who appointed commissars to particular districts.[7] Finally, the prospect of future legal political activity within a semi-constitutional structure, generated by the so-called Bulygin project within the Ministry of Internal Affairs, led to an increased emphasis on recruitment into the National Democratic Party.

These changes, both in organization and in the social composition of the league's governing bodies, could not occur without some fallout. Stanisław Kozicki, the more or less "official" historian of the early Endecja, notes that the influx of propertied members, especially into the National Democratic Party, led to tensions with the old, "democratic" organizations active among the popular classes.[8] The founding of the Polski Związek Ludowy (PZL—Polish People's Union) at the end of 1904 by a group of TON educational activists was an early expression of rank-and-file dissatisfaction with the Endecja leadership, its centralizing tendencies, and its courtship of wealthy and influential landowners. The publication of the program of the PZL coincided, not accidentally, with the dissolution of TON, to provide disenchanted members of that organization's village circles with a "populist" alternative to the envisioned Organizacja Narodowa.[9]

Despite such defections, the Endecja considerably strengthened its mass base during the course of the revolution. Although its leadership distrusted and sought to restrain popular initiative, whether in the communal assemblies or in the movement against the state school system, Dmowski and his colleagues were careful to maintain a public posture of strong support for and even defense of popular causes so long as they conceivably promoted "Polish national interests." Not all popular movements met these select criteria, however. Workers' strikes, whether agrarian or industrial, gradually fell into the category of the politically unacceptable.

During the January–February general strike in industrial areas and the spring agrarian strikes in the countryside, the Endecja leadership openly sympathized with the workers' efforts to improve working conditions. In a well-publicized appeal to the Łódź textile industrialists at the end of January, the National Democratic Party supported workers' demands for

---

7. Andrzej Micewski, *Roman Dmowski* (Warsaw, 1971), pp. 112–113.
8. Stanisław Kozicki, *Historia Ligi Narodowej: Okres 1887–1907* (London, 1964), pp. 276–278.
9. Bronisław Radlak, *Polski Związek Ludowy w rewolucji 1905–1907* (Warsaw, 1962), pp. 20–22.

wage increases, a reduction of working hours, employer-supported retirement and health insurance, and training programs for working-class youth.[10] In the Dąbrowa Basin, representatives of the Endecja went further and joined members of the PPS and SDKPiL on the strike committee that drafted a list of economic demands on behalf of the region's mine workers.[11] In the countryside, the Endecja attempted to adapt more of a mediating role, a tactic occasioned by the need to reconcile conflicting interests, of peasant and landowner, within its own organization. Consequently, it urged employers to make concessions to the "just" demands of farm workers, while calling upon the latter to present demands in the form of petitions rather than strikes.[12]

Within months, the sympathetic and tolerant, if not wholly supportive, attitude of the Endecja leadership toward the strike movement gave way to hostile opposition and dramatic counteraction. The rapid growth in socialist party influence on the labor movement, the socialists' "mania" for political strikes and demonstrations, their active encouragement of class conflict, and the coercive methods employed to achieve strike solidarity forced the Endecja to come out increasingly often against industrial strikes. So, too, did the damage caused to the Kingdom's economy by prolonged walkouts and factory closings. A movement that sought to galvanize the nation's strengths to take advantage of the empire's weakness and force concessions in the direction of self-rule could not long tolerate the social and economic disruptions caused by industrial strikes. Nor could it long tolerate the socialists, who in Dmowski's words, were "quite capable of inciting the crowd but incapable of controlling it."[13]

The National Workers' Union, emerging from the organizational womb of TON, provided the Endecja not only with an embryonic mass working-class organization of its own but also with "our main army in the struggle with revolution," said Dmowski.[14] Within a month of its creation, the NZR became engaged in extensive antistrike and antisocialist counteragitation,

10. APŁ KGP 1515 (cz. 1), Appeal of the Regional Circle of the National Democratic Party to Łódź Industrialists and Factory Owners, January 1905.

11. Adam Kałuża, "Z dziejów walk masowych proletariatu Zagłębia Dąbrowskiego w 1905 r. o 8-godzinny dzień pracy i inne postulaty," *Polska Klasa Robotnicza: Studia Historyczne* 3 (1972): 235–236.

12. Jan Molenda, "Carat i klasy posiadające w walce z rewolucją 1905–1907 r. na wsi polskiej," *Przegląd Historyczny* 46, 1–2 (1955): 146.

13. Dmowski, *Wybór pism*, p. 129.

14. Jerzy Janusz Terej, *Idee, mity, realia: Szkice do dziejów Narodowej Demokracji* (Warsaw, 1971), p. 45.

especially in Łódź, where during the middle of the June "uprising," Okhrana agents circulated three hundred copies of an NZR proclamation.[15] In the aftermath of the violence in Łódź, *Słowo Polskie* (The Polish Word), the nationalist organ from Lwów, declared war against the "anarchy" spread by socialist "criminals" and brandished "the knife and the revolver" as the best arguments against socialism.[16]

Months would pass before the nationalist movement developed the capability to back up its violent rhetoric. In the meantime, the NZR slowly built up its mass organization. Its June program committed it not only to oppose class struggle but also to work for the improvement of workers' conditions, the regulation of labor-management relations through collective bargaining, and the sponsorship of cultural and mutual-aid activities among its working-class members.[17] The NZR's opposition to labor walkouts, especially during the heady days of the autumn of 1905 when the strike movement peaked, necessarily restrained expansion of its membership. For example, the efforts of the Narodowe Koło Kolejarzy (NKK), the nationalist enclave among railworkers, to prevent the Russian rail strike from spreading to the Kingdom in October had little impact. Indeed, many NZR members broke with the organization's leadership and supported the October general political strike.

Two months later, however, during the Moscow uprising and the proclamation of martial law in the Kingdom, the NZR not only maintained discipline within its own organization but together with the NKK was able to neutralize socialist agitation for a general strike in the Kingdom in support of the Moscow insurgents.[18] In the course of 1906, the NZR capitalized on a perceptible shift in workers' attitudes, on the growing opposition among workers themselves to strikes as the means of first resort in resolving conflicts with management, and on the possibilities afforded by legal, trade union activity. By the time of its third congress in June 1906, the NZR could count sixteen thousand members; by October that number had

15. Stanisław Kalabiński, ed., *Carat i klasy posiadające w walce z rewolucją 1905–1907 w Królestwie Polskim: Materiały archiwalne* (Warsaw, 1956), p. 205.
16. Władysław Pobóg-Malinowski, *Najnowsza historia polityczna Polski*, vol. 1 (1864–1914), 2d ed. (London, 1963), p. 568.
17. Kozicki, *Historia Ligi Narodowej*, pp. 260–276; Monasterska, *Narodowy Związek Robotniczy*, pp. 41–62.
18. In the Warsaw region, for example, less than 30 percent of the industrial labor force participated in the December strike; see Stanisław Kalabiński, "Ruch strajkowy robotników przemysłowych Warszawy i gubernii warszawskiej w okresie najwyższego jego natężenia: Próba analizy statystycznej lat 1905–1906 (Część I: Rok 1905)," *Polska Klasa Robotnicza: Studia Historyczne* 4 (1973): 90.

risen to twenty-three thousand.[19] Within a year of its creation, the NZR had become competitive with socialist parties formed more than a decade earlier, and not only in the factories but also in the streets.

Despite being a movement that consciously sought to restrain the popular revolutionary tide of 1905, and in many instances swam against it, the Endecja nevertheless remained the strongest mass political movement at year's end. The centrally orchestrated organizational transformations had caused only slight damage, limited for the most part to defections from the intelligentsia, while paving the way for the creation of a genuine political machine. By early November that machine was capable of organizing massive, yet peaceful, demonstrations of one hundred thousand participants, not only in Warsaw but in every provincial center and county seat throughout the Kingdom where landowners and peasants, workers and intellectuals stood shoulder-to-shoulder in singing the Polish patriotic hymn "Boże coś Polskę" (God Preserve Poland). Within months this machine would win a sweeping victory in the Kingdom's first elections to the Russian State Duma.

## The SDKPiL and PPS

The problem of adjusting to the new era of mass politics confronted not only the Endecja but the two principal socialist parties in the Kingdom as well. The difference was that the Endecja was far more successful in the making that adjustment. For the PPS the organizational strains caused by popular participation ultimately led to a party split in November 1906 as representatives of the party's old insurrectionist tradition collided with proponents of the new politics of mass action. The SDKPiL, unable to reconcile its leadership's addiction to conspiracy with the need for openness in its mass organizations, effectively sentenced itself to a postrevolutionary future on the political fringe.

Several years ago I devoted the major part of a monograph to the political-organizational problems of the SDKPiL, all of which tended to flow to and from the Revolution of 1905, the highwater mark of that party's history.[20] In 1904 the SDKPiL, under the leadership of Feliks Dzierżyński, effectively transformed itself from a loose and highly vulnerable network

19. Monasterska, *Narodowy Związek Robotniczy,* pp. 34–40.
20. Robert Blobaum, *Feliks Dzierżyński and the SDKPiL: A Study of the Origins of Polish Communism* (Boulder, 1984).

of circles into a tightly controlled, centrally directed, and far more disciplined organization that in its strict adherence to conspiratorial principles could withstand tsarist repressive measures. By the end of that year, the SDKPiL finally appeared ready to play on the same field as its more established counterparts, the PPS and the Jewish Bund.

Yet in the first months of 1905, confronted by the challenges of revolutionary mass politics, this lean, conspiratorial organization found itself in danger of "losing its head and bursting open," in the words of its alarmed creator.[21] The growth in membership, modest in comparison with what was to come, led to increased needs for party publications, underground presses, and trained agitators which simply overwhelmed party resources. Unable to secure additional resources from the central party organs abroad, Dzierżyński uncharacteristically argued for granting greater autonomy to local organizations as a temporary expedient in order to better respond to demands of the moment. Nevertheless, as late as July, Dzierżyński referred to the "disparate" state of the party organization "owing to simple exhaustion; absolutely everyone is exhausted."[22]

Accommodating the requirements of a genuine mass organization was simply beyond the SDKPiL's means throughout most of 1905, especially at the local level. In provincial centers like Częstochowa, Radom, and Lublin, local Social Democratic committees were forced to rely on competitors, namely the PPS and the Bund, for the publication of appeals, smuggling operations, and other forms of "technical" assistance. In Lublin, the party did not possess its own printing press until the end of the year; in Radom, it borrowed weapons from the PPS for its "armed defense" units.[23] These were difficult circumstances to accept for a central party leadership determined to set the SDKPiL apart from its socialist rivals, both ideologically and politically. Thus, while local party units entered into agreements and alliances with the PPS and the Bund out of necessity, efforts to achieve cooperation at the national level were repeatedly frustrated by the Social Democratic leadership.[24]

---

21. Feliks Dzierżyński, *Pisma wybrane* (Warsaw, 1951), pp. 113–115.
22. CA PZPR, AM 25/1, Zespół Feliksa Dzierżyńskiego, from a fragment of a letter dated July 19, 1905.
23. Jan Boniecki, "Rewolucja 1905–1907 w Radomiu," *Biuletyn Kwartalny Radomskiego Towarzystwa Naukowego* 11, supplement (1974): 35; Alicja Wójcik, *Ruch robotniczy na Lubelszczyźnie* (Lublin, 1984), pp. 59–60.
24. E.g., the party leadership dismissed an appeal from the PPS for common action against the tsarist government in the aftermath of the January–February general strike with the justification that the SDKPiL could not cooperate with an organization for which "socialism

In struggling to keep pace with the mass movement, the SDKPiL at times appeared to engage in reckless adventurism. Its involvement in an ill-timed and poorly planned mutiny inside the Puławy garrison in April 1905 was more the result of organizational chaos, youthful inexperience, and misleading information than any grand strategy of revolutionary agitation among the troops.[25] Similarly, the SDKPiL's irresponsible behavior in events leading to the "massacre" in Warsaw on May 1 was mainly a response to pressure from below for a mass demonstration and in opposition to the more cautious tactic of general work stoppages planned by the PPS and the Bund. Unfortunately, in trying to score points against its rivals, the SDKPiL knowingly accompanied thousands of marchers into a confrontation with troops and police who had been issued well-publicized instructions to disperse May Day street demonstrations by force. Finally, the needs of a mass party forced the SDKPiL's most experienced and indispensable activists to "come out" into the open, out of their conspiratorial shells, to attend larger gatherings, to meet with various party groups, and to assert their authority. On one such occasion at the end of July, however, the authorities succeeded in rounding up the entire leadership of the party's Warsaw organization.[26]

In 1906, however, the SDKPiL developed the technical and organizational capacity of a genuine mass party, and none too soon, as membership swelled. By the summer of 1906 the SDKPiL counted some twenty-six thousand members in fifty-six organizations, with the greatest expansion occurring in the first six months after the October Manifesto. A second growth spurt that pushed party membership to forty thousand took place in the last months of 1906 as a consequence of both extensive recruitment efforts during the Great Łódź Lockout and the defections that accompanied the split of the PPS. At the same time, party activity assumed less impulsive forms, turning away from the almost blind involvement in strikes and demonstrations which had characterized most of 1905. In 1906, party activity,

is only a facade"; T. Daniszewski, ed., *SDKPiL w rewolucji 1905 roku: Zbiór publikacji* (Warsaw, 1955), pp. 105–110. Later attempts to reach agreements with the PPS and the Bund during the summer were frustrated by the party leadership's jealous protection of its "independence"; see Halina Kiepurska, *Warszawa w rewolucji 1905–1907* (Warsaw, 1974), pp. 142–143, and "Iiul'skaia (1905g.) konferentsiia Bunda s Pol'skoi Sots.-dem.," *Proletarskaia Revoliutsiia* 11 (1922): 182–186.

25. Ignacy Pawłowski, *Wojskowa działalność SDKPiL w rewolucji 1905–1907* (Warsaw, 1956), pp. 133–140; Władysław Kowalski, "Ze wspomnień o próbach powstania puławskiego," *Archiwum Ruchu Robotniczego* 3 (1976): 66–71.

26. Blobaum, *Feliks Dzierżyński*, pp. 137–138; Kiepurska, *Warszawa w rewolucji*, p. 165.

forced by the new requirements of mass politics, shifted to the organization of trade unions, the holding of frequent conferences of party members at all levels, systematic reporting from local organizations, and eventually, participation in elections to the Russian State Duma.[27]

Much of the SDKPiL's newfound organizational strength, however, was deceiving. Party membership followed the geographic faultline of the Kingdom's industrialization; 85 percent of the SDKPiL's members came from Warsaw and Piotrków provinces, 75 percent from Warsaw and Łódź. Outside of a few thousand members grouped in the party's Lublin and Radom organizations, the SDKPiL remained practically nonexistent in the rest of the Kingdom, not to mention Lithuania, where despite its name, the party had failed to maintain an organizational presence. As a radical Marxist party that prided itself on its ideological correctness, the SDKPiL made almost no effort to organize in the vast Polish countryside, even among farm workers. Other nonproletarian elements of the population were similarly ignored. In sharp contrast, the SDKPiL spared no effort in the Łódź industrial region, where it came to possess its most formidable organization. Here, especially, the SDKPiL realized its ambition of being a multinational party able to unite Polish, German, and Jewish workers under one political-ideological roof through a variety of organizational, cultural, and linguistic vehicles.[28]

The SDKPiL thus became a mass party whose influence was far more regional than national. Yet even in the country's industrialized areas, the party leadership's continued insistence on conspiracy-style discipline and loyalty, only now from a new mass membership, served to limit its influence. Unlike the Endecja, for whom the party was considered secondary to the broader national "movement," the SDKPiL quite consciously extolled the primacy of the party over the broader labor movement. Perhaps this was mere wishful thinking, born of the party's experiences of 1905 when the masses, rather than the party, had played the leading role. In any case, the party principle, or partyjność, dominated the organizational conceptions of the party leadership. The most deleterious effect of partyjność was on Social Democratic trade union activity. Rather than seize the opportunity created by the March 1906 laws on unions and associations for participating in legal (and therefore nonparty) trade unions, the SDKPiL leadership insisted on maintaining its own clandestine union organization under strict financial and political subordination to the party. The "He who

27. See J. Krasny, "Stan organizacji SDKPiL w 1905–1907 r.," *Z Pola Walki,* 1 (1926): 35–64.
28. See Samuś, *Dzieje SDKPiL w Łodzi,* pp. 68–114.

is not with us, is against us" attitude thus excluded many workers for whom the effectiveness of a given trade union, rather than its political label, became the primary criterion for participation.[29]

Partyjność, in reality, was a means of maintaining the central control of the party leadership, not only over the SDKPiL's trade unions but over the mass organization as a whole. The centrifugal tendencies that had threatened to tear the SDKPiL apart in 1905 had thus led to an even stronger centripetal organizational reaction in 1906. Excessive centralization, especially the monopolization of power and decision making by a narrow elite, would in turn give rise to an opposition movement within the party; not surprisingly, one of its first manifestations occurred among trade union activists.[30] Five years later, in 1912, the rift between supporters of the party's central executive committee, the main directorate, and proponents of decentralization and local organizational automony would result in a split of the SDKPiL. But by then, the party's mass organization, which had given rise to such issues in the first place, had become a thing of the revolutionary past.

The split of the PPS, in contrast, did not wait for the postrevolutionary era; for it occurred at the peak of that party's development as a mass organization. Indeed, conflict between the party's traditional elite, the Starzy (Old Guard), and the Młodzi (The Young), a group that based itself on the vision—then the reality—of a mass organization, was perceptible as early as 1903. The prerevolutionary origins of the party's dual personality, which would split the party during the revolution, therefore require a brief discussion.

Whereas the SDKPiL developed the organizational forms of a mass party relatively late, racing to catch up with new social and political realities, the PPS already possessed the organizational capacity of a mass party by 1904. In that year, seventeen city workers' committees labored in a territorial structure divided into six regions. In Łódź, where PPS membership stood at five hundred by the end of the year, the party organization was further subdivided into five districts.[31] Moreover, the PPS had created party cells in many of the larger factories, the only socialist party to do so before

---

29. Blobaum, *Feliks Dzierżyński*, pp. 160–161. For a justification of partyjność as it applied to the trade union movement, see Rosa Luxemburg, *Massenstreik, Partei, und Gewerkschaften* (Hamburg, 1906).

30. See Stanisław Pestkowski, "SDKPiL i kwestja związków zawodowych w 1905–1907 r.," *Z Pola Walki*, 7–8 (1929): 96–120; and Wacław Konderski, "Wspomnienia działacza związków zawodowych SDKPiL," ibid., 13 (1961): 71–80.

31. Władysław Lech Karwacki, *Łódzka organizacja Polskiej Partii Socjalistycznej–Lewicy, 1906–1918* (Łódź, 1964), p. 38.

Publishing *Górnik* (The Miner), the PPS Newspaper in Sosnowiec. (Muzeum Nie-podległości 7271)

the revolution. While party members from the intelligentsia continued to contribute 80 percent of the membership dues, party numerical strength was already firmly anchored in a rank and file composed of industrial workers. Finally, the PPS had initiated agitation in the countryside, developing five "activity groups" that hoped to organize workers in the sugar beet plants, distilleries, and breweries scattered throughout rural Poland.[32]

Against this background of a mass organization in the making, a process far more advanced than in the case of the SDKPiL, the PPS was confronted at an earlier stage by the same contradictions that would later plague the

32. Anna Żarnowska, *Geneza rozłamu w Polskiej Partii Socjalistycznej, 1904–1906* (Warsaw, 1965), pp. 21–28, 46.

Social Democrats. In the first years of the century, the Starzy, led by Józef Piłsudski, sat at the top of the PPS hierarchy, dominating the Central Workers' Committee (CKR), especially its three-person executive commission, as well as the party's leading theoretical organ *Przedświt* (Pre-Dawn) and the Foreign Committee of its émigré organization. Reared in the traditions of conspiracy and nurtured by dreams of renewing armed struggle for Polish independence, the party's Old Guard considered the socialist movement and its organizational expression through the PPS a means of recruiting a mass base of support, and potential fighters, for the country's liberation.

Yet as the PPS developed the vehicles for recruiting a mass base, younger activists involved in the organizational spadework began to perceive that effective recruitment of workers required something more than merely raising before them the lofty goal of an independent Poland. For example, Stanisław Jędrzejewski's initial support of Piłsudski's plans for an armed uprising turned to opposition after his experience as head of the party's Łódź Committee.[33] Organizational and political realities soon brought on a theoretical debate, especially within the émigré organization, over two fundamental and related issues: the place of the goal of a democratic independent Polish state in the party's program and the party's relationship to a revived Russian revolutionary movement. More immediately, a minority within the Central Workers' Committee, composed of Feliks Sachs, Jan Rutkiewicz, and Adam Buyno, all with ties to the party organization in the Kingdom, began at the end of 1903 to act in open opposition to the Starzy leadership. Charging that the CKR and especially its executive commission had lost contact with the organization in the Kingdom, the opposition called for the convocation of a new party congress, which, it hoped, would sanction a general democratization of decision making in the PPS.

The Russo-Japanese War and the issues arising from it widened the cleavage between the Starzy and Młodzi during the course of 1904. As mentioned earlier, the Starzy sought to take immediate advantage of the war in the Far East hoping it would escalate into a general European conflict. By supporting the Japanese side, the Starzy intended to give history a push while gaining an ally for its efforts to resurrect an independent Polish state—thus the secret discussions between representatives of the party leadership, including Piłsudski, and Japanese diplomatic and military officials in London and Tokyo, in a vain effort to win Japanese support, moral and material, for PPS armed activity against the Russians. Mean-

---

33. Karwacki, *Łódzka organizacja Polskiej Partii Socjalistycznej*, pp. 39–40.

while, inside the Kingdom itself, the Młodzi discovered through practical experience among the would-be proletarian warriors that workers were more easily mobilized by agitation that focused on declining living standards brought on by the war and on the disruption to their lives caused by mobilization. Thus while the Starzy labored to prolong and extend the Russo-Japanese conflict, the Młodzi organized dozens of successful demonstrations against the war.

These glaringly contradictory responses to the Far Eastern war eventually led in October to a conference of the CKR in Kraków, which resulted in a temporary and unstable compromise. The bankruptcy of its foray into diplomacy forced the Starzy leadership to make concessions to the opposition that had congregated mainly in the party's Warsaw and Łódź organizations. A good deal of controversy had revolved around the party's poorly trained "fighting circles of workers' self-defense," created by the Młodzi to defend demonstrations organized by the PPS but intended by the Starzy to provide cadres for the future Polish legions that were to carry out an armed insurrection. At the Kraków conference the leadership was forced to abandon its grand projects, accept the opposition's emphasis on political agitation and organizational activity, and recognize the burgeoning Russian revolutionary movement as an ally against the tsarist autocracy. At the same time, however, the Młodzi agreed to Piłsudski's newly revised tactics of "armed action" and to engage the Russian government on a limited scale through the aegis of the fighting circles. Piłsudski assumed responsibility for the smuggling of men, arms, and ammunition to the self-defense circles, which would now participate in "armed demonstrations" and in terrorist actions against the regime's most hated representatives. The fighting circles did, however, remain formally subordinate to the directives of the regional party committees controlled by the Młodzi.[34]

The events of 1904, culminating in the October conference of the CKR, had transformed the dual personality of the PPS into a dual power relationship between the party's Old Guard and the representatives of the emerging mass organization. The January–February general strike quickly disrupted this balance of power within the PPS and tipped the scales in favor of the Młodzi. During the strike, taboos disappeared. The SDKPiL and the Jewish Bund, once scorned rivals, were now courted by local PPS organizations as partners in a common revolutionary cause. In the party's

---

34. Żarnowska, *Geneza rozłamu*, p. 149; Władysław Pobóg-Malinowski, *Józef Piłsudski, 1867–1914* (London, 1964), pp. 287–290; Jerzy Pająk, *Organizacje bojowe partii politycznych w Królestwie Polskim, 1904–1911* (Warsaw, 1985), pp. 44–49; Henryk Piasecki, *Żydowska organizacja PPS, 1893–1907* (Wrocław, 1978), p. 106.

published declarations, Poland's national liberation was linked directly to the outcome of the revolution in the empire rather than to the hallowed old conception of armed struggle with Russia.[35] By March, the Młodzi, convinced that the mass organization in the Kingdom stood behind them, decided to move for control of party executive institutions.

To do so, the Młodzi had first to circumvent one such institution, the executive commission of the CKR monopolized by the Starzy. Without the prior agreement of the executive commission, a party conference transformed itself into the Seventh Congress of the PPS, which, in turn, elected a new CKR that excluded the Old Guard with the single exception of Piłsudski. Programmatic pronouncements, moreover, showed the complete lack of support among the party rank and file for the old project of an armed uprising. The independence of Poland remained a goal of the party's political activity, now translated, however, into the demand for a constituent assembly in Warsaw, which itself was made dependent on the victory of the Russian revolution. Finally, the congress entrusted the new CKR with transforming the cadre-type fighting circles into a mass offensive force through the creation of a new fighting organization, the Organizacja Spiskowo-Bojowa (OSB), whose executive, the Wydział, was subordinate to and directed by the CKR.[36]

At first the Starzy treated the Seventh Congress as an illegal "coup" by the Młodzi, ignoring its decisions and opposing the new OSB.[37] For a moment, a divorce of the old and now-dethroned conspiratorial elite from the younger representatives of the party's mass organization seemed imminent. Yet for the next nineteen months, a split was avoided, largely because the Starzy were still left with considerable room to maneuver. Until the June party council, the Starzy maintained their control of *Przedświt* as well as a presence in the CKR.[38] Once these strongholds were lost, developments within the party's fighting organization offered the Starzy an opportunity to rebuild a power base.

The PPS fighting organization, whether in the form of the OSB or its

---

35. Karwacki, *Łódzka organizacja Polskiej Partii Socjalistycznej*, p. 45; Żarnowska, *Geneza rozłamu*, pp. 169–170; Piasecki, *Żydowska organizacja PPS*, p. 132; AGAD KGGW 2501, Appeal of the CKR of the PPS to the Polish Intelligentsia, February 1905.
36. For a discussion of the Seventh Congress of the PPS, see Żarnowska, *Geneza rozłamu*, pp. 176–190. For differing interpretations among Starzy and Młodzi over the meaning of a constituent assembly in Warsaw, see K. J. Cottam, *Bolesław Limanowski, 1835–1935: A Study in Socialism and Nationalism* (Boulder, 1978), p. 157. The creation of the OSB is discussed in Pająk, *Organizacje bojowe*, pp. 55–58.
37. Pobóg-Malinowski, *Józef Piłsudski*, pp. 299–300.
38. Żarnowska, *Geneza rozłamu*, pp. 214, 229–230.

successors, itself became a mass entity. This development was unique to the PPS, from whose general membership at least one-eighth belonged to its fighting organization. As membership in the fighting organization increased, from the 1,345 "fighters" in the OSB (March–October 1905) to the 6,533 "fighters" at the time of the November 1906 party split,[39] the question of the fighting organization's relationship to other party institutions inevitably arose. The relatively open recruitment into the fighting organization also made it vulnerable to provocation and mass arrests. Through adroit manipulation of these issues and problems, the Starzy were able to stage a remarkable political comeback, a comeback that would tear the PPS apart.

The expansion of the fighting organization's activities after the January–February general strike and the shift from a "defensive" to an "offensive" strategy resulted, in practice, in scores of assassination attempts on high administrative and police officials. Most of these actions failed, and the more successful assassinations of police spies, informers, and provocateurs did not lessen the fighting organization's vulnerability. The most dramatic case involved the captured PPS fighter Shlomo Eksztein, from whom the Okhrana extracted information about the fighting organization's leading activists (several of whom were subsequently arrested), their involvement in past assassination attempts, and their plans to kill the new Warsaw governor-general, Konstantin Maksimovich.[40] Already in June, the Starzy began to call for the autonomy of the fighting organization's executive committee, its conversion to a conspiratorial body, and a shift in strategy from the costly acts of terrorism against individual representatives of the regime to disciplined partisan-style action against state institutions.

Such arguments failed to impress the Młodzi-dominated CKR but found growing resonance within the fighting organization itself, especially its Wydział headed by Walery Sławek. After the experience of the Łódź Uprising, which strengthened Piłsudski's position, the Wydział planned and carried out several raids on county treasuries in July and August without the knowledge of the CKR. Only one of these raids was successful, that carried out by Józef Montwiłł-Mirecki at Opatów, which brought the organization over sixteen thousand rubles.[41] In arrests, the raids were as

39. Pająk, *Organizacje bojowe,* p. 108.
40. AGAD KGGW 2492, Warsaw Superintendent of Police to the WGG, July 14 (27), 1905, with enclosed protocol of the Okhrana investigation.
41. Żarnowska, *Geneza rozłamu,* p. 272; Pobóg-Malinowski, *Józef Piłsudski,* p. 323; AGAD KGGW 2572, Radom Governor to the WGG, July 27 (August 10), 1905, and Report of the SDPA to the WGG, August 9 (22), 1905.

costly as the assassination attempts, but a future direction of "armed action" and the means for financing it had been indicated.

By mid-October, Piłsudski and the Starzy had managed to regain a foothold in the fighting organization, which as a result of the Minsk party council, underwent another structural mutation. An Organizacja Techniczno-Bojowa (OTB—Technical Fighting Organization) now replaced the OSB to serve as "a fighting school for the entire party" in preparation for an armed revolution in the Kingdom. Simultaneously, the Minsk council created the Central Fighting Circle under the direction of Piłsudski, whose main tasks were to perfect arms-smuggling operations, train instructors, build laboratories, and create new fighting units for the larger organization. The latter's executive, the Wydział Bojowy (Fighting Department), was organized along the strict conspiratorial lines advocated by the Starzy, which enabled Piłsudski to gradually remove it from the supervision and control of the CKR. The concessions to the Starzy and the return to a power-sharing formula, designed to uphold party unity, proved in the end a recipe for disaster.

In the last months of 1905 and the first months of 1906, when the fate of the revolution appeared to hang in the balance, the CKR and the regional committees looked to the fighting organization as an armed revolutionary force available for immediate action on any number of fronts. Piłsudski and the Starzy, true to their traditional insurrectionary conceptions, sought to preserve, train, and militarize the party's fighting forces for a future uprising. Consequently, the Wydział Bojowy refused to carry out the instructions of the CKR, resulting in endless conflict.

Meanwhile, the Starzy continued to regain lost political ground. The failure of the December general strike and the reimposition of martial law on the entire Kingdom supported the Old Guard's arguments, presented in its factional organ *Nowe Życie* (New Life), for beginning to prepare for an eventual Russo-Polish war by disengaging the party from ineffective participation in empirewide revolutionary manifestations. From Austrian Poland, the venerable Polish Social Democratic leader Ignacy Daszyński came to the aid of the Starzy. In an open letter published in the Kraków-based *Naprzód* (Forward) in early January 1906, Daszyński wrote a blistering attack on the politics and tactics of the Młodzi-dominated CKR. He especially targeted the involvement in the December general strike and support for an autonomous Kingdom within a constitutional and democratic Russia, when, in his opinion, a separate Polish state should be the movement's most important and immediate political goal. Coming from the most respected Polish socialist in Europe and a person whose own fame rested on legal, parliamentary activity and leadership of an open, mass party, Daszyński's open letter stung the Młodzi to the quick.[42]

Placed on the defensive, the Młodzi were forced to make concessions to their opponents at the Eighth Congress of the PPS, which met in Lwów during the second half of February 1906. Although the Młodzi retained a majority on the CKR, its overall composition became decidedly more "centrist." More important, all the party's fighting organizations were made subordinate to the Wydział Bojowy, that is, to Piłsudski. Unfortunately, the congress failed to spell out the relationship between Piłsudski's Fighting Department and the central party organs.[43]

Naturally, the Młodzi and Starzy continued to go their separate ways after the Lwów congress. As the mass organization turned to agrarian strike agitation and legal trade union activity that spring, Piłsudski worked even harder to make the Wydział Bojowy a secret agency with the aim of removing it from the supervision and control of the CKR. Piłsudski's plans for striking a major blow against the Russian state administration, which required both time and a buildup of forces, were undermined, however, within the fighting organization, whose rank-and-file bojowcy itched for immediate action. To maintain his support within the fighting organization, Piłsudski was forced to agree to a series of small-scale terrorist actions carried out during the spring of 1906.[44] These attacks on post offices, armored cars, postal trains, and local administration occurred without the authorization of the CKR and led to constant quarrels between it and Piłsudski's Fighting Department.

A June 1906 party council proved to be the last effort to reach a compromise between the Młodzi and Starzy and avoid a split of the PPS. To mollify the Old Guard, the CKR was again revamped, now constituted entirely of "centrists." Moreover, the OTB and Central Fighting Circle were merged into a single fighting organization, and Piłsudski was reconfirmed as head of the Wydział Bojowy. Much to the chagrin of the Old Guard, however, the June council placed Piłsudski's Fighting Department under the direct supervision of the CKR, and regional units of the unified fighting organization were made subordinate to the regional party com-

---

42. So shocked were the Młodzi by Daszyński's letter that not until a year later, *after* the party split, did they upbraid the socialist veteran for being a "realist" in Galicja but "a romantic and a dreamer regarding our revolutionary struggle" in the Kingdom; see M. Kowieński, "Hasło niepodległości Polski dawniej a dziś," *Myśl Socjalistyczna* (Socialist Thought), no. 1 (May 1907).
43. Żarnowska, *Geneza rozłamu*, pp. 331–337.
44. Pobóg-Malinowski, *Józef Piłsudski*, pp. 338–341.

mittees.[45] To oversee "the reorganization of the party's fighting forces," the council appointed a special commission.

Despite the new "centrist" orientation in the CKR, the Starzy responded to the decisions of the June council by convening a "conference of fighters" in Kraków in July which refused to permit members of the newly appointed commission to attend its deliberations and severely criticized the proposed changes in the fighting organization.[46] The Starzy rejected the idea of a split, however, and would continue to do so until the bitter end. Divorce from the party's mass organization, still considered the main recruiting ground for "fighters" in Piłsudski's guerrilla military organization of the future, was something to be avoided at all costs.[47]

Yet precisely because the bojowcy were recruited from the mass organization, the Starzy could not control the impulse for action among those who, as a leading Piłsudskiite historian put it, "did not know how to gaze into the future."[48] The failure of Piłsudski and his collaborators to restrain the bojowcy had already led to the decisions of the June council. Between August and November, the clamor within the fighting organization for "real activity" would lead to several actions reluctantly sanctioned by the Wydział Bojowy and roundly condemned by the CKR. The first major incident, "Bloody Wednesday" of August 15, 1906, was the fighting organization's coordinated and murderous assaults on unsuspecting Russian police, gendarmes, state officials, and soldiers in various parts of the Kingdom, which left seventy-six dead, including many innocent bystanders.[49] Apart from the hail of public criticism that rained down on the PPS from rival parties across the political spectrum, the CKR was especially embarrassed by the attacks on the Russian army, whose troops it was trying to agitate for the revolutionary cause.

The CKR's decision in the aftermath of Bloody Wednesday to restrict the party's "fighting tactics" to pure self-defense set the stage for the November split. The fighting organization's attack on a postal train near

45. Pająk, *Organizacje bojowe*, pp. 87–88.
46. Żarnowska, *Geneza rozłamu*, p. 417.
47. On the attitude of the Starzy toward a party split, see Teodor Ładyka, *Polska Partia Socjalistyczna (Frakcja Rewolucyjna) w latach 1906–1914* (Warsaw, 1972), pp. 26–30.
48. Pobóg-Malinowski, *Józef Piłsudski*, p. 338.
49. For official reports on Bloody Wednesday, see AGAD KGGW 519, Report of the Płock Governor's Office on Events in the First Half of August 1906; APŁ KGP 1583, Piotrków Governor to the WGG, August 4 (17), 1906; APW WWO 41, Report of the Warsaw Okhrana on the Activities of the PPS, April 1 to October 1, 1906; and Paweł Korzec, ed., *Źródła do dziejów rewolucji 1905–1907 w okręgu łódzkim*, vol. 2 (Warsaw, 1964), pp. 348–349, 370–374.

Imprisoned members of the PPS Fighting Organization in Radom, 1907. (Muzeum Niepodległości 473)

the Rogów station in Piotrków on November 8, the third such action organized not only without the CKR's knowledge but in spite of its prohibition of such action, led to sixteen casualties among the Russian soldiers guarding the train.[50] This time, the CKR suspended the Wydział Bojowy. The Starzy responded by organizing yet another "conference of fighters" in Zakopane, which defended the Rogów action and, in the form of an ultimatum, demanded that the CKR's suspension of the Wydział Bojowy be lifted. When the Ninth Congress of the PPS convened in Vienna on November 19, it not only upheld the suspension but declared the Zakopane conference illegal and rejected Piłsudski's "mandate" to represent the fighting organization. The Starzy then walked out of the Vienna meeting, only to hold a separate conference in Kraków and create the PPS–Revolutionary Faction. The Młodzi and the party centrists who had constituted an overwhelming majority at the Ninth Congress subsequently became known as the PPS-Left.[51]

At the time of the November split, the PPS counted fifty-five thousand

50. Adam Próchnik, *Studia z dziejów polskiego ruchu robotniczego* (Warsaw, 1958), pp. 409–449.
51. For the denouement of the PPS drama, see Żarnowska, *Geneza rozłamu*, pp. 440–458; Pobóg-Malinowski, *Józef Piłsudski*, pp. 353–369; and Ładyka, *Polska Partia Socjalistyczna*, pp. 19–30.

members, making it numerically the strongest socialist party in the Kingdom. The PPS, first and foremost, was a party of the industrial proletariat, maintaining its strongest base among workers in heavy industry and in the larger factories. It had also enjoyed the greatest success of any party in trade union organization. At the time of the split, thirty-seven thousand members belonged to the unions affiliated with, but not directly linked to or controlled by, the Polish Socialist Party.[52] By preserving the "nonparty" label, however fictitious, the PPS-connected unions managed to maintain a precarious legal status that furthered rather than restricted the party's influence on the labor movement. So great was the authority of the PPS on the shop floor that workers in several instances took their conflicts with management to the party for resolution.

This rank and file was at first confused and disoriented by the party split. After the defection of a few hundred members to the SDKPiL, a majority, or approximately thirty-six thousand, sided with the PPS-Left, and nineteen thousand went with the Revolutionary Faction, as the latter took advantage of a good deal of sentiment against the split in several local organizations. But the Revolutionary Faction's numerical support had been inflated by the confusion, and its disinterest in the bread-and-butter issues of wages and working conditions, symbolized by its withdrawal from the trade union movement, quickly led to an erosion of the facade of mass support. Within a year of the split, the Revolutionary Faction would be compelled by its own weakness to dissolve its organization in Łódź.[53]

Through its reluctant divorce with the Młodzi, the Starzy effectively separated from the PPS mass organization as well. Even that part of the fighting organization, numbering more than three thousand, which sided with the Old Guard's tactic of active armed struggle would soon shrink to nothing through provocation and arrests, no longer able to replenish it ranks. After some dramatic sparks in 1907 and a spectacular last hurrah in September 1908 when the armed robbery of a postal train at the Bezdany station near Vilna brought in more than two hundred thousand rubles, the Revolutionary Faction's fighting organization withdrew to Galicja in 1909 with fewer than a hundred members.[54] From there, Piłsudski and his small camp of followers would continue their lonely championship of Polish independence by armed conquest, only now through supraparty agencies.

52. Janina Kasprzakowa, *Ideologia i polityka PPS-Lewicy w latach 1907–1914* (Warsaw, 1965), p. 30.
53. Ibid., p. 28; Ładyka, *Polska Partia Socjalistyczna*, pp. 33–35, 83–88, 126–128.
54. Pająk, *Organizacje bojowe*, pp. 100–101; Ładyka, *Polska Partia Socjalistyczna*, pp. 122–123. On the Bezdany train robbery, see Władysław Pobóg-Malinowski, *Akcja bojowa pod Bezdanami, 26 września 1908* (Warsaw, 1933).

As a consequence, they gave up even the ghost of the PPS, whose legacy had passed long before from the old conspiratorial elite to activists schooled in the politics of a mass organization.

## Other Parties

Just before the revolution, the General Jewish Workers Union, or Bund, was the envy of and, in many instances, the model for other socialist parties in Russian Poland. Although the mainstay of the Bund's organization was its membership in the empire's Lithuanian, Byelorussian, and Ukrainian provinces, its two thousand members in the Kingdom of Poland put it numerically ahead of both the PPS and the SDKPiL. The Bund, moreover, had perfected its agitation, publication, and smuggling operations and had pioneered in the development and deployment of "self-defense" forces. Despite this headstart, the Bund's organization in the Kingdom did not share in the spectacular growth that characterized its Polish counterparts. Bund membership in Russian Poland reached a peak of only eight thousand during the course of the revolution, something less than would be expected of a "mass" party.

The Bund's relative organizational failure in the Kingdom during the revolution was due primarily to stiff competition from numerous rivals for the political support of the Jewish masses. First of all, the two Polish Marxist parties did not hesitate to invade the Bund's turf, despite the latter's repeated insistence on an exclusive right to organize among the Yiddish-speaking poor. The Jewish Organization of the PPS, set up specifically for that purpose, claimed a membership of fifty-two hundred "organized comrades" in October 1906, although fewer than half that number actually paid party dues.[55] Although the "internationalist" mentality of the SDKPiL prohibited it from creating a separate Jewish organization, it too claimed eight hundred active Jewish members and another fifteen hundred "sympathizers" in July 1906.[56] Even greater competition came from the Zionist movement, especially from its leftist, socialist variations. Both the Zionist-Socialist and the Poalei-Zion parties, consisting of only handfuls of members in 1905, underwent rapid organizational expansion in 1906 as they developed local committees, trade unions, and regularly appearing publications. The sudden emergence and popularity of

---

55. Piasecki, *Żydowska organizacja PPS*, pp. 221–222.
56. Krasny, "Stan organizacji SDKPiL," p. 60.

these organizations, according to Okhrana reports, definitely limited the Bund's possibilities of expanding its influence.[57]

Although its potential mass constituency was carved up into so many pieces, the Bund did maintain a more highly visible political presence than its Zionist rivals. Through a variety of terrorist actions, ranging from assassinations of state officials to the organization of popular actions against brothels, the Bund was able to project an image more formidable than its numbers would suggest. The Bund's "self-defense" force of eight hundred "fighters" was equal to that of the SDKPiL, despite the latter's possession of five times as many members in its mass organization.[58] Only the PPS rivaled the Bund in the proportion of party members under arms. The Bund's militancy, however, exposed it to provocation and, like the PPS–Revolutionary Faction, it was forced to disband its Łódź organization at the end of 1907 after a series of arrests.[59]

Although the Bund survived both the revolution and its competition, weakened but intact, the PPS-Proletariat was forced to leave the field by revolution's end. Ludwik Kulczycki's party, which had split from the PPS in 1900, could never expand its organization beyond Warsaw, nor could it develop a program that set it apart from its rivals. Unable to benefit from the revolutionary activity of 1905, the Proletariat became, in the Okhrana's words, "a party in a state of collapse" during the first ten months of 1906, "caught in a struggle for its existence, against the government on the one hand and against other revolutionary parties, especially the PPS, on the other."[60] Reduced to propaganda activity, the Proletariat was unable to stop defections to the mass organizations of the PPS and SDKPiL, especially to their trade unions, nor the subsequent draining of party finances. By the time the Okhrana filed its next periodic report, the PPS-Proletariat had issued its last proclamation.

Even more fleeting were the anarchist and communist groups that emerged in Warsaw during the peak period of the revolution at the end of 1905, only to be returned to oblivion by the martial law repressions of 1906 and 1907. Numbering at most a few hundred young men and women, mainly in their teens and disproportionately Jewish, the membership of these groups engaged almost exclusively in terrorist activities.[61] "The

---

57. APW WWO 41, Reports on the Activities of the Bund and SDPKiL, and Zionist-Socialists and Poalei-Zion, respectively, for the period April–October 1906.
58. Pająk, *Organizacje bojowe*, p. 185.
59. Karwacki, *Łódzka organizacje Polska Partii Socjalistycznej*, pp. 148–149.
60. APW WWO 41, Report on the Activities of the PPS-Proletariat, January–October 1906.
61. According to Jerzy Pająk, 240 "fighters" participated in the anarchist-communist terrorist organizations; see Pająk, *Organizacje bojowe*, p. 202.

Spirit of Destruction is the Spirit of Creativity,'' proclaimed a November 1905 appeal of the group "International," which went on to call for the establishment of an "anarchist commune" by means of individual and mass terror.[62] Such slogans found absolutely no resonance among the general population. Typical was the attitude of the Jews of Kawalaria in Suwałki Province who petitioned the authorities to deport an anarchist who had offended them by his violent language at a mass meeting.[63]

Isolated from the population, the anarchist groups could not hope to survive. Not surprisingly, thirteen members of the "International" group became the logical choice for the first executions under martial law on January 15, 1906, with more to follow at the end of the month.[64] The January executions wiped out the International group, but a series of arrests later that summer revealed the existence of Zmowa Robotnicza (Workers Conspiracy), a group whose members had been recruited mainly from the fighting organizations of other parties.[65] One last flurry of anarchist activity hit Warsaw in the spring of 1907, but the arrest by the Okhrana between June 16 and July 30 of forty-six anarchists from various smaller groups brought an end to this short-lived phenomenon.[66]

Between the socialist and nationalist parties stood populist and liberal parties, the Polski Związek Ludowy (PZL—Polish People's Union) and the Pedecja (the popular acronym for the Progressive Democratic Union), respectively. The PZL, as mentioned earlier in this chapter, was formed in November 1904 by renegades from the Endecja-inspired TON organization. From the beginning, village school teachers played a primary role among the populist rank and file. Conceived as a cadre-style organization that would serve as the basis for the formation of a mass party similar to the Stronnictwo Ludowe (People's Party) in Austrian Poland, the PZL differed in its social and political radicalism from its populist counterpart in Galicja. Populism in Russian Poland thus came to be characterized by a strident anticlericalism, opposition to cooperation with noble landowners in agrarian circles and rural cultural organizations, and a preparedness to collaborate with the socialist parties, especially the PPS.[67]

---

62. See the documentary collection *Anarchizm i anarchiści na ziemiach polskich do 1914 roku,* ed. Herman Rappaport (Warsaw, 1981), pp. 18–21.
63. AGAD KGGW 2524, Report of the SDPA to the WGG, October 28 (November 10), 1905.
64. Rappaport, *Anarchizm,* pp. 24–25, 27–28.
65. Ibid., pp. 37–38; APW WGZŻ 2495 includes files, compiled between September and November 1906, on six members of the group, four of whom were women.
66. Rappaport, *Anarchizm,* pp. 48–64.
67. Radlak, *Polski Związek Ludowy,* pp. 13–21; Jan Molenda, "Miejsce ruchu ludowego

In its first program, published in May 1905, the PZL called for supreme authority to reside in a democratically elected Polish parliament. During the course of 1905, however, the PZL adopted some of the utopian, cooperatist conceptions of the former socialist theoretician Edward Abramowski. Indeed, at the end of the year, Abramowski would draft a revised PZL program that in its statement of maximum goals foresaw a "People's Republic" whose economy would be transformed through a process of voluntary association. Closer to the ground, Abramowski's minimum program called for the Kingdom's political autonomy, realized through both a national legislature and wide-ranging popular self-government at the local level.[68] Regarding the latter, the PZL placed much emphasis on the gmina movement and went far beyond the Endecja's goal of polonization of rural administrative and educational institutions. Instead, the PZL called for equal voting rights for all inhabitants of the gminy, whose affairs should be decided exclusively by the local population. The PZL also called on rural communities to engage in active civil disobedience and asked gmina and village officials not to carry out their responsibilities until the tsarist government conceded home rule to an autonomous Polish administration.[69]

At the Peasants Congress organized by the PZL in June 1906 in Warsaw, the majority of those in attendance were proprietors of medium-sized holdings, people who enjoyed authority in their communities either as model farmers or as elected local officials. Most were literate and some had contributed correspondence to newspapers such as *Gazeta Świąteczna* (Holiday Gazette) which enjoyed broad circulation in the Polish countryside.[70] This emerging rank and file influenced PZL attitudes toward the basic issues of land reform and agrarian strikes. The populists favored the nationalization of church and (Russian) state property and the expropriation of private estates, albeit through legislative acts and with due compensation for the former owners. This respect for property also informed the PZL's ambiguous position on agrarian strikes, which fluctuated between sympathy for the demands of farm workers and fear of the ruinous effects of work stoppages on the agrarian economy.[71]

---

w życiu wsi i wśród innych obozów politycznych," in *Polska XIX wieku: Państwo-społeczeństwo-kultura,* ed. Stefen Kieniewicz (Warsaw, 1982), pp. 353–403.

68. Radlak, *Polski Związek Ludowy,* pp. 25–26.

69. AGAD KGGW 2505, Appeal of the PZL of November 1905, and 2517, Płock Governor to the WGG, December 10 (23), 1905; APW WWO 44, Okhrana translation into Russian of Appeal of the PZL of February 1906.

70. Radlak, *Polski Związek Ludowy,* p. 31.

71. Ibid., pp. 29, 36–37; see also Wiesław Piatkowski, *Idee agrarne ugrupowań politycznych w Królestwie Polskim w latach 1892–1918* (Łódź, 1992), pp. 112–125.

Unfortunately for the PZL, the conditions of martial law and the restriction on legal political activity halted its evolution toward an independent, peasant mass party able to compete at the national level. When the first blows of repression fell in the middle of 1906, the PZL had organized circles in forty-one gminy of Warsaw Province and had made some significant inroads in Lublin and Płock provinces. The party was virtually nonexistent, however, in other regions. Moreover, it lacked the survival instincts of the PPS and SDKPiL, nurtured by years of conspiratorial activity. From mid-1906, the PZL concentrated increasingly on educational, economic, and cultural activity, traditions derived from the movement's prerevolutionary roots in TON, while Stefan Julian Brzeziński and Zygmunt Nowicki vainly struggled to maintain a series of legal press organs. After mass arrests of populist activists in the spring and summer of 1907, the PZL simply ceased to exist.

Despite its short life, the PZL did leave behind a significant legacy, as the organization's remnants found new homes in the educational movement in the countryside, spearheaded by the journal *Zaranie* (The Dawn), and in the "Staszic" circles of peasant agriculturalists.[72] Led by Maksymilian Malinowski and Jadwiga Dziubińska, postrevolutionary populism survived nationalist competition and the active opposition of the Catholic episcopate to form a new political party, the Stronnictwo Ludowe (People's Alliance) in 1915. Mergers with smaller groups and name changes would follow, but in 1918, as a Polish state resurfaced on the political map of Europe, the Polskie Stronnictwo Ludowe—Wyzwolenie (Polish People's Alliance—Liberation) would take its place as the principal peasant party in the former Russian zone. True to its revolutionary roots, the PSL-Wyzwolenie remained throughout its history more radical and anticlerical than its counterparts from the Polish territories previously under Austrian and Prussian rule.

Like the populists, the Progressive Democrats traced their immediate organizational roots to the last months of 1904, when Społeczność Polska (Polish Society), a forum among the liberal Warsaw intelligentsia inspired by the journal *Kuźnica* (The Forge), organized a series of barely disguised political meetings to discuss the crisis created by the Russo-Japanese War and also the possibility of organizing a broad opposition movement. With the exception of the uncompromising SDKPiL, the socialist parties were

72. On the *Zaranie* and "Staszic" movements, see Piatkowski, *Idee agrarne*, pp. 126–139, and Zenon Kmiecik, *Ruch oświatowy na wsi; Królestwo Polskie, 1905–1914* (Warsaw, 1963), pp. 79–151. The Staszic circles were named after Stanisław Staszic, a famous Polish patriot of the late eighteenth and early nineteenth centuries.

drawn to the Społeczność Polska meetings by the prospect of using them as a tribune for their own political propaganda.[73] The association of Polish liberalism with the radical labor movement grew stronger in late January 1905 when *Kuźnica* sponsored the formation of the Committee for Aid to the Strikers. Subsequent strikes by railroad personnel, postal and telegraph workers, and employees in the pharmaceutical and insurance industries brought the liberal intelligentsia into direct contact with the strike movement. Inspired by the promises in the October Manifesto, the formation of unions and associations among these occupational groups, as well as among teachers, lawyers, engineers, and technicians, followed immediately thereafter.

At the end of November, representatives of twelve professional unions, representing six thousand members, met in Warsaw, where five unions immediately joined an umbrella organization, the Union of Unions of the Kingdom of Poland (Zjednoczenie Związków Królestwa Polskiego), created in imitation of the liberal Russian model. By the end of January 1906, eleven unions had joined the Polish variant.[74] In Russia, the Union of Unions provided the liberal movement, represented politically by the Constitutional Democrats, with its primary base of popular support. Such might have been the case for the newly formed Progressive Democratic Union as well, had it not been for a fundamental division over the issue of participation in elections to the Russian State Duma.

Immediately after the October Manifesto, on November 2, 1905, the Pedecja joined the various socialist parties in a mass meeting at the Warsaw Philharmonia attended by some four thousand people. The physical removal of representatives of the Endecja set the tone for the meeting and isolated the Progressive Democrats in their announced intention to participate in the Duma elections. Pedecja speakers, who explained that the party's elected candidates would walk out of the Duma if that body failed to accept demands for the Kingdom's autonomy, a general political amnesty, and the lifting of martial law, nevertheless failed to carry the day against the socialists. The meeting passed instead a series of radical resolutions and resolved to boycott the elections and settle for nothing less than the overthrow of the autocracy and the convocation of a constituent assembly.[75]

Worse still, the Pedecja had failed to gauge the mood of its potential

73. Halina Kiepurska, *Inteligencja zawodowa Warszawy, 1905–1907* (Warsaw, 1967), pp. 64–67.
74. Ibid., pp. 229–238, 294.
75. AGAD KGGW 2493, Report of the SDPA to the WGG, October 24 (November 6), 1905; APW ZOW 34, Internal Memorandum of the Office of the Warsaw Superintendent of Police, October 21 (November 3), 1905.

constituency in the Union of Unions, which a few days after the meeting in the Warsaw Philharmonia, came out in favor of an election boycott.[76] For a time, it appeared that the Pedecja would follow that constituency and adhere to the boycott, but at the last minute its leadership, headed by the journalist Aleksander Świętochowski, decided to enter the campaign. Rather than face the Endecja juggernaut alone, the Pedecja hastily entered into an electoral alliance with the assimilationist Jewish Electoral Committee, which itself had few ties with the mass of Yiddish-speaking Jews. This alliance not only widened the chasm between the Pedecja and the radical parties but encouraged the Endecja, concerned that Jewish votes for Polish liberals could lead to the defeat of its own candidates, to turn to anti-Semitism in its electoral propaganda.[77] The result was a crushing defeat for Polish liberalism in the first Duma elections, a defeat that stood out in marked contrast to the success of the Russian Constitutional Democrats (on which, more below). Although the Pedecja survived to participate in subsequent duma elections, it never managed to elect a single candidate.

Traditional Polish conservatism, whose banner was picked up in October 1905 by the Stronnictwo Polityki Realnej (Party of Realistic Politics), was also pushed to the political margin as a consequence of the revolution. Aristocratic and conciliationist, the Realists were unable to offer a credible alternative to the Endecja. On the one hand, the long campaign of the conciliationist journal *Kraj* for bilingualism in the Kingdom's administration, courts, and schools and for equal rights for the tsar's Polish subjects was largely realized in 1905 as a result of government concessions. Yet these concessions had been achieved by applying active political pressure on the authorities, tactics the conciliationists adamantly opposed. On the other hand, the Endecja's strong and effective opposition to the radical patriotic and socialist movements, especially its propaganda of "realism" and "sobriety" in Polish politics, expropriated what was left of the conciliationist program.[78]

Nevertheless, the Realists challenged the Endecja in the first Duma elections and were swamped, despite the relatively heavy weight assigned by the empire's electoral law to the landowners' curia. The election results forced the Realists to seek an accommodation with the nationalist move-

76. Kiepurska, *Inteligencja zawodowa Warszawy*, p. 333.
77. See Stephen D. Corrsin, "Polish-Jewish Relations before the First World War: The Case of the State Duma Elections in Warsaw," *GAL-ED* 11 (1989): 37–41.
78. Zenon Kmiecik, *"Kraj" za czasów redaktorstwa Erazma Piltza* (Warsaw, 1969), pp. 400–402; Henryk Wereszycki, *Historia polityczna Polski, 1864–1918*, 2d ed. (Paris, 1979), pp. 225–243.

ment. Despite significant differences between the two parties (the Realists had opposed the school strike and boycott yet were far more tolerant toward the Kingdom's ethnic minorities than the Endecja), they entered a multiparty alliance, known as the "National Concentration," for elections to the Second State Duma. The Endecja's manifest domination of the National Concentration led to the last-minute withdrawal of the Realists from the electoral alliance, again with no real effect on the balloting. The identity of traditional Polish conservatism may have been thereby salvaged, but Polish nationalism had established a near monopoly on the right of the political spectrum.

The shared fate of the Pedecja and the Realists is highly illustrative of the transformation of Polish political culture during these years. Traditional liberalism and conservatism had emerged from the old "political nation" of the szlachta and intelligentsia of gentry origin. Already before 1904, the prerevolutionary positivist and conciliationist ideologies of the traditional elite had been eclipsed in political importance by the popular ideologies of nationalism and socialism. When the events of the revolution placed the "mass nation" at the center of the political stage, the liberal and conservative movements, although they took the form of modern political parties, could never acquire the substance of modern political organizations. Without mass support, the progressives and the Realists could at best hope to survive on the political periphery. Indeed, that they survived at all was primarily by virtue of electoral laws that discriminated in favor of the old elite and an imperial political strategy that conferred on these parties a legal and almost protected status to enable them to compete with their mass-based competitors. Yet such competition was at best symbolic, at worst artificial, and in any case without real significance.

## A Question of Violence

Another attribute of the transformation of political culture in Russian Poland denied to and rejected by the conservatives and liberals, but shared in common by the mass-based parties, was the resort to violence as a means of political struggle. The debut of the "mass nation" was accompanied from the beginning by various forms of popular violence that created a climate for the political terrorism waged by the parties. Indeed, the political resort to violence peaked at the same time as the numerical strength of the mass organizations. The decline of the latter, worn down by martial law and dashed hopes, accompanied a circumscribing of party-promoted violence. In a word, the efficacy of terror as a political weapon depended largely on the attitudes and actions of the "mass nation."

Before 1904, only the PPS-Proletariat openly advocated the use of terror for political ends, although it did not possess the organizational means to translate words into deeds. Similarly, the insurrectionary program of the mainstream PPS featured in *Przedświt* represented wishful thinking rather than political reality. Its first fighting circles were created only in April 1904, and their purpose was neither to carry out terrorist actions nor to provide a cadre for an insurrectionary army but, rather, to defend workers' demonstrations. Even this limited task of workers' self-defense could not be realized until the end of the year. The Bund, in contrast, had developed and deployed armed units much earlier, but their purpose was also defensive, namely, to protect the Jewish poor against the violence of pogroms.

The "armed defense" by the PPS of its planned demonstration on Grzybowski Square in Warsaw on November 13, 1904 (see Chap. 2), marked the transition between defensive and offensive action against the authorities. The Grzybowski Square incident also coincided with increasing cases of confrontation betweens crowds and those sent to disperse them. As the authorities resorted to force in breaking up the large street gatherings, violence frequently resulted. The PPS tactic of "armed defense" therefore corresponded with a growing popular mood to fight back when threatened by police and troops.

Already, at the end of 1904, and especially during the January–February general strike of 1905, criminal elements mixed with protestors and demonstrators, adding yet another dimension to the escalating popular violence. In her germinal article on urban crowd behavior during the revolution, Elżbieta Kaczyńska notes that the line dividing the industrial proletariat from socially marginal groups was a very thin one. Economic necessity could blur that line, drawing "occasional criminals" not only from the relatively large number of unemployed but from wage earners as well. By day, these "occasional criminals" might find themselves in a crowd of striking workers. By night, after the dispersal of the crowd by force, the younger members of this group might join with more hard-core criminal elements in knocking out street lanterns and looting private shops. For their part, the socialist parties, without exception, excused such lawlessness and even sanctioned it, in respect to private property, as a form of class struggle.[79]

79. Kaczyńska, "Tłum i margines społeczny," pp. 222–224; see also her chapter "Tłum a władza: Anatomia masowych ruchów społecznych w Królestwie Polskim na przełomie XIX i XX wieku," in *Przemoc zbiorowa, ruch masowy, rewolucja,* ed. Elżbieta Kaczyńska and Zbigniew Rykowski (Warsaw, 1990), pp. 67–104.

The January–February general strike, together with the popular violence that accompanied it, provided an immediate impulse toward armed action within the emerging mass political organizations. In February, the PPS created the first its succession of fighting organizations designed to deal direct blows to the "tsarist apparatus of oppression."[80] Similarly, the Sixth Congress of the Bund, also held in February, envisaged a more offensive strategy for its forces, whose activities were now stepped up dramatically.[81] At the same time, the Endecja created the first of its paramilitary organizations, Baczność (On Guard), primarily as a response to the growing influence and militarization of the socialist movement.[82] Of the major parties, only the SDKPiL continued to lag behind in the formation of armed units, a process that began in earnest only after the abortive June uprising in Łódź.[83]

Already in February, Okhrana agents in Austria and Prussia noted widespread smuggling of revolvers and explosives into the Kingdom, coming from the same operations that for years had provided safe passage for agitators and antigovernment literature.[84] With these weapons, the PPS, in particular, initiated its campaign of assassination, whose intended victims soon became clear: not only targets with high public visibility but also lower-ranking members of the state apparatus whose main distinction had been their cruelty in dealing with popular unrest. The beginning of the terrorist offensive was marked by the wounding of Baron Nolken, the Warsaw superindentent of police, at the end of March during a bomb explosion at the Twelfth Police Precinct in Praga.[85] Attacks on the Siedlce and Częstochowa chiefs of police quickly followed, although lower police functionaries were the most frequent victims. According to data compiled by the Office of the Warsaw Governor-General, more than one hundred police, gendarmes, and soldiers were killed in terrorist attacks between January 1905 and April 1906; by September 1906, the official death toll by political assassination had reached well over two hundred, not to mention an equal number of "others," namely, police spies and informers.[86]

---

80. Pająk, *Organizacje bojowe*, p. 55.
81. Henry J. Tobias, *The Jewish Bund in Russia: From Its Origins to 1905* (Stanford, 1972), p. 313.
82. Pająk, *Organizacje bojowe*, pp. 192–193; APW WWO 21, Appeal and Statutes of *Baczność*, March 12, 1905.
83. Paweł Korzec, *Walki rewolucyjne w Łodzi i okręgu łódzkim w latach 1905–1907* (Warsaw, 1956), p. 152.
84. AGAD KGGW 2488, Report of the SDPA to the WGG, February 1 (14), 1905.
85. AGAD KGGW 2490, Acting Warsaw Superintendent of Police to the WGG, March 13 (26), 1905, and Report of the SDPA to the WGG, March 22 (April 4), 1905.
86. Kalabiński, *Carat i klasy posiadające*, pp. 474–476, 541–542.

Attempts far outnumbered successful assassinations, however, and the biggest fish, including the Warsaw governors-general Maksimovich and Skalon, tended to get away. Moreover, the attacks on lower-ranking Russian state, police, and military personnel, carried out by individuals or small groups primarily from the PPS fighting organization, were at best only indirectly linked to the popular stuggle. Although the crowd might rejoice at the death of a hated police constable, a senior officer of the Land Guard, or captain of the dragoons, it would mourn the fatalities from its own ranks—bystanders caught unaware in the spray of bullets or by an exploding bomb. Indeed the numbers of innocent and intended victims were too often evenly matched in these incidents, and even the most meticulous researcher is hard pressed to find evidence of the crowd actively assisting the assassins.

Having a similarly ambiguous connection to the popular movement was the use of force and violent threats to collect funds for party purposes. Armed units of the Bund and the SDKPiL, in particular, helped meet the financial needs of their parties by aiming a revolver at the class enemy. Although the coerced funds in part provided support for families of arrested workers and other more noble ends, the majority were designated for the purchase and smuggling of more arms.[87] In the last months of 1905 and the beginning of 1906, a time when state authority in the Kingdom nearly collapsed, these same bands not only engaged in "revolutionary" tax collection but transformed themselves into "revolutionary" police and militias as well as into "revolutionary" courts. The terror and expropriation, the violation of human and individual rights by these bands, in time turned a considerable segment of public opinion against the parties they supposedly represented. For example, the Bund's loss of influence to Zionism in places like Suwałki, Częstochowa, Pułtusk, Mazowieck, Mariampol, and Żelechów was accompanied by anger over a terror that intruded even into community religious practices.[88] Similarly, workers at the Miller factory in Rokice Nowe near Łódź in April 1906 rose to the physical defense of its owner against an armed band from the SDKPiL, killing one of his attackers.[89]

---

87. AGAD KGGW 2498, Report of the SDPA to the WGG, September 17 (30), 1905; APŁ KGP 1515 (2), Chief of the Piotrków Provincial Gendarmes to the Department of Police, March 12 (25), 1905.
88. AGAD KGGW 2505, Warsaw Governor to the WGG, December 15 (28), 1905; 2512, Łomża Governor to the WGG, October 10 (23), 1905; 2522, Suwałki Governor to the WGG, May 18 (31), 1905, and Report of the SDPA to the WGG, June 4 (17), 1905; and 2524, Report of the SDPA to the WGG, December 5 (18), 1905.
89. APŁ KGP 1582, Piotrków Governor to the WGG, April 15 (28), 1906.

But certain terrorist actions of the political parties did have widespread popular support, especially those whose original inspiration came from below. The same disorder and weakness of regular police forces that encouraged Mafia-style urban gangsters and bands of rural horse thieves, whose principal victims came from the popular classes, also permitted workers and peasants to engage in bloody retaliatory actions. In the late spring of 1905, the Bund was the first party to realize the possibilities for mass mobilization afforded by popular vigilantism. Its active participation in attacks on prostitution houses in the Jewish sections of Warsaw, Łódź, and Dąbrowa, which also served as havens for gangsters, brought the Bund an instant and popular notoriety. The PPS and SDKPiL soon followed suit. After publicly proclaiming war against criminal gangs, the PPS fighting organization began hunting down people whose activities were well known to both the police and their victims. For example, the PPS eliminated four Ostrowiec gangsters involved in the armed robbery of a local parish priest.[90] Similarly, both the PPS and the SDKPiL assigned fighters to assist the local peasant vigilante movement against horse thieves in Lublin county.[91] Even the Endecja joined in the vigilante movement. Among other actions, its fighters carried out death sentences against five card-playing gangsters aboard the steamer *Wawel* as it cruised the Vistula.[92]

Besides thieves and gangsters, institutions and symbols of Russian state authority provided the proponents of political violence with both vulnerable and popular targets. Terrorist attacks on state vodka outlets, gmina administration offices, the russified schools, state forest headquarters, jails and prisons, and tax collectors were frequently attended by large crowds that both enjoyed and joined in the action. For example, the PPS attack on the Opatów County treasury in July 1905, resulting in the "expropriation" of sixteen thousand rubles, involved as many as sixty people.[93] Similar numbers of participants, mainly from the small and dispersed factories in the countryside, turned out for PPS actions against state vodka outlets and administrative offices in Siedlce Province.[94] After such attacks, rural communities in Kielce Province not only refused to cooperate with the authorities in identifying the main perpetrators but provided them asylum and

90. AGAD KGGW 2520, Radom Governor to the WGG, December 14 (27), 1905.
91. AGAD KGGW 2515, Report of the SDPA to the WGG, November 16 (29), 1905, and Lublin Governor to the WGG, December 4 (17), 1905.
92. AGAD KGGW 512, Report of the Warsaw Governor's Office for the Second Half of March 1906.
93. AGAD KGGW 2572, Radom Governor to the WGG, June 27 (July 10), 1905.
94. Urszula Głowacka-Maksymiuk, *Gubernia siedlecka w latach rewolucji 1905–1907* (Warsaw, 1985), p. 102.

arms; in several gminy, crowds of peasants even attacked jails to free captured party fighters.[95]

Nowhere, however, did the attacks of political armed bands merge with the broader popular movement as much as in the Lithuanian counties of Suwałki Province, where by the end of 1905 the authorities themselves recognized the de facto rule of the Lithuanian Social Democratic Party (LSDP). For the Lithuanian population, the LSDP championed popular aspirations for national self-rule (much like the Polish Endecja) and pressed social grievances against the region's dominant Polish elite. The party's attacks on vodka outlets, and then on primary schools, and its expropriations from Polish landowners and parish clergy received such a degree of popular sanction that the state was forced to resort to the most drastic measures to restore even a semblance of order.[96]

Popular support for political violence began to wane in 1906, in part because of a successful state strategy that made the local population criminally and financially liable for damages caused by terrorist actions in their communities. At the same time, however, the violence itself became increasingly removed from the popular movements from which it drew its sustenance. For the political parties, filling party coffers was a principal object of the expropriations and assaults on state institutions; the attacks on 159 state vodka retail outlets alone had brought to the parties nearly one hundred thousand rubles. It did not take long for greed to replace ideology as a motivation. In Łódź, a PPS fighting unit, formed entirely of workers, transformed itself into a criminal band that continued to expropriate money in the name of revolutionary goals.[97] In Warsaw, a gang of professional criminals actually posed as a PPS fighting unit.[98]

Sometimes, the criminals were not even disguised. All the mass parties, beginning with the Endejca, eventually resorted to hiring gunmen to carry out political assassinations. The SDKPiL fighting units in Warsaw were so riddled with criminal elements that after failing to stop their unauthorized

95. AGAD KGGW 2509, Provisional Governor-General of Kielce Province to the WGG, December 20, 1905 (January 2, 1906) and December 26, 1905 (January 8, 1906).

96. The authority of the LSDP was so great at the end of 1905 that the Lithuanian rural population paid taxes to the party rather than the state. After failing to collect taxes with the help of troops, the state resorted to sequestering peasant livestock, flogging, and ultimately, to courts-martial; see AGAD KGGW 2524, Report of the SDPA to the WGG, December 17 (30), 1905, and Suwałki Governor to the WGG, December 31, 1905 (January 13, 1906).

97. Kaczyńska, "Tłum i margines społeczny," p. 224.

98. AGAD KGGW 520, Warsaw Superintendent of Police to the WGG, April 5 (18), 1906.

activities, the party was forced to dissolve them in August 1906.[99] The infiltration of criminals into these organizations not only blurred the distinction between organized political violence and simple banditry; it also provided a ready means of entry for the Okhrana into the same organizations. Not bothered by political or ideological scruples, the criminals and their information could easily be bought. Through such means, the Okhrana was able to force the dissolution of the organizations of the Bund and PPS–Revolutionary Faction in Łódź in 1907.

More popularly demoralizing, however, was the use of coercion, violence, and terror against political opponents. Political quarrels, once confined to the pages of the underground press, turned rhetorically violent in the aftermath of the October general strike. The SDKPiL and the Endecja, especially, engaged in a war of words that turned into deeds by the end of the year. After months of exchanging political epithets, a shooting incident at the editorial offices of the National Democratic *Goniec* (The Messenger) in Warsaw during the October general strike brought Social Democratic promises of revenge, which were carried out in December.[100] Shortly thereafter, competition between the Endecja and the PPS took a violent turn in Żyrardów after weeks of bitter tension resulting from an incident in which nationalists had prevented socialists from entering a Catholic Church with their red banners.[101] The campaign for elections to the First State Duma would further escalate the interparty fighting in Warsaw, when the PPS, SDKPiL, and Bund, as part of their tactic of "active boycott," sought to disrupt Endecja preelection meetings, incidents that were accompanied with exchanges of gunfire. The bloodiest incident of fratricide in Warsaw, however, occurred in the summer of 1906 when an emissary of Dmowski, sent to act as a mediator in a citywide strike of tanners, was murdered by a PPS unit. The Endecja retaliated on August 2 with a countermove that led to the deaths of nine socialists.[102]

The interparty strife in Warsaw, which peaked during the election campaign to the Second State Duma, nevertheless paled in comparison with the situation in Łódź, which approximated a localized civil war. From the the spring of 1905, labor violence was far greater in Łódź than in Warsaw.

---

99. Kaczyńska, "Tłum i margines społeczny," pp. 226–227; Kiepurska, *Warszawa w rewolucji,* pp. 314–315.

100. AGAD AB, druk 249, Leaflet of the Warsaw Committee of the SDKPiL, October 30, 1905; Micewski, *Roman Dmowski,* p. 115; Pobóg-Malinowski, *Najnowsza historia polityczna Polski* 1:568.

101. AGAD KGGW 2505, Warsaw Governor to WGG, January 2 (15), 1906.

102. Micewski, *Roman Dmowski,* pp. 129–130.

The use of coercion to achieve strike solidarity, the forced ouster of offensive factory foremen and managerial personnel, and the rioting and barricades of the June uprising all formed a climate of violence capable of transforming the fiercely intense competition among the parties for popular support into armed confrontations. The Łódź organizations of the Bund, SDKPiL, PPS, and NZR were numerically the strongest of their respective parties, and surrounding Piotrków Province provided the locale for paramilitary and terrorist activity.

During the October and December general strikes, opponents of the walkouts, belonging mainly to the NZR, were forcibly removed from the factories, an action reminiscent of the earlier ouster of foremen and managers. Later attempts by the socialist parties to organize a series of political protest strikes in the first half of 1906 were met with strong nationalist counteragitation. As armed units of the socialist parties and the NZR either sought to impose the will of the respective majority or to retaliate against the use of force, fighting broke out in several of the larger Łódź factories (including Poznański, Heinzel and Kunitzer, and Karol Scheibler) and spread subsequently to Pabianice, Zduńska Wola, and Będzin in the Dąbrowa Basin.[103] By November, incidents of terror related to interparty strife had become far more frequent than acts against the authorities in Łódź and the surrounding industrial region.

All this was merely a forerunner to the bloodletting that accompanied the Great Łódź Lockout. In December, the first month of the lockout, 57 persons fell victim to the fratricidal struggle in Łódź.[104] Before the lockout ended in May 1907, the interparty warfare had taken another 316 casualties, the largest number in the last three weeks, as the Endecja successfully negotiated a resumption of work.[105] Even then the interparty violence continued. One historian estimates the total number of victims of the civil strife in Łódź from January 1906 through July 1907 at 722 casualties, including 322 deaths.[106] For the Kingdom as a whole, fratricidal warfare claimed at least 1,000 casualties, a figure comparable to the number of soldiers, police, gendarmes, and state administrative personnel struck down during the revolution.

103. Korzec, *Źródła do dziejów rewolucji* 2:20–21, 134–138, 144–145, 192–194, 197–198, 209, 257, 297, 439–441.

104. Stanisław Kalabiński and Feliks Tych, *Czwarte powstanie czy pierwsza rewolucja: Lata 1905–1907 na ziemiach polskich,* 2d ed. (Warsaw, 1976), pp. 565, 569.

105. APŁ KGP 1610, Piotrków Governor to the Department of Police, May 26 (June 8) and July 31 (August 13), 1907.

106. Karwacki, *Łódzka organizacja Polskiej Partii Socjalistycznej,* p. 121.

Victims of fratricidal fighting in the Łódź suburb of Bałuty, 1907. (Muzeum Nie-podległości 8414)

Public opinion reacted to the interparty violence with horror and disgust. It was that opinion which forced the parties to hold a "peace conference" in Łódź after the Great Lockout. Despite a negotiated truce that was observed in the main and promises to return to more acceptable methods of political struggle, membership in all parties involved in the fighting declined precipitously in the second half of 1907; and only part of that decline could be blamed on state repression. By this time, crowds and revolutionaries no longer mingled in search of gangsters. Attacks on state institutions had long ceased to be public spectacles and had instead become isolated acts of terrorism. By the second half of 1907, only the PPS–Revolutionary Faction continued to champion violent political action. Its murder of the Łódź industrialist Mieczysław Silberstein on September 13, resulting in the execution of eight socialist workers without trial ten days later, brought the wrath of public opinion down on the party—and barely a murmur of public protest on behalf of the workers.[107] Without popular support, sanction, and sustenance, political violence came ingloriously to its end.

107. Richard D. Lewis, "The Labor Movement in Russian Poland in the Revolution of 1905–1907" (Ph.D. diss., University of California-Berkeley, 1971), pp. 435–436.

## Legal Political Activity

The violence and party terror of the revolutionary years were in part the result of a frustrating inability to achieve substantive political change through legal means. Indeed, until the October Manifesto, legal and peaceful political expression simply was not possible. The earlier announcement in August of the government's plan for a consultative assembly—an imperial Duma—which had been prepared under the supervision of the Minister of Internal Affairs, Aleksandr Bulygin, raised but few hopes. The severely restricted franchise to the so-called Bulygin Duma, coupled with the Warsaw governor-general's decision to limit participation in preelection meetings to private persons and societies not suspected of antigovernment views,[108] attracted only the clerical-conservative right. As for the Endecja, the initial impulse of the party leadership to participate in the projected election campaign found little support in the mass organization. In the Warsaw region, the mass protests against the "Bulygin Duma" organized by the socialist parties proved sufficiently disruptive that the government felt compelled to impose martial law.

While the statewide October general strike rendered moot the controversy over the Bulygin Duma, the consequent October Manifesto, with its promise both of a statewide legislative Duma elected by universal male suffrage and of proportional representation for the Kingdom, raised genuine hopes. The prospect of real political change contained in the manifesto was celebrated in several dozens of massive demonstrations and processions throughout the Kingdom during the first week of November, including one on November 5 in Warsaw which drew as many as one hundred thousand marchers. Widespread rumors followed, encouraged by the nationalist press, that like Finland, the Kingdom would soon be granted complete political autonomy.[109] In the meantime, the Endecja sponsored a delegation to St. Petersburg, headed by party leader Dmowski, to present the case for Polish autonomy to Count Sergei Witte, the tsar's prime minister and author of the October Manifesto.[110]

Before the delegation could meet with Witte, however, the government responded to the wave of popular demonstrations with the imposition of martial law, for the first time embracing the entire Kingdom, on November

---

108. Kalabiński, *Carat i klasy posiadające,* pp. 290–291.
109. E.g., see *Goniec Łódzki* (Łódź Messenger), no. 287a (November 10, 1905): 1.
110. The Endecja's main organ, *Przegląd Wszechpolski* (All-Polish Review), before the sending of the delegation to Witte, dispatched a message of its own to the Russian government: "Give us authority in the country, and we shall restore order." Quoted by Terej, *Idee, mity, realia,* p. 46.

*Cesarz i Witte.*
*Boleść narodu jest boleścią monarchy*

"The Emperor and Witte. The Pain of the People Is the Pain of the Monarch."
Political cartoon of the signing of the October Manifesto, 1905. (Muzeum Niepodległości 26164)

10. The majority of the delegation opposed the idea of meeting with Witte under such conditions and decided to return to the Kingdom. Dmowski, alone, remained in St. Petersburg, but his conversation with Witte failed to budge the Russian statesman from his position that it was strategically perilous, and therefore impossible, to grant home rule to a territory where one-third of the Russian army was stationed.[111] Already, at this point, a fundamental change of political status within the Russian Empire no longer had a chance, but Dmowski persisted; only now he would place his hopes in the future state duma. This decision to involve the Endecja in the quagmire of the quasi-constitutional political processes of the empire would ultimately cost Dmowski and his party a great deal of accumulated political capital.

The socialist parties, in contrast, adopted a cynical attitude toward the October Manifesto from the very beginning. Their smaller demonstrations demanded—in addition to political autonomy—the immediate end of censorship, a broad political amnesty, and the lifting of martial law in Warsaw and Łódź.[112] The subsequent imposition of martial law on the entire Kingdom, the closing of the short-lived legal socialist dailies, and, above all, the government's proclamation of complicated and antidemocratic election laws in December turned the socialists decisively against the government's constitutional project.[113] The electoral ordinance, with its indirect elections and heavily weighted franchise in favor of the upper and middle classes, ensured that industrial workers especially would have little effect on the balloting and led to separate decisions among all the socialist parties to organize an "active boycott" of the elections to the imperial Duma.[114]

The Endecja's decision to participate and the socialist decision to boycott the elections actively, that is, to disrupt the campaigns of participating parties, made violent confrontations a certainty. A meeting of three hundred residents of Opole in Lublin Province, which appealed for unity among the political parties as the only means of advancing the cause of auton-

---

111. Micewski, *Roman Dmowski*, pp. 116–119.
112. Kalabiński, *Carat i klasy posiadające*, pp. 298–299.
113. See, e.g., the articles "Illegal Elections for the Workers" and "A Duma under the Whip" in the SDKPiL's *Czerwony Sztandar*, nos. 37 (January 5, 1906) and 41 (January 11, 1906), respectively.
114. According to the new electoral ordinance, the thirty-seven seats granted the Kingdom were decided by the vote of colleges comprised of 850 general electors. Of these, 286 came from landed curia, 194 from the peasants' curia, 341 from the urban curia, and 29 from the workers' curia. Of the eighty-three general electors alloted to the city of Warsaw, only three came from the workers' curia. On the electoral ordinance as it affected the Kingdom, see Zygmunt Łukawski, *Koło Polskie w rosyjskiej dumie państwowej w latach 1906–1909* (Wrocław, 1967), pp. 14–16.

omy,[115] probably represented the sentiment of a considerable cross-section of public opinion on the eve of the first Duma elections. Bolesław Prus, the renowned novelist, added his own influential voice to that sentiment in an open letter that criticized both the socialist-led boycott and the nationalist attempts "to monopolize political life" and called upon the nonparty majority to overcome and override the looming interparty strife.[116]

Nevertheless, both the Endecja and the socialist parties, for whom the first and the revolver spoke louder than the silent majority, held fast to their positions. The socialist boycott was largely successful in the workers' curia. In Radom, only railroad workers cast their ballots.[117] In Łódź, the boycott was accompanied by a general strike of more than 50,000 workers from 293 factories; out of nearly 500 factories in the Łódź region, the elections could be held in no more than 20.[118] Balloting took place in only 9 of 114 Warsaw factories, with the result that of 19,500 eligible voters, barely 300 cast their votes.[119] Apart from the workers' curia, however, the boycott failed. In the peasants' curia, only gminy in close proximity to Warsaw sympathized with the boycott. In Lublin Province, the only part of the Polish countryside where the socialists had any tangible influence, elections were held in all but 13 out of 144 gminy.[120] The vast majority of voters in the urban and landed curiae also ignored the boycott, with the exception of landowners in radicalized Łódź County, where only 281 out of 876 eligible voters appeared at the polls.[121]

The results were inevitable. With the election contested only by the Realists and the Pedecja, the National Democrats took thirty-four of the Kingdom's alloted thirty-seven seats, one of which had been reserved for the "Russian" population of the Chełm region; the two remaining seats were won by Lithuanian candidates in Suwałki Province. The Endecja wasted little time in claiming possession of a mandate to strive for its

---

115. APL KGL 267/2, Chief of Nowa-Aleksandrya County to the Lublin Governor, December 2 (15), 1905.
116. AGAD AB, druk 284.
117. AGAD KGGW 2521, Telegram of the Provisional Governor-General of Radom Province to the WGG, April 6 (19), 1906.
118. APŁ TGGW 3, Commander of the Łódź Military Region to the Provisional Governor-General of Piotrków Province, March 29 (April 11), 1906; Korzec, *Walki rewolucyjne,* p. 209.
119. Łukawski, *Koło Polskie,* p. 23.
120. Jan Molenda, "Carat i klasy posiadające w walce z rewolucja 1905–1907 r. na wsi polskiej," *Przegląd Historyczny* 46, 1-2 (1955): 167; Wójcik, *Ruch robotniczy na Lubelszczyźnie,* p. 98.
121. APŁ TGGP 4, Commander of the Łódź Military Region to the Provisional Governor-General of Piotrków Province, March 30 (April 12), 1906. By contrast, 74.3 percent of the eligible voters in Łódź's urban curia participated.

version of legal-political autonomy.[122] Yet once in St. Petersburg, the nationalist-monopolized Polish Circle, even when bolstered by the twelve votes of Polish representatives from Lithuania, Byelorussia, and Ukraine, could not reap any real political dividends from the Endecja's sweeping electoral victory in the Kingdom.

Most important, the Polish Circle alienated all prospective allies who might have backed the Kingdom's autonomy in the First State Duma, beginning with the Russian Constitutional Democrats, or Cadets. The Polish Circle behaved like an embassy in a foreign capital, shunning participation in the Cadet-dominated Duma presidium or in the Duma delegation sent to London to participate in a European parliamentary congress. The Polish Circle also continued Dmowski's flirtation with the Russian government and even joined the pro-government opposition to the Cadet-inspired Duma resolution on agrarian reform. The Cadets consequently backed away from the resolutions of the Russian zemstvo congresses of September and November 1905, which had supported the Kingdom's political autonomy and agreed to bring the issue before the Duma. Not only were the Cadets unwilling to place the matter of Polish autonomy on the Duma agenda, but when the Polish Circle presented its own declaration on autonomy to the Duma on May 12, 1906, it was given a cool reception in the liberal Russian press.

The Poles also isolated themselves from delegations representing the empire's other national minorities, which together with the Polish Circle made up 41 percent of the First Duma. The circle's exclusive interpretation of autonomy was based partly on the conviction that the Russians, whether in the Duma or the government, would more readily agree to narrowly Polish demands than to autonomy for all nationalities. More significant, however, was the Polish Circle's poorly hidden opposition to autonomy for Lithuania, Byelorussia, and Ukraine, where the Polish element would be dwarfed by the non-Polish majority populations. That attitude alienated, for example, the Ukrainian autonomist-federalist group, which otherwise might have supported the circle's declaration on the Kingdom's autonomy, and left the circle open to charges of hypocrisy.[123]

The tsar's abrupt dissolution of the First State Duma in the summer of 1906—which, characteristically, the Polish Circle refused to protest by

---

122. AGAD AB, druk 200, Appeal of the National Democratic Party, May 7, 1906.
123. On the Polish Circle's travails in the First State Duma, see Łukawski, *Koło Polskie,* pp. 37–65, as well his article "Rosyjskie ugrupowanie polityczne wobec sprawy autonomii Królestwa Polskiego w okresie 1905–1907," *Zeszyty Naukowe Uniwersytetu Jagiellonskiego: Prace Historyczne* 9 (1962): 154–158. Less valuable is the discussion in Edward Chmielewski, *The Polish Question in the Russian State Duma* (Knoxville, 1970), pp. 33–36.

signing the Vyborg Manifesto initiated by the Cadets—sent the Poles home empty-handed and set the stage for new elections. In the interim, the SDKPiL and the Bund, after their formal entrance into the Russian Social Democratic Workers Party as autonomous organizations, had reversed their position on the Duma and decided to form an electoral alliance to challenge the Endecja in the workers' and urban curiae. Their prospects were undermined, however, by the decisions of both factions of the PPS to continue the boycott and by their own refusal to join the Pedecja in a Concentration of the Left to oppose the National Concentration centered around the Endecja.

Nevertheless, the appearance of new players on the electoral field made the second election campaign to the Duma in January and February of 1907 far livelier than the first. According to one observer, "There were so many pre-election meetings of all sorts in Warsaw that it was hard to find a suitable hall," and this despite the Warsaw governor-general's ban on such meetings organized by the SDKPiL and the Bund.[124] Police actions and continued PPS boycotts notwithstanding, the SDKPiL-Bund alliance carried the workers' curiae in Warsaw, Łódź, Radom, and the Dąbrowa Basin. In Łódź's urban curia, the alliance received a respectable 26.2 percent of the vote, compared with 48.9 percent for the National Concentration and 23.8 percent for the Pedecja.[125] The SDKPiL also ran a successful campaign in the Puławy region of Lublin Province and managed to elect four of its candidates in the peasants' curia.[126]

Yet despite these successes, the deck was stacked against the socialists in the general electoral college by the weighted franchise. Moreover, by refusing to enter into an agreement with the Pedecja (which, for example, would have defeated the Endecja in Łódź), the socialists let pass their only opportunity to send delegates to the Second State Duma. Consequently, that delegation was dominated once again by the Endecja and its allies. Headed this time by Dmowski himself, who won one of Warsaw's two seats, the Polish Circle returned to St. Petersburg with a revised project of autonomy for the Kingdom of Poland.

The experience of the Polish Circle in the Second State Duma proved even more frustrating. Its new autonomy project, far less ambitious than the first one and containing provisions of equal rights for the Kingdom's national minorities, nevertheless provoked an even more hostile reaction

124. Quoted by Corrsin, "Polish-Jewish Relations," p. 43; Kalabiński, *Carat i klasy posiadające*, pp. 546–548.
125. Korzec, *Walki rewolucyjne*, p. 274.
126. Wójcik, *Ruch robotniczy na Lubelszczyźnie*, p. 128.

in the Russian press.[127] Thus when the tsar's new prime minister, Peter Stolypin, suggested limited self-government based on the Kingdom's "local peculiarities" as an alternative, Dmowski and the Polish Circle took the bait. On the critical issue of calling up 465,000 new conscripts to the colors, the Polish Circle's pro-government position proved decisive in the voting. Recognizing that he held the swing vote between pro- and anti-government forces, Dmowski then began to hold out the enticement of a pro-government vote on the state budget in exchange for Stolypin's support for the polonization of the state school system in the Kingdom. Rather than submit to what he viewed as political blackmail, Stolypin dissolved the Second State Duma and used the intervening period to rewrite the empire's electoral laws, in the process reducing the Kindom's representation to twelve relatively harmless seats (two of which were now reserved for the "Russian" population).[128]

By the time elections were held for the Third State Duma in the fall of 1907, the popular political enthusiasm generated by the revolution had vanished. Although the PPS-Left now joined the SDKPiL and the Bund on the ballot, the majority of voters declined to exercise their rights, which had been rendered farcical by the new electoral ordinance. The disappointed hopes were reflected in Lublin Province, where fifty-five gminy failed to hold elections to the peasants' curia.[129] Only 25 percent of the eligible electorate cast ballots in Warsaw. Where the elections were uncontested, the percentage of participating voters was considerably less.[130] Ironically, the unplanned "passive boycott" of the duma in the autumn of 1907, inspired by popular apathy and disillusionment, proved more widespread than the "active boycott" organized by the socialist parties eighteen months earlier.

Like the resort to violence, participation in the Russian constitutional experiment had failed to change existing political conditions in the Kingdom of Poland, resulting ultimately in the widespread demoralization of

127. Łukawski, "Rosyjskie ugrupowanie," pp. 158–159. Inside the Kingdom, the conservative Catholic press took the Polish Circle to task for its inclusion in the autonomy project of equal rights for Jews; see *Przegląd Katolicki*, nos. 40 (October 3, 1907) and 42 (October 17, 1907): 629–630 and 661–662, respectively.

128. On the Polish Circle's misadventures in the Second State Duma, see Łukawski, *Koło Polskie*, pp. 80–123, Chmielewski, *Polish Question*, pp. 36–38, and Alfred Levin, *The Second Duma: A Study of the Social-Democratic Party and the Russian Constitutional Experiment* (Hamden, Conn., 1966), pp. 128, 132, 139, 193, 339–340.

129. Wójcik, *Ruch robotniczy na Lubelszczyźnie*, p. 129.

130. Łukawski, *Koło Polskie*, p. 129.

groups and individuals who, only a few years earlier, had become politically active for the first time. Yet like the mass mobilizations and demonstrations of political enthusiasm of 1905, the popular apathy of 1907 and the subsequent postrevolutionary years would also form part of the modern Polish political experience. On many future occasions, during the interwar period, the postwar communist era, and in the most recent postcommunist years, a majority of Poles would act in similar fashion. Similar, too, is the subsequent history of polarization and fragmentation, those other phenomena that marked the birth of modern Polish mass politics in the first years of the twentieth century.

Before 1905, the main issue was whether the "mass nation" could participate in public life. After 1905, the question has been the extent to which it would chose to, by what means (legal or illegal, peaceful or violent), and in how many different factions and configurations. The ultimate significance of the Revolution of 1905, therefore, is that, for the first time, the popular classes were confronted with such choices, thus altering forever the course of a political experience that for centuries had been the preserve of an ancient elite.

# The Church and the Revolution

For the Roman Catholic Church—the only traditional "Polish" institution to survive successive nineteenth-century insurrections and subsequent waves of Russian repression—adjusting to the demands of the modern era and the new postrevolution political culture proved especially troublesome. With its independence compromised, its finances controlled, its practices closely scrutinized, and its official ties with Rome forcibly severed by the Russian autocracy after the January Insurrection of 1863, the Polish Church had, by the turn of the century, already found it increasingly difficult to satisfy the spiritual needs of its rapidly growing and changing flock. Although Russian state policies did much to restrict the church's access to that flock, the ultramontane conservatism of the hierarchy, coupled with an aging clergy's addiction to routine, had further engendered an ignorance of and an indifference toward the modern set of social problems, aspirations, and concerns confronting many Polish Catholics.[1]

As a result, the church was surprised by its inability to exercise any significant influence on the population at the onset of the revolution in January and February of 1905. In subsequent months, the church experienced a profound crisis that seemed to endanger its traditional relationship with Polish society. Faced with the prospect of complete political isolation on the one hand and a schismatic movement of disillusioned clergy on the other, the church was eventually forced to make room for reformist im-

---

1. An earlier version of this chapter appeared under the title "The Revolution of 1905–1907 and the Crisis of Polish Catholicism," *Slavic Review* 47, 4 (1988): 667–686, and is reprinted here, with some modifications, by permission of the American Association for the Advancement of Slavic Studies.

pulses based on western European models and experience. In the end, the church survived the revolutionary crisis and even emerged somewhat strengthened. It failed, however, to take full advantage of the opportunities for Catholic social action afforded by the revolution, as old methods, ways of thinking, and personnel continued to dominate clerical practices.

### Church, State, and Society before the Revolution

The crisis that suddenly confronted the church during the revolutionary era was the direct consequence of a long period of intellectual and organizational stagnation at a time of rapid population growth, internal and external migration, urbanization, and industrialization. The failure of the church to adapt to the fluidly changing times had several causes, principal among them, the church's relationship with the Russian state after the January Insurrection of 1863. The church's supporting role during that insurrection made it a likely target of subsequent Russian retribution. The post-January crackdown subsequently devastated the church in the Kingdom, tearing apart an organization carefully constructed over centuries. The exile of members of the hierarchy along with hundreds of diocesan chaplains and monks, the confiscation of church property, the liquidation of 124 out of 176 cloisters, a decade of forced vacancies in six of seven bishoprics, the closing of the Theological Academy in Warsaw, and the placing of the hierarchy under the authority of the Theological College in St. Petersburg all had paralyzing effects on many of the church's activities.[2] Designed to deny the church an independent base and freedom of action in Russia's Polish provinces, these repressive measures also created a leadership vacuum and an internal organizational instability that undermined traditional discipline.

Russian policies also attempted to isolate the church in the Kingdom from the outside world and from its own parishioners. Official contacts, not only with Rome but with Catholic institutions elsewhere in Europe (including, most significantly, Prussian and Austrian Poland), were strictly prohibited. Inside the Kingdom, contacts between bishops and diocesan clergy were carefully restricted and supervised by the Russian government after 1864. A bishop could not undertake a visitation of his diocese or appoint and transfer clergy without the permission of the state authorities.

---

2. By 1870, 227 clerics had been exiled, 37 sentenced to death, 200 imprisoned, and 44 forced to flee the country; see Ryszard Bender, *Społeczne inicjatywy chrześcijańskie w Królestwie Polskim, 1905–1918* (Lublin, 1978), pp. 38–39.

The nomination of professors at theological seminaries was also subject to
state confirmation. Finally, the authorities created obstacles to the clergy's
access to the Catholic population. Until 1905, pastoral letters from the
bishops to the faithful were prohibited. In addition, priests could not accept
newcomers from other parishes on their own initiative (this at a time of
dynamic migration), nor could they administer sacraments to the ill in
"public places" such as hospitals and sanatoriums.

If this were not enough, measures of russification were introduced to
loosen the traditional bonds tying the Catholic Church to Polish language,
history, and culture. The church was required to conduct its official business and correspondence in the Russian language, which in turn justified
the obligatory study of Russian at theological seminaries. Beginning in
1875, Russian also became the language of instruction for the study of
history in the seminaries. Eventually, even the required prayers for the tsar
and members of the imperial family had to be said in Russian.

The Vatican initially responded to the Russian assault on the Polish
church by breaking diplomatic relations with St. Petersburg, but in 1882
those ties were restored when Leo XIII reached an accommodation with
the Russian government which brought little relief to the Polish clergy.
Terrorized by Russian repression and virtually abandoned by Rome, the
hierarchy in the Kingdom was forced to make a fundamental change in its
political strategies toward the Russian state, to exchange its late-1850s and
early-1860s policy of moderate opposition and cautious confrontation for
one based on fear of reprisal and calculated loyalism. The main fear, of
course, was that even the most modest form of clerical protest could result
in more drastic measures against Roman Catholics, including the closing
of churches.[3] Reinforcing the hierarchy's reluctance to cross swords again
with the Russian government was the fact that Wincenty Chościak-Popiel,
the titular head of the church in Russian Poland as archbishop of Warsaw,
shared in the bitter experience of Siberian exile after the January Insurrection. A policy of loyalism toward the autocracy seemed the only way to
provide insurance against further repression. Repeated demonstrations of
loyalty, it was also hoped, might eventually win the church some breathing
room in its relationship with the state.

The hierarchy's accommodation to the post-January status quo reflected
at the time a larger trend in the opinion of a traditional political elite still

---

3. Such fears were not baseless. In 1905, Warsaw governor-general George Skalon threatened to close all churches that had become forums for patriotic demonstrations and the
singing of national hymns; see APL KGL 1905:18, WGG to the Polish Bishops, September
30 (October 13), 1905.

unchallenged by the practitioners of modern mass politics, and not only in the Congress Kingdom but in Prussian and Austrian Poland as well. "Triple Loyalism," the conservative-clerical backlash to the failure and tragic consequences of the January Insurrection, as mentioned in Chapter 1, was intended to conciliate Poland's foreign rulers with expressions of political loyalty in exchange for modest concessions in the national-cultural sphere. Similarly, Warsaw positivism, the more liberal and progressive intellectual tendency of the immediate post-January era, also rejected political confrontation with the Russian authorities and concentrated instead on "organic work." Thus, the church's adoption of a loyalist stance and its resignation from political activity in pursuit of limited and "realistic" goals fit squarely the prevailing mood of the 1870s and early 1880s.

The embrace of a loyalist strategy by the church nevertheless restricted its activities to the performance of narrowly defined pastoral duties, and even these became increasingly difficult to fulfill because of the weak state of church finances and rapid demographic change that outstripped church resources. The population explosion of the last decades of the nineteenth century in Russian Poland, combined with migration from the countryside to industrial centers, stretched traditional parish organization beyond its limits. By 1905, gigantic and overpopulated urban-industrial parishes had become commonplace. Holy Cross parish in Łódź, frequently cited in the Catholic literature of the period as a prime example, contained 142,000 parishioners served by only eight clergy.[4]

To make matters worse, the demographic explosion in urban and industrial parishes came at a time when the church's independent financial base (which consisted mainly of income derived from landed property and tithes before the January Insurrection) had been largely eliminated and replaced by inadequate state subsidies. The possibilities for new capital construction in these parishes were consequently limited. For example, the Warsaw district of Powiśle in 1905 contained one hundred thousand Catholics belonging to three parishes. Yet all of Powiśle was served by only three small churches, the largest of which could accommodate only twenty-seven hundred believers at a time. Other major urban parishes suffering from severe shortages of clergy and places of worship included Resurrection parish in Łódź (90,000 parishioners); Praga (82,000), Wola (65,000), and All Saints (62,000) in Warsaw; St. Zygmunt's in Częstochowa (50,000); Radom (34,000); and Sosnowiec (31,000).[5] The fulfillment of normal pas-

4. "Trudności duszpasterstwa w wielotysiącznych parafiach," *Wiadomości Pasterskie* 3, 5 (1907): 298–302.
5. Ibid.; see also Aleksander Wóycicki, *Chrześcijański ruch robotniczy w Polsce* (Poznań, 1921), pp. 71–72.

toral duties in these primarily working-class parishes became nearly impossible, and thousands of parishioners were left with many of their
religious needs unattended. When Franciscan missionaries from Kraków
were allowed by the Russian authorities in 1906 to visit urban-industrial
parishes in the Kingdom, they were shocked to discover that most workers
had not had their confessions heard in over a year.[6]

Though many of the reasons for the sad situation in urban parishes can
be attributed directly to the policies of the Russian government, the needs
of urban parishioners were not the first priority of the church itself. Too
often the limited funds available to the church for capital construction were
spent instead on expensive monuments or shrines and the adornment of
cathedrals, a practice termed "building the material church."[7] Unfortunately, the "material church" left many urban areas without even the most
elementary wooden structures.

Nor was the cadre policy of the hierarchy designed to meet the needs
of urban parishioners. No effort was made to redress the growing imbal-
ance between the relatively large number of priests serving in rural areas
as well as at the residences of bishops and the dramatically small number
of clergy serving in the large urban-industrial parishes. At the same time,
the ecclesiastical authorities tended to nominate as administrators to these
parishes older men whose origins and experience were far removed from
the cities and working-class elements of the population. Placement in urban
parishes had become, in fact, a reward for years of service in poor, more
sparsely populated rural parishes. Because the collection of fees (*opłaty*)
for the performance of certain pastoral duties (marriages, funerals) was a
major supplement to the otherwise meager income of the lower clergy, the
large number of Catholics in an urban parish could lead to a marked improvement in the financial status of the new parish priest.[8]

These older chaplains, accustomed to the long-established practice in
rural areas of sitting in their churches and waiting for their parishioners to
come to them, possessed neither the energy nor the temperament to satisfy
the more elusive religious needs of urban parishioners, let alone understand
their specific social concerns and aspirations. Evidence drawn from files
on clergymen which came across the desk of the Warsaw superintendent
of police as part of the process of state confirmation of appointments and

6. See Czesław Bogdalski, *Wspomnienia z misyi odprawianych od 1906–1908 r. w Królestwie Polskim* (Kraków, 1908).

7. Marian Fulman, "Wielkomiejskie i fabryczne parafie," *Wiadomości Pasterskie* 2, 2
(1906): 77.

8. Ibid., p. 80.

transfers supports this conclusion. The aggregation of data from 124 of these files for the period 1905–1907 provides, moreover, an excellent profile of the Warsaw clergy during the years of the revolution.[9] The data demonstrate clearly that the Warsaw clergy was aging, nearly 60 percent of its members having been born before the January Insurrection of 1863. In their fifties and sixties by 1905, they had completed their seminary studies and entered the priesthood at a time of the most intense Russian repression against the church. Even more striking are their geographic and social origins: more than 90 percent originated in the provincial nobility. As might be expected, only a small minority (slightly more than 10 percent) engaged in extrapastoral social activities, which were, of course, scrupulously noted by the police. Significantly, those deemed "active" outside their churches (thirteen priests) came from a variety of social backgrounds, not excluding the nobility, and were born without exception after the January Insurrection.

In addition to the effects of age and social background, a profound intellectual inertia also left the church ill equipped to deal with major social issues once they had been so forcefully raised by the revolution. The prohibition of all official contacts with Rome and European Catholicism isolated the church in the Kingdom from the leading currents of contemporary Catholic thought. Hence, at a time when the rest of Catholic Europe (including Prussian and Austrian Poland) was discussing and putting into limited practice the social encyclicals of Leo XIII, especially *Rerum Novarum* with its call for adapting the church's mission to the industrial age, the "social question" had yet to find an audience among the overwhelming majority of Catholic clergy in Russian Poland. Because of state censorship, *Rerum Novarum* itself was not discussed in the Catholic press in the Kingdom until the revolution, fourteen years after its pronouncement. The first bishop to comment officially on the "social question" was Tomasz Kuliński of Kielce diocese, but this came in late November 1905, ten months into the Revolution.[10] Furthermore, the curricula of Catholic seminaries completely ignored social studies before the revolution, leaving the clergy as a whole intellectually unprepared to absorb the Catholic social teachings

9. APW ZOW 1549, 1552, 1556–7, 1563, 1565, 1577, 1579, 1586, 1588, 1592, 1594–6, 1598–1600, 1602, 1606, 1617, 1619, 1627, 1629–33, 1636, 1638, 1640–3, 1645, 1649–50, 1655–6, 1659, 1663–4, 1672, 1675, 1678, 1680, 1682–4, 1688–9, 1695–7, 1701–2, 1704, 1707–9, 1713, 1716–7, 1721, 1723–4, 1726, 1728, 1730, 1732–3, 1735–7, 1744, 1747, 1750, 1752, 1754, 1761, 1763–7, 1770–3, 1776–8, 1780–1, 1788–90, 1795–6, 1799, 1801, 1807, 1809, 1812, 1814, 1817, 1822, 1824, 1826, 1829, 1832–4, 1840, 1842, 1853, 1862, 1878, 1882, 1884, 1889, 1900, 1902–3, 1907.
10. ADK AK OA-2/9, Bishop of Kielce to the Diocesan Clergy, November 23, 1905.

of Wilhelm Ketteler, Gaspard Marmillod, Henry Manning, James Gibbons, Ludwik Windhorst, and other contemporary theologians.[11]

This is not to imply that there were no Catholic social initiatives undertaken in the Kingdom of Poland before the revolution. The indefatigable Honorat Koźmiński, father superior of the Capuchin monastery of Nowe Miasto, organized a network of semiconspiratorial assemblies of monks and nuns which acted as a substitute for the cashiered cloisters earlier engaged in social work. By 1895, sixteen such assemblies had been formed, including the Factory Sisters and the Servants of Mary, both active among urban industrial workers. At the turn of the century, Father Karol Bliziński initiated missionary activity aimed specifically at the Warsaw proletariat, organizing two religious conferences for workers attended by three thousand and five thousand people respectively in 1898 and 1899.[12] Undoubtedly these initiatives touched as many if not more Polish workers than the prerevolutionary socialist movement. Nevertheless, these initiatives were uninformed by a broader theory or plan of action and lacked the official support of the hierarchy. As such they were bound to remain sporadic, isolated, and confined to a few thousand workers.

## A Church in Crisis

This long period of organizational stagnation, political paralysis, and intellectual inertia prepared the way for a church crisis during the revolution which took several forms: the striking unpopularity of the church's continuing adherence to loyalist policies toward the Russian government; the embrace of a new and—in the eyes of the church—"heretical" faith called socialism by tens of thousands of Polish workers; the end of church monopoly over popular opinion in the countryside as a result of the penetration and expansion of the nationalist and populist movements; and finally, internal divisions among the clergy, including the first and only schism in the history of Polish Catholicism since the Reformation.

In 1904 there already were clear signs that the church hierarchy's position of calculated loyalism not only lacked popular support but could provoke violent opposition. The official support of the hierarchy for Russia in its war against Japan, symbolized by Archbishop Popiel's sponsorship

11. The problem of absorbing Christian sociology "in one gulp" was addressed by Ks. K. Max, "Działalność społeczna kapłana," *Wiadomości Pasterskie* 2, 6 (1906): 321–328.
12. Bender, *Społeczne inicjatywy,* pp. 46–51, 59–60.

of a train of medical supplies and personnel to the Far Eastern front, flew in the face of popular sympathy for Japan, growing resistance to mobilization, and a general boycott of government fund-raising efforts. Hostility to the church's policy became glaring when, at the end of March 1904, windows were smashed in the Warsaw homes of Prince Włodzimierz Czetwertyński, Baron Leopold Kronenberg, Ludwik Górski, and other "conciliationists" authorized by the archbishop to collect contributions for the medical train.[13]

The lower clergy, meanwhile, displayed little enthusiasm for the Russian war effort in general and for contributions to the archbishop's medical train in particular. In reports by provincial governors to the chancellory of the Warsaw governor general, the attitude of the parish clergy toward the war was described merely as "correct." Provincial governors complained that the clergy lacked fervor, expressing neither sympathy for nor opposition to the cause of Russian arms in the Far East. Typical was the behavior of Father Józef Szczęśnik, who in the Church of the Holy Cross in Łódź read imperial wartime proclamations in such a muffled voice that police constable Pilipenko, sitting a couple of rows from the pulpit, could not hear a word.[14]

The hierarchy's failure to elicit support for the Russian war effort in 1904 was followed by its complete inability to influence an aroused public opinion in 1905. Appeals to striking workers in January and February to return to their jobs had no effect and displayed a woeful lack of familiarity with or concern for working-class conditions. The episcopate willingly attributed the cause of the strikes to outside agitation, completely ignoring depressed wages and exploitative practices in the factories.[15] Naturally, that appearance of siding with management only fed the anticlerical propaganda mills of the socialist parties, which in turn served only to reinforce the episcopate's obsession with socialist "agitators" and "subversives."

The hierarchy's opposition to the simultaneous strike and boycott movement against the russified school system proved even more unpopular than its useless appeals to the workers. The archbishop's pastoral letter of July 27, 1905, while expressing sympathy toward the desire of Polish youth to have instruction in their native language, nevertheless called for an end to

13. AGAD KGGW 2280, Warsaw Superintendent of Police to the Acting WGG, March 18 (31), 1904.
14. AGAD KGGW 2308, Piotrków Governor to the WGG, February 28 (March 12), 1904.
15. AGAD AB 2311, plik XIII, Pastoral Letter of the Archbishop of Warsaw to the Polish People, undated; see also Archbishop Popiel's appeal, "Orędzie Arcypasterskie," *Przegląd Katolicki*, no. 11 (March 16, 1905): 154.

the boycott of the Russian schools, arguing that "a bad school is better than no school at all."[16] Instead of heeding the archbishop's advice, public opinion in the Kingdom greeted his letter with protests from across the political spectrum.[17]

The success of socialism in capturing the imaginations of thousands of Polish workers during the revolution was, from the church's point of view, the most alarming aspect of its "troubled times." Given the weakness of the church and its mission in urban-industrial areas, the popularity of socialism during this period can be at least partly explained by its ability to pose as a new religion. The Polish socialist movement's active and largely unconscious borrowing of religious symbols and metaphors; its self-reference as a "new faith," a "new creed," and a "new gospel"; its quite conscious use of traditional religious melodies for "proletarian hymns"— all were important, even crucial, elements in its efforts to reach industrial workers in the first years of the twentieth century. And whereas the traditional religion seemed to offer only old, mechanical sacramentalism, the "apostles" of socialism conjured up visions of "the Kingdom of God on earth," which is how they often described their final goal.[18] In this sense, the popularity of socialism during the revolutionary era cannot be equated with a tendency toward a decline of religiosity among Polish workers. On the contrary, the spiritual needs of a still very traditional working class, although insufficiently attended by traditional religious institutions, were greater than ever before, as demonstrated by an equally enthusiastic receptivity to later Catholic missionary activity.[19] A large proportion of Polish workers during the revolution, unlike their political and religious leaders, did not necessarily perceive a contradiction between socialism and Catholicism. Rather, the evidence suggests that socialist sympathies and tra-

16. AGAD AB, druk 257, The Archbishop of Warsaw to Polish Parents, June 10, 1905. Popiel's position contrasted starkly with that of the episcopate in Prussian Poland, which despite its similarly loyalist inclinations, publicly condemned Prussian school policies aimed at germanization and tacitly supported the Poznanian school strikes of 1906–1907; see William W. Hagen, *Germans, Poles, and Jews: The Nationality Conflict in the Prussian East, 1772–1914* (Chicago, 1980), p. 183.

17. At the same time, however, Archbishop Popiel urged the tsar through private channels to allow the introduction of Polish into the schools; see Tadeusz Krawczak, "Rewolucja a życie społeczno-religijne: Powstanie mariawitów" (Seminar paper, Institute of History, Warsaw University, 1985), p. 10.

18. Andrzej Chwalba, "Krzyż i czerwony sztandar," *Znak* 341 (April 1983): 651.

19. In the large working-class parish of Chojny near Łódź, fifteen to twenty thousand participated in evening Masses conducted by Kraków Franciscans at the end of 1907; see Bogdalski, *Wspomnienia,* p. 322.

ditional religious beliefs could be and were entirely compatible in the working-class culture of the early twentieth century.[20]

Yet precisely because socialism posed as a new religion that could solve not only socioeconomic problems but metaphysical ones as well, the Catholic Church treated it as the most dangerous of heresies. In the pastoral letters of the bishops to the Polish population and the diocesan clergy during the revolution, the socialists were seldom referred to by name but were labeled conversely as "false prophets," "agitators of evil," and "wolves in sheep's clothing."[21] The lower clergy could be even less sparing in epithets, frequently condemning the socialists as "messengers of Satan" or personifications of the "horned enemy" himself.[22] Yet simplistic condemnations of socialism in pastoral letters and from the pulpit, even the use of confessionals against suspected socialist sympathizers, could not alter the fact that the church was failing to minister to the religious needs of the urban population and only served to illuminate its ignorance of the conditions in which that population lived and worked.

The church also began to lose ground in the countryside to the competing ideologies of nationalism and populism. Lulled to sleep by its ancient position of unquestioned authority in the villages and the traditional indifference of the peasantry to national issues, the church was caught off guard by the awakening of national consciousness among rural inhabitants during the revolution. As a consequence, the village clergy exercised little influence on the movement in the communes for local self-government and the polonization of rural institutions. The leadership of the gmina action movement, especially in 1905, included surprisingly few parish priests.[23] Instead there were several reported cases of active opposition of individual clergymen to the gmina movement. A few even informed the Russian authorities of "illegal" actions taken by communal assemblies.[24] In retaliation, the homes of such priests became targets of local vandals.

---

20. For an excellent analysis of the confluence of religious and class consciousness among Polish workers during the revolution, see Maria Dorota Kowalska, "Świadomość religijna klasy robotniczej Królestwa Polskiego w latach 1904–1907," *Przegląd Powszechny* 5 (May 1986): 213–224. For a more general discussion of popular religiosity at the turn of the century, see Daniel Olszewski, "Stan i perspektywy nad religijnością XIX i początku XX wieku," *Nasza Przeszłość* 59 (1983): 45–67.

21. ADK AK OA-2/13, Bishop of Kujawy-Kalisz to the Catholic Population, December 20, 1905; ADP PWD, Bishop of Płock to the Polish People, December 31, 1905.

22. ADK KD OD-2/1.

23. Richard D. Lewis, "Revolution in the Countryside: Russian Poland, 1905–1906," *Carl Beck Papers in Russian and East European Studies* 506 (1986): 7.

24. Such instances were reported in *Polak*, no. 9 (September 1905); see also Stanisław

If the attitude of the church toward the gmina movement was ambivalent at best, its reaction to the agrarian strikes that swept over large parts of rural Poland in the spring of 1905 was unambiguously hostile. The church viewed all strikes, industrial and agrarian, as violations of divinely sanctioned property rights as well as of the seventh and tenth commandments. Yet the vehemence with which it greeted strikes by farm laborers, unquestionably the most impoverished segment of the entire population, can only be explained by the noble origins of the vast majority of the Polish clergy. For similar reasons, the church denounced arbitrary actions by peasants to settle long-standing disputes with noble landowners over easement rights. In a letter of March 1905 to the diocesan clergy, the bishop of Kielce portrayed the Polish countryside as a scene of wild revolutionary anarchy, a place of "vigilantism in the place of justice, hatred in the place of love for one's neighbor, violence in the place of order."[25] This reaction from one of the more politically moderate members of the episcopate typified the church's response to the agrarian social issues of the revolution.

Such attitudes were no help to the church in its efforts to prevent the nationalist and populist movements from making significant inroads in the Polish countryside, even though the allegiance of rural inhabitants to the church in matters spiritual remained unshaken. Actually, the church shared a certain common ground with Polish nationalism and its chief exponents in the National Democratic Party. Both favored a "realistic" approach to the Russian government, seeking to move it to concessions while strongly opposing efforts to overthrow it by revolutionary means. Both despised the socialist movement and assumed combative positions toward those political parties advancing and promoting it. Both were fundamentally anti-Semitic. Still, the church distrusted the nationalist movement, particularly its secular emphasis, its past links to freemasonry, and its demagogic appeal to the masses. Despite the avowedly pro-Catholic tactical stance the National Democrats assumed during the revolution, the bishops continued to denounce the ideology of "integral nationalism" which called upon the church to play the role of a "national institution" subordinate to the "national interest."[26] As a result, conservative Catholic

Kalabiński and Feliks Tych, eds., *Walki chłopów Królestwa Polskiego w rewolucji 1905–1907*, vol. 1 (Warsaw, 1958), pp. 892–894.

25. ADK AK OA-2/9.

26. On the relationship between the Endecja and the Roman Catholic Church, see Bogumił Grott, "Rola katolicyzmu w ideologii obozu narodowego w świetle pism jego ideologów i krytyki katolickiej," *Dzieje Najnowsze* 12, 1 (1980): 63–94; and Teodor Mistewicz, "Rola

publicists did not hesitate to label Polish nationalism "areligious," "pagan," and "pantheistic," though they refrained from condemning it outright as a heresy (a charge reserved for socialism).[27] The well-publicized conflict of the Catholic hierarchy with the National Democrats, peaking in their bitter dispute over the role of the church in a private Polish school system, and particularly in the Polska Macierz Szkolna (see Chapter 5), clearly illuminated the differences between the two camps for all those who cared to see. The church's disapproval, however, did little to undermine the growing popularity of nationalism among rural Polish Catholics, who voted overwhelmingly for the National Democrats in successive elections to the Russian State Duma in 1906 and 1907.

In its numbers, territorial range, and organizational depth, the populist movement posed a far lesser threat than nationalism to the church's traditional position in the countryside. As already noted, the Polish People's Union, the political arm of the populist movement, lasted barely two years before it was effectively suppressed by the Russian authorities in early 1907. Yet because of populism's social and class overtones, including its support for agrarian strikes and radical land reform, the church treated it as an enemy far more dangerous than Polish nationalism. In particular, the populist slogan *"Sami sobie"* (We by ourselves) was interpreted by church officials to mean not only "without the nobility" but also "without the clergy."[28] The church therefore sought to remove populist publications such as *Siewba* (Sowing) and *Zaranie* (The Dawn) from peasant cottages and to eliminate schools and cooperative circles organized by the populists. In Kielce diocese, the bishop resorted to the excommunication of four populists; elsewhere, the clergy, acting on its own, often refused to administer the sacraments to readers of the populist press.[29] This was not enough, however, to prevent the growth of a populist readership in the years after the revolution, nor was it sufficient to restore rural parish priests to their previous position of unchallenged authority in the villages.

While the church focused on the external challenges posed by the mass political movements to its traditional position in society, it remained rel-

religii i kościoła rzymsko-katolickiego w świetle publicystyki polskiego ruchu nacjonalistycznego," *Kwartalnik Historyczny* 91, 4 (1985): 765–789.

27. "Błędy 'Myśli Polskiej,'" *Przegląd Katolicki,* no. 39 (September 27, 1906): 593–595; Ks. dr. Wł. Namiotko, "Demokracya narodowa i jej zasady," ibid., no. 5 (January 31, 1907): 69–71.

28. Ks. A. Brykczyński, "Ważny obowiązek," *Przegląd Katolicki,* no. 52 (December 26, 1907): 827.

29. Zenon Kmiecik, *Ruch oświatowy na wsi: Królestwo Polskie, 1905–1914* (Warsaw, 1963), pp. 140–147.

atively blind to the far greater danger of growing divisions and dissent within its own ranks. At one end of this spectrum, the revolution promoted the emergence of what was later called the "modernist" tendency, personified almost totally by the figure of Izydor Wysłouch.[30] A Capuchin monk and a product of one of the semiconspiratorial assemblies organized by his father superior, Honorat Koźmiński, Wysłouch appointed himself the "conscience" of the church during the years of the revolution. Writing for lay publications under the pseudonym of Antoni Szech, Wysłouch subjected the church and its conservative social policies to a scathing criticism. He also expressed strong sympathies for the ideals, if not the practices, of the socialist movement and collaborated openly with various populist enterprises. Perhaps only a tiny fraction of the Polish clergy shared Wysłouch's social radicalism, but his articulate attacks on the church's inertia in the face of contemporary social and political questions had a much broader appeal, particularly among reform-minded members of the younger clergy.[31]

Alarmed by the resonance of Wysłouch's uncensored criticisms, the church authorities finally took disciplinary action against him in the spring of 1906. In April, Wysłouch was sent to a Jesuit academy in Innsbruck for "continuing education." At the same time, he agreed under pressure to submit all of his future writings to ecclesiastical censorship. With Wysłouch effectively silenced, the conservative Catholic press embarked on what amounted to a mud-slinging campaign against him.[32] To respond to his attackers, Wysłouch returned to Russian Poland at the end of 1907, having decided once again to circumvent the censors. Within a year, however, Wysłouch was forced to leave the Capuchin order, and all of his publications were placed on the Index. Henceforth, the Polish church's struggle against "Szechism" in the Kingdom was made synonymous with growing conservative attacks on "modernism" in larger European Catholic debates.[33]

30. For a popular but slanted biography of Wysłouch, see Henryk Syska, *Przechodzień z góry duchu: O księdzu Antonim Szechem* (Warsaw, 1955). A more scholarly approach to his career may be found in Józef Keller and Zygmunt Poniatowski, eds., *Studia o modernistach katolickich* (Warsaw, 1968), pp. 169–236.

31. See Marian Fulman, "Szakale, czy ludzie?" *Wiadomości Pasterskie* 3, 2 (1907): 124–126, for an impassioned defense of Wysłouch's "pure and honest" intentions as well as his striving for "Catholic reform that would correct the impotence of the Polish church at a most critical moment for society."

32. See esp. Ks. Kajetan Szymkiewicz, "List otwarty," *Przegląd Katolicki*, no. 18 (May 3, 1906): 268–270; and J. Popiel, "O p. A. Szechu, i do niego," ibid., no. 45 (November 8, 1906): 689–691.

33. Bishop Apolinary Wnukowski of Płock, even before Wysłouch's departure from the

At the opposite extreme from "modernism" was the Mariavite movement, led by a group of forty young priests whose rebellion against the hierarchy and traditional discipline was based on an idealized medieval model of a devout and ascetic clergy. Whereas Wysłouch inveighed against the church for ignoring the affairs of this world, the Mariavites (from the Latin *Maria vita*) believed that the clergy's preparation of Catholics for the other world was lacking in devotion. Yet the Mariavites also struck a social chord in their substitution of Polish for Latin in the liturgy, their opposition to receiving fees for the performance of routine pastoral duties, and their attacks on the "noble" lifestyles of the parish clergy. And in contrast to Wysłouch, the Mariavite clergy eventually commanded the allegiance of tens of thousands of believers in twenty-two parishes.[34]

The source and inspiration of the Mariavite movement can be traced to the visions of the nun Felicja Kozłowska, whose career, like Wysłouch's, began in one of Honorat Koźmiński's semisecret assemblies. Engaged in missionary and social work among the parishioners of Płock, Kozłowska by 1900 had convinced several young vicars—many of them recent graduates of the Theological Academy in St. Petersburg—of the validity of her visions. They were also attracted to the practices Kozłowska derived from those visions, which she deemed essential to salvation: continual adoration of the Most Holy Sacrament through daily personal communion and the daily intercession of Mary achieved through round-the-clock prayer shifts of believers in their churches or chapels. From the beginning, Kozłowska's followers among the clergy were characterized by an extraordinary pastoral zeal that gained for the movement many adherents, particularly in urban and mixed urban-rural parishes, where the church had not shown much initiative. The Mariavites, by contrast, served free meals to the poor, opened up shelters for the children of working-class families, and organized cooperative shops among the unemployed.[35]

Initially the Mariavite movement attracted little attention from the hierarchy and other members of the clergy. Only once the movement began, without the approval of the episcopate, to assume organizational form, through the creation of the Assemblies of Mariavite Chaplains and Mariavite Sisters, did the church react. In the summer of 1903, the archbishop of Warsaw transferred six Mariavite priests to less densely populated rural

---

Capuchin order, banned his publications along with other "modernist" brochures, books, and newspapers that "aim at the overthrow of revealed religion"; see APD PWD, Bishop of Płock to the Diocesan Clergy, December 31, 1907.

34. "Statystyka sekty mariawitów," *Miesięcznik Pasterski Płocki*, no. 10 (1906): 282–283.
35. "Społeczna działalność Matki Marii Franciszki," *Mariawita* 6, 3 (1962): 29–31.

parishes. Shortly thereafter, in a letter to the diocesan clergy, Archbishop Popiel warned against participation in the Mariavite assemblies, which, he argued, had violated church discipline and had departed from the principles of Catholic theology.[36] Meanwhile, the Mariavites strove hard behind the backs of the Polish episcopate for formal recognition of their movement in Rome, and in August 1903, Pius X granted a special audience to Kozłowska and seventeen accompanying priests. The Polish bishops, nevertheless, quickly regained the pope's ear through intensive lobbying. In August 1904, a year after his audience with Kozłowska, Pius rejected her visions and dissolved the Assembly of Mariavite Chaplains, leaving the fate of the Mariavite Sisters in the hands of the Polish episcopate.[37] Formalized by a November 1904 decree of the Holy Inquisition, the papal decision also banned any further contacts between Kozłowska and her adherents among the clergy.

The following January the Mariavites issued a formal declaration of submission to the sentences of the Inquisition. Despite the submission to Rome, however, the subordination of the Mariavites to episcopal authority at home proved only superficial. Instead they redoubled their pastoral activity, spreading further the censored Mariavite cults in predominantly mixed rural-urban parishes. They also began to criticize the "depraved" lifestyles of the non-Mariavite clergy openly from the pulpit, propagating among parishioners a new model of the priesthood. As a result, the episcopate in January 1906 suspended the Mariavite priests in their functions, and both sides once again turned to the Vatican. There, the Polish bishops continued to enjoy the upper hand. On April 5, 1906, Pius X issued an encyclical against the Mariavites, giving them fifteen days to unite with the church and demanding their submission to interviews with their bishops. When Father Jan Michał Kowalski, in the name of six Mariavite priests in Płock diocese, rejected these demands, the first schism in Polish Catholicism since the Reformation became a fact, formalized by the Inquisition's official sentence of excommunication on December 5, 1906.[38]

Meanwhile, the revolution had brought laymen into the quarrel between the Roman Catholic hierarchy and the rebellious Mariavite priests. Denied a hearing in Rome, the Mariavites turned for support directly to the population, resorting frequently to the slogans of class struggle popularized by the revolution. For its part, the church also sought to mobilize public opin-

36. Krawczak, "Rewolucja a życie społeczno-religijne," p. 14.
37. Ibid., p. 15. The Assembly of Mariavite Sisters was dissolved in Płock diocese but allowed to continue a tenuous existence elsewhere.
38. ADK AK OA-2/9.

ion through pastoral letters to the faithful, agitation from the pulpit, and a series of vicious attacks on the Mariavite "heresy" in the Catholic press.[39] With inflamed passions leading to a search for more radical solutions on both sides, Catholic loyalists and Mariavites engaged in a struggle for the control of churches, chapels, shrines, and cemeteries which at times assumed the form of fratricidal warfare. The most violent incident occurred in the Warsaw suburb of Leszno, where in April 1906 fighting between Mariavites and their Catholic opponents for control of the parish church left eight dead. The Russian authorities finally intervened at the end of 1906 to contain the religious strife and bloodletting.[40] The Mariavites achieved legal recognition by the tsarist government in exchange for the restoration of disputed places of worship to Roman Catholic jurisdiction. For its part the autocracy gained a potential weapon to use as leverage against the church in the postrevolutionary period.

### Revolution and Catholic Reform

The Mariavite controversy and schism, however costly to the church, was not entirely detrimental, for it forced a reexamination of clerical practices, lifestyles, and ethical behavior. In particular, it led to a reconsideration of the "devotionalist" direction of theological training in the seminaries, which advocates of reform held partially responsible for the Mariavite deviation.[41] It also focused attention on the generation gap and on a lack of communication between older and younger members of the clergy. Similarly, the successes of the mass political movements during the revolution pressured the church to rethink its position on national and social issues and to build new organizational bridges to the popular classes. Ironically, the revolution, while confronting the Polish church with one of the most profound crises in its history, also created opportunities for the church to emerge from that crisis.

Most significantly, the revolution loosened some of the more stringent state controls on the Catholic Church and Catholic religious practices. The

---

39. See Ks. Br. O., "Wichrzenia herezyi 'mankietników,'" *Przegląd Katolicki*, no. 9 (March 1, 1906): 125–127; as well as "Pseudomarjawici, ich początek i odstępstwo od Kościoła," *Miesięcznik Pasterski Płocki*, no. 1 (1906): 18–32.
40. Already, by the end of February 1906, the Warsaw governor-general had issued a circular to provincial and police authorities, instructing them to remain neutral in the religious quarrels of the population but firmly act to prevent and eliminate incidents of violence; see APW ZOW 1938.
41. Ks. M. Szkopowski, "Czarny mankiet," *Wiadomości Pasterskie* 1, 10 (1905): 613–619.

most important development affecting religion during the revolution, the Edict of Religious Toleration issued by the tsar in April 1905, eased a number of the restrictions against the church which had accumulated since the January Insurrection of 1863. Designed to retain the neutrality of non-Orthodox Christian churches, if not their loyalty, during the Russian government's struggle against revolutionary forces throughout the empire, the edict specifically conceded to the Catholic Church in Poland some much-needed breathing room. Separate statutes involving the construction of places of worship in ethnically mixed areas, clerical appointments and transfers, religious processions, missionary activity, the formation of religious brotherhoods, and the travel of clergy outside their parishes were liberalized. Legal limits were also placed on punitive action the state could take against individual priests, excluding them, for example, from hard labor camps and Siberian exile.[42]

The principal provisions of the edict, however, rescinded earlier measures of russification. In this regard, state recognition of the right of Orthodox subjects to convert to another Christian denomination allowed the long-persecuted Uniates, residing mainly in the ethnically Byelorussian and Ukrainian counties of the Kingdom's eastern provinces, to join the Roman Catholic Church. As previously mentioned, the edict also restored the exclusive right of Catholic clergy to provide Polish-language religious instruction in the public schools.[43] Although this latter concession could hardly satisfy the national aspirations of a society striving for Polish as the language of instruction of all subjects, it went a long way toward meeting the church's own more-limited agenda.

Besides the Edict of Toleration with its specific concessions, other developments during the revolution were beneficial to the Catholic Church. The relaxation of press laws and state censorship enabled the church to expand its publications dramatically and to discuss previously prohibited topics, including social and national issues. Further concessions on education, eventually permitting the formation of private schools with Polish as the language of instruction for most subjects, vastly improved the church's chances to influence the direction of youth. And finally, the October Manifesto, with its provisions on freedom of assembly and association, allowed the church to sponsor the formation of new organizational entities to reach Catholics whose needs could no longer be accommodated solely by traditional institutions and practices.

42. "Zniesienie ograniczeń religijnych," *Przegląd Katolicki*, no. 17, supplement (April 27, 1905).
43. Ibid., no. 18, supplement (May 4, 1905).

Meanwhile, events and an aroused public opinion pressured the church to take advantage of the opportunities presented by the revolution. As the palpable unpopularity of its loyalist policies clearly demonstrated, the church could no longer afford to ignore the national and self-governing aspirations of Polish society, especially as those aspirations were frequently expressed in patriotic demonstrations and popular protests at Catholic places of worship.[44] Once the Edict of Toleration allowed the church greater maneuverability in its relationship with the Russian state, the church did begin to rethink its position and gradually, but ever so carefully, to identify itself with selected national causes. Although this change came about only after the October Manifesto, the shift in policy from calculated loyalism to cautious support of "national work" did produce some immediate benefits. For example, the episcopate's quiet abandonment of its opposition to the school strikes and boycott, replaced by public calls and private lobbying for Polish language concessions, helped ensure for the church an important voice in the subsequent debate over a future private Polish school system. Similarly, the church recovered some of its lost ground in the countryside as the clergy began to involve itself in larger numbers in gmina action.[45] But the most important consequence of the church's shift in strategy came after the imposition of martial law throughout the Kingdom in December 1905, when a growing number of Poles, again denied the opportunity for legal and unrestricted political activity, turned to the church as a means of expressing their national identity. In 1906, the first full year of martial law, the number of pilgrims to the ancient shrine of the Black Madonna in Częstochowa jumped fourfold in comparison with the previous year (from 262,041 pilgrims in 1905 to 1,064,232 pilgrims in 1906).[46]

Although partial accommodation to the national aspirations of society enabled the church to offer a more viable alternative to the program of the National Democrats, the crisis of the church in industrial centers as well as the challenge of socialism could be alleviated only by the adoption of a countervailing social evangelism. Given the nature of the times and the

---

44. Demonstrators often demanded crosses, church emblems, and banners from the clergy as well as the participation of priests in patriotic processions; see ADK AK OA-2/12, Circular of the General Consistory of the Warsaw Archdiocese to the Clergy, November 15, 1905.

45. E.g., some clergy in Piotrków Province, supported by the bishop of Kujawy-Kalisz, Stanisław Zdzitowiecki, "illegally" began to record civil documents in Polish as an act of solidarity with the gmina movement; see APŁ KGP 1565.

46. APŁ KGP 1566, Częstochowa Chief of Police to the Piotrków Governor, October 11 (24), 1906.

institution, the only available model came in the form recommended by Catholic social teachings in western Europe. This meant, above all, the popularization and realization of the social encyclicals of Leo XIII.

A group of moderate reformers, also drawn primarily from the younger ranks of the Polish clergy, emerged during the revolution to assume such a mission. Predicating their efforts on the support of the episcopate (in contrast to Wysłouch and the Mariavites), these reformers, or "social workers" (społecznicy) as they called themselves, sought to use the concessions granted to the church by the tsarist government for the broad implementation of Christian Democracy on Western (particularly French, Belgian, and German) models and experience. Closer to home, they drew practical lessons from the social and political activism of the Catholic clergy in Prussian Poland, who through their involvement in institutions of "organic work" had fully maintained for the church a position of national leadership.[47] Grouped around the monthly periodical *Wiadomości Pasterskie* (Pastoral News) and led by Marian Fulman and Bronisław Marjański among others, the clerical reformers in the Kingdom also favored wide-ranging changes in the curricula of theological seminaries, in the personnel and recruitment policies of the hierarchy, and in the financial practice of "building the material church."[48]

To promote their ideas as well as the discussion of national and social issues, the reformers became vocal advocates of frequent conferences of the clergy at all levels. As an intended model, the reformers organized a nationwide congress of the clergy which convened in Warsaw on December 12, 1905. Despite the absence of the episcopate's expressed approval, the congress was attended by 417 clerics. Here, at least a part of the clergy put itself on public record in support of ambitious political reform, calling for "the widest possible administrative and legislative autonomy [for the Kingdom of Poland], with a separate parliament in Warsaw elected on the basis of universal, equal, direct, and secret suffrage."[49] In the same vein, the congress also backed popular demands for the elimination of capital punishment and a general amnesty for political prisoners. In keeping with the slogan "With the Polish people—the Polish priest," the congress justified its resolutions with the argument that the obligations of the clergy were not merely pastoral and religious but also those of general citizenship.

47. See Hagen, *Germans, Poles, and Jews*, pp. 118–158, as well as Richard Blanke, *Prussian Poland in the German Empire, 1871–1900* (Boulder, 1981), pp. 22–26, 81.
48. Ks. A. Szymański, "O pracy społecznej," *Wiadomości Pasterskie* I, 3 (1905): 153–176; Marian Fulman, "Nasza praca społeczna na dobie," ibid., I, 6 (1905): 389–395.
49. "Uchwały I-go krajowego zjazdu duchowieństwa w Warszawie," *Wiadomości Pasterskie* I, 12 (1905): 806–811.

Above all, the reformers sought to build new organizational bridges to Polish Catholics with the aims of familiarizing the clergy with the living, working, and "religious-moral" conditions of the common people and of improving those conditions through a combination of direct social action and missionary work. The most successful Catholic social initiative of the revolutionary era was the Association of Christian Workers (Stowarzyszenie Robotników Chrześcijańskich—SRCh), founded by Father Marceli Godlewski at the end of 1905. The SRCh fought adult illiteracy, created mutual-assistance funds, provided job-placement service as well as free medical care and legal advice, established savings and loan institutions, and formed cooperatives among its working-class members. To raise the moral-religious level of its membership, the SRCh not only promoted participation in religious processions and traditional Catholic brotherhoods but also organized clubs, theaters, choirs, orchestras, excursions, and other "morally uplifting" activities.[50]

As a result of the firm belief of Godlewski and other clerical "patrons" of the association that industrial-labor relations should be based on cooperation rather than confrontation, the SRCh refrained from developing a trade union organization. Nevertheless, it did seek to mediate disputes between labor and management while calling upon the state to create courts of arbitration. Such ideas gained currency among a growing number of industrial workers, especially once the strike movement failed to achieve the desired results in 1906 and 1907. Within a couple of years of its founding, the association counted 22,207 members organized in seventy-nine circles, placing it third among workers' organizations behind the PPS and SDKPiL but slightly ahead of the National Workers' Union (NZR) sponsored by the Endecja.[51]

After 1908, the SRCh experienced a decline (though not nearly as dramatic as that which afflicted the socialist parties) as the euphoria and hopes of the revolutionary years gave way to general disillusionment with all organized activity and a tendency among workers to retreat to the shelter of private lives. In the meantime, other promising social initiatives promoted by the reformers, such as a projected Christian association of farm workers modeled after a similar organization in Prussian Poland, were never realized.[52] Indeed, just as their efforts were beginning to bear fruit

50. APW ZOW 667, Statutes of the Association of Christian Workers in Warsaw Province, December 8 (21), 1906.
51. Wóycicki, Chrześcijański ruch robotniczy w Polsce, p. 97.
52. Marian Fulman, "Stowarzyszenie robotników rolnych," Wiadomości Pasterskie 2, 12 (1906): 729–735.

among the population, the reformers ran into obstacles that proved insurmountable.

Understandably, the Russian government, recalling the role of the church in the January Insurrection of 1863, did not look kindly on Catholic social activity and the clergy's involvement in mass organizations. It therefore held up the legal registration of the SRCh until the end of 1906, meanwhile placing many of its "priest-patrons" under the surveillance of the secret police. Godlewski himself was repeatedly harassed in subsequent years, and Fathers Jan Gralewski and Józef Kownacki, both strong proponents of Catholic social work in Warsaw, were confined by order of the Warsaw governor-general to a Carmelite monastery in Płock Province. Marceli Ryniewicz, vicar of Holy Trinity parish in Warsaw, was deprived of the right to teach religion in private schools because of his involvement in a Polish teachers' union. More frequently, the Russian authorities simply refused to confirm appointments and transfers, as in the case of Piotr Wojtkowski of St. Anthony's parish in Warsaw when he used a state subsidy to provide food and lodging for the children of political prisoners.[53] A more serious blow to the reformers came in January 1906 with the suspension of the progressive Catholic periodical *Dzwonek Częstochowski* (The Częstochowa Bell) for violation of martial law press codes, which forced its talented editor and eloquent spokesman for social Catholicism, Father Józef Adamczyk, to flee the country.[54]

Despite state persecution and harassment, the reformers might have persevered had they enjoyed the solid support of the hierarchy. The attitude of the Polish episcopate toward Catholic social action remained, however, ambivalent at best. Bishop Stanisław Zdzitowiecki of Kujawy-Kalisz was the only consequential advocate of reformist causes, exercising his authority to sponsor initiatives such as the publication of *Wiadomości Pasterskie,* with its pronounced social profile.[55] Tomasz Kuliński, bishop of Kielce, sought to familiarize his diocesan clergy with Catholic social teachings and expressed support for society's "just demands" in pastoral letters before his death in early 1907, but he otherwise wavered in his commitment to the cause of reform, frequently retreating to a position more in line with that of the rest of the episcopate.[56] The episcopal majority, for its part, paid

53. APW ZOW 1617, 1629, 1680, 1801, and 1878.
54. APŁ KGP 1589, Częstochowa Chief of Police to the Piotrków Governor, December 29, 1905 (January 11, 1906).
55. Roman Dzwonkowski, *Listy społeczne biskupów polskich* (Paris, 1974), pp. 145, 162.
56. The bishop of Kielce was also a prime mover behind the organization of four-day "social courses" for the clergy, which were held in Warsaw in the summer of 1907; see ADK AK OA-2/9.

lip service to the principles embodied in papal encyclicals while refusing to take the steps necessary to promote their realization beyond the formation of the Commission for Social Work in October 1905. Reform of the seminaries, including the introduction of social studies in their curricula, did not occur until 1908 and then on a much more limited scale than envisioned by the reformers.[57] Meanwhile, construction of churches in urban parishes increased only marginally as available funds continued to be channeled into "building the material church."[58] The shortage of personnel in working-class parishes, and particularly of young, energetic priests, remained acute. This prompted Bronisław Marjański to complain bitterly about the episcopate's indifference to the challenges confronting the church's mission in factory centers, "which is why they continue to send to such places the usual old, sick, backward, and incompetent parish priests."[59]

The episcopate also disapproved of the reformers' political tendencies, particularly their ties to the National Democrats.[60] The assistance of the Endecja in the organization of the Warsaw congress of the clergy in December 1905, for example, was enough to compromise the gathering in the eyes of the episcopate.[61] As the hierarchy's polemical war against the National Democratic ideological postulates and education policies gained momentum in 1906, the reformers found themselves in a most unenviable position. Those reformers who participated in the myriad organizations sponsored by the Endecja were publicly criticized and called upon to resign from whatever functions they held.[62] Meanwhile, *Wiadomości Pasterskie* felt compelled to join, though with considerably less enthusiasm, in the chorus of Catholic press attacks against the nationalist movement.[63]

Contrary to their expectations, the reformers were also unable to draw effectively on the moral support of the Holy See in their efforts to imple-

---

57. Wóycicki, *Chrześcijański ruch robotniczy w Polsce,* pp 144–145.
58. Fulman, "Wielkomiejskie i fabryczne parafie," p. 77.
59. Ks. Bronisław Maryański, "Sprawa robotnicza," *Wiadomości Pasterskie* 2, 11 (1906): 641–650.
60. These ties can be traced to the involvement of several dozen priests in the Collegium Secretum, a circle of clergymen organized under nationalist auspices at the turn of the century, which stressed cooperation with the lay intelligentsia in national, social, and educational work; see Bender, *Społeczne inicjatywy,* pp. 55–56.
61. E.g., Bishop Wnukowski of Płock scolded reformers for "participating in nationalist meetings well outside their parishes and diocese"; see ADP PWD, Bishop of Płock to the Diocesan Clergy, December 23, 1905.
62. Ibid., February 1, 1907; Ks. dr. Wł. Namiotko, "Polska Macierz Szkolna," *Przegląd Katolicki,* no. 10 (March 7, 1907): 149–153.
63. See, e.g., the moderate tone of "Stronnictwo narodowe-demokratyczne a Kościół," *Wiadomości Pasterskie* 3, 6 (1907): 377–381.

ment the principles of *Rerum Novarum*. The papacy of Pius X, Leo XIII's successor, was one of general retrenchment and emphasis on traditional doctrine that effectively blunted the edge of earlier "progressive" encyclicals. In this respect, the reformers were dealt a major blow by the pope's December 3, 1905, letter to the Polish bishops denouncing "anarchist unions" and "the extreme nationalist party" for pushing the Polish population to "barbaric, criminal activity." To counteract such behavior among the population, Pius called upon the Polish church to stand for law and order as well as the integrity of the Russian state.[64] Although Pius continued to recommend the clergy's involvement in "Catholic social action," his interpretation of extrapastoral social and political activity lacked clear instructions for putting the doctrines of Christian Democracy into practice. The reformers were disappointed to discover that the Vatican itself was still profoundly conservative, especially once Pius made his first pronouncements against social "modernism" in 1910.

Lack of support from their bishops and the Vatican naturally left the reformers vulnerable to an assault from their older and more conservative colleagues. Known variously as "super-Catholics" or "churchmen" (*kościelnicy*) by their opponents, these conservatives remained generally unimpressed by the "social gospel" of Leo XIII. Grouped around the weekly periodical *Przegląd Katolicki* (Catholic Review), they intended to use the concessions granted by the tsarist government for the pursuit of more traditional goals. They believed, for instance, that the problem of incorporating the Uniates from the eastern provinces should take precedence over the needs of urban parishioners in personnel assignments and financial decisions.[65] To deal with the religious needs of industrial workers, the conservatives preferred to rely on traditional missionary activity carried out by teams of Redemptionist and Franciscan monks brought in from Austrian Poland with the temporary blessing of the Russian government.

Not surprisingly, the conservatives deemed initiatives such as the Association of Christian Workers "too radical." Instead, they threw their complete support behind the organization of parishioners in an all-embracing Catholic Union which, according to its statutes (and in contrast to the SRCh), was directly subordinate to the authority of the bishops. Designed to merge all existing Catholic organizations, thereby providing the church with a more viable political base in its competition with the modern mass movements, the Catholic Union instead became a tool of the

---

64. *Przegląd Katolicki*, nos. 1–2 (January 11, 1906): 1–3, nos. 3–4 (January 25, 1906): 25–28, and nos. 5–6 (February 8, 1906): 49–51.
65. Ks. Antoni Szaniawski, "Pilna potrzeba," ibid., no. 20 (May 18, 1905): 297–298.

conservatives in their struggle with the reformers. The Association of Christian Workers indeed became the principal target of attacks by leaders of the Catholic Union, who did not hesitate to accuse Father Godlewski and his collaborators of "modernism."[66]

The conservatives also equated the idea of frequent conferences of the clergy with "modernism," while continuing to regard the episcopal chancellory as the only reliable source of knowledge and information. They believed, moreover, that politics should be left entirely in the hands of the episcopate. Political activity of individual clergymen, especially in mass organizations, was considered degrading to the clerical profession. Such positions were naturally very much in line with the opinion of the episcopal majority.

Unfortunately for the reformers, conservative positions were also in line with views held by the majority of the lower clergy. In the spring of 1906 the chancellory of the bishop of Kielce circulated questionnaires among the parish clergy in an attempt to poll clerical opinion in the diocese on some of the key political and social issues confronting the church. Though this experiment was not repeated elsewhere in the Kingdom of Poland, the written responses from both rural and urban areas of Kielce diocese (which included the Dąbrowa Basin industrial region) provide a revealing sample of contemporary clerical attitudes.[67] The following questions, in particular, drew long essay-type responses: How should a chaplain respond to anticlerical agitation? Should the clergy promote reading among parishioners and of what kinds of literature? Should chaplains participate in secular social, educational, and religious organizations, in recreational associations and sporting clubs, and especially, in political parties? And most important, should involvement in extrapastoral activities require in all cases the prior permission of the bishop?

Significantly, the answers indicate a limited familiarity with the encyclicals of Leo XIII and Catholic social teachings in the West, which are referred to in fewer than 25 percent of the responses studied (though one can imagine what that percentage might have been before the revolution). This minority tended to approve participation in secular organizations as another means of reaching parishioners, particularly the lower classes and youth groups. According to Franciszek Staszkiewicz of Książnice Wielkie parish, such participation was necessary "in order to measure the pulse of

---

66. Wóycicki, *Chrześcijański ruch robotniczy w Polsce*, pp. 152–154.
67. The responses were sent to the Consistory of Kielce diocese and are contained in the collection ADK KD OD-2/1. Unfortunately, data on the age and social background of the respondents are not available.

social life and to counteract social ills." Father Józef Zalewski of
Sułoszowa parish agreed, adding that "in the struggle of life and death for
the Faith, a pastor must act among the people, he must go to the people—
to the workers, to the poor; he must seek out ways to help them, to make
their lives less difficult." Citing Roman Catholic practices in western Europe, one respondent argued that clerical involvement in secular organizations did not require the permission of the bishop, as it was already
justified by earlier papal appeals to the clergy.

At the same time, these priests called for the active engagement of the
clergy in the fight against illiteracy through the establishment of libraries
and reading rooms at the parish level, and they favored clerical involvement in the publication of a diocesan daily newspaper. They also considered that the best way to fight anticlerical propaganda and agitation was
through exemplary behavior, modest living, and conscientious performance
of pastoral duties, rejecting the use of the pulpit, altar, confessional, and
other "holy places" for "counteragitation." Most significantly, although
they agreed that the church as an institution should stand above partisan
politics, they believed that priests as individuals and citizens should be
permitted to exercise their political rights and participate in political parties.

The majority of respondents however, argued that the spiritual mission
of the clergy ruled out involvement of its members in partisan politics.
According to Stanisław Zamojski of Oleśnica parish, membership in a political party was "beneath the dignity" of a chaplain, who "must be everything for everyone." Father T. Dybowski of Bydlin parish went even
further, condemning the involvement of clergymen in politics as "harmful
for both the church and the country." General opposition to clerical participation in political activities, however, did not exclude the use of the
pulpit to fight the church's real and imagined enemies nor that of the
confessional for the "private instruction" of parishioners. "Political agitation in defense of the rights of the church," according to Father Dybowski, "does not contradict the teachings of the church nor the dignity
of the clergy."

Most respondents were indifferent to participation in nonpolitical secular
organizations and could not see how a priest's involvement in such activities served the aims of the church. Wawrzyniec Nowakowski of Pacanów
parish thought the only safe arena for "social activity" of the clergy was
the conservative Catholic Union. Others maintained that the clergy had no
time at all for activity outside the church. The priority given to traditional
pastoral duties was expressed most succinctly by Father M. Wilamowski
of Mierzwin parish: "Participation in associations, trade unions, cooperatives, and sporting clubs should be left in the hands of laymen. Let the

chaplain take care of the altar, pulpit, and confessional.'' Above all, the majority of respondents stressed the absolute necessity of "unity with the bishop," which effectively translated into a willingness to abdicate all initiative—political, social, and religious—to episcopal authority.

In the end, the contest between the reformers and the conservatives in the Polish clergy was unequal, symbolized by the voluntary folding of *Wiadomości Pasterskie* at the end of 1907 because of general lack of support and interest in its further publication. With the decline of the revolution and the pressures generated by it, the hierarchy backed away from its initial and cautious endorsement of Western-style Catholic social action, thus killing any possibility of introducing the more far-reaching changes in traditional practices called for by the advocates of reform. Conservative retrenchment in the Vatican of Pius X, indeed throughout European Catholicism in the years before World War I, could not but strengthen the hand of Catholic traditionalists in the Kingdom. The subsequent offensive against "modernism" in Poland, designed to silence radical critics like Izydor Wysłouch, was bound to have a sobering effect on the more moderate proponents of change as well. And finally, the general age and social profile of the clergy, coupled with its indifference to anything outside the performance of routine pastoral duties, denied reformers the broad support necessary to overcome the hesitation and tentative policies of the episcopate. In the final analysis, the conservatives' victory over the reformers represented the loss of significant opportunities created by the revolution for the church to expand its mission in neglected areas and to tap an undeniably deep reservoir of popular religiosity. Having survived the crisis of the emergency years of the revolution, the church in Russian Poland was inclined to retreat into its ancient shell and return to its traditional methods of saving souls.

# THE IMPACT OF
# MARTIAL LAW

During the first ten months of 1905, the government responded to the various manifestations of upheaval in the Kingdom of Poland with both concessions and measures of repression. The carrot-and-stick approach, however, was the result not of a carefully considered policy but of inconsistent attitudes within the government about how best to deal with the crisis in the Polish provinces. Generally, the central government in St. Petersburg inclined toward compromise in the linguistic, cultural, and religious spheres, a tendency that, if realized in full, could have satisfied the national aspirations of most politically conscious Poles. The provincial bureaucracy in the Kingdom, however, generally opposed such concessions and fought a rearguard action against them. Through their control over the flow of information to St. Petersburg, the provincial authorities sought to present a compelling case for repressive measures, especially as they applied to the political expression of Polish national identity. Their lobbying efforts were not without effect, especially among key officials in the Ministry of Internal Affairs, who then turned to the whimsical and vacillating Nicholas II for the appropriate edict.

The inability of the government to resolve upon a firm course of action, reflected in the alternating currents of compromise and crackdown, exacerbated tensions in the Kingdom. St. Petersburg's concessions of religious toleration and bilingualism in education and local administration raised expectations for more fundamental change, whereas the emergency powers granted the provincial bureaucracy proved sufficient only to embitter ever-increasing numbers. In early November, during the ten days immediately after the October Manifesto, the government appeared to be left with but two choices, both of them extreme. The first was to crown the earlier concessions with a manifesto similar to that of November 4 to the Finns, restoring statutory political autonomy to the Polish provinces. The second was to proclaim a "state of war," or martial law, throughout the Kingdom of Poland and to suppress, once and for all, the movement for Polish home rule. The decision, reached on November 10, to impose martial law, had calamitous repercussions. As it turned out, it killed the last opportunity for a peaceful "Russian" solution to the proverbial Polish question. Instead, Russian rule in the Kingdom thereafter rested irrevocably on military occupation.

## The "Victory" of the Provincial Bureaucracy

The imposition of martial law resulted, in large part, from the attitudes of those who reported to St. Petersburg, that is, those important members of the administrative and police apparatus responsible for maintaining Russian government in the Kingdom. These bureaucratic attitudes, in turn, helped shape the way in which events in Poland were reported. A particular spin was thus put on the flow of information received by St. Petersburg, which because of the regularity of that flow, could not but influence central officials, such as Russia's first prime minister, Sergei Witte, who otherwise tended to favor conciliatory gestures toward the Poles. In short, bureaucratic reporting from the Kingdom, rather than a supposedly uncompromising central government in St. Petersburg, created the principal obstacle to the possibility of an autonomous Kingdom emerging from the Revolution of 1905.

To get at the mentality of these provincial officials, it is necessary to recall briefly the dual function of the Russian administrative and police apparatus in the Kingdom as it evolved after the 1863 insurrection. On the one hand, that apparatus governed the Kingdom with the help of an army of occupation; that is, it implemented and maintained the law, ensured order and security, supervised the development of industry and commerce, kept the social peace, and systematically provided the central ministerial agencies with summary reports based on information received from its lower-ranking officials. In the absence of Poles, who had been purged and then blocked from administrative appointments of any significance, the provincial Russian bureaucracy effectively became the Kingdom's ruling class. On the other hand, however, the bureaucracy in Russian Poland became the principal agency in charge of implementing the official state policy of russification. Placed in the front lines of the struggle against Polish language, culture, and religion, the provincial bureaucrats became zealots for the cause of russification, eventually exceeding the expectations of St. Petersburg in this regard. More than once, a relatively moderate central government would force their temporary retreat. Nevertheless, anti-Polish attitudes hardened and stereotypes became fixed among these provincial officials—attitudes and stereotypes that were to figure prominently in their reporting during the Revolution of 1905.

To the typical 1905-era Russian bureaucrat in the Kingdom, the principal enemies were the noble landowner, the Catholic priest, and the urban-based intellectual, all representatives of those social groups that, some forty years earlier, had provided political and moral leadership for the January Insurrection. Not surprisingly, as a new ruling class, the provincial bureaucracy felt continually threatened by the displaced native elite. In reporting Polish attitudes toward the Russo-Japanese War, for example, local officials concentrated almost exclusively on monitoring the behavior of landowners, clergy, and intelligentsia. When unmistakable signs of discontent appeared from below, responsibility for it was readily assigned to one of the aforementioned groups.[1] By extension, the bureaucracy saw little danger coming from the "mass nation" in its own right, especially from the Polish peasantry, whose eternal gratitude for favorable terms of emancipation was taken for granted.

Throughout most of 1905, the course of events and the policies of the central government placed the ruling bureaucracy in the Kingdom on the defensive. Although St. Petersburg never got around to an official renunciation of russification, it did much to dismantle existing policy and thereby undermine the position of its agents in the Kingdom. The Edict of Religious Toleration, conceived as early as 1903 and promised at the end of 1904, was finally issued the following April. By removing restrictions on public religious manifestations, the movement of clergy, and especially the conversion of former Uniates to Roman Catholicism, the Edict of Toleration undercut russification. In the eyes of the provincial bureaucracy, however, religious toleration played into the hands of the traditional enemy, the Polish Catholic priest. In an effort to force St. Petersburg to modify the edict, provincial governors readily identified the Catholic clergy as leaders of the national and separatist movements in Poland. Meanwhile, bureaucratic harassment of the clergy was stepped up, despite the edict. Provincial officials demanded from central authorities the transfer of troublesome priests, sought to use their limited emergency powers to restrict the clergy's newly attained freedom of movement, insisted on the use of

---

1. These reports, compiled for each of the ten Polish provinces, are located in AGAD KGGW 2308.

Russian in all official church correspondence, and threatened to close places of worship that permitted the singing of the forbidden national Polish hymn, "Boże coś Polskę" (God Preserve Poland). Beyond increasing the red tape for the legal conversion of Uniates to the Roman rite, however, the central government stayed the course of toleration.

Worse still, from the vantage point of the provincial bureaucracy, was the decision of the Committee of Ministers of June 19, 1905, which further undercut earlier russification measures. The popular movement against the russified school system, accompanied by the demands of gmina assemblies for expanded use of the native language, convinced the central government to offer the Poles limited, yet significant, concessions. The principle of bilingualism was introduced in public elementary and secondary schools, in gmina administration, and in the commissariats of peasant affairs. Discrimination in state approval of land purchases based on religion or nationality was also terminated. Meanwhile, the Council of State agreed to consider the question of introducing, in the Polish provinces, institutions of rural and municipal self-government as well as independent justices of the peace.[2]

Once again, central government policy ran contrary to the interests of the Russian bureaucracy in the Kingdom. Earlier, that bureaucracy had tried to stem the movement against the schools, which it blamed on the Polish intelligentsia, through closings and mass expulsions of students. To undermine the gmina action movement in the countryside and its perceived leading "agitators" from the noble landowning class, some Russian officials had even resorted to informing the peasants that the end result of their "illegal action" would be the restoration of serfdom. All of this had little impact either in the Kingdom or in St. Petersburg. Rather than retreat from their language demands, the Poles subsequently enlarged them. On October 14, the central government responded with legislation permitting the establishment of private schools with Polish as the language of instruction for nearly all subjects, thus providing the legal basis for what would become the Polska Macierz Szkolna (Polish Motherland Schools) and other independent educational initiatives.[3]

While fighting the concessions to the Polish national movement and its perceived representatives among the Polish elite, the bureaucracy in the Kingdom continued to court its supposed "friends" among the lower

2. The decision of the Committee of Ministers of June 6 (19), 1905, as confirmed by the tsar, is found in AGAD KGGW 2621.
3. On the concessions of October 14, see Edmund Staszyński, *Polityka oświatowa caratu w Królestwie Polskim: Od powstania styczniowego do I wojny światowej* (Warsaw, 1968), pp. 170–171.

classes. Peasants and industrial workers, it reasoned, were basically apolitical and would remain aloof from the revolutionary and national movements if their economic grievances were addressed. Hence, during the January-February general strike and throughout the spring of 1905, the governors of Piotrków, Warsaw, Radom, and Lublin provinces actively sought to mediate industrial labor disputes, to the point of pressuring employers to make concessions. In the countryside, although provincial authorities remained convinced that agrarian strikes and mass trespassing incidents would not have occurred without "outside agitation," many of them expressed sympathy for the demands of the rural poor. In Lublin Province, local authorities were particularly slow to intervene in agrarian disputes and moved only after complaints of their "inactivity" reached St. Petersburg.[4] In neighboring Siedlce Province, by contrast, officials moved quickly enough, but in response to the alarming prospect that landowners and farmhands would reach agreement without their participation.

When the behavior of the lower classes belied the provincial bureaucracy's belief in the continuing efficacy of a policy of divide and rule, however, appeals to St. Petersburg for emergency powers became exceedingly commonplace. The Warsaw superintendent of police was calling for the imposition of martial law, literally "a state of war," already by the end of February, even though the industrial general strike had run its course. In his mind, the "national movement" embodied in the school strikes posed a far greater threat to Russian rule than the discontent of industrial workers.[5] The best that he and the rest of the provincial authorities received from St. Petersburg was agreement to proclaim a "state of intensified security," the lowest level of emergency rule. "Intensified security" was proclaimed in Warsaw and Piotrków provinces at the end of January; in Kalisz, Radom, and Siedlce provinces on February 4; and in the rest of the Kingdom by the end of February.

"Intensified security" increased the powers of the provincial authorities, but more on paper than in actuality. On the basis of Article 15 of the statutes providing for this form of emergency rule, provincial governors

---

4. AGAD KGGW 2513, Minister of Internal Affairs to the WGG, March 21 (April 3), 1905; Stanisław Kalabiński, ed., *Carat i klasy posiadające w walce z rewolucją 1905–1907 w Królestwie Polskim: Materiały archiwalne* (Warsaw, 1956), pp. 88–89. In response to St. Petersburg, rather than the Polish landowners, the Lublin governor finally issued a proclamation announcing that cases involving attacks on private property and employers of farm labor would be turned over to military courts. In reality, however, those arrested in connection with the agrarian strikes either received short jail terms or were placed under temporary police surveillance.

5. AGAD KGGW 2489, Warsaw Superintendent of Police to the WGG, February 15 (28), 1905.

and superintendents of police were empowered by the Ministry of Internal Affairs, through the Warsaw governor-general's office, to issue "binding decisions" and to sentence and fine, without reference to the courts, those who violated their decrees. As the most progressive features of the Russian legal reforms of the 1870s had never extended to the Kingdom in the first place, the power of administrative sentencing itself meant very little in the Polish context. Moreover, the maximum sentence that could be imposed under Article 15 was three months in jail and/or a five-hundred-ruble fine. Only those deemed guilty of "terrorist" acts, that is, outright physical assault against the state and its representatives or against private individuals and their property, could be transferred to military courts for sentencing. Theoretically, this meant that under "intensified security," the wearing of a traditional Polish national emblem during a religious procession and the illegal sale and possession of weapons and explosives could result in the same maximum jail sentence or fine.[6] Consequently, the very arbitrariness of "intensified security" aggravated popular discontent instead of pacifying it, whereas the later concessions of the central government of April and June seemed to condone many of the acts of civil disobedience punishable under its statutes.

At the same time, the central government proved reluctant to grant the provincial bureaucracy in Poland greater emergency powers, not those provided by the statutes regulating "a state of extraordinary security," let alone those embodied in "a state of war." To be sure, martial law was proclaimed in Łódź and Łódź County on June 24, but even then as a belated response to a very real breakdown of law and order. Martial law provided the then-Warsaw governor-general Lt. Gen. Konstantin Maksimovich (who had replaced Mikhail Chertkov three months earlier) sweeping authority, which he immediately delegated to Gen. Nicholas Shuttleworth, the commander of those army units that had suppressed the local insurgency.[7] Shuttleworth's "rule" in Łódź was far from draconian, however, and extended little beyond the enforcement of a strict curfew, a ban on demonstrations and other public gatherings, and a hunt for revolutionaries and terrorists. Although martial law led to an immediate decline in strike activity in Łódź as troops were posted in the factories, it did not prevent a revival of the strike movement in the fall.

6. Cf., e.g., APW ZOW 1778, Directives of the Warsaw Governor-General of March 18 (31), 1905, with AGAD KGGW 2577, Circular of the WGG to the Provincial Governors of June 30, 1905.

7. Paweł Korzec, ed., *Źródła do dziejów rewolucji 1905–1907 w okręgu łódzkim,* vol. 1, pt. 2 (Warsaw, 1957), pp. 244–246.

Martial law was also introduced in Warsaw on August 23, 1905, in response to the increasingly large protest demonstrations and strikes organized by the socialist parties against the Bulygin duma, the consultative assembly announced by imperial decree four days earlier. Again, however, martial law had only a local resonance. Requests by the Siedlce and Kalisz governors to extend martial law to their provinces were rejected as "unjustified" by the Ministry of Internal Affairs.[8] More to their liking, however, was the ministry's critical appointment on August 28 of George Skalon as Warsaw governor-general.

Skalon was hardly a stranger to the Polish provinces. The descendent of a French noble family, long russified by generations of service to the Russian crown, Skalon first served in the Kingdom as a special affairs officer to Governor-General Iosif Gurko in the early 1890s, during the most intense period of the campaign against Polish language, religion, and culture. After typical service transfers into and out of posts in the Kingdom, he returned to Warsaw at the end of May 1905 as deputy to Governor-General Maksimovich. Known as a proponent of "the strong arm," Skalon's replacement of the ineffective Maksimovich three months later became the first important step in the ultimate resort to exclusively repressive measures of rule. Skalon would remain in the office of Warsaw governor-general until his natural death in February 1914, having survived several earlier attempts on his life.[9]

Although Skalon's appointment came too late to influence the decision of the Ministry of Internal Affairs to deny the Kalisz and Siedlce governors' requests to impose martial law in their jurisdictions, the new Warsaw governor-general proved more successful in defeating a planned concession that would have permitted Polish as the language of instruction for all subjects in officially permitted private schools.[10] Otherwise, Skalon's first month in office proved relatively calm. By the end of September, he was sufficiently confident to recommend for the ministry's consideration the eventual lifting of martial law in Łódź and Łódź County and its replace-

8. AGAD KGGW 2507, Kalisz Governor to the WGG, August 13 (26), 1905, and 2584, Minister of Internal Affairs to the WGG, August 19 (September 1), 1905.
9. Halina Kiepurska, *Warszawa w rewolucji 1905–1907* (Warsaw, 1974), pp. 303–304. The most serious and nearly successful attempt was undertaken by the PPS on August 18, 1906, when a bombing of Skalon's carriage left the Warsaw governor-general with a mild concussion; see Adam Próchnik, *Studia z dziejów polskiego ruchu robotniczego* (Warsaw, 1958), pp. 450–492.
10. Zygmunt Łukawski, "Rosyjskie ugrupowanie polityczne wobec sprawy autonomii Królestwa Polskiego w okresie 1905–1917," *Zeszyty Naukowe Uniwersytetu Jagiellońskiego: Prace Historyczne* 9 (1962): 151.

ment with a state of intensified security.[11] Skalon's confidence, no doubt, was bolstered by a dramatic increase in troop strength in eight of the Kingdom's ten provinces since June.[12]

The Kingdom's tenuous and superficial tranquillity was soon disrupted by the October general strike, less than two months into Skalon's tenure in office. The resulting Imperial Manifesto of October 30 then sparked an extraordinary chain of events in the Kingdom. Although Warsaw itself technically remained under a "state of war," censorship effectively evaporated the next day, and the first of several large-scale demonstrations in support of the Kingdom's political autonomy proceeded through the streets of the Polish capital. On November 1, the Catholic Church expressed its gratitude for the October Manifesto with the singing of "Te Deum Laudamus" and prayers for the House of Romanov in the country's major cathedrals. On November 2, a large crowd responded to the appeal of the socialist parties to demand the release of political prisoners in front of the Warsaw magistrate's office on Theater Square. Cossack attempts to disperse the demonstrators resulted in rioting and many fatalities, prompting Skalon to plead with Sergei Witte, the recently appointed chairman of the Council of Ministers, to maintain a state of intensified security in the entire Kingdom and martial law in the Warsaw and Łódź regions.[13] Nevertheless, the next day the tsar granted a general amnesty that led to the release of more than a thousand persons in Warsaw alone. This was followed on November 4 by the largest of the Warsaw demonstrations, a peaceful procession of as many as one hundred thousand organized by the National Democrats and headed by cross-bearing priests. This demonstration, in turn, provided a model for dozens of mass processions held in provincial capitals and district towns on November 5, which began with expressions of gratitude to the tsar in Catholic churches and ended with the illumination of candles in the windows of Polish, as well as Jewish, homes.

Particularly after the tsar's manifesto to the Finns of November 4, rumors of impending autonomy permeated the political air of the Kingdom. The demonstrations of November 5 were accompanied by the resolutions of factory crews and peasant assemblies calling for Polish home rule. The popular movement for autonomy was capped by the dispatch of a delegation of Polish dignitaries, organized by the National Democrats and led by Roman Dmowski, to meet with Count Witte. As the Polish delegation set off for St. Petersburg, the bureaucracy in the Kingdom, headed by the

11. Korzec, *Źrodła do dziejów rewolucji* I (2): 381–382.
12. Kalabiński, *Carat i klasy posiadające*, pp. 273–279.
13. Ibid., pp. 298–299.

Political demonstration in Warsaw, November 1905. (Muzeum Niepodległości 22957)

determined Skalon, labored even harder for a military solution to the Polish question. On November 6, despite the relatively peaceful nature of events since the October Manifesto, Skalon on his own initiative ordered the provincial governors to disperse all street demonstrations with armed force.[14] It remained, however, to convince St. Petersburg that the restoration of order in the Kingdom depended not on further concessions but on the immediate application of repressive measures. "Three years at my post have convinced me," the Kalisz governor Novosiltsev reported to an agreeable Skalon, "that the Poles, by virtue of their character, can never be satisfied and must be ruled by a consistently strong hand."[15]

As high as Polish expectations for autonomy ran, fears among the provincial bureaucracy that the imperial government might actually concede autonomy ran even higher. In his telegram to Witte of November 2, Skalon reported that "extremist parties" were behind the demand for political au-

14. Ibid., p. 301.
15. AGAD KGGW 2507, Kalisz Governor to the WGG, October 29 (November 11), 1905.

Artist's depiction of the Theater Square Massacre in Warsaw, November 1, 1905. (Muzeum Niepodległości 43297)

tonomy voiced in the Warsaw demonstrations—this in an attempt to justify the retention of the various forms of emergency rule already in place. For the next week, Skalon bombarded St. Petersburg with his agents' reports of absolute chaos in the Kingdom. Throughout the country, according to the special deputy to the Warsaw governor-general for police affairs, local government authority was collapsing as a result of the "paralysis" of the regular police and insufficient troop strength.[16] In Piotrków Province, the population of Częstochowa reportedly was "arming itself to the teeth with Austrian weapons" in secret preparation for an armed uprising, while the Dąbrowa Basin had fallen to "socialist rule."[17] "Complete anarchy" was said to embrace the Puławy region of Lublin Province.[18] Meanwhile, the

16. AGAD KGGW 2512 and 2525, Reports of the SDPA to the WGG, October 19 (November 1) and October 28 (November 10), 1905, respectively.
17. AGAD KGGW 2498, Telegram of the Provisional Governor-General of Łódź and Łódź County to the Chief of Staff of the Warsaw Military Region, October 29 (November 11), 1905, and 2499, Commander of the Częstochowa Garrison to the Chief of the Okhrana of Piotrków Province, October 23 (November 5), 1905; Kalabiński, Carat i klasy posiadające, pp. 307–308.
18. APL KGL 1905:250, Telegram of the Chief of Nowa-Aleksandria County to the Lublin Governor, October 21 (November 3), 1905; AGAD KGGW 2515, Report of the SDPA to the WGG, October 28 (November 10), 1905.

eight thousand inhabitants of Żelechów in Gawrolin County of Siedlce Province had become "completely terrorized" by the activity of the "socialist party."[19]

This steady stream of exaggerated reports of anarchy, terrorism, the breakdown of civil administration and police authority, and above all, preparations for a general uprising finally made an impact in the Russian capital, particularly in the Ministry of Internal Affairs. It was here that Skalon won the critical support necessary for a crackdown. While preparing his ground by sounding alarms within the ministry, Skalon simultaneously called on General Voronin, chief of staff of the Warsaw Military Region, to present him with a detailed plan for the defense of the "Vistulaland" in the event of an armed uprising—in effect, a blueprint for martial law.[20] On November 8, before receiving Voronin's report, Skalon sent an urgent wire to D. F. Trepov, head of the Department of Police within the Ministry of Internal Affairs, arguing that martial law was "the only way out"— that is, the only way to avoid an imminent insurrection.[21] Skalon's case for a "state of war" and "strong repressive measures" easily won over Trepov and Minister P. N. Durnovo, who then secured the tsar's approval on November 10. Thus, before Dmowski and the Polish delegation ever had an opportunity to present to Witte their case for autonomy as the best means of preserving political stability in the Kingdom, the decision to impose martial law had already been made.

## From False to Real Alarms

Skalon's purpose in imposing martial law was not to forestall an uprising but to defeat Polish efforts to obtain political autonomy. Three weeks later, after the much-invoked justification of a general uprising failed to materialize, martial law was lifted. The intended damage to the cause of Polish autonomy had been accomplished. The imposition of martial law, however, had created such bitterness among the general population that the earlier, highly exaggerated prophecies of anarchy and revolt now became self-fulfilling. The gmina assembly of Sielce (Płońsk County, Warsaw Province) best expressed popular attitudes when it claimed that the provincial bureaucracy was responsible for all subsequent disorders in the country

19. AGAD KGGW 2527, Report of the SDPA to the WGG, October 23 (November 5), 1905.
20. Kalabiński, Carat i klasy posiadające, pp. 305, 310–311.
21. Ibid., pp. 302–303.

The delegation to Count Witte. Political cartoon, November 1905. (Muzeum Niepodległości 35873)

because it had failed to implement reforms in the spirit of the October
Manifesto.[22]

The same provincial officials who had demanded strong repressive measures in early November now questioned whether martial law had brought
about the expected results. In Warsaw Province, the crackdown on the

22. AGAD KGGW 2505, Warsaw Governor to WGG, December 29, 1905 (January 11,
1906).

gmina action movement and its leaders exacerbated existing tensions. In mid-December, assembly meetings in all gminy of Sochaczew County passed a uniform set of resolutions that amounted to a declaration of independence from the ruling bureaucracy.[23] Gmina assemblies resolved, among other things, to forbid the presence of the police at their meetings, and many members of the rural Land Guard were persuaded by individual threats against their lives and unrestrained crowd violence to leave the Kingdom altogether. Incapable of carrying out their responsibilities unless accompanied by military patrols, those members of the Land Guard in Łowicz County who had not abandoned their posts remained confined to their homes, revolvers in hand, in anticipation of assassins or a mob siege.[24]

Authorities in Kalisz Province, too, were disappointed with the results of martial law, which they clearly had expected to pacify the popular movement, especially in the countryside. Although major eruptions of violence were avoided, the provisional military governor-general requested the removal of "priest-agitators" from parishes where gminy continued to be particularly recalcitrant in fulfilling their obligations to the state.[25] Whereas martial law failed to change the mood of the population in Kalisz Province, it transformed the "abnormal relationship" between the population and local officials in Kielce Province to one of "open hatred," according to its governor. As in Warsaw Province, the exceedingly vulnerable rural police became the principal target of popular anger, "even on their quarters at night."[26]

In Łomża Province, where in many counties the ranks of the Land Guard had been reduced by nearly half, the lifting of martial law at the end of November was accompanied by Polish patriotic demonstrations in towns, villages, and settlements that had not participated in the earlier celebrations sparked by the October Manifesto. This time, however, there were no expressions of gratitude to the tsar for the new freedoms. The subsequent radicalization of gmina action in the province and, especially, of the movement against the state schools were sufficient to convince police officials of the existence of plans for an uprising, despite the contrary views of the Łomża governor.[27]

In Lublin the imposition of martial law was answered with a one-day general strike on November 13 and the forced suspension of instruction in

23. AGAD KGGW 2505, Report of the SDPA to the WGG, December 17 (30), 1905.
24. AGAD KGGW 2505, Warsaw Governor to the WGG, December 11 (24), 1905.
25. AGAD KGGW 2507, Provisional Governor-General of Kalisz Province to the WGG, November 11 (24), 1905.
26. AGAD KGGW 2509, Kielce Governor to the WGG, November 7 (20), 1905.
27. AGAD KGGW 2512, Report of the SDPA to the WGG, December 10 (23), 1905.

all city schools. All proclamations announcing martial law were torn down. Although socialist efforts to call a second general strike on November 16 failed, patrols of police and troops were constantly harassed by snipers. Outside the provincial capital, vigilantism experienced a sharp upsurge in Lublin, Krasnystaw, and Lubartów counties.[28] In Płock Province, martial law met with little active resistance, but its lifting at the end of November was accompanied by a peasant tax revolt and other, bolder forms of gmina action. Gmina administrators and court officials refused any further use of the Russian language in the performance of their duties, leading to mass dismissals and arrests.[29]

A succession of "binding decrees" issued by the provisional military governor-general of Radom Province indicates the growing severity of the crisis in that region. These proclamations to the population began by listing bans and punishments for such matters as possession of antigovernment publications, the failure to close gates and entrances to buildings at the appropriate hour, and the wearing of school uniforms by expelled students. Within days, however, the "binding decrees" turned to the possession and use of explosive devises and handguns as well as the defense of telegraph lines, railroad track and bridges, and other state property. Consequently, the inhabitants of Radom Province, an early center of terrorist activity, were among the first to be assigned collective responsibility for the state's material losses "regardless of the circumstances."[30] State efforts to collect the subsequent fines levied on the population, however, met with resistance. Residents of Białobrzegi in Opatów County, fined nineteen hundred rubles for refusing to defend telegraph lines in their community, submitted only when confronted by half a company of Cossacks. Moreover, the use of Cossacks to collect not only fines but also taxes from the rural population left many towns in the province without adequate troops.[31]

In Siedlce Province, where the national movement had long been accompanied by a religious movement among the Roman Catholic and Uni-

---

28. AGAD KGGW 2515, Reports of the SDPA to the WGG, November 10 (23) and 16 (29), 1905; Provisional Governor-General of Lublin Province to the WGG, November 9 (22) and November 15 (28), 1905; and Lublin Governor to the WGG, December 4 (17), 1905.
29. AGAD KGGW 2517, Provisional Governor-General of Płock Province to the WGG, November 11 (24) and December 11 (24), 1905; Reports of the SDPA to the WGG, November 22 (December 5) and December 16 (29), 1905; and Senior President of the Warsaw District Court to the WGG, December 16 (29), 1905.
30. AGAD KGGW 2520, Proclamations of the Provisional Governor-General of Radom Province of November 1 (14), November 2 (15), November 4 (17), November 6 (19), and November 13 (26), 1905.
31. AGAD KGGW 2520, Provisional Governor-General of Radom Province to the WGG, November 9 (22) and 12 (25), 1905; Kalabiński, *Carat i klasy posiadające*, p. 388.

ate population against the official Russian Orthodox Church, the imposition of martial law and its ill-timed lifting led to a dramatic upsurge in ethno-religious tensions, especially in the eastern counties of the Chełm region. In the immediate aftermath of the Edict of Religious Toleration, missionary work, nationalist propaganda and voluntary mass conversions had already resulted in the departure of 68 percent of the province's East Slavic population from Orthodoxy in the spring and summer. Now, in the last months of 1905, the remaining Orthodox minority became subjected to coercion and terror from a Catholic majority increasingly bent on eliminating Orthodoxy from the region altogether. Gmina assemblies, dominated by Roman Catholics and Uniates, arbitrarily disenfranchised their Orthodox neighbors by making membership in the Catholic Church a prerequisite for holding local elective office. As a result, many mayors, plenipotentiaries, and village elders converted to retain their posts. When the authorities refused to confirm the converted officials in their positions and installed Orthodox candidates in their place, the latter became targets and casualties of popular violence. Meanwhile, the agricultural employers of the region, almost uniformly Polish and Roman Catholic, openly discriminated against Orthodox farm workers in hiring, wage payments, and the granting of pasturing rights. And where employers failed to discriminate, crowds of Catholic villagers frequently blocked Orthodox laborers from working on nearby estates. By December the Orthodox minority in Siedlce Province was said to be "in a state of near panic" as a result of rumors of "impending pogroms" against them.[32]

If civil administration was breaking down throughout the Kingdom, in the Lithuanian counties of Suwałki Province it collapsed altogether. From early November to mid-December 1905, provincial authorities recorded no fewer than seventy-five armed attacks, including several cases of arson, on local administrative offices, courts, primary schools, vodka retail outlets, and headquarters of the Land Guard.[33] In Wyłkowyszki County, all twenty-four members of the rural police had to be transferred to the county seat for their personal safety, and troop strength was deemed sufficient only in the towns. In the abandoned countryside, gmina assemblies openly declared their independence from state taxation and threatened death to police and gendarmes who dared to appear at their meetings. Everywhere Russian

32. AGAD KGGW 2527, Siedlce Governor to the WGG, November 24 (December 7), 1905; see also Robert Blobaum, "Toleration and Ethno-Religious Strife: The Struggle between Catholics and Orthodox Christians in the Chełm Region of Russian Poland, 1904–1906," *Polish Review* 35, 2 (1990): 120–123.
33. AGAD KGGW 345, Summary Reports of the Suwałki Governor's Office for November and December 1905.

signs and portraits of the imperial family were vandalized and destroyed by Lithuanian armed bands, who also carried out acts of expropriation against preponderantly Polish landowners and parish priests.[34] On December 15, after dozens of "disorders" over a five-day period, Skalon requested permission from the Ministry of Internal Affairs to reimpose martial law in Władysławów, Wyłkowyszki, Kawalaria, and Mariampol counties, which had fallen victim to a "complete anarchy" fanned by the Lithuanian Social Democratic Party.[35] Two days later, the tsar approved the restoration of military rule in these counties inhabited by a majority of Lithuanians, whose "days of freedom" proved even more short-lived than for the tsar's other subjects in Russian Poland.

In retrospect, the renewed resort to a "state of war" in Suwałki Province on December 17 served as a mere prelude to the reimposition of martial law throughout the Kingdom of Poland. Within four days, all ten provinces were returned to military rule while Skalon lobbied St. Petersburg for even greater emergency powers. Shocked by the near collapse of state authority which accompanied the first experience with martial law, both in its precipitous imposition and its equally precipitous lifting, Skalon and the military governors took to their task with far greater seriousness of purpose the second time around. If, in its first enactment, martial law had been called upon to defeat the movement for Polish autonomy, it now faced the even more formidable challenge of restoring basic law and order. And while the first, mild dose of martial law had managed to kill the prospects for a self-governing Kingdom in the course of three weeks, it would take several years of sweeping repressive measures to restore the confidence of provincial authorities and to permit a return to civilian administration.

## The Rule of the Provisional Governors-General

The period of military rule, which lasted in varying degrees until 1909, extends beyond the strict chronological confines of this book. Even with the extension of a restored civilian administration to all ten provinces in the middle of that year, parts of the Kingdom still remained under "civilian" forms of emergency rule in 1914, when the outbreak of the Great War created a new and far different challenge to the maintenance of Russian power in the Kingdom. Nevertheless, because the goals of martial law

34. AGAD KGGW 2524, Suwałki Governor to the County Chiefs, December 3 (16), 1905, and Report of the SDPA to the WGG, December 5 (18), 1905.
35. Kalabiński, *Carat i klasy posiadające*, pp. 378–381.

were largely accomplished by 1907, a discussion of the salient features of
military rule is in order.

As in November, the reimposition of martial law resulted in the transfer
of all civil and military authority in the provinces to ten "provisional"
military governors-general.[36] Martial law vested these military governors,
usually district commanders, with sweeping administrative, police, and judicial powers exercised under the scrutiny of the Warsaw governor-general
in his dual capacity as commander of the Warsaw Military Region.
Although the provisional governors-general delegated certain of their responsibilities to the civilian provincial governors "in the aim of restoring
order as quickly as possible," there were few cases of competing and
conflicting jurisdictions.[37] On their own initiative, the provisional military
governors could issue binding decrees and, in the event of their violation,
administer maximum sentences of three months in jail and fines of three
thousand rubles without referring to the courts or, for that matter, to the
Warsaw governor-general.

These "normal" repressive measures were supplemented by the nearly
dictatorial powers entrusted to the Warsaw governor-general, particularly
through his exercise of Articles 12 and 19 of the emergency statutes affecting territories under a "state of war." Under Article 19, in cases involving armed opposition to the authorities, attacks on police, military, and
public officials, premeditated armed assaults on private property, and the
looting, robbery, and theft of public property, the Warsaw governor-general
could deprive citizens of all rights and transfer their cases to the military
courts. Upon a guilty verdict from the latter, the Kingdom's chief military
and civilian official was then empowered to impose the death sentence.
Article 12 permitted the Warsaw governor-general to dispense with the
military courts and impose capital punishment without any trial so as to
respond quickly to political murder, attempted assassinations and their
preparation, and all activity "aimed at terrorizing the authorities and the
population."[38]

36. Later subdivisions were created in Radom and Piotrków provinces in the course of 1906,
leading to the appointment of two additional provisional governors-general.
37. One such instance involved the submission of police protocols of evidence in criminal
cases to the judicial authorities, which was still required by martial law statutes and upheld
by the Warsaw governor-general; see AGAD KGGW 2585, WGG to the Provisional
Governors-General, February 7 (20), 1906.
38. For Skalon's own understanding of Articles 12 and 19, see AGAD KGGW 2584, Circular of the WGG to the Provisional Governors-General, November 7 (20), 1905, and 2585,
WGG to the Provisional Governor-General of Opatów, Iłża, Końskie, and Sandomierz Counties in Radom Province, January 1 (14), 1906.

From the beginning, Skalon sought to limit the restrictions that St. Petersburg, through the person of Prime Minister Witte, might place on the exercise of his extraordinary powers, while never tiring of reminding the provisional governors-general of his exclusive prerogatives. With the reimposition of martial law on December 22, Skalon's right to exercise Article 19 was initially confined by the exclusion of six instances otherwise specified by statute.[39] This limitation, together with early reports from the provinces that the "normal" repressive measures imposed by the provisional governors-general were having little immediate effect, prompted Skalon to lobby the Ministry of Internal Affairs for "strong repressive measures" to accompany martial law. Lifting the restrictions on his exercise of Article 19 and the liberal resort to Article 12, according to the Warsaw governor-general, was "the only way to restore internal order."[40] Such arguments convinced Minister P. N. Durnovo, who on January 12, 1906, informed Skalon of his "guaranteed support" for "all severe and decisive measures" to restore order in the Kingdom.[41]

Having received Durnovo's telegram, Skalon proceeded on the same day to order the execution of the Piekalski brothers, workers of the Saturn Mining Company, held in connection with the murder of a member of the Land Guard, and of Jan Markowski, for the killing of the Lublin stationmaster.[42] Three days later, thirteen anarchist-communists from the International group were executed by firing squad in Warsaw. Before the month was out, twenty-four persons, mainly anarchists, had been sentenced to death by administrative fiat.[43]

For Count Witte, who had already sought to restrain the arbitrary exercise of the prerogatives granted Skalon by the martial law statutes, the executions in Poland constituted an abuse of power. Fearful that Skalon's actions would turn moderate Russian opinion against his government and undermine the fledgling constitutional experiment, Witte successfully outflanked Durnovo in convincing the tsar on February 19 to suspend the Warsaw governor-general's application of Article 12 and to restore the earlier restrictions on his exercise of Article 19.[44] These restraints on Ska-

39. AGAD KGGW 2585, Circular of the WGG to the Provincial Governors, December 8 (21), 1905.
40. Kalabiński, *Carat i klasy posiadające*, pp. 399–401.
41. AGAD KGGW 2585, Minister of Internal Affairs to the WGG, December 30 (January 12), 1906.
42. Kalabiński, *Carat i klasy posiadaj*ące, pp. 421, 423.
43. Herman Rappaport, ed., *Anarchizm i anarchiści na ziemiach polskich do 1914 roku* (Warsaw, 1981), pp. 24–25, 27–28.
44. Ibid., p. 30.

George Skalon, Warsaw Governor-General from August 1905 to February 1914.
(Muzeum Niepodległości 35971)

lon, however, proved short-lived. With Witte's fall from grace several
weeks later, followed by the ascendancy of Peter Stolypin in the Ministry
of Internal Affairs and then as head of the government, Skalon had little
trouble in restoring his prerogatives. Thereupon, the Warsaw governor-
general's right to resort to Article 12 was loudly proclaimed as a public
warning but exercised only once more, in September 1907, when eight
socialists were executed for the murder of a Łódź industrialist.

Skalon's subsequent self-restraint in his use of Article 12 is explained,
in part, by the introduction in Poland of the field courts-martial, legal
justification for which was provided by Article 87 in Stolypin's revision
of the empire's Fundamental Laws after the dissolution of the Second
Duma. For Skalon's purpose in the Kingdom, this legal mechanism combined the semblance of due process with the means to respond quickly to
crimes against the state. Accordingly, in all localities under martial law,
civilians accused of a crime who otherwise would have been tried by a
regular military court under Article 19 could be turned over to a provisional
"field" court, established on an ad hoc basis and made up of a chairman
and four officers. The accused were to be tried within twenty-four hours
of their arrest, with sentences passed no later than forty-eight hours after
the court had convened. The proceedings were to be entirely secret, and
the sentence, once submitted to and approved by the commander of the
military region (in the Kingdom's case, the Warsaw governor-general), was
to be executed within twenty-four hours of its pronouncement. Needless
to say, procedures and the administration of punishment became quick and
simplified, meeting the requirements of both summary justice and the rights
of the accused to a "trial." The field courts were therefore made to order
for Skalon, and ideal blending of Articles 12 and 19, which shielded him
from accusations of arbitrary action while maintaining the full range of his
emergency powers.

To argue that the field courts were extremely active in Russian Poland
would be an understatement. The interwar socialist and historian Adam
Próchnik studied the 347 cases and 1,168 accused persons tried by the field
courts in the Kingdom in 1908, the year for which he found the most
complete documentation. Unfortunately for the contemporary historian, the
data retrieved by Próchnik, embracing the courts' verdicts and sentences
in 76 percent of the cases, are no longer extant. Nevertheless, of the 885
individual verdicts and sentences examined by Próchnik, 391 resulted in
the death sentence. Of these, 171 were subsequently commuted by the
Warsaw governor-general to life sentences in hard-labor prisons. We are
therefore left with a minimum of 120 executions (there may have been as
many as 150) by verdict of the field courts in Russian Poland in 1908

alone, which amounted to slightly less than 11 percent (and perhaps as much as 14 percent) of all such executions in the entire Russian Empire between 1906 and 1914.[45]

Although the loudly proclaimed purpose of the field courts was "to fight terror with terror," only 40 percent of the cases examined by Próchnik involved accusations of subversive political activity (terrorist actions, armed expropriations, political assassinations). By party affiliation, of those accused of political crimes against the state, 167 belonged of the PPS, 101 to the SDKPiL, and 63 to anarchist organizations of various hues. They were joined, in descending order, by 22 Bundists, 13 Zionists, and one member of the National Workers' Union. The majority of those brought before the field courts, however, were accused of violent, but nonpolitical, criminal offenses. Here, Próchnik's data confirm the dramatic upsurge in the activity of criminal gangs at the end of the revolution discussed in Chapter 6.

Although the activity of the field courts and the application of the "Stolypin necktie" in Russian Poland appear in bold relief against the backdrop of the empire as a whole, their effectiveness against the state's political enemies—and violent criminal bands, for that matter—ultimately depended on the success of the "normal" repressive measures of the provisional governors-general in restoring order among the general population. In the first weeks of reimposed martial law at the end of 1905 and the beginning of 1906, these measures only served to encourage popular rebellion in large parts of the Kingdom, especially in Suwałki, Radom, Kielce, and Siedlce provinces, which in turn caused the excitable Warsaw governor-general to lose patience quickly. Over the long term, however it was the punitive action of the provisional governors-general, rather than the extraordinary powers demanded by Skalon, that restored Russian state authority in the Kingdom.

Foremost among the concerns of the martial law governors was the illegal possession, sale, and purchase of firearms. Weapons smuggling had already reached epidemic proportions in the first months of 1905 when the first steps were taken to control their further proliferation by banning all sales of firearms and ammunition.[46] Subsequent confiscations of illegally possessed or sold firearms during the course of 1905—in Lublin Province

45. Próchnik, *Studia z dziejów polskiego ruchu robotniczego*, pp. 527–556. The total of 1,102 executions for the empire as a whole for the duration of the field courts is taken from Alfred Levin, *The Second Duma: A Study of the Social-Democratic Party and the Russian Constitutional Experiment*, 2d ed. (Hamden, Conn., 1966), p. 261.
46. APW ZOW 1078, Directive of the WGG of March 18 (31), 1905.

alone there were more than four hundred documented cases[47]—had little real impact. When, at the end of December, the provisional governor-general of Siedlce Province reported that "almost the entire population" of the town of Ryki in Gawrolin County was armed, he was hardly exaggerating.[48] His counterparts could and did make similar claims, whether for the northern counties of Kielce Province, whose inhabitants were said to provide arms to terrorist bands; the peasants of Janów County in Lublin Province who provided arms to militias to protect their villages from the rumored, impending attacks of "Black Hundreds"; or factory workers in Radom, where two battalions conducted mass searches for illegal weapons.[49]

Disarming the general population thus became the first priority of the martial law governors. Of the 165 cases that came before the provisional governor-general of Piotrków Province for administrative sentencing between April 12 and May 12, 1906, more than one-third (57) involved illegal possession of firearms, explosive devices, and other weapons. The sentences for illegal weapons possession in the most urban and industrialized of the Polish provinces during this period nearly doubled those in the next-highest of the thirteen categories of martial law violations—participation in illegal meetings (30). The remaining categories included strike agitation (20), possession of illegal publications (18), disruption of trade and commerce (9), illegal solicitation (8), distribution and posting of illegal publications (8), illegal street sales of newspapers (5), resisting authorities (3), anti-duma agitation (3), participation in street demonstrations (2), tearing down government publications (1), and gmina agitation (1).[50]

Illegal weapons possession, however, was an even greater problem in rural areas. Between January 10 and March 19, 1906, the provisional governor-general of Kielce Province handed down 204 administrative sentences for various martial law infractions. Of these, 140 cases could be adequately documented, and nearly half of them (65) involved the illegal carrying and possession of weapons, mainly firearms. Moreover, of the 73

---

47. APL KGL 1905:121.
48. AGAD KGGW 2527, Provisional Governor-General of Siedlce Province to the WGG, December 15 (28), 1905.
49. AGAD KGGW 2509, Provisional Governor-General of Kielce Province to the WGG, December 20, 1905 (January 2, 1906); 2515, Provisional Governor-General of Lublin Province to the WGG, December 24, 1905 (January 6, 1906); and 2521, Telegram of the Provisional Governor-General of Radom Province to the WGG, December 29, 1905 (January 11, 1906).
50. APL TGGP 4, Administrative Sentences of the Provisional Governor-General of Piotrków Province, March 30 (April 12) to April 30 (May 12), 1905.

Street arrests in Warsaw, 1906. (Muzeum Niepodległości 35887)

sentences between February 20 and March 19, 42 (nearly 60 percent) concerned weapons charges.[51]

But the main purpose of the military governors was not so much the punishment of those arrested as the reduction of the number of weapons in circulation and the prevention of their falling into the hands of the fighting organizations of the political parties. An examination of twenty-four sentences by the Kielce provisional governor-general for weapons violations between March 8 and March 21, 1906, reveals unexpectedly light punishments, far removed from the maximums of three months in jail and fines of three thousand rubles permitted by martial law statutes. Only twice were persons sentenced to more than a couple of weeks in jail, and the highest fine imposed was twenty-five rubles.[52] Yet for a peasant whose illegal possession of a hunting rifle had led to arrest, several days in jail during spring planting, coupled with a fine of ten rubles, could and did have a significant economic impact. Already by early summer, the specter

51. APK TGGK 21, 22I, 22II, 23, 23A, and 74.
52. APK TGGK 23A.

of an armed population sustaining terrorist bands had been put to rest through effective measures of confiscation, interdiction, and deterrence.

Viewed from below, the principal goal of martial law was to drive a wedge between the general population and the opposition political movements. The imperial Russian version of divide-and-rule, as it applied to the Polish provinces, rested on the principle of collective responsibility. In the first place, the extraordinary expenditures necessitated by military rule were covered by special levies imposed on the towns and gminy. Although reliable data are available only for Lublin Province, such assessments for the first two months of 1906 amounted to more than two thousand rubles. Although the average levy of thirty-five rubles per gmina does not sound like a large sum, when extended over the duration of martial law, it constituted a major drain on already strapped community budgets. Within a couple of months, the treasuries of several gminy could no longer contribute their "fair share" to martial law government in Lublin Province, so Skalon simply imposed higher charges on the towns.[53]

One reason community resources were so strained was that the population was also made financially liable for all damage to state and private property. This principle, applied only occasionally in November 1905, mainly in Radom Province, now applied to the entire Kingdom. Such liability could vary widely with the losses suffered: from the 1,891 rubles levied retroactively on the town of Białobrzegi in Radom Province for damages resulting from "rioting and looting" on November 12 and 13, 1905, to the less than 15 rubles demanded from the villagers of Czartyszew in Kielce Province as their share of responsibility for the robbery of the Łopyszno gmina treasury.[54] Actual collection, regardless of the sums involved, frequently required the use of military force. In Suwałki Province, where Lithuanian gminy were particularly recalcitrant in paying taxes, let alone fines, authorities warned in early January 1906 that all resistance would be treated as insurgency, with arrested persons to be tried by courts-martial. Nevertheless, the chief of Mariampol County, although accompanied by dragoons, managed to collect a mere five rubles in his entire jurisdiction. In Wyłkowyszki County, authorities managed to collect two hundred rubles, but only when they went for the economic jugular by sequestering peasant livestock—and even then, the local population boycotted state attempts to auction the sequestered property. After January 20, the martial law authorities in Suwałki Province were forced to resort to

---

53. APL KGL 1905:254/2 and 1906:136.
54. AGAD KGGW 2520, Radom Governor to the WGG, February 22 (March 7), 1906; APK TGGK 7, Kielce Governor to the Chief of Kielce County, October 11 (24), 1906.

additional punitive measures, including flogging, to collect taxes and fines.[55]

It proved equally difficult for the authorities to convince communities to cooperate actively with the authorities in defending state property. When the inhabitants of Pruszków in Warsaw County were assigned responsibility for the security of a state vodka outlet, the village assembly "illegally" resolved to close it down.[56] In Lublin County, gmina assemblies were similarly uncooperative, and this despite a good deal of official arm-twisting of the sort successful in neighboring Lubartów and Biłgoraj counties. Here, the local population "continually" refused to provide "volunteers" for "security units" of night watchmen at gmina administration offices, to finance jail maintenance, or to hire new guards.[57]

Eventually, however, the principle of collective responsibility succeeded in its main goal of eroding the social base that had provided support to the state's revolutionary political opponents, especially in the countryside. Accordingly, once a semblance of order had been restored among rural inhabitants, the state demonstrated a more flexible, even charitable, attitude in dealing with the villages. Already in early April 1906, the military governor of Piotrków Province, on the advice of his civilian counterpart, rescinded a fine of 642 rubles levied on the gmina of Popień.[58] Sentences were suspended against persons arrested earlier for gmina action agitation in those areas where "the use of the state language has been restored and the mood of the population pacified."[59] Similarly, gmina officials exiled for proclaiming their solidarity with the gmina action movement were allowed to return to their places of residence. Peasants, arrested for various martial law infractions, were released to return to spring field work. Fines and sentences, especially for minor violations of martial law, were substantially reduced, by Skalon's order, beginning in February 1906. Martial law excesses and the abuse of power now came under the highest scrutiny, as in the case of the gmina of Skarbiewo in Warsaw Province, which had been subjected to successive three-thousand-ruble fines as well as requisitioning and where the protests of the gmina assembly eventually led to

---

55. AGAD KGGW 2524, Provisional Governor-General of Suwałki Province to the WGG, December 20, 1905 (January 2, 1906), and Suwałki Governor to the WGG, December 31, 1905 (January 13, 1906).
56. APW WGZŻ 1724, Chief of the Gendarmes in Warsaw, Nowominsk, and Radzymin Counties to the Chief of the Warsaw Provincial Gendarmes, March 9 (22), 1906.
57. APL KGL 1906:47i, Chief of Biłgoraj County to the Lublin Governor, June 28 (July 11), 1906, and Chief of Lublin County to the Lublin Governor, June 17 (30), 1906.
58. APŁ TGGP 3, Provisional Governor-General of Piotrków Province to the Chief of Brzeziny County, March 19 (April 1), 1906.
59. AGAD KGGW 2517, Memorandum of the Director of the Chancellory of the WGG, April 12 (25), 1906.

the dismissal of the chief of Płońsk County.[60] By the end of November, repressive measures of rural tax and fine collection came to an official end.[61]

While the government attempted by such means to neutralize the rural population, it also moved to beef up the police, whose weakness in both numbers and morale had played a major part in the near collapse of state authority at the end of 1905. During the course of 1906, the number of police functionaries more than doubled, from approximately 4,700 at the beginning of the year to nearly 10,000 by early 1907.[62] In Lublin Province, where complete data are available, the Land Guard was increased from 388 members at the beginning of 1905 to 557 members in December 1906, leaving it still short of the projected rural police force of 660. Nevertheless, the composition of the police according to nationality did not change, as "Roman Catholics" (i.e., Poles) continued to make up less than 10 percent of the Land Guard. The preponderantly "Orthodox" Land Guard remained an alien force.[63]

By the summer of 1906, if not earlier, the state had clearly restored order among the population at large. The countryside had been effectively pacified, and in urban-industrial areas the strike movement had subsided dramatically. Armed bands continued to wage a campaign of political terror, but with obviously diminishing effects and with less and less popular support, as the authorities themselves acknowledged when Skalon lifted the ban on the sale and possession of firearms by "law-abiding" citizens in the late spring.[64] The state had won its "war," and many of the desiderata for the proclamation, or, more accurately, the reimposition, of martial law in December 1905 had been satisfied. Why, then, did the "state of war" remain in effect, indeed, for another three years?

This question assumes added poignancy when it is realized that Skalon himself broached the question with his subordinates as early as March 1906. The compilation of the responses of the provisional governors-

60. AGAD KGGW 2609, Minister of Internal Affairs to the WGG, January 28 (February 11), 1906; Provisional Governor-General of Warsaw Province to the WGG, February 8 (21) and March 11 (24), 1906; Warsaw Governor to the WGG, March 7 (20), 1906; WGG to the Warsaw Governor, March 5 (18), 1906; and Protocol of the Gmina Assembly of Skarbiewo, March 10, 1906 (N.S.).
61. AGAD KGGW 2585, Circulars of the WGG to the Provisional Governors-General, January 23 (February 5), 1906, and November 16 (29), 1906.
62. Jerzy Pająk, *Organizacje bojowe partii politycznych w Królestwie Polskim, 1904–1911* (Warsaw, 1985), pp. 122–123.
63. APL KGL 1905:64 and 1906:94.
64. APL KGL 1906:17, Lublin Governor to the County Chiefs and the Lublin Chief of Police, May 11 (24), 1906; Stanisław Kalabiński and Feliks Tych, *Czwarte powstanie czy pierwsza rewolucja: Lata 1905–1907 na ziemiach polskich,* 2d ed. (Warsaw, 1976), p. 402.

general by Skalon's chancellory reveals a near unanimity of opinion opposed to an early lifting of martial law. Only the military governor of Płock Province favorably considered the possibility. In stark contrast, the Piotrków provisional governor-general was "decisively against" a return to civilian rule, which was also considered "completely impossible" by his counterpart in Warsaw Province. Such adamancy is understandable, given the relative instability that still afflicted the Kingdom's two most urbanized and industrialized provinces. But the military governors of the remaining and predominantly rural provinces also argued for postponement: until after the elections to the First Duma (the Łomża, Kalisz, and Kielce provisional governors-general), or until after the actual convening of the Duma (the Suwałki provisional governor-general), or until after the completion of spring field work (the Lublin provisional governor-general).[65] The prevailing opinion that the time was not right, that the lifting of martial law would be "premature," requires brief explanation.

Fear of terrorism undoubtedly contributed to the extreme caution of the martial law officials, especially in March 1906, when the activity of armed bands was peaking. Slightly more than a year later, however, when most of these bands had been liquidated, there would be no renewed discussion of the possibility of returning to civilian rule. More significant was the bitter experience of lifting martial law after a mere three weeks in November 1905, which had helped bring on the popular revolutionary upsurge, especially in the countryside, and an unprecedented destabilization of Russian authority in the Polish provinces. Fearful of repeating that mistake, the Warsaw governor-general and his subordinates now erred on the far side of caution, even though the situation had changed in fundamental ways since the previous December. This overreaction, induced by the alarm of recent memory, paralyzed any proclivity within Skalon's administration to think in bolder political terms, whether in March 1906 or after the various scenarios outlined by the military governors as the year wore on. This political paralysis, most unfortunately, would freeze the Kingdom in a "state of war" long after any conceivable justification for its continuation. When the country was finally freed from the rigors of military rule several years later, many of the gains from the revolutionary era had been lost.

Lost, but not necessarily irretrievable. Beyond denying the Kingdom statutory political autonomy, martial law in subsequent years did much to arrest, if not reverse, the development of civil society. That society, which

---

65. Kalabiński, *Carat i klasy posiadające*, pp. 456–461.

had emerged in piecemeal fashion at the end of the nineteenth century and the beginning of the twentieth, perhaps had been brought to premature blossom by the revolution. Like a warm, early, but also stormy spring, the revolution fostered the sudden cropping out of a multitude of associations, societies, and organizations, many of them with roots in the underground, while it transformed others already legally and publicly in existence. These bodies, intermediate between state and society, whether in the form of political parties, trade unions, professional associations, cooperatives, cultural and educational organizations, or communal assemblies, were strained, sometimes violently, by a too-rapid growth and by the pressures of popular participation, in unprecedented numbers, by many whose only experience had been that of subjects, and not that of citizens. Ambiguous and uncertain state policies, alternating between forced acquiescence and repression throughout 1905, further destabilized conditions under which both the notion and the phenomenon of citizenship struggled to express and consolidate themselves.

Independence, whether in the form of territorial political autonomy or a separate state existence, was not necessarily a precondition for the further and healthy development of civil society in Russian Poland. Far more indispensable were legal guarantees and recognition of intermediate, autonomous, and public institutions and organizations, regardless of the state or governing structure providing them. In this sense, the March 1906 "provisional" laws on unions and associations were the best available means for the nurturing and consolidation, under the stabilizing conditions of extended experience, of the fragile flowers of civil society in Russian Poland which had taken various forms, as well as many deformities, during the revolution.

Yet despite the existence of the March laws, together with other, earlier state concessions affecting religious toleration, rural self-government, public and private educational institutions, and proportional political representation of the Polish provinces in the Russian State Duma, martial law in the Kingdom, as a result of its long duration, effectively undermined the very conditions made possible by these concessions for the further, peaceful, and stable development of civil society. This is where martial law, which by 1907 could no longer be justified by its original intentions of restoring order in Russian Poland, caused real social damage. The subsequent and prolonged night frost of military rule, lifted only in stages between 1909 and the outbreak of the Great War, became the extended experience, rather than that promised in the October Manifesto and the March laws, under which the remaining offshoots of civil society in Russian Poland now struggled to survive.

Many did not make it. Two political parties, the PPS-Proletariat and the Polish People's Union, were eliminated by 1907. The main parties constituting the socialist movement—the two factions of the PPS, the SDKPiL, and the Bund—although they survived the aftermath of the revolution, were crippled by mass arrests, declining memberships, and further fragmentation. The nationalist movement, despite its now-thorough rejection of revolutionary means, fared little better in the political climate created by martial law, especially after Stolypin's constitutional revisions denied the population of Russian Poland proportional representation in the State Duma. Even the Association of Christian Workers, which never claimed the status of a political party, as well as its competitor, the conservative Catholic Union, suffered under the intense scrutiny, restrictions, and harassment of the state authorities. Revolutionary or not, these organizations were repressed simply because they engaged, or were perceived to engage, in politics, an autonomous activity that the still-autocratic Russian state was not altogether willing to concede to the tsar's subjects in Poland, even at the local level. Hence, zemstvo-style assemblies and elected municipal councils would never be extended to Russian Poland. Although legally recognized political parties would continue to exist, together with those that retreated to the underground, they were rendered largely incapable of acting politically.

Political parties and organizations were not the only institutions of civil society that struggled to survive martial law. Trade unions and professional associations, despite their disavowal of party ties as required by the March laws, shared the fate of the mass political organizations. As a consequence of their political inspiration and, more significantly, of their potential as bases for recruitment into the political parties, Skalon's martial law government between 1907 and 1910 not only rendered the process of registering new unions and associations virtually impossible but closed down even more whose statutes had earlier been approved, including twenty-three in Łódź alone.[66] For similar reasons, many of the promising independent educational and cultural initiatives and organizations discussed in Chapter 5, including the Polska Macierz Szkolna, the University for All, and the Światło circles, were all suppressed. The periodical press, which had mushroomed toward the end of the revolution after the lifting of preventive censorship, too, was never permitted to realize its potential to act as a civic forum for the exchange of opinion on important political and

66. Ignacy Orzechowski and Aleksander Kochański, *Zarys dziejów ruchu zawodowego w Królestwie Polskim, 1905–1918* (Warsaw, 1964), pp. 156–182; Władysław Lech Karwacki, *Łódź w latach rewolucji 1905–1907* (Łódź, 1975), p. 345.

social issues. Already in 1906, forty-one periodicals of wide-ranging diversity were closed down in Warsaw.[67] Even the seemingly innocuous cooperative movement under the aegis of the Association of Christian Workers encountered a most uncooperative state. Of the 160 cooperative stores created in Łódź under its sponsorship, not a single one had survived by 1910.[68]

Still, state repression of the would-be institutions of civil society was not indiscriminate. Ironically, some even grew and developed. Foremost among these were the gmina assemblies. Despite the political activization of the communes during the revolution and disregarding all evidence to the contrary, the state continued to view the peasantry as essentially apolitical, if not a base of social support for imperial rule. Convinced both by their own attribution of the gmina action movement to outside agitation and of the efficacy of concessions to bilingualism in rural self-government and primary education, state officials pursued policies in the Polish countryside that alternated between lenience and negligence. After the restoration of order in rural areas, some repressive measures were suspended, and peasants arrested on martial law violations were released. Then, having established by those measures that rural self-government and primary schools would adhere to the recently established rules of bilingualism, the state essentially turned its back on the gminy, which enabled communal institutions to carve out areas for real local self-government. For example, the gminy displayed considerable initiative in expanding the network of elementary schools in the countryside, especially in the last two years before the outbreak of World War I, and, even more significantly, in the absence of any tangible financial assistance from the state.

A second example, again drawn from the countryside but also from provincial towns, is the uninterrupted growth of the volunteer firemen's movement. The associations of volunteer firemen had not been inactive during the revolution. One need only recall the peaceful processions and demonstrations of November and December 1905, accompanied by the "orchestras" of volunteer firemen intoning "Boże coś Polskę" and from whose ranks came the marshalls who, far more than the despised rural police, maintained public order. Despite the role of volunteer firemen as civic and, therefore, political leaders in their local communities, including their participation in gmina action, their associations were also of irreplaceable

---

67. Halina Kiepurska, *Inteligencja zawodowa Warszawy, 1905–1907* (Warsaw, 1967), p. 338.
68. Władysław Lech Karwacki, *Związki zawodowe i stowarszyszenia pracodawców w Łodzi.* (Łódź, 1972), pp. 372–389.

"Freedom of the Press." Political cartoon from 1906. (Muzeum Niepodległości 37079)

social and economic utility. Although the state remained skeptical of the volunteer firemen, its unwillingness or inability to commit its own resources to fighting fires outside the major urban areas left it little choice but to tolerate the proliferation of the associations. Thus between 1900 and 1911, the number of volunteer firemen's organizations increased from 128 to 452, and ultimately to 557 associations on the eve of the Great War.[69]

Because other independent and autonomous initiatives in the countryside, including agricultural circles and rural cooperatives, similarly prospered, the balance sheet for civil society does not look nearly as bleak, especially in the light of the fact that the majority of the population of Russian Poland continued to live and work in rural areas. Yet even in the major urban and industrial centers, though institutions important for the development of civil society may have been emasculated, they were never completely uprooted and destroyed. Even at the height of Skalon's repressive military rule, political parties, trade unions, associations, and independent publications continued to exist, sometimes beyond the legal margins, but also within them. Once martial law was lifted, and despite the continuation of lesser forms of emergency rule, these urban-based institutions of civil society displayed a remarkable capacity for revival and expansion between 1911 and 1914.

How, then, does one weigh the ill fortunes of a political party, incapacitated by the arrest of its leaders in the summer of 1907, against the simultaneous legal registration of an organization like the Society for the Advancement of Equal Rights of Polish Women or the appearance of a volunteer firemen's association in a few locality? Even a partial answer will require extensive social research and creative analytic approaches to the postrevolutionary period in Russian Poland. Yet given the preoccupation of the historiographic literature with narrowly defined political outcomes, there is some satisfaction in raising the question.

---

69. Józef Ryszard Szaflik, *Dzieje ochotniczych straży pożarnych* (Warsaw, 1985), pp. 178–181.

# INDEX

CPSIA information can be obtained
at www.ICGtesting.com
Printed in the USA
FFOW03n2345160117
31311FF